Java Data Mining: Strategy, Standard, and Practice

D1466141

The Morgan Kaufmann Series in Data Management Systems
Series Editor: Jim Gray, Microsoft Research

Java Data Mining: Strategy, Standard, and Practice

A Practical Guide for Architecture, Design, and Implementation

Mark F. Hornick
Erik Marcadé
Sunil Venkayala

AMSTERDAM · BOSTON · HEIDELBERG · LONDON
NEW YORK · OXFORD · PARIS · SAN DIEGO
SAN FRANCISCO · SINGAPORE · SYDNEY · TOKYO

MORGAN KAUFMANN PUBLISHERS

Publisher   Diane D. Cerra
Publishing Services Manager   George Morrison
Project Manager   Marilyn E. Rash
Assistant Editor   Asma Palmeiro
Cover Design   Brian May, Maycreate LLC
Production Services   Graphic World Inc.
Composition   diacriTech
Illustration   diacriTech
Interior Printer   The Maple-Vail Book Manufacturing Group
Cover Printer   Phoenix Color Corp

Morgan Kaufmann Publishers is an imprint of Elsevier.
500 Sansome Street, Suite 400, San Francisco, CA 94111

This book is printed on acid-free paper.

Java Specification Request 73. Copyright © 2004. Oracle Corporation. Used with permission.

Java Specification Request 274. Copyright © 2005. Oracle Corporation. Used with permission.

Library of Congress Cataloging-in-Publication Data
Hornick, Mark F.
   Java data mining : strategy, standard, and practice : a practical guide for architecture, design, and implementation / Mark F. Hornick, Erik Marcadé, Sunil Venkayala.
      p. cm.—(The Morgan Kaufmann series in data management systems)
   Includes bibliographical references and index.
   ISBN 0-12-370452-9 (acid-free paper)
1. Data mining. 2. Java (Computer program language) I. Marcadé, Erik.
II. Venkayala, Sunil. III. Title.
   QA76.9.D343.H67 2007
   005.74—dc22   2006050783
   ISBN-10: 0-12-370452-9
   ISBN-13: 978-0-12-370452-8

For information on all Morgan Kaufmann publications,
visit our Web site at *www.mkp.com* or *www.books.elsevier.com*

Printed in the United States of America
06 07 08 09 10   10 9 8 7 6 5 4 3 2 1

To Suzanne, Amanda, and Tim for their enthusiasm and support.
– M.H.

To Caroline, Laetitia, and Guillaume.
– E.M.

To my parents, wife Meera, and daughter Shreya.
– S.V.

Contents

Chapter 9   Using the JDM API   **199**

Preface

The birth of a standard is an amazing event, highlighting the ability of individuals from vastly different and often competing companies to come together to design an interface for a domain such as data mining. For JSR-73, we drew on experts from data mining tool and application vendors, as well as users of data mining technology. Data mining, as a field, is remarkably diverse in scope, encompassing capabilities from a broad range of disciplines: artificial intelligence, machine learning, statistics, data analysis, and visualization. Producing a standard in such a space is a challenging and fascinating adventure.

Within a year or so of embarking on the JDM 1.0 standard, various expert group members suggested that we'd have to write a book about Java Data Mining (JDM) someday. And indeed, here we are. Our main motivation for writing this book is to introduce data mining to a much broader audience, one that may have never used or encountered data mining before. As such, we focus less on the technical and scholarly details of data mining than on its practical understanding and application. We have tried to include a reasonably broad set of references for individuals who want to dive down to the next level of detail. However, we have strived to make data mining concepts, process, and use through JDM more accessible to Java developers, who usually do not encounter data mining, and the colleagues they will work with to develop advanced analytic applications.

Advanced analytic applications—those augmented with advanced and predictive analytics such as data mining—provide greater business intelligence, yielding insight into business problems and guidance for improved decision making. Such applications are becoming most valuable to businesses, and hence can increase revenue and profits—both for the vendors who sell them and for the businesses that use them.

Readers of this book will find a somewhat unconventional approach to data mining. Other books on data mining provide much detail on algorithms and techniques. Although this information is important to those studying machine learning or wanting to become a data analyst, other potential users of data mining are left wondering how these algorithms or techniques will be applied to solve problems. As vendors of data mining technology strive to make data mining more accessible to a broader range of users, such as business analysts, information technology (IT) specialists, and database administrators (DBAs), it is no longer the details that users require, but the big picture. Users ask, "How can I use this powerful technology to provide value within my business?" In this book, we strive to approach this and other questions from several perspectives: the software developer, the software and systems architect, and the business and data analyst. We explore these perspectives in the following section, "Guide to Readers."

In this book, we provide insight into three key aspects of the Java Data Mining standard. The first aspect, covered in Part I, focuses on strategies for solving data mining–related business and scientific problems, and on the strategy the JDM Expert Group pursued in the design of the JDM standard. After an introduction to the data mining field, we discuss solving problems in various industries using data mining technology.

Although every industry has unique problems to solve, requiring custom and innovative solutions, each industry also shares many problems that can benefit from cross-industry solutions. For example, industries such as retail, financial services, and healthcare, as well as the public sector, all have customers. The cross-industry solution spaces include customer acquisition, customer retention, customer lifetime value, and targeted marketing.

Because data mining solutions typically do not take form or produce value in a vacuum, we then discuss the overall process, based on the industry standard data mining process CRISP-DM. Because users of data mining technology need to be minimally conversant in the terminology and concepts to problem solve with their colleagues, we introduce the mining functions and algorithms defined in JDM. With this foundation, we explore the JDM strategy, answering questions such as: What drove the design of JDM? What is the role of standards? Lastly, before embarking on details of the Java Data Mining standard, we provide a "getting started" code example that follows the CRISP-DM process.

The second aspect, covered in Part II, focuses on the standard itself. This part introduces various concepts defined by or assimilated into the standard using examples based on business problems. After this, we explore the design of the JDM API and more detailed code examples to give readers a better understanding of how to use JDM to build applications and solve problems. Although JDM is foremost dedicated to being a standard Java language API, Java Data Mining also defines an XML schema representation for JDM objects, as well as a web services interface to enable the use of JDM functionality in a Services Oriented Architecture (SOA) environment. Part II also discusses these with specific examples of their use.

The third aspect, covered in Part III, focuses on using JDM in practice, building applications and tools that use the Java Data Mining API. We begin this part with several business scenarios (e.g., targeted marketing, key factor analysis, and customer segmentation). Because JDM is designed to be used by both application designers and data mining tool designers, we introduce code for building a simple tool graphical user interface (GUI), which manipulates JDM-persistent objects as well as enables the building and testing of a model. Having introduced web services in Part II, we give an example of a web services based application. Since data mining can impact the Information Technology (IT) infrastructure of most companies, we explore the impact of data mining along several dimensions, including hardware, software, data access, performance, and administration tools. Since the practice of using data mining often involves the use of commercial implementations, we introduce two such JDM implementations, from Oracle and KXEN. We also provide some guidelines or insights for implementers new to JDM.

Wrapping up in Part IV, we explore the evolution of data mining standards, which puts JDM in the broader context of other data mining standards. We also contrast the approaches taken by various data mining standards bodies. Since we note that no standard is ever complete, and JDM 1.1 itself covers only a subset of the possible data mining functions and algorithms, we highlight directions for JDM 2.0. We introduce features under consideration such as transformations, time series, and apply for association models, among others.

Acknowledgments

We first want to acknowledge the Java Data Mining expert group members who participated in the long process required to produce the JSR-73 standard. Their unwavering support through weekly conference calls and face-to-face meetings over the 4 years of the standards development is greatly appreciated. We also acknowledge the additional contributions of Hankil Yoon, Ka Kit Chan, Jim Dadashev, and Somesh Marepalli to the Technology Compatibility Kit (TCK) implementation, and Marwane Jai Lamimi to the Reference Implementation (RI).

We are very grateful for the general and specialist input provided by Frank Byrum, Jim Melton, and Osmar Zaiane on the developing manuscript. Over the past year, their detailed comments on both structure and content were a tremendous asset. We thank Jacek Myczkowski and Don Deutsch for their valuable comments on the final manuscript, as well as their support of the standards efforts for JSR-73 and JSR-247 at Oracle. We thank the JDM expert group members Michal Prussak, Alex Russakovsky, and Michael Smith who also provided valuable comments on the final manuscript, and David Urena and Samy Mechiri who contributed to the source code used in Part III of this book.

Of course, all remaining errors (which we expect exist despite careful review) are entirely our responsibility.

We offer our appreciation and gratitude to the wonderful people at Morgan Kaufmann Publishers as they guided us through the process of book writing and publishing. We thank Jim Melton, one of our reviewers, for putting us in contact with Diane Cerra, our talented and patient publisher, to begin this journey. We thank Diane, Asma Palmeiro, Misty Bergeron, Marilyn Rash, and Bruce Siebert who worked to make this book possible.

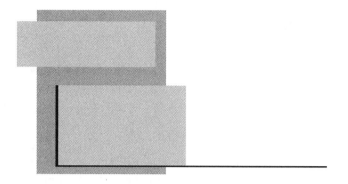

Guide to Readers

Data mining is becoming a mainstream technology used in business intelligence applications supporting industries such as financial services, retail, healthcare, telecommunications, and higher education, and lines of business such as marketing, manufacturing, customer experiences, customer service, and sales. Many of the business problems that data mining can solve cut across industries such as customer retention and acquisition, cross-sell, and response modeling. Due to the cost, skillsets, and complexity required to bring data mining results into an established business process, early adopters were typically big companies and research labs with correspondingly large budgets and access to statisticians and machine learning experts. In recent years, however, data mining products have simplified data mining considerably by automating the process—making the fruits of the technology more widely accessible. New algorithms and heuristics have evolved to provide good results with little or no experimentation or data preparation. In addition, the availability of data mining has increased with in-database data mining capabilities.

Java Data Mining (JDM) furthers the adoption of data mining by providing a standard Java and web services Application Programming Interface (API) for data mining. This book introduces data mining to software developers and application architects who may have heard of the benefits of data mining but are unsure how to realize these benefits. This book is also targeted at business and data analysts who want to learn how JDM helps in developing vendor-neutral data mining solutions. It does not require a reader to be familiar with data mining, statistics, or machine learning technologies.

We have organized this book into three main parts: *strategy, standard*, and *practice*. In Part I, JDM Strategy, we introduce data mining in general, uses of data mining in solving industry problems, data mining processes and techniques, the role of data mining standards, and a high-level introduction to the JDM Application Programming Interface (API). Most of this part doesn't require the reader to know the Java language.

In Part II, JDM Standard, we explain the concepts used in JDM by example, explore the JDM API design and its usage, and introduce the Java Data Mining XML schema and web services. This part requires readers to know the Java language, XML, and XML schema. It gives a brief introduction to web services in Chapter 11 before discussing the JDM web services.

In Part III, JDM Practice, we illustrate practical problem solving using the JDM API. We begin by developing a sample data mining tool using JDM and a sample data mining web service using JDM. We then introduce two JDM vendor implementations, exploring their functionality, architecture, and design tradeoffs before giving some guidance to others interested in implementing a JDM-compliant system.

In Part IV, Wrapping Up, we discuss the evolution of data mining standards, where they have been and where they might go. We give a preview of some of the features proposed for JDM 2.0.

For the Software Developer

 For software developers, and in particular Java and web services developers, this book introduces data mining and how to use JDM to develop data mining solutions. Part I introduces data mining and various types of business problems that can be solved using data mining, illustrates a standard process used to conduct a data mining project, describes data mining techniques used to solve business problems, explains the JDM standard strategy and why the JDM standard is necessary, and provides an overview of the JDM API. Even though software developers are not typically involved in the initial solving of a data mining problem, it is important to know

about concepts to understand the JDM API and how to develop data mining solutions.

Part II will familiarize developers with JDM concepts and the API. Readers of this part are required to know the Java language, Object Oriented Programming, the Unified Modeling Language and XML to understand the Java examples, API design concepts, JDM XML schema, and web services. This part introduces JDM concepts using examples, describes the design and usage of the Java API, and illustrates the Java Data Mining XML schema and web services interfaces.

Part III describes the use of the JDM API in practice with sample applications and detailed code examples both for the Java and web services API. It also provides JDM vendor implementation details and explains the process for other data mining vendors in adopting the JDM standard.

After reading this book, we expect the data mining knowledge gap between developers and data analysts will be greatly reduced to help them communicate more effectively when developing a data mining solution.

For the Software Architect

 Data mining is often integrated with existing software applications and business processes. Understanding of data mining processes provides greater insight for architects to enable this technology in existing or new applications. For example, an architect needs to understand how data mining works to add intelligent customer offers using data mining to an existing call center application.

For architects who want to be hands-on with the JDM API (e.g., to develop prototypes), all parts of this book are useful. Part I and Part III are particularly useful for architects. Part I introduces data mining in general and provides examples of how it is currently being applied to solve business problems. Most important, it introduces the data mining process and the role of the information technology department in implementing a data mining project.

Part II will be useful to understand the API-level concepts for the architects who want to be hands-on with the API, to develop prototypes, or to mentor the developers about the use of the API.

In Part III, we provide deeper insight into how JDM can be used in practice. Chapter 16, which discusses vendor implementations, is particularly useful for data mining software architects who are interested in developing JDM compatible API's and extensions.

After reading this book, architects should be comfortable in integrating JDM-based data mining solutions with their applications and be able to develop a strategy to operationalize data mining results with their existing applications.

For the Business/Data Analyst

 For business and data analysts who want to extract actionable information from corporate data, this book provides an introduction to data mining and how it is used to solve various business problems across industries. In Part I, the data mining usage scenarios and process of implementing a data mining project will be particularly useful for the analyst unfamiliar with data mining. Chapter 5, JDM Strategy, enables analysts to understand why the JDM standard is important in implementing a data mining solution. Typically, analysts are not involved in the software implementation of the solution, yet Part II may be useful for understanding the data mining concepts used by JDM to facilitate communication with developers and data mining experts, and for using tools based on JDM.

For an analyst who is already familiar with data mining and who has expertise in data mining and statistics, this book gives details of Java Data Mining and its usage in developing data mining solutions. Data mining tools can often generate JDM-compatible code to easily deploy a solution to a JDM-compatible Data Mining Engine (DME).

After reading this book, an analyst previously unfamiliar with data mining should be able to better understand how data mining can help in solving business problems. A data mining expert analyst will be able to understand the supported data mining features in JDM and be able to communicate easily with the software architects/ developers to implement a data mining solution.

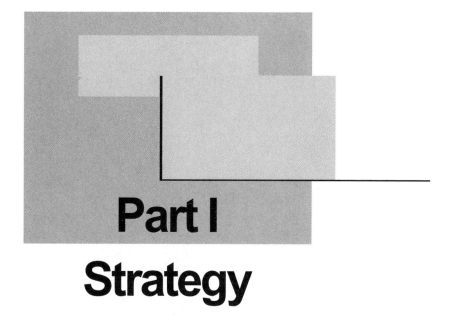

Part I
Strategy

In this part, we frame data mining as a strategy for solving complex business problems and discuss the role of standards that support such a strategy. It addresses the needs of both the business analyst and the architect.

Chapter 1

Overview of Data Mining

*The most incomprehensible thing about the world
is that it is at all comprehensible.*

—Albert Einstein

Imagine one's surprise at discovering which genes determine susceptibility to a certain type of cancer by running an algorithm on data consisting of 5,000 genes from each of a hundred patients. Imagine one's surprise at being able to predict with high accuracy which customers will purchase a specific product. Einstein's comment on *comprehensibility* fits well with the world of data mining. What is so amazing is that by amassing data from the real world on just about anything, patterns can be determined that provide insights into the world the data represents, making the world more *comprehensible*. Using data mining to gain insight into seemingly random data points is an increasingly common strategy among business analysts, scientists, and researchers.

Although the complexity of some data mining algorithms is great, using them has been greatly simplified through automation and higher level abstractions, such as those found in Java Data Mining 1.1 (JSR-73) [JSR-73 2004]. Java Data Mining (JDM) provides a standard application programming interface (API) and design framework to provide developers, application architects, data analysts, and business analysts greater access to data mining technology.

This chapter discusses why data mining is relevant today, both to consumers of data mining results and users of the technology. It then introduces and explores data mining at a high level, contrasting data mining with other forms of advanced analytics and reviewing the basic data mining process. Since the mining metaphor is often used, we digress to contrast the data mining process with the gold mining process. To be relevant, data mining must provide value. We discuss the reliability of data mining results and highlight ways in which data mining adds value to businesses.

1.1   Why Data Mining Is Relevant Today

Today's business landscape is highly competitive. Product margins are typically low due to increased competition and commoditization. Consumers have more information about competing offers and more channels such as the Web to pursue them. Customer loyalty exists either as long as the customer experience [Shaw/Ivens 2002] remains positive or until a better alternative comes along.

Savvy businesses have long taken advantage of advanced analytics and data mining to give them an edge in the marketplace. Major retailers know which customers to target with ad campaigns. Manufacturers know how to determine which aspects of their manufacturing process are yielding inferior results and why. Financial services providers, such as banks, know which customers are a high risk for a loan [Davenport 2006].

Companies that do not leverage data mining in their business processes are not likely to realize their revenue and profit potential. Their customers' experiences may be inferior as they become fatigued by what appear to be random solicitations or irrelevant offers. Companies may be missing key insights into ways to determine why customers are leaving or what customer profile yields the highest customer lifetime value.

From another angle, various regulatory compliance measures (e.g., Sarbanes-Oxley [SOX 2006], Basel II [BIS 2004]) require the keeping of large quantities of historical data. As such, multi-terabyte data repositories are becoming commonplace. Many companies make dramatic efforts to collect almost everything about their businesses, and to ensure that the data are clean. Consequently, corporate executives want to put this costly asset to good use. One such use is in the area of Business Intelligence (BI), which traditionally involves extracting information, generating reports, and populating dashboards with key performance indicators from these repositories to assist with business decisions.

More recently, the concept of BI is being expanded to include data mining techniques to extract knowledge and generate predictions for business problems, thereby enabling companies to make better use of a costly corporate asset, their data. With the advent of fast and inexpensive hardware, the ability to mine large volumes of data is not only possible, but the building of models and the scoring of data can often be performed in real time. Advances in data mining techniques and Moore's Law [Webopedia 2006] help to ensure that businesses and researchers will be able to keep pace with data repositories doubling at about the same rate as hardware performance.

On the other side of the spectrum are the marketers, financial analysts, and even call center representatives—generally application users—who leverage data mining increasingly through intelligent applications. These users either know nothing about the techniques of data mining or do not need to know anything about data mining to reap its benefits. The algorithms and the data mining process are concealed by business-centric user interfaces, which present the results of data mining, not its mechanics. For many, this is the only way to take advantage of the benefits of data mining—through verticalized solution applications.

Data mining is also relevant today as the technology becomes more accessible to a broader audience. Traditionally, data mining has been the realm of statisticians, data analysts, and scientists with Ph.D.'s in machine learning. These users wrote their own algorithms and graphical tools, leveraged complex commercial graphical user interfaces and application programming interfaces. Their process for mining data was often ad hoc, stitching together analytic workflows using Perl [Perl 2006], AWK, Python, Tcl/Tk, among others [SoftPanorama 2006].

With modern advances in data mining automation technology and the introduction of standard interfaces and processes, data mining is being made accessible to a new class of users: application architects and designers, and mainstream developers. Although the role of the data analyst will likely always be in fashion for superior results, technology is at the point where nonexperts can get good results. Here, *good* is defined as results that could be achieved by a junior statistician and sometimes much better. This empowers architects, designers, and developers to experiment with mining the data available to their applications and to enhance those applications with predictive analysis, presenting new insights to application users.

Once application owners see the potential of data mining in these applications unleashed, through the efforts of their application creators, the application owners may choose to apply more expert data mining skills to determine whether the quality of the results can be further enhanced. Oftentimes, even small insights can have a significant impact on a business or scientific problem.

1.2 Introducing Data Mining

Data mining is the process of finding patterns and relationships in data. At its core, data mining consists of developing a *model*, which is typically a compact representation of patterns found using historical data, and applying that model to new data. We apply a model to data to predict individual behavior (classification and regression), segment a population (clustering), determine relationships within a population (association), as well as to identify the characteristics that most impact a particular outcome (attribute importance). These and other data mining capabilities are explored in detail in subsequent chapters.

> *Data Mining grew as a direct consequence of the availability of large repositories of data. Data collection in digital form was already underway by the 1960s, allowing for retrospective data analysis via computers. Relational Databases arose in the 1980s along with Structured Query Languages (SQL), allowing for dynamic, on-demand analysis of data. The 1990s saw an explosion in growth of data. Data warehouses were beginning to be used for storage of data. Data Mining thus arose as a response to challenges faced by the database community in dealing with massive amounts of data, application of statistical analysis to data and application of search techniques from Artificial Intelligence to these problems. [Wikipedia-DM 2006]*

Motivations for undertaking data mining include reducing costs, increasing revenue, making new discoveries, automating laborious human tasks, identifying fraud, and improving customer or user experiences. As such, data mining is a competitive strategy for all industries and ventures.

1.2.1 Data Mining by Other Names

Data mining goes by several aliases, for example, *advanced analytics, predictive analytics, artificial intelligence,* and *machine learning.* Advanced analytics is commonly thought of as referring to sophisticated statistical analysis, online analytical processing (OLAP), and data mining. In the next section, we elaborate on the difference between OLAP and data mining.

Predictive analytics focuses more on the data mining elements of predicting outcomes or making assignments [SearchCRM 2006], but it has also come to mean a more automated data mining process [Oracle-PA 2006]. Such automated data mining processes relieve the data miner[1] of data preparation or model quality checks, allowing the focus to be mainly on desired results (e.g., making predictions or ranking attributes by relative importance).

Artificial Intelligence (AI) is described as "the science and engineering of making intelligent machines, especially intelligent computer programs. It is related to the similar task of using computers to understand human intelligence, but AI does not have to confine itself to methods that are biologically observable" [McCarthy 2004]. AI is very broad and dates back to at least the 1950s. As such, there are several branches of artificial intelligence: logical AI, search, pattern recognition, representation, interference, common sense knowledge and reasoning, learning from experience, among others. Aspects of data mining may find their way into each of these, but the true emphasis is *learning from experience*. Machine learning [Mitchell 1997] falls into this category, where computer programs examine historical data in an effort to *learn* or derive patterns from the data that can be used to solve specific problems.

1.2.2 Data Mining Versus Other Forms of Advanced Analytics

When we talk to customers new to data mining and ask whether they mine their data, we'll sometimes hear, "Yes, of course." But when we ask how they mine their data or which tools they use, we hear that they have a very large database that they analyze with complex queries. To some, this is data mining. The area of query and reporting addresses relatively simple *deductive* analysis, that is, the extraction of detail and summary data based on human-formulated questions. For example, answering questions such as "which stores sold portable DVD players in the past quarter" and "how much did each sell" is common. We draw a distinction that querying is not data mining in the machine learning sense. Answering such questions can be accomplished through a straightforward SQL query, as shown in this code, which is based on the schema of Figure 1-1.

---

1   We will sometimes refer to the user of a data mining tool or the person who mines data as a "data miner."

```
SELECT store.name, sum (sale_amount) AS sales_sum
FROM store, sales, date, product
WHERE product.name = 'Portable DVD Player' AND
    product.id = sales.product_id AND
    sales.store_id = store.id AND
    sales.date = date.date AND
    date.quarter = '2Q06'
GROUP BY store.id
ORDER BY sales_sum
```

Figure 1-1 shows four tables: SALES, PRODUCT, STORE, and DATE. The SALES table contains the sales amount and keys into the other three tables, indicating the product sold, the store that sold it, and the date that it was sold. The PRODUCT table provides the name of the product as well as a hierarchical grouping of that product into higher-level categories. A product belongs to a particular group, which belongs to a more general category (e.g., Coca-Cola 20-ounce soda may have a product group of "colas" and be in the product category of "soft drinks").

Another technology to distinguish from data mining is Online Analytical Processing (OLAP) technology [Wikipedia-OLAP 2006]. OLAP supports summaries, forecasts, and trend analysis. For example, summaries often involve "rolling up" data to different levels of granularity as defined by a *dimension*, such as Date, which can

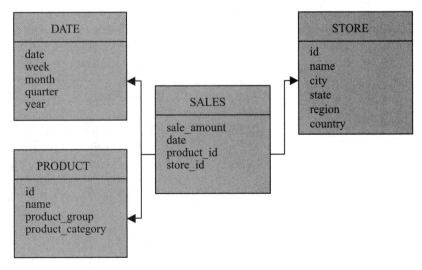

Figure 1-1 *Example of a star schema.*

provide a summary of dollar sales by day, week, month, quarter, or year. Multiple dimensions can be used to form a data *cube;* for example, the store where the sale was made and the product that was sold are each dimensions, as depicted in Figure 1-2. The sale amount is called a *measure,* and a cube may have multiple measures. Once the cube is defined, business and data analysts can "slice and dice" it to provide different views of the data (e.g., sales by month by geographical region by product category). Like querying large databases, OLAP is also deductive in nature. Users formulate questions or organize data to retrieve answers. The underlying data representation for OLAP is often in the form of a star or snowflake schema, as shown in Figure 1-1.

In contrast, data mining supports knowledge discovery of hidden patterns and insights. It takes an inductive approach to data analysis, building up results by analyzing each of potentially millions of records. Data mining allows the answering of such questions as how much revenue will each store generate for portable DVD players in the next quarter, or which customers will purchase a portable DVD player and why. Although OLAP generally supports trend analysis and forecasting, it may rely on simple moving average or percentage

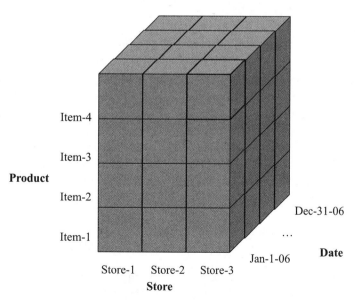

Figure 1-2 *Example of an OLAP cube.*

growth calculations considering aggregated or summarized data. In other cases, it may leverage more advanced time series analysis.

Like query and reporting and OLAP, data mining solutions exist in every industry—for example, predicting the likelihood of a customer buying a particular product, switching to a competitor's product, or defaulting on a loan; identifying false insurance claims; contracting a certain type of leukemia.

The results of data mining can be fed back into the data warehouse, data mart, or other data repositories to enrich query and reporting and OLAP analysis. In query and reporting, once we predict which customers are likely to purchase a portable DVD player, we can sort customers by their likelihood to purchase that product or accept a related offer, and then select the top N customers for a marketing campaign. In OLAP, we can use data mining to identify which dimensions are the most predictive for a particular measure. If there are many, perhaps dozens, of dimensions to choose from, this can guide selecting dimensions to include in a particular cube analysis.

In addition, the predictions from data mining models on the individual data records can be fed back into the cube, perhaps as additional measures that can be included in subsequent roll-ups. For example, we could predict which offer a given customer is likely to accept and then include a dimension that rolls up these offers into an offer hierarchy.

1.2.3   Process

For business people and C-level[2] executives, the details of data mining are likely to be a curiosity at best. What these individuals desire are tangible results that they can use to make better business decisions. From their perspective, knowing which customers are likely to become next month's attrition[3] statistics is more important than the technique used to get that information—as long as the methodology used is sound and the tools trustworthy. At this level, we can view data mining as a "black box," as illustrated in Figure 1-3.

---

2   "C-level" refers to top corporate management, including the Chief Executive Officer (CEO), Chief Marketing Officer (CMO), Chief Information Officer (CIO), and so on.

3   *Attrition* occurs, for example, when a customer terminates service or stops purchasing a product, an employee resigns, or student does not return the following term. Attrition is often the term used in the industries financial services and higher education. In the telecommunications industry, attrition is referred to as "churn."

Figure 1-3 *A workflow involving data mining.*

There is a comprehensive, recognized process for data mining—CRISP-DM—which we cover in detail in Chapter 3. For now, we can consider a simplified process that begins with defining the problem and its objectives, identifying data for mining, and assessing data quality. The *availability of data* for mining is not the same thing as *appropriateness of data* for mining. If the data is *dirty* (i.e., contains errors and inconsistencies), it likely must first be cleaned. Note that the adage "garbage in, garbage out" is most applicable to data mining.

This data is then transformed as required by the data mining tool and/or according to the creativity of the data miner. Transformations include, for example, replacing misspelled values with correct ones, identifying outlier values, and create attributes derived from other attributes. The knowledge extraction process continues with mining the transformed data to produce a data mining model, which is then evaluated for quality and relevance to the problem's objectives. The knowledge extraction step could involve the labor of dozens of statisticians in a back room crunching numbers, or a data mining algorithm iterating over the data to produce a *model* of the data.

The model itself may be used directly to understand, for example, customer segments, or what the factors are that most influence customers to accept an offer. The model may also be used to generate *scores* (i.e., make predictions or classifications). Scoring can be performed in batch (i.e., all at once over a given dataset such as a large customer dataset), or integrated into applications for real-time scoring such as in call center applications or online retail product recommendations.

Solving business and scientific problems often requires many components in a complex process flow—for example, customer interaction, data collection and staging, data analysis and summarization, report generation and distribution, decision making, and deployment. As such, data mining does not exist by itself but is often integrated with a business process to provide value.

Operational systems collect data, typically in relational databases, that is then cleaned and staged into the corporate data warehouse.

Various reporting tools can issue queries about data, both in operational data stores and the data warehouse. OLAP cubes may be refreshed with the latest data to facilitate slicing and dicing the latest results. Data mining, as described earlier, not only plays a key role in understanding the interactions between historical data and outcomes, but also in characterizing those interactions in a way that can predict future outcomes and feed those outcomes back into other analysis and decision making.

Although corporate data available for mining may be considerable, when assessing the data available for mining you may need to supplement it. Banks, for example, know every transaction their customers have ever made, their account balances, and details from customer loan applications. One could say that a bank has plenty of data to mine. However, the "availability of data" may not be sufficient to build a useful data mining model, or a model that satisfies a particular need. If a bank is trying to understand its customers based on demographics, such as personal interests as part of a marketing campaign, those demographics are not typically part of the bank's operational data stores or data warehouse. Before mining the data, a bank may have to acquire demographic information, either through direct solicitation from customers or by purchasing customer information from third-party providers.

1.2.4   What Is a Data Mining Model?

We have used the term *model* several times already and defined it as a compact representation of the patterns found in historical data. To illustrate the concept of a data mining model more concretely, consider a simple *linear regression* problem — that is, predicting a continuous numerical value from one or more inputs. Basically, we have a set of points on a graph and we want to fit a straight line to them. This functionality was provided in the Texas Instruments TI-55 scientific calculator of the 1970s and had been around long before that. Essentially, the algorithm iterates over the data to collect statistics and then determines the coordinates of the line that best fits the set of two-dimensional points; this is illustrated in Figure 1-4.

The model that represents this line is simply expressed as two values from the equation $y = mx + b$, where m is the slope, and b is the y-intercept. A model that consists of m and b is sufficient to make predictions for y given a value of x. For example, if $m = 2$ and $b = 5$, then if x (or age) $= 25$, we predict the value of y (or income) $= 55$ (thousand).

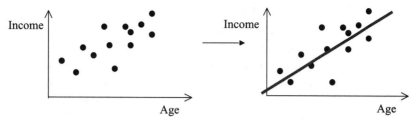

Figure 1-4 *Fitting a regression line to a set of data points.*

In two dimensions,[4] involving the attributes age and income, and with a small number of data points, the problem seems fairly simple. We could probably even "eye" a solution by drawing a line to fit the data and estimating the values for *m* and *b*. However, consider data that is not in two dimensions, but a hundred, a thousand, or several thousand dimensions. The attributes may include numerical values or consist of categories that are either numbers or strings. Some of the categorical data may have an ordering (e.g., *high, medium, low*) or be unordered (e.g., *married, unmarried, widowed*). Further, consider cases where there are tens of thousands or millions of cases. It is intractable for a human to make sense of this data, but it is relatively easy for the right algorithm executing on a sufficiently powerful computer. Here lies the essence of data mining.

Now, data mining algorithms are typically much more complex than that of linear regression; however, the concept is the same: there is a compact representation of the "knowledge" present in the data that can be used for prediction or inspection.

1.2.5 Some Jargon

Every field has its jargon—the vernacular of the "in crowd." Here's a quick overview of some of the data mining jargon.

At one level, data mining experts talk about things like models and techniques, or *mining functions* called classification, regression, clustering, attribute importance, and association. *Classification* models predict some outcome, such as which offer a customer will respond to. *Regression* models predict a continuous number, such as what is the predicted value of a home or a person's income.

---

4   This use of the term "dimension" here should not be confused with the same term as used in OLAP, which has a different intent. Here, the term "dimension" is synonymous with "attribute" or "column."

Clustering models contain descriptions of groups of records that share similar characteristics, such as the naturally occurring segments in a customer database. *Attribute importance* models rank the input attributes according to how well they are able to predict an outcome or assist in defining clusters. *Association* models contain rules for common co-occurrences in data, such as the determination that customers who purchased products A and B also purchased product C 90 percent of the time.

Data mining often is characterized as being *predictive* or *descriptive* and *supervised* or *unsupervised*. The predictive nature of data mining is that the models produced from historical data have the ability to predict outcomes such as which customers are likely to churn, who will be interested in a particular product, or which medications are likely to affect the outcome of cancer treatment positively.

The descriptive nature of data mining is where the model itself is inspected to understand the essence of the knowledge or patterns found in the data. As in the regression example of Section 1.2.4, we may be more interested in the trend of the data and hence knowing that the slope of the line is positive is sufficient—as *age* increases, *salary* increases.

Some models serve both predictive and descriptive purposes. For example, a decision tree not only can predict outcomes, but also can provide human interpretable rules that explain why a prediction was made. Clustering models provide not only the ability to assign a record to a cluster, but also a description of each cluster, either in the form of a representative point called a *centroid*, or as a rule that describes why a record is considered part of the cluster. These concepts are explained more fully in Chapter 7.

The notion of *model transparency* is the ability of a user to understand how or why a given model makes certain predictions. Some algorithms produce such models, others algorithms produce models that are treated as "black boxes." Neural networks are a good example of *opaque* models that are used solely for their predictive capabilities.

A second characterization is *supervised* and *unsupervised* learning. Supervised learning simply means that the algorithm requires that its source data contain the correct answer for each record. This allows some algorithms (e.g., decision trees and neural networks) to make corrections to a model to ensure that it can get as many of the answers correct as possible. The correct answers *supervise* the learning process by pointing out mistakes when the algorithm uses the model to predict outcomes. Other algorithms (e.g., naïve bayes) use the known outcomes to compute statistics which enable subsequent predictions. Supervised models use data consisting of *predictors* and *targets*. The predictors are attributes (columns) used to predict the *outcome* – the target attribute (also a column).

Unsupervised learning does not require, and does not accept, knowledge of any correct answer. It merely looks at all the data and applies an algorithm that performs the appropriate analysis. Clustering is an unsupervised technique that determines the clusters that naturally exist in the data.

In data mining, several terms have evolved to mean the same thing. For example, when referring to a column of data, the typical relational database term, we will see the terms *attribute, field,* and *variable*. Similarly, when referring to the rows of data, we will see the terms *case, record, example,* and *instance*. They typically can be used interchangeably.[5] In JDM, we have adopted the terms *attribute* and *case*.

The Mining Metaphor

Data mining is the process of extracting knowledge from data. That knowledge can be used to understand the nature of a business or scientific problem, or applied to new data to make predictions or classifications. Just as mining in the physical world involves a process of going from raw earth to refined material (e.g., gold, steel, and platinum) to end-products (e.g., jewelry, electronics), data mining involves a process of going from large volumes of raw data to extracted knowledge to knowledge applied in practice. This section takes this metaphor to its limit by contrasting a description of the gold mining process [Wells 2006] with data mining.

> *Gold mining involves the science, technology, and business of the discovery of gold, in addition to its removal and sale in the marketplace. Gold may be found in many places, most commonly rock but even sea water; in very small quantities. More often it is found in greater quantities in veins associated with igneous rocks, rocks created by heat such as quartzite.*

"Data Mining" is somewhat of a misnomer since we are not trying to discover "data," but the knowledge that is present in data. In any

---

5   There are some distinctions to be made, for example, a case may be comprised of multiple records when the data is stored in *transactional format*. Here a case corresponds to a transaction consisting, perhaps, of multiple items as purchased at a grocery store checkout.

case, making use of this knowledge is key to realizing a return on investment (ROI) with data mining. Like gold mining, some corporate data are rich with patterns and insights, others have nothing. Unlike some gold mining, however, data mining doesn't have "veins" of knowledge waiting to be pulled out. Rather, the knowledge is dispersed in the data, waiting to be discovered by various data mining techniques.

Since the costs can be high in the exploration and removal of gold from the hard rock mines, large companies are created in order to raise the money necessary for the development of the mines, rather than the solitary individual or small group associated with placer mining.

The machinery brought to bear in data mining, of course, is computer hardware, software algorithms, and often experienced data analysts. Traditionally, companies specialized in their ability to mine certain domains of data, using certain techniques; for example, the retail domain for customer segmentation and response modeling, banking for fraud detection and credit scoring, genomics for cancer cell similarity analysis, or homeland security for text document analysis. Other companies cover a much broader range of domains and techniques. Still, the image of statisticians or data mining experts in the back room working creative magic with the data and producing mind-boggling results is prevalent.

Mining for gold is only worthwhile financially where there is a significant concentration of it found in ore. The fixed price of gold in 1934 increased from $20.67 U.S. to $35 U.S. per troy ounce. This price remained fixed until 1968 which discouraged hard rock mining for gold because increased inflation (which raised the cost of mining production) prevented the mining companies from making a profit.

The price of gold can be likened to ROI in business. An IDC report [IDC 2003] shows the *median* ROI for advanced analytics projects, such data mining, to be 145 percent. This makes an investment in such projects a worthwhile venture in general. It is when competition becomes so fierce, and margins so slim, that not leveraging data mining becomes a practice dangerous to corporate survival. Like gold mining, data mining results may miss ROI targets for numerous reasons: the quality of the raw material (data) from which knowledge is to be extracted, using the wrong tool(s), applying the wrong technique to the problem, the skill of the individuals performing the mining, the inability to use the mining results effectively in the business process, and so on. This can require paying more attention to the data being collected, using the right tools or tools that have more automated intelligence for the mining process, or hiring more skilled or experienced individuals.

> *Before hard rock mining operations have even begun, companies explore areas where gold may be found and scientifically analyse the rock. The actual gold originates deep within the earth in places called pockets. These pockets are filled with gold, heavy ore, and quartz. If enough gold is discovered in the ore, the technological process of hard rock mining begins.*

As we discuss later in Chapter 3, the data mining process begins with a clear understanding of the business objectives and data mining goals. Like gold mining, we then need to survey the corporate landscape for available data. Sometimes needed data may be readily available in repositories such as data warehouses and data marts. Other times, data resides in various databases that support operational systems. In less sophisticated organizations, data may reside in Excel spreadsheets or flat files. Once sources have been identified, we need to analyze the data for quality (e.g., missing values, consistency of values, etc.) and prepare it through data cleansing and other transformations. An assessment can be made for correlation between combinations of attributes as to whether the data is likely to contain any useful patterns or knowledge; then the process of data mining begins.

> *First, miners dig a tunnel into the solid rock. During the 1930s, miners working for the companies dug these tunnels by hand, a very labour-intensive undertaking. Miners often risked their health, digging with picks and shovels during long shifts in these dark, damp tunnels, building the shafts and carting out the ore.*

Data miners have it a little easier. However, in the early days of data mining, statisticians applied various combinations of univariate (single attribute) and multivariate (multiple attributes) statistics. They also hand-coded algorithms, such as linear regression, to fit a line to a set of data points. Visualization was often crude, sometimes relying on only numerical outputs. Due to hardware and software limitations, the number of attributes and cases mined was often relatively small, perhaps tens of attributes. Producing useful models could take weeks or months using complex analysis. Getting the results of mining into the hands of business people, or into operational systems, often required teams of people to process the results, produce high-level reports, and include models in operational systems.

Today, there are commercial tools with standard and state-of-the-art algorithms that can automate much of the data mining process. Such tools can produce good results, but the expert data miner may be able to produce superior results through custom analysis and crafty techniques. In addition, including data mining results in applications or operational systems has also become simpler as a result of standard interfaces and model representations.

 The gold milling process may be broken down into three basic procedures:

1. *Sorting the ore by size*
2. *Crushing the rock*
3. *Extracting the gold*

A simplified data mining process can be broken down into four basic procedures:

1. Acquiring and preparing the data
2. Building the model
3. Assessing model quality and reviewing the model details
4. Applying the model to new data for predictions or assignments

First, miners raise the ore out of the mine in wheeled carts pushed on rails and take it down to the mill. The rock fragments are sorted according to size in a grizzly—a device consisting of a series of spaced bars, rails, or pipes—above a forward moving conveyer belt to a crusher machine.

In large companies, and even some smaller ones, the IT department's database administrators (DBAs) help to identify available data from operational systems and data warehouses. Data is "sorted" according to quality, completeness, and applicability to the problem to be solved. Once data is identified, it needs to be unified by joining different data tables, often into a single table, or perhaps a set of tables related by a single case identifier or as part of a star schema.

After secondary washing, a shaker screen filters out fragments of less than 1/2 inch diameter into a fine ore bin, or box. Larger ore fragments are pulverized or crushed in the crusher. The fine ore is fed by conveyer belt to a ball mill, a rotating steel cylinder filled with tumbling steel balls which further crushes the fragments to a consistency of fine sand or talcum powder. This powder is fed into a thickener with a cyanide and water solution to create a sludge (a sticky, mudlike material). The liquid sludge is diverted into holding tanks and referred to as the pregnant solution—a liquid sludge containing 70% of the gold.

Like rock and ore, raw data needs to be prepared. The mechanisms for refining it to enable knowledge extraction involve data analysis technology, data cleansing, transformations, and attribute synthesis. These are big terms for problems such as graphing data values, correcting typos, dealing with missing values, categorizing data values (e.g., age) into buckets instead of continuous values, and creating new attributes based on other attributes (e.g., customer lifetime value).

[The liquid sludge] is drawn from holding tanks through a clarifier, a device that removes all the remaining rock or clay from a pregnant solution. In the next step, the material is taken to a de-areator tank that removes bubbles of air and further clarifies the solution.

The dataset as presented to the data mining algorithm can be viewed as the "pregnant solution." As a data mining algorithm executes, it makes finer and more precise distinctions about the data to extract knowledge. This can be in the form of, for example, rules that define customer profiles, common co-occurrences of product sales enabling cross-sell, or a representative case that describes a set of patients susceptible to a type of cancer.

Zinc is added in dust form to the de-areated solution, which is drawn under pressure through a filter press; which causes the gold and zinc to precipitate onto canvas (heavy cloth) filter leaves. This zinc-gold precipitate (condensed into a solid) is then cleaned from the filters while extreme heat burns off the zinc.

The purified "precipitate" of data mining is the emerging model, which contains the extracted knowledge. It needs to be tested and possibly refined through changing of parameters or further preparation of the data to produce a sufficient knowledge yield.

Water passing through the filters is chemically tested for gold residue before being discharged into tailings ponds. Gold bearing water may be passed through the filtering process several times to remove all of the gold and separate it from impure substances.

Mining algorithms will often make several passes over the data to continually tune or refine the model. Algorithms, such as neural networks, decision trees, and K-means clustering, make multiple passes over the data until any further improvements are determined insignificant or some other *stopping criterion* is met.

> *Gold recovered from the ore through the milling process is poured into bricks that are shipped to be assayed and sent to the mint in Ottawa, where coins are struck (made).*

Data mining models can be shipped from the lab to the field, or components of which can be packaged up in reports or dashboards for management and operations staff. From there, some models can be used to score new data (i.e., make predictions or classifications). These scores can be used in applications such as predicting customer response.

After reviewing this metaphor, you should have a physical grounding in the data mining process and perhaps have learned something about gold mining you did not know before.

1.3 The Value of Data Mining

The true value of data mining does not reside in a set of complex algorithms, but in the practical problems that it can help solve. Too often, data mining solutions are presented through the eyes of the data analyst—the person who massages and prepares the data and builds the models—where the emphasis is on the algorithm and techniques used to solve the problem. However, in the business world, true *value* is realized with *return on investment*, when we see that $2 million was saved for a $300,000 investment to predict which customers will default on a loan, or when we see that consumer fraud was reduced 50 percent resulting in a savings of $22 million.

1.3.1 How Reliable Is Data Mining?

For a technology to be truly valuable, it needs to be reliable. Few technologies are foolproof in practice, including data mining. However, data mining is based on a firm foundation in mathematics and statistics. Data mining algorithms withstand tests on both real and synthetic datasets, where results are rigorously analyzed for accuracy and correctness. The reliability of results more often depends on the availability of sufficient data, data quality, and the technique chosen, as well as the skills of those preparing the data, selecting algorithm parameters, and analyzing the results. If the data provided contains erroneous values (e.g., false data entered on warranty cards, or a lot of missing values), data mining algorithms may have difficulty discovering any meaningful patterns in the data. However, over the past several decades, data mining techniques have been used extensively in industry. For example, credit card transactions and mortgage applications are often approved with input from data mining models.

When a model is first produced, it can be quite reliable in terms of the accuracy of its predictions on new data. However, is the predictive quality of a model invariant? Does model accuracy remain constant over time?

Few things remain constant, especially when humans are involved. Tastes change, needs change, technology changes, life-altering events force change. For example, a model that may have been excellent at predicting credit risk for a given month may start to show signs of degraded performance. When this happens we say that such a model is *stale*. In this case, the model may need to be rebuilt, taking into account more recent data. The data mining process and its artifacts require periodic review and maintenance to maintain reliable results.

1.3.2   How Can Data Mining Increase Profits and Reduce Costs?

Let's consider an example from campaign management, first without the use of data mining and then using data mining. One of the objectives for campaign management is to determine which customers to contact with regard to a particular sales campaign, with goals to minimize costs and maximize response and profits. If you knew in advance which customers would respond, you may likely contact only those customers.

Consider Company DMWHIZZ with a base of a million customers. Based on previous campaign responses, DMWHIZZ generally gets a 2 percent response rate. With a million customers, this produces about 20,000 responses. A proposed DMWHIZZ campaign will require mailing costs of $1.50 per item, with a total campaign cost of $1.5 million. If the average profit per customer who responds is $50, our expected total profit is $1 million (20,000 × $50). But, since the net profit of the campaign is a *negative* $500,000, DMWHIZZ will not proceed with the campaign.

Let's see how applying data mining can make this campaign profitable. Selecting those customers most likely to respond is a classification problem (i.e., classify each customer as responding or not with an associated probability). As with any classification problem, DMWHIZZ will need to have actual response data from a similar campaign to learn customer behavior. To achieve this,

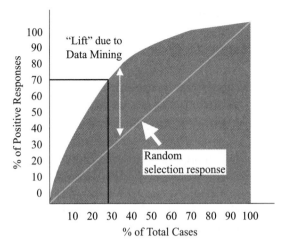

Figure 1-5 *Cumulative positive targets representing model "lift."*

DMWHIZZ takes a 1 percent sample of customers for a trial campaign. Reviewing the data from the 10,000 customers they received their expected 2 percent, or 200 responses. Using the data mining model and a held-aside or test set of customers, we find that the model can return 80 percent of the likely responders contacting only 40 percent of the customers, or 70 percent of likely responders contacting 30 percent of the customers, as illustrated in Figure 1-5.[6]

Armed with this information, DMWHIZZ data miners build a classification model using customer demographic and other data in their customer and sales databases. The resulting model is used to predict the likelihood of response for each of the remaining 990,000 customers. Now, let's add up the results.

The cost of the trial campaign was $15,000 (10,000 × $1.50). Using the data mining model, DMWHIZZ scores the 990,000 customers and takes the top 40 percent as likely to respond (400,000). Recall that this model provides 80 percent of the likely responders within that 40 percent. Since we expect 20,000 responses out of a million customers, we should get 80 percent of these, or 16,000 — less the 200 we already received in the trial, or 15,800. At an average profit of $50 per

---

6 Note that predicting a customer's response is one aspect of the solution. Another aspect is often profitability. This scenario can be augmented to predict profit per customer and multiply by the probability of response, thereby producing an expected profit per customer. Customers can be ordered based on this expected profit.

response, this produces $790,000 in revenue.[7] The cost of the campaign is $600,000 (400,000 × $1.50), so the projected profit is $175,000 ($790K − $600K − $15K).

But what if we are more selective? Can we further increase profit? If we restrict the campaign to the top 30 percent of customers likely to respond (300,000), we will obtain 70 percent of the likely responders, or 13,800 responses (20,000 × 70 − 200). Projected revenue is $690,000 (13,800 × $50), but cost of the campaign is only $450,000 (300,000 × $1.50). So, the projected profit is $225,000 ($690K − $450K − $15K). In this case, we actually increased profits by running a campaign for fewer customers.

1.4   Summary

This first chapter discussed how data mining is particularly relevant to businesses today in solving complex problems. Competition and the need to improve customer experiences and interactions are among the motivations, along with a better evaluation of the risks associated with business processes. We discussed other terms that are often used for data mining or are related to it. We then introduced data mining, contrasting it with other forms of advanced analytics such as OLAP and highlighting a basic process for extracting knowledge and patterns from data. We introduced the notion of a *model* as a compact representation of the knowledge or patterns found in the data. To set the stage for our subsequent discussions, we introduced typical data mining jargon, which will be revisited in more detail in later chapters.

As gold mining has been performed through the centuries, so has it been codified into a repeatable process. Similarly, data mining has evolved to the stage where the process of mining data has also been codified. Since data mining has parallels with gold mining, we compared and contrasted the process of data mining with that of gold mining.

We finished with a discussion on the value of data mining, exploring reliability as well as a specific example in monetary terms.

---

7   In an actual modeling, the $50.00 expected profit would be multipled by the probability of response assigned to each customer. This gives a more precise expected outcome.

The next chapter takes a more in-depth look at solving problems in industry.

References

[BIS 2004] Bank for International Settlements, "Basel II: Revised International Capital Framework," http://www.bis.org/publ/bcbsca.htm, June 26, 2004.

[Davenport 2006] Thomas Davenport, "Competing on Analytics," *Harvard Business Review,* January 2006.

[JSR-73 2004] "Java Specification Request 73: Java Data Mining (JDM)," Maintenance Release v1.1, June 2005, http://jcp.org/en/jsr/detail?id=73.

[McCarthy 2004] John McCarthy, "What is Artificial Intelligence," Department of Computer Science, Stanford University (http://www-formal.stanford.edu/jmc/whatisai/whatisai.html), November 24, 2004.

[Mitchell 1997] Tom Mitchell, *Machine Learning,* McGraw-Hill, Boston, 1997.

[Oracle-PA 2006] http://www.oracle.com/technology/products/bi/odm/pa-addin/odm_pred_analytics_addin.html.

[Perl 2006] http://www.perl.org/about.html.

[SearchCRM 2006] http://searchcrm.techtarget.com/sDefinition/0, sid11_gci1070868,00.html.

[Shaw/Ivens 2002] Colin Shaw, John Ivens, *Building Great Customer Experiences,* Great Britain, Palgrave Macmillan, 2002.

[SoftPanorama 2006] http://www.softpanorama.org/Scripting/index.shtml.

[SOX2006] http://www.soxtoolkit.com/sox-mail.htm.

[Webopedia 2006] http://www.webopedia.com/TERM/M/Moores_Law.html.

[Wells 2006] Wells Historical Society and Wells Museum, "Hard-Rock Mining: The Process," http://wells.entirety.ca/mining.htm.

[Wikipedia-DM 2006] http://en.wikipedia.org/wiki/Data_mining.

[Wikipedia—OLAP 2006] http://en.wikipedia.org/wiki/OLAP.

[Wikipedia—OpenStd 2006] http://en.wikipedia.org/wiki/Open_standard.

[XML.com 2006] "Service Oriented Architecture," http://www.xml.com/lpt/a/ws/2003/09/30/soa.html.

Chapter 2

Solving Problems in Industry

No problem can stand the assault of sustained thinking.

—Voltaire

Data mining has long been used to solve important problems across industries [Apte+ 2002] [Berry/Linoff 2004] [Gloven 2002]. One of the biggest challenges to using data mining is knowing to which types of problems it can readily be applied. Too often, a discussion of data mining delves into a specific algorithm and its myriad features. However, success with data mining goes beyond choosing the right algorithm. Understanding the requirements in a particular domain, and the types of problems and approaches to solving those problems, is the best starting place to reap the benefits of data mining technology. This chapter explores various business problems that are common to many industries and that can be addressed with a strategy based on data mining.

As Internet and digital storage technology enables volumes of data to grow astronomically, so does the need for analyzing that data to extract useful information. However, data mining is not only for large institutions with terabytes of data. Data mining's benefits can be leveraged by companies both big and small, from large financial institutions to local car dealerships, those with millions of customers, and those with hundreds, and those with scientific as well as manufacturing process data analysis needs.

Java Data Mining (JDM) is geared toward providing a rich set of capabilities that allow applications to integrate data mining processes and results to solve a wide variety of problems. As such, JDM fits well with a solution strategy involving data mining.

2.1   Cross-Industry Data Mining Solutions

Data mining can solve a wide variety of problems either to gain understanding or insights from business and scientific data (what is the root cause of failures), or to predict certain outcomes (will the customer purchase the product?) or values (what is the predicted real estate value?). Knowing how to adapt even a small set of canonical problems to specific industries enables taking advantage of the power of data mining. This section explores several cross-industry solutions where data mining is being applied. We use the term "cross-industry" since most industries can tailor each of these solutions for their particular domain.

2.1.1   Customer Acquisition

Obtaining new customers is the hallmark of growth for many companies. However, not all customers are equally profitable. Business marketers may select a subset of customers using some basic criteria, such as income and age constraints, but may prove to be not loyal, that is, not stay with the company for a long time or purchase products exclusively from that company. Providing generous offers to attract such customers may result in high acquisition costs while providing no long-term benefits. Some customers simply jump from offer to offer to take advantage of discounts or "freebies."

Others may be loyal, but may purchase infrequently or purchase only low-margin products. Targeting low-value customers with generous offers may also prove to be counterproductive. Targeting the right potential customers can result in greater customer retention, greater customer lifetime value, and more profitability in the most desirable product and customer segments.

Consider the customer groups in Figure 2-1. A potential customer population for a marketing campaign is represented by the large oval. A company could attempt to acquire all these customers, but that may be prohibitively expensive. Moreover, many of the potential customers may quickly leave for a competitor, purchase only low-margin products, or introduce more costs (through call center or

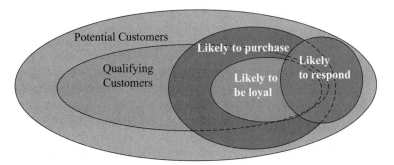

Figure 2-1   *Identifying your customers.*

support line interactions) than profits for the business. If we use traditional query techniques, we may select a subset of these possible customers and target those of a certain age or in a particular income bracket or household size. This type of segmentation is often based on intuition or business experience. Yet, only a subset of these customers are likely to purchase such a product or respond to a campaign, whether contacted by mail, phone, or e-mail.

Where customer acquisition costs are high, either due to the means of customer contact or incentives offered to them, knowing which customers are likely to respond (see Section 2.1.3, "Response Modeling") and the potential value of those customers can greatly reduce costs. Yet still, only some of the customers who purchase or respond will be loyal. A goal for customer acquisition is to target those customers who will have the greatest probability for response, loyalty, or lifetime value.

For a moment, let's go back to the simple query approach. Forming precise boundaries to determine which customers to target based on intuition or business experience may be accurate some of the time, but likely leaves out some customers, perhaps many, who may prove to be highly valuable, simply because they didn't meet a preconceived set of constraints.

Data mining is a key component of any modern customer acquisition strategy and revolves around several techniques. Given a set of potential customers, perhaps obtained as data acquired from a third party, data mining techniques such as clustering and classification can be used to identify the various customer segments that exist among those customers. After analyzing each of those segments, we can determine the likelihood that each customer segment, and each individual customer, will purchase specific products. To achieve this requires having historical data on the types of products existing customers have purchased and various attributes of those customers such as demographics, behaviors, etc.

Once we have identified the customers who are likely to purchase, we can further assess which of these customers are likely to be profitable. This also requires historical data containing the profiles of customers deemed to be profitable and unprofitable. Certain classification techniques, such as decision trees, can produce a set of profiles, or *rules*, highlighting the characteristics of profitable customers. This information can then be used to select profitable customers.

Now that we know which customers are likely to purchase, which of those are likely to be loyal, and which will be the most profitable, we can perform response modeling to determine who is likely to respond to a campaign. Then, we may even go one step further to determine which channel is best for contacting such customers.

2.1.2 Customer Retention

Once a business has customers, one of the next problems is how to keep those customers. Customer retention, or answering the question "how do I keep my current customers?" is a problem faced by businesses in most every industry. For example, in financial services, a customer who leaves is called an "attriter" and the problem is referred to as "attrition." In telecommunications, a customer who leaves is called a "churner" and the problem is referred to as "churn." Regardless of the terminology, the basic problem is the same: which customers are likely to leave and why?

Customers may leave for many reasons, for example, poor service, moving out of the area, or the availability of more competitive offers. However, these reasons are not always obvious until after the fact. An effective customer retention effort often requires identifying customers before they leave so that some action can be taken, if warranted, to retain those customers. We say "if warranted" because some customers may not be worth retaining. Customers who have low value or represent a net loss to the business when considering support and maintenance costs fall into this category.

Data mining can be applied to identify characteristics of individuals and their past and current behavior to determine much more subtle indicators of attrition or churn. For example, in wireless phone service, a customer whose minutes of usage drop from a four-week moving average of 500 minutes per week to 50 minutes per week could have many reasons: the person is on vacation, lost his job for which the phone was largely used, started using other means of communication such as Internet, or switched to another service provider for work-related calls, but still uses the service for personal calls. Figure 2-2 illustrates a pattern in minutes of usage that a possible churner may exhibit before terminating his account. However, different groups of individuals may be exhibiting this behavior, for example, teenage girls with large family and friend circles, 30-something single male professionals, etc. Understanding the particular characteristics of each of these groups enables businesses to develop campaigns to retain such customers or to increase their service usage. Data mining can identify the important factors or attributes that lead to a specific behavior, as well as group individuals according to their behavior.

A customer retention or loyalty strategy can revolve around several techniques. Customer loyalty can be increased when that customer purchases more products. Identifying which other products existing customers are likely to purchase, called *cross-sell* (see Section 2.1.5), can meet this objective. The data mining technique *association*, as discussed in Section 4.5, can help here.

We have already noted that some customers are more valuable than others, that is, they purchase products in greater quantity or purchase more profitable products. Helping to prevent the loss of such high-value customers is another area where data mining can help. First, one needs to be able to identify high-value customers. Being able to *classify* individuals efficiently as *high*, *medium*, or *low* value, or as representing a specific dollar amount to the business, is a

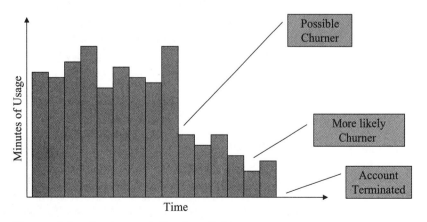

Figure 2-2 *Customer J. Doe's cellphone usage pattern.*

first step. Once we know which customers are high value, we can take steps to encourage them to remain customers, especially if we've identified them as likely to leave. Just as important as knowing which customers to keep is knowing which customers to let go. As noted above, low-value customers can be costly to maintain. For example, if a customer frequently uses your call center with questions or problems yet buys minimal product or services, it may be more cost effective to allow such customers to leave. Both active and passive actions can help to reduce low-value customers. Combining data mining results with rule-based systems can help to automatically recommend actions for certain customers.

For customers who are likely to leave, businesses need to understand if there are any common factors (e.g., a certain age or ethnic group, geographic region, or type of products sold) that are common among dissatisfied customers. If such factors are identified, businesses may be able to take more effective actions to avert a customer's decision to leave. Data mining can be used to identify the factors that play most heavily in determining an outcome. The data mining technique *attribute importance* can help here (see Section 4.4) as well as the decision tree algorithm which produces rules that highlight the specific attribute values that result in a dissatisfied customer. For example, a decision tree rule may indicate that high-income, 30-something female customers from the Northeast who purchased the latest product offering and had an unsuccessful call center experience cancelled their service.

Knowing in aggregate the number of customers likely to leave, say in the next three months, can give a manager a reasonable estimate for resource allocation, either in the number of support staff needed to try to retain these customers or budget to provide incentives to customers at risk. In this case, classification techniques allow the building of models that generate a probability of each customer to leave. Summing these probabilities provides the estimate of total attrition.

2.1.3   Response Modeling

The essence of response modeling is to determine whether or not someone will respond positively to a request or offer. That request may be to purchase a product, complete a survey, donate money, or participate in a clinical trial. The motivations for response modeling are simple: reduce costs by soliciting fewer people who have a greater likelihood of responding, increase return on investment by getting more positive responders for the money expended, and reduce customer fatigue by contacting only those customers most likely to show interest.

From a data mining perspective, the goal is to classify each individual as a *responder* or *nonresponder* with an associated probability. Data mining classification algorithms are well suited for this task. Customers can then be ranked from those with the highest probability of response to the lowest probability of response. Choosing those customers at the top of the list provides a high concentration of responders. This is reflected in a "lift" chart as depicted in Figure 2-3. The notion of lift is discussed in detail in Chapter 7, but in short, lift provides a simple understanding of how much better the predictions of the data mining model are than a random selection of customers.

To use data mining for response modeling, it is important to have relevant historical data about which customers responded and did not respond to campaigns in the past. "Relevant data" means that the data is for a similar situation, for example, purchase of a product or type of product, completing a survey, etc. Moreover, there needs to be sufficient demographic and other customer-related information from which data mining algorithms can "learn" the patterns or types of customer that respond. If there is no historical data available, a trial campaign can be performed on a random subset of the potential customers. Assuming there are a sufficient number of responders, the data mining algorithm can learn what distinguishes a responder from

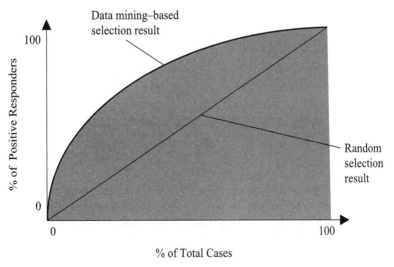

Figure 2-3 *Getting "lift" on responders.*

a nonresponder. It is from this trial, or sample, of the population that we can also test model accuracy and obtain a lift chart.

Response modeling can be combined with a value prediction, such as dollar amount of order, donation size, etc., to derive an expected return on the campaign. A *regression* model can be built to predict, for example, the amount each customer spends or each alumnus donates. Multiplying this value by the probability that a given customer will respond to the campaign produces an expected value for that customer. Customers can be sorted not only by likelihood to respond, but by expected value to identify the highest likely spenders or donors.

Another refinement of response modeling is to determine which channel is best to approach these customers, for example, mail, e-mail, or phone. Once again, based on historical data, we can learn the pattern of customers who respond best to mail, e-mail, or phone.

2.1.4   Fraud Detection

Anywhere money is involved, the potential for fraud exists; all industries are vulnerable to individuals who abuse established procedures for personal gain, often illegally. Healthcare, financial services, and taxation are just a few areas where fraud is found.

One approach to fraud detection involves clustering. The objective is first to group the data into clusters. We can then review each of the clusters to see if there is a concentration of known fraud in any one cluster, indicating that fraud is more likely to occur within a given cluster than another. In addition, we can look for cases that don't match any of the known clusters particularly well, or at all. These *outliers* become prime candidates for investigation.

A second approach to fraud detection involves classification. We first identify examples of fraud manually in historical data. With classification, the goal is to learn to distinguish between fraudulent and nonfraudulent behavior. Consider a dataset consisting of various predictor attributes, such as "age," "income," "wire transfer within last 10 days," and a target attribute indicating if the case was fraudulent or not. A classification algorithm like decision tree or support vector machine can then predict the likelihood of fraud on new data. Cases with a high probability of fraud are then good candidates for investigation. However, we can also predict the likelihood of fraud on the original data. This allows for a comparison between actual target values and the predicted values.

Where there are discrepancies (i.e., the case was believed to be nonfraudulent, but predicted to be fraudulent), there are opportunities for investigation.

In fraud detection, we want to ensure we catch fraud (minimize false negatives, which incorrectly identify fraud events as nonfraud events), while avoiding investigating too many red herrings (minimize false positives, which identify nonfraud events as fraud events), since the costs associated with investigating fraud can be high.

We digress briefly to discuss the types of errors possible for a classification model. Figure 2-4 illustrates a typical report on prediction accuracy, where *Type I error* is considered a false negative prediction and *Type II error* is considered a false positive prediction. The columns are labeled with the possible predicted classes, in this binary case, "0" corresponds to the negative (nonfraud) prediction, and "1" the positive (fraud) prediction. The value reported where actual and predicted equals "1" indicates the number of times the positive class was predicted correctly. Similarly, the value reported where the actual and predicted equals "0" indicate the number of times the negative class was predicted correctly. More than two values are possible when predicting multiple outcomes. In this case, the matrix is $n \times n$, instead of 2×2, where n is the number of possible values.

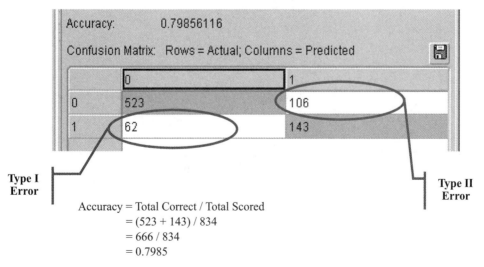

Figure 2-4 *Assessing prediction accuracy via Type I and Type II error.   Source: Screen capture from* Oracle Data Miner *graphical interface.*

As a percentage of transactions or cases, fraud is normally quite small, perhaps less than a few percent among all cases. A challenge for some data mining algorithms using predictive modeling for fraud detection is this imbalance between the number of known fraudulent cases and nonfraudulent cases. When using classification to identify fraud, such data can require special data preparation. A technique called *stratified sampling* can be used to obtain a dataset that contains a better balance. For example, if a million-case dataset contains 1 percent known fraud cases, this means that for the 10,000 examples of fraud, there are 990,000 examples of nonfraud. Many algorithms have difficulty with this imbalance, producing models that cannot distinguish fraud from nonfraud well. Consider that if the model simply predicted all cases to be nonfraud, the result would be 99 percent accurate, yet would not detect any fraud. By sampling the data for 25 percent (10,000) fraudulent cases and 75 percent (30,000) nonfraudulent cases, the algorithm can learn more effectively. When stratified sampling is introduced, *prior probabilities* can be used to inform the algorithm of the original population distribution, as illustrated in Figure 2-5. In this example, the priors are 1 percent for *fraud* and 99 percent for *nonfraud*. We revisit this concept of prior probability in Chapter 7. There are other techniques that can support fraud detection such as anomaly detection, which is being introduced in JDM 2.0.

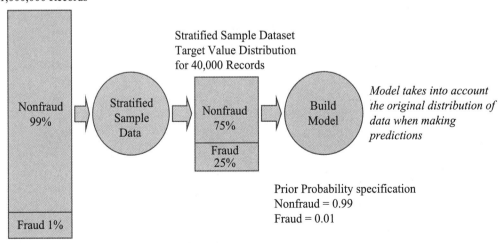

Figure 2-5 *Example of stratified sampling and prior probabilities.*

Perhaps the biggest problem in performing data mining is in the availability of useful data. Even if a company is willing to pursue a data mining project, that project can quickly come to a standstill due to either a total lack of data to mine, or poor quality data. Data with many missing values or inaccurate entries can make extracting meaningful information nearly impossible until the fundamental data quality or availability issues are resolved. This can involve anything from establishing a data warehouse, instituting business processes to collect certain information, or going back to the data sources to clean up "dirty" data. However, the problem of data availability and quality is beyond the scope of this book. We refer readers interested in this topic to [Kimball1 2004, Phonniah 2004] on data warehousing, and [Pyle 1999] on data preparation.

2.1.5 Cross-Selling

Getting customers to buy more of a company's products is a key goal for many marketing managers. Cross-selling is quite prevalent in online retailers, or e-businesses, where purchasing one product gives the company an opportunity to sell other products to that same customer. Cross-selling can involve identifying complementary or related products, or even premium products—called *up*-selling. For some products, suggestions for cross-selling may be obvious, for example, staples with staplers and mouse pads with computer mice. However, others are not so obvious, sometimes involving multiple products being purchased together.

The term *market basket analysis* is often applied to this problem. The data typically used is *transaction data*, a collection of records identified by a transaction identifier and containing the set of products or items that were purchased in that transaction. Consider a supermarket visit at customer checkout. Each customer's shopping cart or "market basket" contains some set of items. The data mining technique *association rules* leverages these buying patterns of customers to provide insight into which products are commonly purchased together, known as *product relationships*. Once we know these relationships, they can be used to position products on the same Web page, suggest other products at checkout time, or result in a separate solicitation via e-mail, mail, or phone.

Another use of identifying product relationships involves understanding product demand given promotions on certain products. For example, consider a store that decides to put a certain computer game on sale that uses a steering wheel input device. If the retailer does not foresee the relationship, there may be plenty of computer games in stock (what the retailer planned to promote), but customers may not be able to buy the complementary steering wheel input device since the product may have sold out prematurely. As a result, the retailer loses additional sales from customers who want that input device, or even loses the sale of the computer game from customers wanting both items and purchasing none.

2.1.6   New Product Line Development

Answering which bundle of products should be offered to customers, perhaps with pricing discounts, is a challenging task. Knowing which products are normally purchased together, possibly out of thousands, is daunting. Since not all customers behave the same, a bundling strategy should start with groups of similar customers. The first step is to identify a set of customer segments or target markets.

Consider a typical customer database, including individuals with a wide range of ages, incomes, and interests. Using clustering techniques, we can automatically identify customer segments. These segments might include such groups as "wealthy seniors who enjoy the outdoors," "young families in the suburbs," "college students who rent," and "large families in cities who use public transportation." We then partition the *market basket* data associated with each customer according to the customer's assigned segment. The next step is to use an association technique to find those products that are frequently purchased together within each segment. For example, we may find that "young families in the suburbs" may purchase several life insurance policies on family members as well as home insurance, but not car insurance. These now form the candidate product bundles that can be targeted for each of the customer groups. In the example, this could lead to a product bundle for multiple life insurance policies or a more complete bundle that includes car insurance to get this customer segment to purchase car insurance from this insurance company as well. The basic process is depicted in Figure 2-6.

Usually it is not enough to just identify possible product bundles. It is important to understand how likely a customer group is to purchase the new product bundle, and how much profit we can expect to make from such customers. To determine the success of a product bundle, a test marketing campaign can be performed, much like the response modeling problem of Section 2.1.3. From this we can determine not only if a significant percentage of customers will purchase

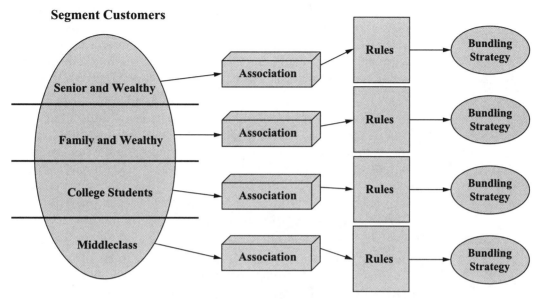

Figure 2-6   *Developing new product lines using segmentation and association.*

the new product bundle, but also develop a subprofile of customers in the segment most likely to purchase.

2.1.7   Survey Analysis

Thousands of surveys are conducted every day. The value of these surveys is often realized through straightforward statistical analysis and deductive reasoning. For example, consider a customer service satisfaction survey for a wireless telecommunications provider. Typically, such survey results are provided as bar charts of the population according to age group, income level, household size, and marital status. Questions are often summarized, for example, 50 percent of respondents rated quality of service low. Sometimes, results will even be correlated with a particular demographic, for example, 15 percent of 20- to 30-year-olds rated quality of service low while 80 percent of 30- to 40-year-olds did so. However, there may be more complex combinations of demographics that could shed more light on a particular response. For example, 75 percent of those who rated quality of service low have income between $75K and $100K, have a household size of 5, have over 1,000 minutes of usage per month, and travel for work more than 50 percent of the time. This kind of information helps to target a specific profile of persons and possibly even helps to pinpoint the reason for the low quality of service rating.

To this end, data mining technology can be applied to identify the profiles of respondents who answered one or more questions a certain way. It can also be used to understand how respondents are grouped or segmented. Such results enable focused sales and marketing efforts to well-defined groups, as well as corrective action [SPSS 2003].

Data in surveys is often *structured* but can also be *unstructured*. Structured data contains discrete responses such as multiple choice questions involving demographic data, for example, age and income level, or statements to be rated from "strongly agree" to "strongly disagree." Unstructured data can consist of short free-form responses, for example, the "other" category with a line to specify a value, or longer free-form questions such as "What was your best and worst experience with our company?" where the user responds with text.

To address free-form responses, text mining can be introduced by extracting important terms from the text and combining it with structured data before mining. Some data mining vendors will perform this term extraction automatically, others may require explicit preprocessing.

2.1.8   Credit Scoring

Every time you apply for a loan, mortgage, or credit card, your credit history is checked and your current financial situation is assessed to determine a "credit score." This score indicates the type of *risk* you represent to the financial institution issuing the credit. Credit scoring takes into account various information such as customer demographics, loan history, deposits and assets, total credit line, outstanding debt, etc.

The more accurate the score, the more likely the financial institution is to make a correct decision on a customer. Although there are always unexpected factors for individuals defaulting on loans, such as job loss or illness, the credit score provides important input to the loan decisioning process.

Historically, statistical methods were employed for credit scoring. Today, data mining plays an increasingly important role in determining credit worthiness due to the large number of predictor attributes that exist on customers.

A typical approach for building credit scoring models uses supervised learning, where first a credit score for each of a set of customers is computed manually. This score is combined with customer demographic and other data as noted above. If we were interested in classifying customers as a high, medium, or low credit risk we could use a classification technique. If we wanted to predict a numerical score, we could use a regression technique that predicts a continuous numerical value.

Another approach uses historical data on customers who either failed or succeeded in fulfilling their loan obligations in the past. Instead of using manually computed "scores," a classification algorithm learns to predict the probability of default on a loan. After these probabilities have been established, a scale can be introduced for ranking customers (assigning a credit score), usually based on a desired distribution of scores (e.g., 5% must be in the top range— "AAA" rating according to some classifications; 25% in the next range, and so on).

2.1.9 Warranty Analysis

Anyone who buys products has likely had some of those products break. Some of those products will be under warranty, which means that someone—the retailer, manufacturer, or independent warranter—will make certain repairs free of charge. Many products come with warranties automatically, for example, you will see "the manufacturer warranties this product to be free from defects for a period of 90 days from purchase." More common today are customer-purchased, or extended, warranties. Although extended warranties are often regarded as a "cash cow" for retailers, depending on the industry, the costs associated with servicing products are, to some extent, a gamble. The warranter expects a certain percentage of products to fail within the warranty period, and builds the cost for that into either the product cost or the cost of the extended warranty. By using advanced analytic techniques, warranters can better manage the seemingly unpredictable and uncontrollable expenses associated with warranties. Manufacturers and retailers need good algorithms for predicting future claims, very reliable products, or dramatically overpriced warranty offerings.

To reduce internal warranty costs where multiple suppliers, assemblers, dealers, and repair centers are involved, it is important to understand where product failures originate to improve cost recovery and processes. Because data mining can attribute problems to the various parties in the product path, data mining can be used to identify the root causes behind warranty repairs, for example, a particular supplier's parts or even the repair process itself. Using attribute importance, we can identify the factors that best determine valuable and problem parties. Using association, it is possible to determine which types of problems typically occur together and from which parties. By identifying the causes of failures faster, overall costs can be reduced by taking corrective action sooner. In addition, data mining can be used to forecast warranty reserves.

Warranty claims processing is often labor intensive, especially where invalid or fraudulent claims must be analyzed manually. By quickly classifying claims as invalid or potentially fraudulent, using techniques discussed in Section 2.1.4, both time and claims paid can be reduced.

2.1.10   Defect Analysis

Any company that manufactures products is interested in understanding the root causes of product defects. Data mining provides several techniques for uncovering root causes, including association, clustering, and predictive modeling. In association, the resulting rules identify co-occurring items, features, or events that typically accompany defects. Whereas the number of factors associated with each production run may be large, on the order of hundreds or thousands of factors, such that examining these manually is intractable, the association data mining technique extracts rules highlighting the most frequent factors that, in this case, result in product failure.

In clustering, defective parts or production runs may share common properties. Clustering analysis produces groupings of items according to common attribute values. Reviewing the distribution of data values for each cluster and the rules that define each cluster may give clues as to what each of these defects has in common. In predictive modeling, one can build a classifier to predict which items are likely to be defective. If the classification model provides transparency, such as the rules, one can identify what determines a failure. Moreover, for any given production run, users could predict if a defect is likely given certain conditions such as temperature or humidity. Other benefits of data mining for defect analysis are well-stated in [Wu 2002]:

> Through the use of data mining techniques, manufacturers are able to identify the characteristics surrounding defective products, such as day of week and time of the manufacturing run, components being used and individuals working on the assembling line. By understanding these characteristics, changes can be made to the manufacturing process to improve the quality of the products being produced.

High-quality products lead to improved reputation of the organization within its industry and help to drive sales. In addition, profitability improves through the reduction of return materials allowances and field service calls.

2.2 Data Mining in Industries

The cross-industry solutions presented in the previous section are readily applicable to a variety of industries. In this section, we characterize some specific industry problems for which data mining can be applied. In the discussion, we highlight some of the cross-industry solutions as well as other problems where data mining can be applied.

2.2.1 Financial Services

Financial services is an umbrella term that includes banking, insurance, and capital markets. Within banking, many opportunities exist for the use of data mining, including credit scoring, credit card fraud detection, cross-sell, as well as customer relationship management issues including response modeling, acquisition, and retention [SAS 2001] [SAS 2002].

In [Wu 2002], we find that

within the financial services industry, credit card issuers have been using data mining techniques to detect potentially fraudulent credit card transactions. When a credit transaction is executed, the transaction and all data elements describing the transaction are analyzed using a sophisticated data mining technique called neural networks to determine whether or not the transaction is a potentially fraudulent charge based upon known fraudulent charges. This data mining technique yields a predictive result. While the prediction may or may not be correct, this technique requires the system to learn various patterns and characteristics of transactions so to fine-tune its prediction capabilities. By utilizing data mining, credit card issuers have decreased and mitigated losses due to fraudulent charges.

While neural networks have traditionally been used in this industry, they also suffer from problems such as scalability and difficulty converging on an optimal solution. Other algorithms, like Support Vector Machine as discussed in Chapter 7, overcome these types of problems.

Within banking, the advent of the Basel II accord, final version issued June 2004, created a huge opportunity for data mining. Basel II is the result of deliberations among central bankers from around the world and the Basel Committee on Banking Supervision in Basel,

Switzerland. One of the outcomes of Basel II is to allow banks to move away from stringent reserve requirements and rely more on the risk actually assumed by the individual banks for their specific customers. However banks must be able to prove to regulators that their risk estimates are well grounded. Accurately calculating the "loss given default," that is, the amount of money the bank is likely to lose if a customer defaults on his loan, for an individual bank's customers can result in reduced reserve requirements, thereby freeing up capital for other investment. In one aspect of the accord, banks must maintain 5 years of what is called "customer default" data from which to build models that produce a probability of default, where "default" refers to the customer's inability to pay back a loan. The results of these models must be available for auditing and to provide the required proof to regulators that risk used is based on actual data [BIS 2004] [Wikipedia 2005].

Within insurance, beyond typical customer acquisition and retention, one goal is to increase the number of policies held by customers. This can be achieved through the development of successful policy bundles, as well as cross-sell and up-sell of policies as described in Section 2.1. Regression techniques can be used to set rates for insurance premiums using customer demographics and psychographics, and claims history. Setting rates too high results in lost business, setting rates too low can result in overexposure on claims. Insurance claims fraud detection is another area where data mining plays an important role [SAS 2002a].

Within capital markets, data mining can assist with bundling stocks into a mutual fund portfolio by clustering stocks, yielding sets of stocks with common characteristics. By assigning stocks to clusters, each cluster can be the starting point for further analysis and assessment of which stocks to include in a particular portfolio. Data mining has also been used to perform trader profiling to understand the type and styles of traders, as well as trader abuse through insider trading monitoring [NASD 2006].

2.2.2 Healthcare

It is practically a cliché to comment on the skyrocketing costs of healthcare. Costs are often attributed to inefficiencies in process, errors, fraud, and generally a lack of knowledge of what treatments are necessary or appropriate for a given patient. With increasing momentum, healthcare institutions and health plans are turning to data mining to solve such important problems and contain costs [Hagland 2004].

To realize these benefits requires a certain infrastructure, one that is able to collect electronically meaningful data about patients, their treatments, and healthcare providers such as labs, doctors, and nurses. Hospitals and other care providers are slowly moving into the digital age. For those who have, they can use this data to identify the important factors that determine a patient's likelihood of responding to a particular treatment. Using the association technique, providers can determine probable causes of a patient's death that may be a result of external factors such as staffing shortages, prescription mix-ups, or process flaws.

As for financial institutions, fraud is a major concern for healthcare insurance companies, specifically in the area of billing fraud [SPSS 2003a]. Being able to identify which providers are likely billing incorrectly and by how much is an area where data mining can be readily applied. A fairly common technique is to cluster healthcare providers to identify those with unusual billing patterns. There may be a few clusters of providers that warrant investigation since they are outside the norm of other providers. There may be individual providers that do not fit any particular cluster and warrant further investigation. Association can be used to identify uncommon relationships expressed as rules that appear with low support, that is, few cases exhibit that behavior. Using regression techniques, an expected number of claims or monetary value of claims for each provider can be predicted. By comparing the actual number of claims or monetary value to the predicted, those providers who significantly differ from the predicted value are identified as candidates for investigation.

Still other areas for healthcare fraud involve doctors prescribing unneeded medications, perhaps due to receiving kickbacks from drug companies. Developing predictive models on patients who legitimately use certain drugs can yield profiles of such patients. When a drug is prescribed, the profile of the patient can be matched against known profiles for legitimate users of the drug. Mismatches are candidates for investigation.

2.2.3 Higher Education

Higher education institutions such as colleges and universities are faced with a growing number of concerns, including reducing operations costs and the resultant tuition increases, attracting students who will flourish in their respective environments and complete a degree program, and increasing alumni donations.

Using the classification technique, colleges and universities can identify the types of students that tend to enroll in and complete particular course programs. When determining which students to solicit or admit, one consideration can include their likelihood to graduate. Understanding which course programs are likely to be pursued can enable projecting future revenues, more efficient planning in terms of number of sections offered, and the corresponding needed staff.

Another concern involves student attrition, with a goal to identify the profile and likelihood of students who will drop out of a degree program or transfer. A critical time for many students is between the second and third year in an undergraduate program. If students likely to drop out or transfer can be identified at this juncture, appropriate measures can be taken to address the need for tutoring or scholarships. Data mining can also be used to understand why certain groups of students drop out or transfer, or what are the important factors leading to a higher turnover ratio one year compared to another.

A common activity in higher education is soliciting donations from alumni. Response modeling can be used to identify which alumni are most likely to donate. Regression can be used to predict how much each alumnus is likely to donate. Multiplying the predicted donation amount by the probability to donate yields an expected donation amount. Ranking alumni by this expected donation amount enables prioritizing who to contact and how. Using classification and regression algorithms that provide transparency, we can identify the characteristics of alumni who donate and alumni who make relatively large donations.

2.2.4   Public Sector

Within the public sector is a wide range of possible data mining applications, from crime analysis to lottery systems [SPSS 2005].

In crime analysis, law enforcement is getting much more sophisticated in data collection and management, leveraging this data for "tactical crime analysis, risk and threat assessment, behavioral analysis of violent crime, analysis of telephone and Internet records, and deployment strategies" [McCue 2003]. By extracting patterns over large datasets, it is possible, for example, to identify relationships between events (association) or the attributes associated with increased threat levels (attribute importance).

In the area of homeland security, data mining is often met with skepticism. There are concerns over privacy and accuracy. In particular, Seifert [2004] notes,

> One limitation is that although data mining can help reveal patterns and relationships, it does not tell the user the value or significance of these patterns. These types of determinations must be made by the user. A second limitation is that while data mining can identify connections between behaviors and/or variables, it does not necessarily identify a causal relationship. To be successful, data mining still requires skilled technical and analytical specialists who can structure the analysis and interpret the output that is created.

Despite these limitations, data mining is being used for identifying terrorists and for analyzing large volumes of text documents, including the Web and e-mail, for possible breaches in national security.

In lottery systems, data mining is employed to increase revenues by predicting customer color or game preferences, to acquire and retain customers, and to determine in which regions certain games are most successful [SPSS 2005]. Attribute importance can be used to determine which customer demographics most affect game success. Classification techniques can predict which customers are likely to prefer certain types of games.

2.2.5 Communications

The communications industry is one of intense competition. Many of the cross-industry problems noted above apply: customer retention/attrition referred to as "churn," response modeling, fraud detection, and cross-sell. As noted in Peppers/Rogers [1999],

> GTE developed a data mining product called ChurnManager that scans all the data in a customer's file and summarizes it in an easy-to-use graphical interface that is prominent on the very first customer record screen displayed to the service rep answering the call. / Every customer's relationship with GTE is summarized ... to provide [the customer service representatives] with instant notification of potential customer dissatisfaction, as well as customer value and vulnerability to leaving the service.

Another specific communications industry problem is in the area of network performance management.

> A leading US operator uses [data mining] to ensure that calls are routed effectively. This is done by continuous monitoring of performance rules and the analysis of data, both data on the history of component and trunk usage, and on the current network activity metrics. This operator has seen "false" service and engineering call-outs decrease and the number of successful calls on their network increase. [Morgan 2003]

2.2.6   Retail

Many players in the retail industry already leverage data mining extensively. Customer relationship management (CRM) and the desire for one-to-one marketing [Peppers/Rogers 1999] make good use of various cross-industry solutions: customer acquisition and retention, response modeling, and new product line development, among others. Loyalty programs such as those providing affinity cards (frequent buyer cards) allow retailers to understand the buying habits of customers and predict future behavior and needs.

Retail problems, however, go beyond CRM. Efficiently processing and managing inventory can make a significant difference in profit margins. Wu [2002] states,

> *In retail, every time merchandise is handled it costs the merchant. By incorporating data mining techniques, retailers can improve their inventory logistics and thereby reduce their cost in handling inventory. Through data mining, a retailer can identify the demographics of its customers such as gender, martial status, number of children, etc. and the products that they buy. This information can be extremely beneficial in stocking merchandise in new store locations as well as identifying 'hot' selling products in one demographic market that should also be displayed in stores with similar demographic characteristics. For nationwide retailers, this information can have a tremendous positive impact on their operations by decreasing inventory movement as well as placing inventory in locations where it is likely to sell.*

2.2.7   Life Sciences

Life sciences typically involves research that analyzes the structure, function, growth, origin, evolution, or distribution of living organisms and their relations to their natural environments [NCCS 2005]. It is a fruitful area for applying data mining techniques amidst the deluge of data confronting the life sciences industry [Lanfear 2006]. Problems cover a wide range of areas including disease diagnosis [Chan+ 2002] [Lerner+ 2001] and treatment, genomics, drug interactions, drug discovery, and cancer research [May/Heebner 2003].

For assessing disease treatments [Hamm 2004], attribute importance techniques can rank treatments, treatment factors, and treatment efficacies. For example, factors associated with positive diabetes treatments are ordered based on the drug received, full patient history, number of hospital admissions, gender, etc. In addition, association techniques can identify correlations between a particular treatment and patient outcome. Rules may be of the form, "if number of visits to provider > 5 then outcome = improvement in 36 percent of cases."

In cancer research, data mining has been applied to cluster different types of cancer cells according to hundreds or thousands of attributes on the cancer cells. This data can consist of visible aspects of the cancers, as well as gene-level data. Those cancer cells that appear in the same cluster as cancer cells with known treatments may be treated similarly. Accurately diagnosing cancer in patients is essential for selecting optimal treatment. However, accurate diagnosis is often difficult since tumor appearance and location are not always sufficient to properly classify a tumor. Moreover, clinical data can be incomplete or misleading. Data mining has also been successfully employed to reduce error by using molecular classification of common adult malignancies. Using microarray-based tumor gene expression profiles, classification techniques using data from over sixteen thousand genes have been analyzed to yield more accurate diagnoses [Ramaswamy+ 2001].

For drug discovery and drug interactions, data mining is being employed "to predict properties such as absorption rates, metabolites, liver toxicity, and carcinogenicity" [Pinsky 2005].

2.3 Summary

In this chapter, we identified and discussed several cross-industry solutions where data mining plays a central role. Understanding such common data mining scenarios is a beginning for identifying uses of data mining in your individual application domains. We also highlighted several industries and their particular uses of data mining. Each of these industries can apply the cross-industry solutions cited, tailored to its own domain-specific needs.

We have so far discussed various mining techniques at a high level. In the next chapter, we go to the next level of detail, discussing data mining functions and algorithms that are provided in JDM.

References

[Apte+ 2002] C. Apte, B. Liu, E. Pednault, P. Smyth, "Business Applications of Data Mining," *Communications of the ACM*, vol. 45, no. 8, August 2002.

[Bakin+ 1999] http://citeseer.ifi.unizh.ch/bakin99mining.html.

[Berry/Linoff 2004] M. Berry, G. Linoff, *Data Mining Techniques for Marketing, Sales, and Customer Relationship Management*, New York, John Wiley & Sons, Inc., 2004.

[BIS 2004] Bank for International Settlements, "Basel II: Revised International Capital Framework," http://www.bis.org/publ/bcbsca.htm, June 26, 2004.

[Chan+ 2002] K. Chan, T. Lee, et al., "Comparison of Machine Learning and Traditional Classifiers in Glaucoma Diagnosis," *IEEE Transactions on Biomedical Engineering*, vol. 49, no. 9, September 2002.

[Gloven 2002] M. Gloven, "Mining for Knowledge—Revealing the Secrets of Information," *Proceedings of IPC2002*, International Pipeline Conference, September 2002.

[Hagland 2004] M. Hagland, "Data Mining," *Healthcare Informatics Online*, http://www.healthcare-informatics.com/issues/2004/04/hagland.htm, April 2004.

[Hamm 2004] Carolyn Hamm, Walter Reed Medical Center, presentation at Oracle Life Sciences User Group Meeting, June 2004.

[Lanfear 2006] J. Lanfear, "Dealing with the Data Deluge," in *Nature Reviews Drug Discovery*, Nature Publishing Group, 2006. http://www.nature.com/drugdisc/nj/articles/nrd832.html.

[May/Heebner 2003] M. May, G. Heebner, "Drug Discovery and Biotechnology Trends," *Science*, September 26, 2003.

[McCue 2003] Colleen McCue, "Data Mining and Crime Analysis in the Richmond Police Department," SPSS, www.spss.com, 2003.

[Morgan 2003] M. Morgan, "Revenue-Generating Networks" *Telecommunications International*, http://www.findarticles.com/p/articles/mi_m0IUL/is_5_37/ai_101862365, May 2003.

[NASD 2006] http://www.nasd.com/AboutNASD/CorporateInformation/CorporateDescription/index.htm.

[NCCS 2005] http://nccs2.urban.org/ntee-cc/u.htm#u50.

[Peppers/Rogers 1999] Don Peppers, Martha Rogers, Bob Dorf, *The One to One Fieldbook*, New York, Currency/Doubleday, 1999.

[Pinsky 2005] S. Pinsky, "Mining Data via n-Tier Architecture," Bio-IT World.com, http://biodev.telepathy.com/public/index.php/intro/13, 2005.

[Ramaswamy+ 2001] S. Ramaswamy, P. Tamayo, et al., "Multiclass Cancer Diagnosis Using Tumor Gene Expression Signatures," *PNAS*, vol. 98, no. 26, pp. 15149–15154, December 18, 2001.

[SAS 2001] "Customer Relationship Management in Banking—Key Challenges Facing Banking Executives," SAS, www.sas.com, 2001.

[SAS 2002] "Advanced Marketing Automation for Banking," SAS, www.sas.com, 2002.

[SAS 2002a] "Data Mining in the Insurance Industry," SAS, www.sas.com, 2002.

[Seifert 2004] J. Seifert, "Data Mining: An Overview," CRS Report for Congress, Order Code RL31798, December 16, 2004.

[SPSS 2003] "How to Get More Value from Your Survey Data," SPSS, www.spss.com, 2003.

[SPSS 2003a] "Data Mining Techniques for Detecting Fraud, Waste, and Abuse," www.spss.com, 2003.

[SPSS 2005] "Data Mining for Lottery Systems," http://www.spss.com/vertical_markets/government/lottery.htm.

[Wikipedia 2005] http://en.wikipedia.org/wiki/Basel_II.

[Wu 2002] J. Wu, "Business Intelligence: The Value in Mining Data," http://www.dmreview.com/article_sub.cfm?articleId=4618, DMReview.com, February 2002.

Chapter

3

Data Mining Process

To learn is to change. Education is a process that changes the learner.

—George B. Leonard, 1986

Historically, data mining has been viewed as the territory of gurus and Ph.D.s and not for the techno-phobic or faint of heart. Fortunately, increased understanding of the data mining process and advances in automating many aspects of the traditional data mining process are making data mining more accessible to mainstream application developers. The data mining process involves learning and, as the chapter-opening quotation notes, learning leads to change—in the case of data mining, change in our understanding of the business problem, change in our understanding of the data and what it represents. To reap this understanding requires giving sufficient thought to the problem to be solved as well as how to integrate the data mining process and its results into the business process. The ability to understand whether the data mining results meet the business objectives and can be integrated with the business process are key aspects of a successful corporate business intelligence strategy.

In this chapter, we characterize a rather complete and sophisticated data mining process through the CRISP-DM standard, a popular data mining process model, going from problem definition to solution deployment [CRISP-DM 2006]. The standard largely approaches the data mining process from the perspective of what a consultant should do for a customer engagement, complete with knowledge- and solution-transfer to the customer. For smaller-scale data mining projects, portions of the process may be omitted; however, the general flow still applies. Having a well-defined and thorough process is a critical part of a successful data mining strategy.

Also in this chapter, we highlight specific advances that simplify the traditional data mining process, thereby making data mining more accessible to application developers. We then highlight those parts of the data mining process that are supported by Java Data Mining (JDM). Two of the phases, data analysis and data preparation, are covered in more detail in Section 3.2, followed by a more in-depth review of the modeling phase. Section 3.5 discusses how the data mining process fits into enterprise software architectures. Section 3.6 discusses advances in automated data mining that facilitate the overall data mining process, and concludes with a discussion of how some vendors present and integrate data mining into business applications.

3.1   A Standardized Data Mining Process

The *Cross Industry Standard Process for Data Mining,* or CRISP-DM, was a project to develop an industry- and tool-neutral data mining process model [CRISP-DM 2006]. The CRISP-DM concept was conceived by DaimlerChrysler (then Daimler-Benz), SPSS (then ISL), and NCR, in 1996 and evolved over several years, building on industry experience, both company-internal and through consulting engagements, and specific user requirements. Although most data mining projects traditionally had been one-off design and implementation efforts by highly specialized individuals, they suffered from budget and deadline overruns. CRISP-DM had as goals to bring data mining projects to fruition faster and more cheaply. Since data mining projects that followed ad hoc processes tended to be less reliable and manageable, by standardizing the data mining phases and integrating and validating best practices from experts in diverse industry sectors, data mining projects could become both reliable and manageable.

We should note that data mining project success depends heavily on the data available and the quality of that data. As a whole, placing greater emphasis on current and future data analysis requirements during system and application design can greatly reduce future data mining effort. Poor data design and organization poses one of the greatest challenges to data mining projects.

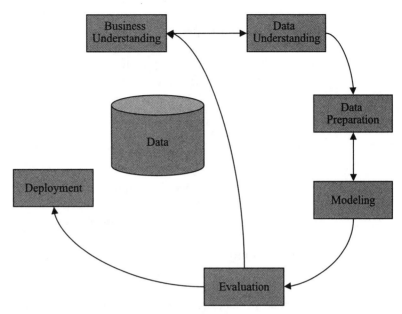

Figure 3-1 *CRISP-DM process: the six phases.*

As illustrated in Figure 3-1, CRISP-DM presents the process of a data mining project through a life cycle with six distinct phases. It highlights the tasks associated with each phase as well as the relationships between the phases and tasks. As with most standards, CRISP-DM does not claim to cover every relationship between phases and tasks, since this depends on project goals, the user's experience and needs, and the peculiarities of the data. It is highly likely that movement between any of the defined phases may be required. The arrows in the figure indicate common or the most important phase relationships.

The data mining process itself typically forms a continuum as indicated by the outer circle of Figure 3-1. Once a solution has been deployed, new insights into the problem typically emerge, yielding more questions that can be answered by data mining or refinements of the existing solution to improve result quality. With each iteration of the data mining process, improved skills and experience help improve subsequent efforts.

3.1.1 Business Understanding Phase

In the first phase, CRISP-DM begins with the problem to be solved, called *business understanding*, which includes defining business objectives and requirements followed by the definition of a data mining problem, project planning, and an assessment of effort. CRISP-DM distinguishes between business goals and data mining goals. Business goals are stated in business terms, for example, "reduce the cost of fraud in insurance claims." Data mining goals are stated in technical terms, for example, "determine which factors (attributes) occur together on a claim form, combined with submitter demographics, to identify fraudulent claims; then predict which claims are fraudulent and order by predicted fraud monetary value."

This first phase is the most important, and often the most challenging. Without a clear understanding of what problem needs to be solved and how results will be used, expectations may be fuzzy and unrealistic. Business and technical people typically work together to define the problem and how it can best be approached. Some problems, such as campaign response modeling, can be easy to define. Others, as noted for the "churn" problem discussed in Chapter 2, require a deeper assessment of what is predicted—has the customer churned?—and is not always immediately clear. For example, does churn only occur when a customer has terminated all service, some service, or merely reduced minutes of use? In these cases, domain and business expertise is necessary to provide such answers.

Another aspect of the business understanding phase includes identifying available resources: human, hardware, software, and data. Knowing which domain and technical experts can be drawn upon to work on the problem is an initial step. However, available computing resources, appropriate software, and access to needed data sources can make or break a data mining project and need to be assessed early on.

Since most data mining projects expect a significant return on investment (ROI), having such expectations defined up front is key. Ensuring that costs are properly balanced with expected benefits avoids false starts or inflated expectations. In large-scale projects, it is not uncommon for data mining projects to result in cost savings or increased profits of tens of millions of dollars with a small percentage of that devoted to the data mining project itself. IDC, an analyst organization in the information technology and telecommunications industries, notes that both predictive and nonpredictive analytics projects yield high median ROI—with predictive analytics topping out at 145 percent [IDC 2003]. IDC also notes that predictive analytics projects dramatically improve business processes with an emphasis on the quality of operational decisions.

JDM addresses aspects of this first phase by providing a framework for thinking about data mining problems in terms of mining functions: the inputs they require and the outputs they produce. The business problem itself requires domain-specific knowledge and creativity to decide what should be done. JDM, being an application programming interface (API), enables the specification of *how* the solution will be implemented, and through the use of *settings* and *data* objects JDM can assist in the capture of some outputs from the business understanding phase.

3.1.2 Data Understanding Phase

Once we understand the problem and expected results, we need to determine what data is available, its quality, and appropriateness for solving the stated business problem. This is covered in the *data understanding* phase. Often, once the data is better understood, the problem may need to be refined, or even redefined. Important data may be missing or corrupt; such data is referred to as *dirty*. This may result in new requirements to clean the data or to obtain new data, or different types of data, with careful attention paid to accuracy or completeness.

With data understanding, we strive to gain insights into the data through basic and possibly advanced statistical methods. For example, we need to understand the range of values in each attribute as well as frequency counts of values, often referred to as the *data distribution*. Continuous attributes, like *age* and *income*, may be bucketized (or binned) to provide a better sense of the overall distribution. Frequency counts provide insight into the existence of extreme values, called *outliers*, that can adversely affect data mining results. We also need to assess how the data should be interpreted; for example, should a number attribute be treated as a continuous value, like *age* or *income*, or a discrete value, perhaps movie rating or multiple choice survey question response? Some data mining tools will automatically address issues such as outliers and missing values, as well as provide heuristics for guessing how the data should be interpreted.

In many situations, data may be coming from multiple sources that need to be integrated before further analysis is possible. It is at this point that data inconsistencies may be most pronounced because the joining of data tables may be hindered if keys are not properly maintained. For example, joining two tables based on customer name may prove impossible if names such as "John Smith" are common, or if customers are identified with name and address and addresses are not entered correctly or consistently across data sources. Having common unique identifiers greatly simplifies this effort.

JDM supports data understanding through its statistics interface. Users can compute statistics such as mean, median, standard deviation, etc., as well as frequency counts on all attributes in a dataset. Since these statistics are collected on individual attributes, they are referred to as *univariate* statistics. These statistics can be inspected directly as numerical values provided through the API, or through a vendor tool–provided graphical interface. JDM 2.0 [JSR-247], as discussed in Chapter 18, further extends the statistics interface to include *multivariate* statistics (i.e., those involving two or more attributes). JDM specifies data to be presented as a single table; however, vendors are free to extend this capability to support multiple tables, online analytical processing (OLAP) cubes, or nested tables.

3.1.3   Data Preparation Phase

Once the problem is defined and we believe there is reasonable data to support solving that problem, we enter the *data preparation* phase. In this phase, one goal is to produce one or more datasets suitable for mining from the raw data identified in the *data understanding* phase. Through an iterative approach, many such datasets may need to be produced with various refinements to achieve the desired model quality. Data transformations within data preparation can be as simple as ensuring that similar values are coded the same way (e.g., "married," "Married," and "M" are all converted to "married" so they are considered the same value). This type of data cleaning is essential to avoid poor results such as inaccurate predictions or meaningless clusters. As noted in Chapter 1, the adage "garbage in, garbage out" is no more fitting than in data mining.

At the other end of the spectrum, data preparation may involve computing missing values or deriving new attributes from others, for example, defining a new target attribute called ATTRITER defined as "yes" if 50 percent or more of a customer's accounts have been closed within the past month, and "no" otherwise. The amount of data preparation can vary from virtually none, where data mining tools perform automated data preparation, to extremely elaborate preparation involving complex or creative transformations. The effort required by the data preparation phase can often dwarf the effort required by the other phases depending on how dirty or primitive the data is. We expand our discussion of data preparation in Section 3.2.

JDM distinguishes between data that is *prepared* and data that is *unprepared*. Data miners may specify that their data is already prepared, perhaps through various *extraction, transformation, and load* (ETL) tools, and that the data mining tool should not transform it further. For example, if a user already normalized a data attribute — perhaps the range of attribute *age* between 10 and 90 has been mapped to values between 0 and 1 — the data mining tool typically should not normalize it again. Alternatively, users may specify that some data attributes are unprepared, meaning that the tool should perform transformations it deems appropriate. JDM 2.0 further extends support for data preparation by including a framework and an explicit interface for performing common data mining transformations.

3.1.4 Modeling Phase

Once a dataset is sufficiently prepared, the *modeling* phase begins. Practitioners often consider this phase the "fun part." Here, the user gets to specify settings for mining functions, and if more control is desired, the user can further select algorithms and their specific settings for building models. These settings can be automatically tuned by the data mining tool, or tuned explicitly by the user. Since there are many possible algorithms or techniques for a given problem, users may try several to determine which produces the best result. Some mining algorithms may have specific data preparation requirements. As such, users may switch back and forth between the modeling and data preparation phase.

Also included in the modeling phase is model assessment. Normally, a data mining tool will produce *some* model for almost any data thrown at it, whether or not there are any meaningful knowledge or patterns in the data. To safeguard against this, users can *test* supervised models, that is, those supporting classification and regression. On *unsupervised* models, like association and clustering, users can inspect the models to determine if the results are meaningful. For example, are the clusters defined in a clustering model helpful in understanding customer segments, or are these segments different enough to develop a marketing strategy around them? We explore the details of the modeling phase further in Section 3.3.

JDM provides extensive support for the modeling phase. For those users new to data mining, they can specify problems at the mining function level. In this case, the data mining tool is responsible for selecting an appropriate algorithm and corresponding algorithm settings. JDM also provides algorithm level settings, where a user can select a specific algorithm and adjust settings manually. JDM also provides detailed attribute-level specifications, called *logical data*, for defining how the input *physical data* should be interpreted. For example, in Section 3.1.2, we gave an example involving whether to interpret a number attribute as continuous (age) or discrete (rating). This can be specified as input to model building using the logical data specification.

For model assessment, JDM provides capabilities to test supervised models using a variety of techniques, as well as to inspect model details such as cluster definitions, or the rules associated with a decision tree. Specifically, JDM provides interfaces for assessing classification models via the confusion matrix, lift, and receiver operator characteristics (ROC); regression models via error metrics; clustering models by viewing cluster rules and centroids; association models by filtering and inspecting rules; and attribute importance models by viewing the ranking of attributes. Models produced using specific algorithms may also have corresponding model details to provide greater insight into the results produced. These concepts are discussed in detail in Chapters 7, 8, and 9.

3.1.5   Evaluation Phase

Whereas building and testing models is the fun part, the next phase, *evaluation*, cannot be overlooked. Before unleashing a model in a business application or process, we need to assess how well it meets the business objectives set out in the business understanding phase. Although we may have high quality models from the modeling phase, they may still not satisfy the business objectives. For example, an exploratory model may produce superior results using attributes fully populated with values in the data sample, but that are not populated for most customers in practice. During the evaluation phase, we review the steps leading up to the model and its quality assessment to determine if some aspect of the business problem has not been addressed, or not addressed adequately. The objective for this phase is to decide whether or not the model can be deployed in the business application or process.

As noted for the modeling phase, JDM provides much of the raw information needed to support the evaluation phase, in terms of test metrics and model details. The evaluation phase relies on domain knowledge and critical thinking to assess whether the data mining models will address the business need.

3.1.6 Deployment Phase

The deployment phase in CRISP-DM focuses on packaging the results of the data mining project — both the knowledge extracted from the data as well as the process and experience mining the data for the specific business problem — for the business users, IT department, or business application consumer. The deployment phase may culminate in a report, or some degree of an implementation, perhaps as complete as an implemented and repeatable data mining solution integrated with a business process. CRISP-DM stresses the need to define a monitoring and maintenance strategy as part of this phase. This involves, for example, defining when and how models will be *refreshed*, that is, rebuilt, and under what conditions. Rebuilding may be conditional on a model meeting accuracy requirements as determined by further model testing. For unsupervised models, rebuilding may be done on a periodic basis with manual review of the model details. In either case, models may need to be rebuilt when data statistics such as range of values or distribution changes significantly as illustrated in Figure 3-2. In Figure 3-2(a) we see the attribute income with a fairly normal distribution. However, in Figure 3-2(b) the distribution changes to what is called multimodal data and may affect an existing model's quality.

Although some data mining results are useful for the knowledge or insight they provide, businesses reap some of the most important benefits of data mining technology when the results are deployed in a business application or process, especially in a repeatable manner. This may involve the ability to rebuild and assess models automatically, or to move models from the system where they are built to another system where data scoring occurs. For example, the

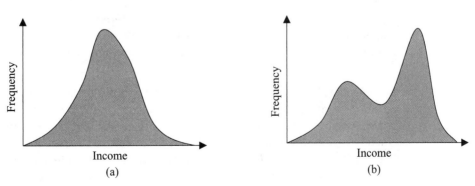

Figure 3-2 *Attribute frequency distribution changes.*

deployment of a data mining solution in a call center application may involve rebuilding models with the latest customer data on a weekly basis at the central data center, and exporting these models to geographically local call centers. The customer service representative (CSR) application accepts new data obtained by the CSR's interaction with a customer. The application uses the data mining model to generate predictions indicating anything from products the customer is likely to buy, to whether the customer is likely to terminate service or leave for a competitor, to what is the customer's frustration index.

By virtue of being an API, a JDM program captures the sequence of data mining operations performed, which can be useful for developing a report, or more importantly, for deploying a functioning system. However, JDM also defines an array of data mining objects, such as models, settings, and tasks. JDM also defines result objects, which when combined with the other mining objects can be used to recount the data mining process the user went through to develop the solution. JDM further supports the deployment phase through interfaces for exporting and importing models and other mining objects, applying models to data (i.e., scoring), and, of course, building models.

3.2   A More Detailed View of Data Analysis and Preparation

We have just explored the data mining process according to CRISP-DM, end to end. When planning a data mining project, consider that particular phases require a disproportionate percentage of the overall time and effort. For example, among the data analysis, data preparation, and modeling phases, it is often said that 80 percent of the time is spent in data analysis and preparation, and only 20 percent on modeling. Given this, no discussion of data mining is complete without a discussion of data preparation. However, to do justice to the topic of data analysis and preparation requires more space than we will devote to it here. Indeed, entire books are written on the subject, as data preparation is viewed as an art as much as a science [Pyle 1999].

Section 3.1 discusses how JDM supports both data analysis and data preparation. However, JDM 1.1 does not support any specific data mining transformations. The expert group decided to limit the scope of the first release of JDM, making it more manageable and, as a result, the general *data transformation problem* was deferred to a subsequent Java Specification Request (JSR) or JDM release. As such, transformations are now being addressed in JDM 2.0.

As noted before, JDM does allow the specification on a per attribute basis whether an attribute has been prepared by the user or not. If the user does not want the data mining engine (DME) to further manipulate an attribute's data values, perhaps by binning or normalization, the attribute is flagged as *prepared*. If the DME cannot work with the data as presented—perhaps a neural network requiring normalized data was presented with data in an invalid range—the DME may choose to throw an exception or produce a poor model.

Some DMEs may be able to accept data in a more "raw" form and perform automated transformations within the DME. In this case, the user may flag the data as *unprepared* and expect the DME to preprocess the data. One benefit of allowing the DME to prepare the data is that such DME-performed transformations are typically embedded in the model. Consequently, when data is scored or model details examined, values are presented in terms of the original data value. Contrast this with an example of user-provided transformations: if a user binned the attribute *age* into 5 bins labeled bin-1 through bin-5, the model may contain rules that refer to those bins, not the original values. This makes directly interpreting model detail difficult. Moreover, when scoring data, the user must explicitly bin *age* before providing those values to the model. Note that identifying data as unprepared does not mean that the user did not, or could not, prepare the data in some way, perhaps by removing or replacing missing values, or by computing new attributes.

What to Look for in Data

One of the reasons for performing data analysis is to understand the degree to which data contains useful values, or is rife with errors and inconsistencies.

Constants and Identifiers

A simple type of analysis involves locating attributes that are *constants* or *identifiers*. If an attribute contains all null values or the same value, such an attribute, called a *constant*, contains no information for the data mining model. For example, it may be interesting to know all customers are from the United States, but a data mining algorithm will not find such an attribute useful. On the other hand, an attribute that contains all distinct values, forming a key, is called an *identifier*. It can be useful to identify a case, but should not be used as a predictor in the mining process. For example, the attribute *social security number* can be used to predict which customers will attrite *perfectly* for a given build dataset. However, such a model will not generalize to different social security numbers and therefore is not useful. Some attributes are *near* constants or *near* identifiers, meaning that a high percentage of the values are the same or unique, respectively. What constitutes high is often determined by the user or DME, but generally can be around 95 percent depending on the dataset. Both constants and identifiers should be excluded as predictors from a dataset prior to mining.

Missing Values

Missing values are common in real data. For any given record, or *case*, data may not have been provided, for example, a customer not specifying his income on a warranty card. Also, data may have been lost, for example, a temperature recording device that failed for a period of time would collect no data. If a case has too many missing values, it may not be worth including. Similarly, if an attribute has too many missing values, it too may be worth excluding from the build data.

Similar to constants and identifiers, what constitutes *too many* missing values in a case or attribute is subject to experience or trial and error. In some cases, missing values can be replaced with a constant such as the average value for the attribute, or even a value predicted from another model likely built using other predictors in the same dataset. Using a model to predict and populate missing values is called *value imputation* and may, of course, produce incorrect values for a given case and thus bias the dataset. However, it may still produce better results than leaving the values as missing. Experience, trial and error, and resulting model quality can guide the decision on how to treat missing values. If a target attribute in a supervised mining function has missing values in the build dataset, the corresponding cases should be removed since the model does not know the correct answer for these cases. Some data mining algorithms handle missing values automatically, requiring no user preprocessing.

Errors and Outliers

Like missing values, data that contain errors are common in practice. Errors can result from data entry mistakes, such as mistyping the name of a town ("Bostin" instead of "Boston"), transposing digits in a customer's social security number, or specifying an invalid date ("13/32/06"). Errors can also be deliberate where customers misstate income, age, interests, or even gender. Data mining techniques can tolerate some degree of error in the data, referred to as *noise;* however, too much noise and not enough valid signal can result in poor quality models.

Various errors can be detected and corrected through data cleaning techniques [Rahm/Do 2000] [Pyle 1999]. For example, reviewing the unique values in a column may expose spelling mistakes or invalid values. Comparing names and addresses across tables for small differences, where most of the information is the same, can highlight matching cases. Once many of the errors have been addressed, duplicate cases can more easily be identified and ultimately removed.

Another common plague on data involves *outliers*. The term outlier can be applied to values within an attribute or to entire cases in the data. The effects of outliers differ depending on the data mining technique or data preparation technique. For example, consider an attribute *income* with a distribution centered around $100,000, but also with some very high income values in the millions of dollars. If we need to bin this data into discrete bins, we may choose to take the maximum and minimum values, and divide the range into equal subranges. If the minimum income was zero, and the maximum was $10,000,000, we can divide this into five bins: 0–2M, 2M–4M, and so on. However, with the bulk of the entries centered around $100,000, we could find that the first bin (0–2M) contains 99 percent of the data. Such an outcome is not very useful when mining data since this would result in an attribute that contains values that are 99 percent the same, in effect a *constant!* The original distribution is illustrated in Figure 3-3, and the binned distribution is illustrated in Figure 3-4(a).

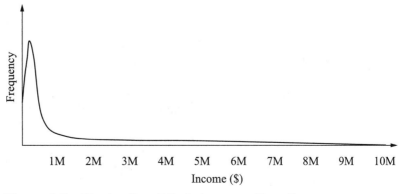

Figure 3-3   *Binning the attribute income with outliers.*

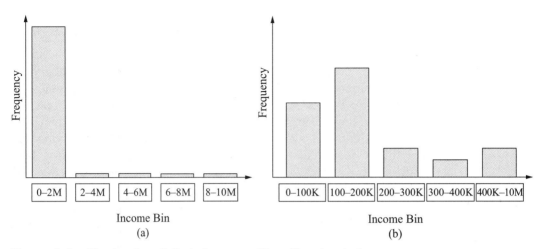

Figure 3-4   *Binning the attribute income with outliers treated.*

An alternative is to transform, or assign a *treatment* to, values that are too far away from the average, or *mean,* value. Standard deviation is a typical statistic. Data values that are, say, more than 3 standard deviations from the mean can be replaced by NULLs, or edge values (i.e., the value at 3 standard deviations from the mean). This allows binning to produce more informative bins. As illustrated in Figure 3-4(b), if we replace the outliers with edge values, we see the distribution of data in the bins can be more telling.

Derived Attributes

Sometimes, the data analyst or domain expert may be aware of special relationships among predictor attributes that can be explicitly represented in the data. Whereas some algorithms may be able to determine such relationships implicitly during model building, providing them explicitly can improve model quality. Consider three attributes: *length, width* and *height.* If we are trying to mine data involving boxes, it may be appropriate to include the *volume* (length × width × height) and *surface area* (2 × [(length × width) + (width × height) + (height × length)]) as explicit attributes. We may decide to leave the original attributes in the dataset to determine if they provide any value on their own.

Further, we may apply a specific mathematical function such as log to an attribute that has a very large range of possible values, perhaps that grow exponentially. Other attributes may be derived from simple calculations, for example, given a person's birth date, we can compute their current age; or we can compute total minutes of usage per year by summing the minutes of usage per month.

Derived attributes may also be used to construct a target attribute. For example, we may compute a "churn" attribute which is set to 1 if the percentage in minutes of usage drops by 75 percent, indicating churn, and 0 otherwise.

Generating derived attributes often depends on the data miner's domain understanding, creativity, or experience.

Attribute Reduction

Another common data preparation step involves reducing the number of attributes used in mining. Some data mining tools can scale to include large volumes of data for mining—millions of cases and thousands of attributes. While it is possible to mine such data volumes, it may not always be necessary or beneficial. If nothing else, more data, either in cases or attributes, requires more time to build a model, and often requires more time to apply that model to new data. Moreover, some attributes are more predictive than others. Models built using nonpredictive or noisy attributes can actually have a negative impact on model quality. Consider a dataset with 1,000 attributes, but only 100 of the attributes are truly useful/necessary to build a model. In a best case scenario, building the model on the 1,000 attributes wastes 90 percent of the execution time, since only 100 attributes contribute positively to model quality. Identifying those 100 attributes is key.

Previously, we discussed manually removing attributes that are constants or identifiers, or contain too many missing values. However, the data mining function *attribute importance* can be used to determine which attributes most contribute to model quality. In supervised techniques such as classification and regression, attribute importance identifies those attributes that best contribute to predict the target. In unsupervised techniques such as clustering, it can identify which attributes are most useful for distinguishing cases among clusters. Since attribute importance ranks the attributes from most important to least, a decision needs to be made as to what percentage of the top attributes to include. In some cases, attributes may be identified as negatively impacting model quality; these can easily be removed. Others may contribute nothing; these too can easily be removed. If there are still a large number of attributes, it may still be appropriate to build models on different subsets of the top attributes to decide which subset produces the best or most suitable model. Data miners may trade off greater speed of scoring for a small reduction in model accuracy.

Some algorithms, such as decision tree, identify important attributes by the very nature of their processing. Providing a large number of attributes to such algorithms can work as well as, or better than, attribute importance for supervised learning. In subsequent model builds, perhaps when refreshing the model or building a production model, it may be reasonable to include only those attributes actually used in the initial model.

Transforming Data

Much of what we have discussed in this section involves transforming data. There are some fairly standard data mining transformations we should introduce in more detail: *binning, normalization, explosion, sampling,* and *recoding*. Binning involves reducing the *cardinality* — the number of distinct values — of an attribute. Some algorithms, like naïve bayes, work best when provided a relatively small number of distinct values per attribute. Consider the attribute *age,* with a continuous value range from 0 to 100. A person's age can be any number in this range. If real numbers are allowed, there are an infinite number of possible values, which make understanding the distribution of ages difficult. Binning of numbers involves defining intervals or ranges of numbers that correspond to a *bin,* or single value. In the example involving *age,* we could define four bins: $0-25, 25-50, 50-75, 75-100$, where the lower endpoint is excluded (e.g., $25-50$ means $25 < x < = 50$). Producing a bar chart of binned age frequencies gives us a more meaningful view of the distribution. Alternatively, binning can also be applied to discrete values to reduce cardinality. For example, consider the 50 states of the United States, we may want to bin this into five bins: *northeast, southeast, central, southwest, northwest*. Here, we can explicitly map CT, MA, ME, NH, NJ, NY, PA, RI, and VT to Northeast.

The normalization transformation applies only to numerical data where we need to compress or normalize the scale of an attribute's values. Normalization allows us to avoid having one attribute overly impact an algorithm's processing simply because it contains large numbers. For example, a neural network requires its input data to be normalized to insure that an attribute *income,* with a range from 0–1,000,000, doesn't overshadow the attribute *age,* with a range of 0 to 100. Normalization proportionally "squeezes" the values into a uniform range, typically 0 to 1 or −1 to 1.

The explosion transformation applies only to discrete data such as strings or numbers representing individual categories. The goal is to transform such attributes into numerical attributes. This is necessary for those algorithms, like k-means, that work only with numerical data. As such, explosion is used on *categorical* data. Some category sets do not have any order among them (e.g., attribute *marital status* with values *married, single, divorced, widowed*). These can be exploded using what is called the *indicator* technique. For marital status, four new attributes, created with names of the categories, replace the original attribute. For each case, the new attribute corresponding to the value in *marital status* is set to 1; all others are set to 0. If a case has the value *married*, then the attribute named "married" is given a 1, and the other three new attributes are given a zero.

If an attribute contains values that are ordered, such as *customer satisfaction* with values *high, medium,* and *low,* that attribute can be exploded using a technique called *thermometer*. For customer satisfaction, three new attributes are created with names of the categories: high, medium, and low. These replace the original attribute. For each case in the dataset, the new attribute corresponding to the value in *customer satisfaction* is set to 1, as well as those new attributes ordered less than it. Remaining new attributes are set to 0. For example, if a case has the value *medium*, then the attributes named "medium" and "low" are set to 1 and the "high" attribute is set to zero. These are illustrated in Figure 3-5.

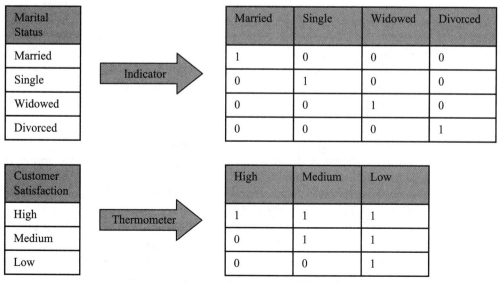

Figure 3-5 *Exploding attribute: indicator and thermometer approach.*

Sampling

Companies are amassing huge volumes of data on everything from manufacturing processes and product defects to maintaining a 360-degree view of operations and customers. However, some algorithms are better at dealing with large volumes of data than others. Similarly, some implementations scale better than others. In general, the more data that needs to be processed, the more time it will take to build a model; it also will likely require more computer memory and disk space. One way to reduce the amount of time and resources needed to build a model is to take a sample of the data. This is especially useful in the early phases of model building where a user should get a feel for how a particular algorithm responds to the provided data. Building a model on 1 million customers may take minutes or hours depending on the technique. It would be better to get a quick assessment of whether the mining technique yields any results using a small sample than waiting for dubious results. Once the user is convinced the technique and the data are appropriate, building a model on more or all of the data can be pursued with greater expectations for success. In other cases, a sample of the data may be all that is required to produce a good model. For example, if you have a population of 10,000,000 customers, it may not be necessary to build a clustering model on all 10,000,000 in order to segment your customer base. A sample of even 50,000 may produce statistically sound results.

When randomly sampling records, there is no guarantee that a given attribute will contain all the possible values contained in that attribute. This is particularly important when building classification models. For the model to be able to predict a given target value, it needs to have learned from data that contains examples of those values. In addition, a dataset skewed with too many of one category may not allow a given algorithm to learn the desired pattern (i.e., the negative signal drowns out the positive).

Recall the sampling technique called *stratified sampling*, introduced in Section 2.1.4, which allows you to specify how many of each target value to provide in the resulting data sample. Consider a dataset with target attribute *customer satisfaction*. The goal is to predict a given customer's satisfaction level based on other customer demographics and other customer experience metrics. If the values are *high*, *medium*, and *low*, we should ensure we have a reasonable number of each category. In Figure 3-6(a), we see a histogram of the original data: high (4,654 cases), medium (130,954 cases), and low (50,348 cases). We can then sample the data to ensure that we have a

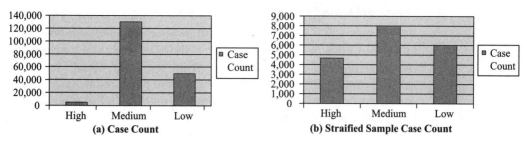

Figure 3-6   *Customer satisfaction data: histogram of target attribute.*

relatively equal number of each category. Since we have few cases in the *high* category, we will want to use all of those, and we may decide to take 8,000 of the medium cases, and 6,000 of the low cases, as illustrated in Figure 3-6(b). The "correct" number of cases to specify is more of an art than a science. Trying several variations can help identify an appropriate mix.

Recoding

In several of the transformations above, we discussed replacing one value with another. In its most general form, this is called *recoding*. The binning transformation on categorical data mentioned above (the 50 United States into regions) is also a form of recoding that enables manual roll-up of data. Typically, recoding is performed on categorical data (e.g., replacing the attribute values *H*, *high*, *hi*, and "***" with *HIGH*). This can be useful for cleaning data, as in the previous example, or to help in the interpretability of a model. For example, when looking at the rules produced from market basket analysis, it is much easier to understand a rule like "BEER implies PIZZA" than one like "Prod-3425 implies Prod-5593." Recoding can also be useful for numerical data when non-numerical data is mixed in with numerical data. For example, it is not uncommon to see "999" or " " used for a missing age value. These may be more appropriately be replaced with null.

Integrating data

An important step in data preparation often involves integrating two or more datasets into one. If the data contain well-defined keys and use the same data conventions, integrating the data can be as simple as performing a database join on the two tables, producing a new table or view. However, real data is seldom so clean and requires various data cleaning techniques as noted in the previous section about errors and outliers.

3.3   Data Mining Modeling, Analysis, and Scoring Processes

In Section 3.1.4, we discussed the CRISP-DM modeling phase at a relatively high level. In this section, we explore the modeling process in more detail, as well as process details for assessing supervised model quality and applying models to new data. In JDM, we characterize these activities as data mining *tasks*.

3.3.1   Model Building

In model building, we start with a dataset—a collection of cases—where each case typically corresponds to a record and has a set of attribute values. A case can be data we have collected on a customer, house, disease, or anything that we wish to understand better through data mining. The amount of data required for mining varies depending on the algorithm and the nature of the problem. For example, in a clinical trial to assess health improvement, there may be only 200 cases, one for each participating patient. On the other hand, a company may have a database of 10 million customers and want to segment these customers using a clustering algorithm. Similarly, some problems may have very few attributes, such as observable traits of mushrooms, while others may have thousands of attributes, such as the output of a microarray chip exploring the human genome.

To extract knowledge or patterns from data, we begin with a dataset, called the *build data,* as illustrated in Figure 3-7. Depending on requirements of the *data mining engine* (DME) or the problem to be solved, the data may be sampled and transformed, producing a transformed dataset ready for model building.

The process of model building requires not only the data, but also a group of settings that tell the DME what type of model to build, for example, a classification model with a particular target attribute. The settings may include what algorithm to use, among other settings. The output of this process is a *model* — a compact representation of the knowledge or patterns contained in the data. Depending on the mining function and algorithm, the model can then be used to make predictions, or inspected to understand the knowledge or patterns found in the data.

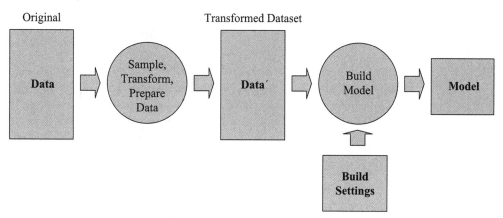

Figure 3-7 *Data mining model build process.*

3.3.2 Model Apply

In model apply, the objective is to use the model to make predictions or classify data. This is often referred to as *scoring*. The data used is called the *apply data*. When using a data mining model for apply, the apply data should have characteristics similar to the build data (e.g., the same or a subset of the attributes used for model building). We include "subset" here because some algorithms, like decision trees, produce models that use only the most relevant attributes. Hence, during apply, only those attributes need be included.

The apply data must be transformed in the same way as the build data was transformed, using the same statistics gathered for the transformations from the build data. Consider an attribute *age* with values ranging from 10 to 90. If this attribute were binned into 8 bins, each with a range of 10 years, this same transformation must be applied to data used for applying the model. If we did not bin the data, or binned it into, say, 12 bins, the model would likely produce incorrect results, if not explicitly raise exceptions. Note that it would not matter if the apply data contained different age ranges, say from 5 to 75; the original bin boundaries must be used.

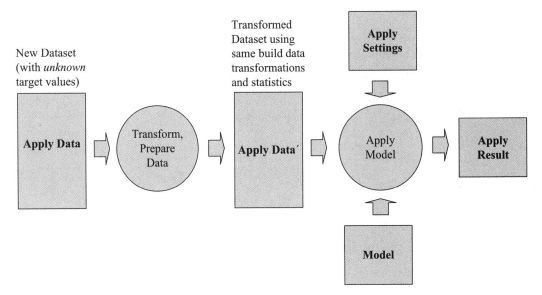

Figure 3-8 *Data mining model apply process.*

As illustrated in Figure 3-8, we begin with a new dataset that we wish to apply the model to—the *apply data*. The apply data must be transformed using the same transformations as for the build data. This transformed dataset is then used with the model and *apply settings* to produce the *apply result*. The apply settings describe the contents that the user wants in the apply results (e.g., the top prediction(s) for a case, the probability that the prediction is correct, additional attributes carried over from the apply data, and so on). These are explained further in Chapters 8 and 9.

The apply result is typically a table where each input case from the apply data has a corresponding output case. A unique identifier of the case is normally provided in the apply result so that results can be matched to the apply data. For example, you likely want to know which customer is predicted to respond favorably to a campaign.

3.3.3   Model Test

Model test applies only to supervised models—classification and regression. The reason for this is that in order to test a model, you need to know the *correct* outcome to determine how accurate the model is. In unsupervised models, we do not have a target (known outcome) and so there is no known value to compare. In general, we do not know whether an unsupervised model is correct or not, only if it is useful through manual inspection.

The notion of testing a supervised model is simple. Take a set of cases with known outcomes and apply the model to those cases to generate predictions. Compare the known, or *actual,* outcomes with the predicted outcomes. Simplistically, the more predictions the model gets correct, the more accurate the model. However, there are a variety of *test metrics* that can be used to understand the *goodness* of a model. Metrics such as confusion matrix, lift, and ROC for classification, and various error metrics for regression are explored in Chapter 7.

To test a model, we use what is called a *held-aside* or *test* dataset. When building a model, the original data with known outcomes can be split randomly into two sets, one that is used for model building, and another that is used for testing the model. A typical split ratio is 70 percent for build and 30 percent for test, but this often depends on the amount of data available. If too few cases are available for building, reserving any records for test may lessen the accuracy of the model. There is a technique known as *cross validation* for addressing this situation [Moore 2006]. However, we do not discuss it further here as cross validation is not currently defined in JDM.

Just as in model apply, the same transformations must be applied to the test data before providing the test data to the model. The model test phase compares the predictions with the known outcomes. From this, the test metrics are computed.

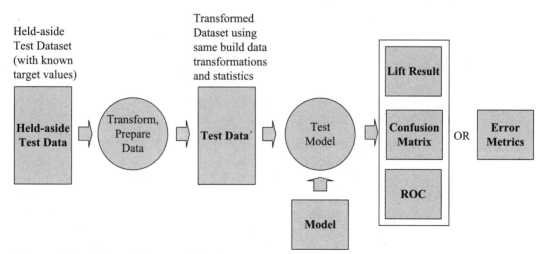

Figure 3-9 *Data mining model test process.*

3.4 The Role of Databases and Data Warehouses in Data Mining

An abundant source of data for mining is found in relational databases and data warehouses. Historically, data mining tools have focused on data contained in flat files. Flat files, however, can be difficult to manage and control. Database management systems (DBMSs) offer query capabilities, security, correctness guarantees, and access control, among other features. In addition, DBMSs, like some other tools, provide metadata control for data tables, explicitly capturing column names, data types, and comments as part of the table definition. Today, virtually all data mining tools are capable of accessing data stored in commercial relational databases, such as Oracle Database, IBM DB2, and Microsoft SQL Server. Querying and transformations, using languages like SQL, facilitate analyzing data and preparing it for mining. Multiple tables can be joined easily to produce a single table—often a key step in data preparation.

Whereas individual databases readily support data mining needs, large organizations often have dozens, hundreds, or even thousands of databases spread across geographical locations and numerous operational systems. The designers of these databases may have adopted local conventions for schema design, naming, values used in columns, etc. As such, trying to integrate data from multiple databases to obtain a global picture becomes quite a challenge. A *data warehouse* [Inmon 1995, Ponniah 2001] is designed to provide a common view of all the relevant data in an organization. Here, *relevant* is defined as whatever is needed to run the business more effectively or provide management insight into the health of the business. For example, businesses implementing a customer-oriented data warehouse strive to get a "360-degree" view of their customers (i.e., being able to see all aspects of a customer's interaction with the business). Designing a data warehouse with advanced analytics and data mining requirements in mind can greatly increase the value of the data warehouse and reduce efforts to extract knowledge once completed.

When building a data warehouse, most database vendors provide ETL tools for collecting and cleaning data. However, data mining can be leveraged in the creation of a data warehouse to identify data quality issues, or populate missing values. To populate missing values, the user can build predictive models from the other associated attributes, using what is called *value imputation*. Data mining can also be used to determine what data should be given special attention for accuracy due to its value in model building and scoring. Further, it can help identify which attributes should be included in the data warehouse in addressing business problems such as attrition, fraud, or cross-sell.

Unfortunately, many businesses strive to first design and implement a data warehouse, then introduce OLAP, and lastly consider data mining. Although this phasing of introduction may, at first glance, seem reasonable, it can greatly delay, and in some cases preclude, ever reaping the benefits of data mining. Data mining can place unique requirements on the design of the data warehouse, such requirements that are better to take into account during data warehouse requirements and design time. Unfortunately, given the cost and effort involved, some data warehouse projects have produced disappointing results. This is due largely to merely cleaning and assembling *available* corporate data instead of selecting data that is actually *needed* to answer key business questions — the types of questions that data mining–based solutions can answer. Since data mining can contribute to the data warehouse design and population itself, as well as to the design and understanding of OLAP cubes, businesses should include data mining at the outset.

3.5 Data Mining in Enterprise Software Architectures

At this point, we have discussed a standard data mining process, some of the details surrounding data preparation and modeling, and the role of databases and data warehouses. Any discussion of data mining process would be incomplete without a discussion of how data mining fits into enterprise software architectures. Enterprise software architectures today are driven to provide current and accurate information in a manner that is digestible by business users. Businesses spend millions of dollars building data warehouses to unify their data under a coherent data model. The ability to issue queries over all customer data or to obtain up-to-the-minute sales reports from all regional stores is now possible. However, looking at data to understand the past and present is only part of the value present in a data warehouse. A typically dormant and untapped source of value involves looking at data to understand the future as well. Data mining not only provides insight into past and present data, but also provides an arsenal of techniques for accurately predicting the future. We are seeing a steady increase in the use of data mining, especially in businesses that have invested the time and money in a data warehouse. C-level[1] executives want to get more return on their investment.

So, how does the data mining process fit into enterprise software architectures?

3.5.1 Architectures

Data mining tools provide a wide range of options for integrating with enterprise software architectures and processes. First, we take a look at data mining tools themselves and then how they interact with data sources.

As illustrated in Figure 3-10, we can view data mining tools as consisting of four parts: a graphical user interface (GUI) for interactive data mining, an application programming interface (API) for building applications, a data mining engine (DME) where the core processing or data mining algorithm execution occurs, and a mining object repository (MOR) where persistent mining objects are stored. Some tools may provide multiple APIs based on different programming languages (e.g., Java, SQL, C#, C) or may involve Web services.[2] Some may build their GUIs directly accessing the data mining engine, as shown in Figure 3-10(a); others have the GUI using the public API, as shown in Figure 3-10(b). Ideally, a tool should

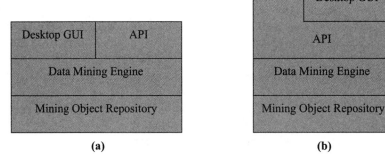

(a)　　　　　　　　　　　　　　　　**(b)**

Figure 3-10　*Data mining tool architectures.*

1　"C-level" refers to executive management (e.g., Chief Executive Officer, Chief Information Officier).

2　A detailed discussion of JDM web services and architectural implications is provided in Chapter 11.

allow full interoperability among the objects produced either through the GUI or API(s).

Tools can further be characterized along other dimensions: *data access options, DME location,* and *mining object storage.* Historically, data mining tools were file based, storing all mining objects and metadata in flat files at the operating system level. With the prevalence of data stored in databases, nearly all tools support accessing data in commercial relational databases. A DME that accesses remote data exists as a standalone server, an operating system process or set of processes that loads data from files or extracts data from the database. Such a DME then mines the data and saves any results back to the file system. This is illustrated in Figure 3-11(a). Other systems leverage the relational database itself to store all mining objects and metadata, thereby keeping the mining process under database control, as illustrated in Figure 3-11(b).

Other vendors take a database-centric approach where the algorithms are moved to the data, instead of the data to the algorithms, as illustrated in Figure 3-12. As data volumes continue to grow, the time and space required to move data outside the database also grow, sometimes dwarfing the data mining execution time. In-database mining also avoids the management of extracted data, which includes disk space, memory, and security.

With this foundation in place, we now take a look at an enterprise architecture involving data mining. In Figure 3-13, we see several *operational data stores* (ODSs), containing perhaps customer, sales, service, account, etc., that support various applications, such as online retailing, call centers, business intelligence dashboards, business activity monitoring (BAM), mobile customers, campaign

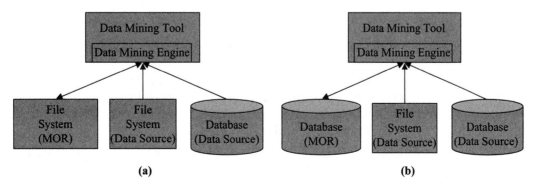

Figure 3-11 *Data mining tool data access and mining object storage architectures.*

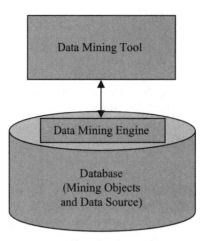

Figure 3-12 *In-database data mining tool architecture.*

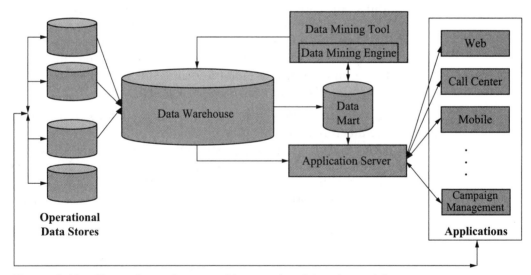

Figure 3-13 *Enterprise software architecture involving data mining.*

management, to name a few. The ODSs provide data to the data warehouse. This data is normally cleaned and merged into an integrated data schema. Subsets of this data may be moved to a *data mart* – a database populated with a subset of warehouse data dedicated to a specific purpose, in this case performing data mining [Firestone 2002]. Results from data mining may be returned to the data mart or the data warehouse for use by the application server in supporting the various applications.

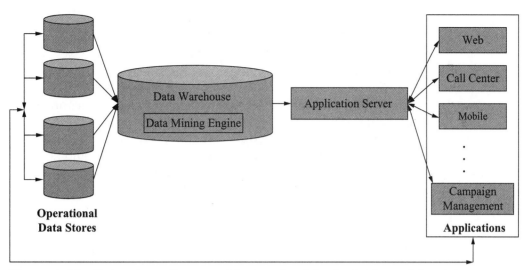

Figure 3-14 *Enterprise software architecture involving in-database data mining.*

Of course, the architecture just described is only one of the many possible architectures. If an in-database data mining tool architecture is used, as illustrated in Figure 3-14, either the data mining engine and data mart are merged, or the data mining engine, data mart, and warehouse components are merged to further simplify the architecture. Some businesses have concerns over how the mining activity may impact data warehouse performance. However, with newer technologies [Oracle 2006], processors can be effectively partitioned to separate mining from query and reporting demands on the data warehouse. The need for a data mart as opposed to mining the data warehouse directly may depend on the concerns of the database administrator (DBA) for managing machines, disk space, and overall system performance.

We have seen where data mining fits into an overall enterprise architecture. But as a matter of process, how do we incorporate data mining into an operational system?

3.5.2 Incorporating Data Mining into Business Operations

If we have followed the CRISP-DM process, we will have identified the data needed for mining, determined the steps necessary for preparing the data for mining, performed enough experimental mining to know which models work well for the business problems at hand,

and assessed which specific results should be deployed into business operations. We will also have identified the hardware and software resources for performing data mining in production.

It is at this point that having an API is critical for *operationalizing* data mining. If a graphical user interface was used for the exploratory mining, you either need to have kept very good notes about the steps and settings used to obtain your results, or be able to generate a script of the steps performed. In some cases, this script is a combination of structured and free form text. Ideally, the tool should generate an executable script in an appropriate programming language. This is where JDM re-enters the picture. The generated program can then be incorporated in the business workflow.

3.5.3 Business Workflow

At its simplest, a *workflow* is a sequence of tasks that are executed when certain conditions are satisfied. For example, a workflow may involve human actions: obtain customer information, call customer, present offer, record response, if response positive then take order, repeat. A workflow may also be completely automated, involving no human interaction: receive Internet purchase order, check inventory database if order can be fulfilled, if yes then submit shipping order. Workflows, especially involving data mining, introduce additional dependencies among tasks as well as a combination of automated and manual tasks. Such dependencies may be based on time, success or failure of previous tasks, or explicit human approval. Time dependencies include starting a task at a specific time or after a specific duration. Workflows may also be set up to be performed repetitively (e.g., once per week).

Consider the data mining workflow illustrated in Figure 3-15, which supports refreshing a predictive data mining model—used for cross-sell or response modeling—on a monthly basis using the latest data from the data warehouse. On the first of each month at midnight, the system retrieves needed data for mining. It then prepares that data using the transformations determined from the exploratory phases of the data mining process. To increase the chances of getting a model with adequate accuracy, we build three models in parallel using different settings, perhaps even different algorithms: decision tree, neural networks, and support vector machine. These models are tested on the test data and the results automatically compared to select the most accurate model.

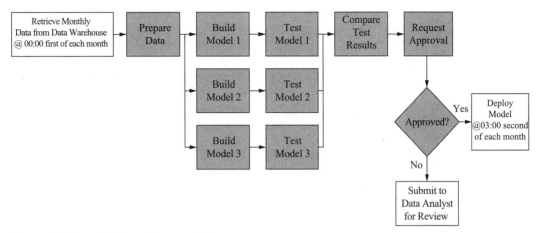

Figure 3-15 *A data mining workflow.*

To ensure against deploying an inadequate model, which, for example, could impact customers contacting a call center, we introduce a manual approval step. If the model is approved, it is deployed to the operational system. If not approved, the problem is submitted to a data analyst for review. Since approval or disapproval is expected within one day, we have a time dependency to deploy the model at 3:00 A.M. on the second day of the month. If a decision is not made in time, the task does not execute.

3.6 Advances in Automated Data Mining

"Why can't I just point a data mining tool at my data warehouse and say, 'Find something interesting' or 'Solve my business problem'? We can map the human genome, but I still have to spend countless hours, days, weeks, even months, extracting knowledge from my data warehouse or solving data mining problems, many of which must have been solved before. With all the intelligence put into applications today, why don't the data mining vendors produce software that automates this data mining process?"

These are the rantings of many a novice in data mining. In fact, more and more applications *are* building in data mining–based intelligence, providing industry-specific and problem-specific interfaces, without users even being aware of data mining's presence. However, there are many situation-specific problems that still warrant customized solutions. For these, data mining software is increasingly getting better at automating much of the data preparation required by algorithms. Advances in algorithms also include automated settings tuning to obtain optimal models relative to the data provided. Some tools even select the "best" model from a set of candidate models. However, the process of defining the business problem, selecting the mining function to be used, and ensuring that suitable data exists and is coalesced into a dataset for mining cannot currently be automated. People knowledgeable in the domain must lead the charge in these areas.

Another advance in automated data mining is in the area of *guided analytics,* which typically consists of a wizard-driven graphical user interface. Such an interface systematically prompts the user for information needed to define a data mining problem and then guides the user through the various data mining steps, for example, sampling, outlier treatment, algorithm-specific transformations, building, testing or assessing, and applying. Tools supporting guided analytics allow business analysts and non–data mining experts to obtain reasonable results.

The JDM interface enables vendors to provide a great deal of automation for users. The separation of mining function from mining algorithm allows vendors to intelligently select an algorithm and corresponding settings based on the problem and data provided. Many of the settings for both functions and algorithms include an option *systemDetermined*. This instructs the DME to determine the most appropriate setting value automatically.

3.7 Summary

In this chapter, we introduced the CRISP-DM standard data mining process and characterized how JDM supports the various phases of this process. We then looked at data analysis and preparation in greater detail exploring what to look for in data and how to address typical data quality issues. Since modeling is the main focus of JDM, we explored three principal tasks—model build, test, and apply.

In preparation for the discussion on enterprise software architectures, we discussed the role of databases and data warehouses on data mining. We characterized the architectures of data mining tools and their interplay with file systems and databases. We then looked at a larger scale enterprise system involving data mining and how workflow can be used to include mining tasks in the enterprise.

Lastly, we characterized advances in automated data mining, noting the use of guided analytics interfaces and support for automation in JDM.

References

[CRISP-DM 2006] http://www.crisp-dm.org.

[Firestone 2002] J. Firestone, "DKMS Brief No. Six: Data Warehouses, Data Marts, and Data Warehousing: New Definitions and New Conceptions," http://www.dkms.com/papers/dwdmed.pdf.

[Han/Kamber 2001] J. Han and M. Kamber, *Data Mining: Concepts and Techniques,* San Francisco, Morgan Kaufmann, 2001.

[IDC 2003] Henry D. Morris, "Predictive Analytics and ROI: Lessons from IDC's Financial Impact Study," IDC, Framingham, MA, 2003.

[Inmon 1995] W. H. Inmon, "What Is a Data Warehouse?" *Prism Tech Topic,* vol. 1, no. 1, 1995.

[JSR-247] http://jcp.org/en/jsr/detail?id=247.

[Moore 2006] Andrew Moore, "Cross Validation Tutorial Slides," http://www.autonlab.org/tutorials/overfit.html.

[Oracle 2006] Real Application Clusters, http://www.oracle.com/database/rac_home.html.

[Ponniah 2001] Paulraj Ponniah, "Data Warehousing Fundamentals: A Comprehensive Guide for IT Professionals," New York, John Wiley & Sons, 2001.

[Pyle 1999] Dorian Pyle, *Data Preparation,* San Francisco, Morgan Kaufmann, 1999.

[Rahm/Do 2000] Erhard Rahm, and Hong Hai Do, "Data Cleaning: Problems and Current Approaches," University of Leipzig, Germany, http://dbs.uni-leipzig.de.

Mining Functions and Algorithms

*I believe the States can best govern our home concerns,
and the General Government our foreign ones.*

—Thomas Jefferson to William Johnson, 1823

Just as federal and state governments serve their separate functions, mining functions and mining algorithms play distinct roles. Mining functions provide the ability to specify *what* is to be done, providing a high level of interoperability and commonality among vendors. Mining algorithms provide the ability to specify *how* it should be done, often with vendor-specific features. Algorithms allow users to tailor data mining results, and allow vendors to expose details of their algorithms supporting a given function.

Java Data Mining (JDM) separates the notion of mining function from mining algorithm to simplify the specification of model building. Vendors are able to automate the selection of which algorithm would work best on the provided data. This helps novices at data mining obtain good results without knowing details of the underlying algorithms. Yet, data mining experts are able to control which algorithm is used and tune specific parameters.

Once we appreciate the type of industry problems that data mining can solve, as discussed in Chapter 2, and the overall data mining process, as discussed in Chapter 3, users applying the technology as part of their business strategy need to understand the more general class of problems they will encounter when trying to mine data in new situations. In data mining, there are several fundamental functions and associated algorithms. In this chapter, we characterize mining functions at a high level along several dimensions, and explain the data mining functions provided in JDM. These mining functions include *classification, regression, attribute importance, clustering,* and *association*. In the first version of JDM, the expert group felt these five functions were most commonly used, as well as most mature and amenable for standardization. Moreover, these functions form a core supporting many common data mining solutions. We also note algorithms that are typically associated with these mining functions, especially those specified in the standard.

4.1   Data Mining Functions

As introduced in Chapter 1, data mining functions can be classified along several dimensions. For example, *supervised* and *unsupervised, descriptive* and *predictive, transparent* and *opaque*. At some level, all mining functions are implemented using one or more algorithms, whether the algorithm details are exposed to the user or not. The choice of algorithm can impact some of these dimensions, as we discuss below.

Supervised functions are typically used to predict a value and require the user to specify a known outcome or *target* for each case to be used for model building. Examples of targets include binary attributes with categories indicating buy/no-buy, churn/no-churn, and success/failure. A target may also be a *multiclass* attribute, containing multiple values, for example, indicating likely salary ranges in $30,000 increments; expected reaction to a drug such as *highly favorable, favorable, no response, unfavorable,* or *highly unfavorable;* or favorite color. A target may also be a continuous numerical value, for example, house price, temperature, or the number of copies of a book to print. The target allows a supervised data mining algorithm to learn from "correct" or "actual" examples, those with known outcomes. Some algorithms assess how well they predict the provided target values as they build models and adjust the resulting model accordingly. Others simply count co-occurrences between values in each non-target attribute, called a *predictor attribute*, and target attribute values, ignoring how well it is able to predict.

Supervised functions are of two types: *classification* and *regression*. Classification predicts categorical values; regression predicts continuous values. As we discuss in Sections 4.2 and 4.3, classification and regression also differ in how model quality is assessed.

Unsupervised functions do not use a target, and are typically used to find the intrinsic structure, relations, or affinities in a dataset. Unlike supervised mining functions, which predict an outcome, unsupervised mining functions cover a wide range of analytical capabilities including clustering and association. Clustering may be used to identify naturally occurring groups in the data, for example, similar proteins or cancer cells, or retail customer segments. Association models return items and rules that can be used, for example, to identify products for cross-sell to retail customers. There are other unsupervised mining functions, such as sequential patterns [Wang+ 2005], feature extraction [Lui+ 1998], and anomaly detection [Margineantu+ 2005], not yet officially covered by JDM.

Another dimension of data mining involves whether the resulting model is *descriptive* or *predictive.* Descriptive data mining describes a dataset in a concise, enlightening, and summary manner, and presents interesting generalized properties of the data. Descriptive data mining results in models that provide *transparency,* that is, the ability to understand why the model behaves as it does. The extent to which a model is descriptive often depends on the algorithm used to produce it. For example, in supervised learning, decision trees typically provide human interpretable rules that explain why a given prediction was made, whereas a neural network used on the same data provides no readily discernable understanding, and are considered "black-box" or *opaque.* Most unsupervised mining functions, such as clustering or association rules, by definition are descriptive. Mining functions and algorithms can be both descriptive *and* predictive, such as the decision tree algorithm.

Predictive mining functions perform inference on the available data, and attempt to predict outcomes or assignments for new data. In addition to the prediction, predictive mining functions may also provide a probability or confidence as to how strong the prediction is based on what the model knows. For example, a clustering model may assign a case to Cluster 5 with a 95 percent probability (a strong assignment), or a classification model may predict the customer will churn with a 55 percent probability (a weak prediction). Supervised mining functions by definition are predictive. Supervised algorithms supporting predictive data mining include naïve bayes, neural networks, support vector machine, and decision trees. The clustering mining function, with algorithms such as k-means, may also be considered predictive when used to assign new cases to clusters. Even association rules can be used for prediction [Lui+ 1998, Li+ 2001, Antonie/Zaiane 2002], although this is not covered by JDM 1.1. See Chapter 18 on JDM 2.0 features for a brief description.

4.2   Classification

Classification can be used to make predictions involving a wide range of problems, including campaign response, customer segmentation, churn and attrition modeling, credit analysis, and patient outcomes. Many of these were discussed in Chapter 2.

The notion of classification is to *classify* cases according to a fixed set of *categories*. A category, or *class*, is simply a discrete value with some well-defined meaning. For example, the problem to determine "will the customer respond to a campaign" typically has two categories: *yes* and *no*. As a supervised mining function, the data used to build a classification model needs to include a *target attribute*, containing the known outcomes. From the response modeling example in Chapter 2, "yes" in the target attribute of build or test data indicates that the customer responded to the campaign; "no" indicates that the customer did not respond.

In the apply results, where the predictions are placed, "yes" indicates that the model predicted the customer will respond to a similar future campaign. This prediction is often accompanied by a probability; for example, the customer is 80 percent likely to respond to this campaign. This can be taken to mean that out of 100 customers with similar probability, 80 of those customers should respond to the campaign. Probabilities are quite useful since they can be used to compute, for example, expected return on a campaign by multiplying the probability by the expected order value of each customer and summing the results. Problems like response modeling normally have two possible outcomes, a *binary classification problem*, but classification can also be used to predict more than two possible outcomes, a *multiclass classification problem*.

Let's take a look at the data used to build a classification model. As a type of supervised learning, classification algorithms build a model from a set of *predictors* used to predict a *target*. As illustrated in Figure 4-1 for the response modeling problem, a set of predictors may include demographic data such as age, income, number of children, and head of household (yes or no), to predict a customer's response to a campaign. The data for classification contains attribute

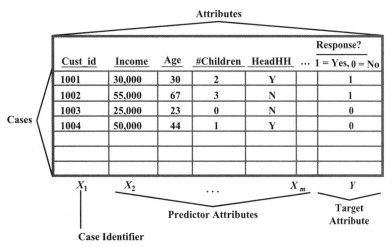

Figure 4-1 *Characterization of a dataset used for classification.*

values for the predictors and target in each *case*. Additional attributes, such as *name* or some *unique identifier*, may be provided to identify each case. The resulting model creates in effect a functional relationship between the predictors and the target:

$$Y = f(X_2, ..., X_m).$$

Determining the quality of classification models is based on comparing the historical, or *actual*, target value with the *predicted* value. Chapter 7 explores specific metrics used to assess classification model quality.

Algorithms that support classification in JDM are decision trees, naïve bayes, support vector machine, and feed forward neural networks.

4.3 Regression

Regression is used to make predictions for continuous numerical targets. It is valuable, for example, in financial forecasting, time series prediction, biomedical and drug response modeling, house pricing, customer lifetime value prediction, and environmental modeling such as predicting levels of CO_2 in the atmosphere.

Like classification, regression is a supervised mining function and requires the build data to contain a set of predictors and a target attribute, as illustrated in Figure 4-2. The target attribute contains

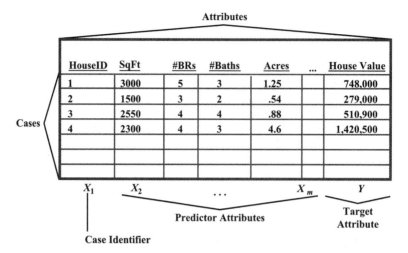

Figure 4-2   *Characterization of data used for regression.*

known numerical values, such as *house value*. In this house pricing example, the predictors may include attributes for house square footage, number of bedrooms, number of bathrooms, land area, and proximity to school.

Also like classification, regression produces a functional relationship between the predictor attributes and the target attribute, $Y = f(X_2, \ldots, X_m)$. When getting a prediction from a regression model, some models may return only the numerical prediction, for example, a specific predicted house value such as $976,338. Others may also be able to return a confidence band surrounding this value. For example, the model may provide a confidence of $15,478, which means the prediction for the house price is most likely correct between the range $960,860 and $991,816.

Determining the quality of regression models is based on comparing the size of the difference between the *actual* target value and the *predicted* value. Since predictions are continuous, it is highly unlikely the model will predict a target value exactly, unlike classification models that have few discrete values. As such, there are metrics that assess the overall error the model makes when predicting a set of values. Chapter 7 explores specific metrics used to assess regression model quality.

Algorithms that can support regression in JDM include support vector machine, neural networks, and decision trees. Other popular regression algorithms are *linear regression* and *generalized linear models* (GLM) [StatSci-GLM 2006].

4.4 Attribute Importance

Which attributes most affect the outcome of my prediction? Which attributes contribute most to defining good clusters? Which attributes should I eliminate when building a model? These are some of the questions answered by attribute importance for both supervised and unsupervised learning.

Business analysts often want to know what factors, or predictor attributes, most influence an outcome, such as a customer's decision to churn, buy a product, or respond to a campaign. Knowing which attributes most influence an outcome enables business analysts to focus their attention on the data most relevant to their problem, perhaps when querying data, manipulating it in an OLAP cube, or building a model. Attribute importance can identify where greater effort should be made to ensure the accuracy of certain data. Similarly, it can identify the attributes that do not contribute useful information to model building and consequently these attributes can be eliminated from the build data. Attribute importance results may influence what data is maintained in the data warehouse, or what data is purchased from third-party data providers.

Consider a company that purchases data from a third-party supplier. This data may be quite rich, consisting of hundreds if not thousands of attributes. But, which ones are most useful for data mining? Since data can be expensive to purchase, instead of purchasing as much as possible, a business analyst may choose a relatively small sample of data with a wide range of attributes. Using attribute importance, the analyst can determine which of the attributes are most useful for building models to solve particular problems. Then, only those attributes that add value to the accuracy of the models need to be purchased for the remaining cases.

As noted above, attribute importance can assist in determining which attributes are most relevant for building a model. Eliminating unnecessary attributes in the build data can reduce model building time. If fewer attributes are used to build a model, fewer are required to apply that model, hence scoring will be faster as well. Studies have shown that eliminating "noise" attributes from data can also improve model accuracy or quality. Noise attributes are those reported by attribute importance as not contributing to the model, or actually reducing model quality.

Attribute importance produces a model that ranks attributes according to how each attribute contributes to model quality, for example, how effective each predictor attribute is at predicting the target. Attribute importance results are often depicted graphically using a bar chart. For example, Figure 4-3 illustrates the attribute ranking available through JDM involving the attribute name, rank, and importance value. A bar chart provides an immediate sense of the relative importance of the attributes. Obviously, a higher ranked attribute is more important than a lower ranked attribute. However, there is typically no real sense of magnitude in the importance value, meaning for example, one attribute being twice as important as another does not hold. JDM specifies no precise interpretation of attribute importance values other than attributes with a greater numeric value are relatively more important than those with lesser values.

From this ranking, users can select the attributes to be used in building models. For example, a percentage of the top attributes may be used to construct a new dataset, or perhaps visual inspection will

Predictor	Rank	Attribute Importance Value
household size	1	0.19
marital status	2	0.18
promotion	3	0.16
...	...	...
workclass	17	0.008

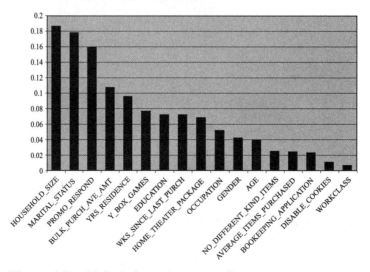

Figure 4-3 *Attribute importance result.*

indicate a sharp drop-off in the importance value. Some algorithms may produce negative attribute importance values. Such attributes are likely noise, actually making the model accuracy or quality worse than if they were not present.

4.5 Association

Association analysis is widely used in transaction data analysis for directed marketing, catalog design, store layout, and other business decision-making processes. Association is the mining function used for market basket analysis, that is, the analysis of consumer behavior for the discovery of relationships or correlations among a set of items. For example, the presence of one set of items implies the presence of another item or set of items, such as 90 percent of the people who buy milk and eggs also buy bread in the same transaction. Association identifies the attribute value conditions (items) that frequently occur together in a given dataset by providing *rules*.

The rules returned from an association model are different from the rules produced from clustering models or classification decision tree models. For example, decision tree rules are *predicate-based*, meaning that they consist of a series of true or false boolean-valued expressions, such as "age < 45 AND income > 80,000 AND owns_home = TRUE." Association rules deal with discrete items, specifically, consisting of two sets of items. One itemset, called the *antecedent*, implies another itemset, called the *consequent*. If we have an antecedent A and a consequent B, the rule can be written as A ➜ B. These two itemsets are found to occur together in some number of transactions or market baskets in the provided data.

Support and confidence metrics are used as quality measures of the rules within an association model. The *support* of a rule indicates how frequently the items associated in the rule occur together, for example, milk, eggs, and bread occur together in 22 percent of the transactions. The *confidence* of a rule indicates the probability of finding both the antecedent itemset and consequent itemset in the same transaction, given that the antecedent alone is found. An example is illustrated in Figure 4-4 where there are four transactions, each with some purchased items. The association algorithm found the rule "milk implies bread," where milk is the antecedent, and bread is the consequent. First, we count the number of transactions that contain milk and bread. Since there are two, we say the support for this rule is 50 percent (2/4). The confidence of this rule is determined by

Transaction ID	Purchased Items
1	{milk, eggs, bread}
2	{milk, cheese}
3	{milk, bread}
4	{eggs, ham, ketchup}

- Support:
  $(A \rightarrow B) = P(AB)$

- Confidence:
  $(A \rightarrow B) = P(AB)/P(A)$

- Rule Length:
  number of items in the rule
  $AB \rightarrow C$
  Rule Length = 3

milk → bread:

   Support = 2/4 = 50%
   Confidence = 2/3 = 66%

bread → milk:

   Support = 2/4 = 50%
   Confidence = 2/2 = 100%

Figure 4-4   *Computing support and confidence of an association rule.*

taking the number of times we saw both milk and bread (the support) and dividing it by the number of transactions that have milk alone, which is 3. This gives us a confidence of 66 percent (2/3). Intuitively, we want to know that if we see milk, how likely are we to also see bread. In the dataset provided, we see that 2 out of 3 times.

Let's turn this around for a moment. The association model also contains the rule "bread implies milk." You could ask, why is this different? The support is the same as in the previous rule; however, the confidence is 100 percent. This is because every time we saw bread (2 times), we also saw milk, as in transactions 1 and 3.

Input data for association models typically comes in one of two forms. Figure 4-5 illustrates a standard one-row-per-case format, referred to as *single record case*, which has also been used for the other mining functions above. In the association data, however, each predictor attribute indicates whether the product was purchased or not. A "1" indicates the item was purchased in the transaction, a "0" indicates it was not.

Another representation, more common for association data, is often called "transactional format" and referred to as *multirecord case* in JDM. In this format, we capture only the items purchased, as opposed to those purchased and not purchased. Each item purchased has a row in the table. The items are linked together by their transaction or case identifier. This is illustrated in Figure 4-6.

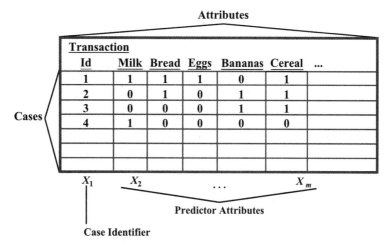

Figure 4-5 *Characterization of data used for Association—single record case.*

Transaction Id	Milk	Bread	Eggs	Bananas	Cereal	
1	1	1	1	0	1	
2	0	1	0	1	1	
3	0	0	0	1	1	
4	1	0	0	0	0	

Transaction Id	Attribute Name	Value
1	Milk	1
1	Bread	1
1	Eggs	1
1	Cereal	1
2	Bread	1
2	Bananas	1
2	Cereal	1

...

Figure 4-6 *Characterization of data used for Association— multirecord case.*

The choice of data format depends on how the data was originally maintained, perhaps in the data warehouse. But more importantly, it depends on the ability of the algorithm to handle a particular format. Multirecord case format is considered a *sparse* representation of the data since it only contains the items of interest. Single record case format is considered a dense representation since it contains all the information. As you may expect, sparse representations can be more space efficient depending on the data. Consider a grocery store that sells 10,000 different products and where customers purchase on average 10 products at a time. If we maintained the data in single record case, we would require space for 10,000 entries per transaction. If we have 1,000 transactions in our dataset, this is a total of 10,000,000 entries. However, if we use multirecord case format, we store only data on 20,000 items (20 items/transaction × 1,000 transactions). Each item requires 3 entries (two minimally), which amounts to 60,000 entries. Clearly, 10,000,000 greatly exceeds the sparse representation of 60,000.

Association rules are interesting for showing relationships among items, but can also be interesting for showing relationships among item categories. To generate association rules that include category rules, some association algorithms can take a *taxonomy* as input which shows the relationships among items. Each item is associated with one or more categories. Categories in turn can belong to one or more other categories. The overall taxonomy cannot contain any cycles; that is, a category can end up being its own parent, directly or indirectly.

Consider the example in Figure 4-7, which illustrates four subcategories of food: *fruits, meats, grains,* and *dairy.* Fruits are further subcategorized into *native* and *imported* fruit, and *fresh* and *canned* fruit. Pineapple exists in both fresh and imported forms. Apples are both fresh and native fruits. Each of the categories provided may further be subdivided into finer categories or linked to specific items, for example, *Royal Gala* apples.

Whereas association models normally find rules among items, given such a taxonomy, an association algorithm can also identify rules among categories. For example, "dairy implies grains" (one category implies another category), "dairy implies Rice Krispies"

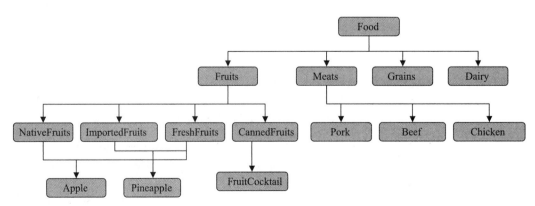

Figure 4-7   *Taxonomy for food items.*

Table 4-1 *Example Association Rules*

Rule ID	Antecedent	Consequent	Support	Confidence
1	Milk	Bread	.50	.66
2	Ham, Bacon, Bread	Eggs	.14	.45
3	Apples, Grapes	Oranges	.37	.25
4	Cereal, Bananas	Milk	.44	.78
5	Steak	Steaksauce	.19	.39
6	Cakemix, Oil	Eggs	.08	.78

(one category implies an item), or "angus filet mignon implies steak sauce" (one item implies a category).

The mining function for association provides most of the functionality for specifying inputs to model building and retrieving rules. As such, JDM does not specify any algorithm settings for association; however, the most popular algorithm is Apriori. For retrieving rules, JDM focuses on filtering rules using various criteria; for example, users may want to see only rules that meet a minimum support or confidence value. Others may also want rules involving some minimum number of items in the antecedent for more interesting rules, or having a specific set of items in the antecedent or consequent. The rules filter may be simple or complex, depending on the needs of the user or application. For example, consider the rules in Table 4-1.

If we are interested in only "long" rules, we may select all rules with length 4 or greater. This returns only one, rule 2. If we are interested in rules with high support and confidence, we may select all rules with support > 0.3 and confidence > 0.5. This returns rules 1 and 4. If we are interested in any rules involving the item "milk," we may select those containing "milk" in the antecedent or consequent. This returns rules 1 and 4 again. If we are interested only in what results in the purchase of eggs, we may select those containing "eggs" in the antecedent only. This returns rules 2 and 6.

4.6 Clustering

Clustering has been used in customer segmentation, gene and protein analysis, product grouping, finding taxonomies, and text mining. Typical goals for clustering can include finding representative cases from a large dataset to support data reduction, identifying natural clusters in a dataset to give insight into what cases are grouped together, as well as finding data that either does not belong to any of the found clusters or belongs to a cluster of only a few cases providing a kind of outlier or anomaly detection [DEI 2005]. The data format used for clustering is similar to that used for supervised learning, except that no target attribute is specified.

Essentially, clustering analysis identifies clusters that exist in a given dataset, where a cluster is a collection of cases that are more similar to one another than cases in other clusters. A set of clusters is considered to be of high quality if the similarity between clusters is low, yet the similarity of cases within a cluster is high [Anderberg 1973]. As illustrated in Figure 4-8, it can be fairly easy to understand clusters in two dimensions. Here we have two numerical attributes: *income* and *age*. The figure depicts two clusters each with its respective *centroid*, that is, representative center point. Cluster C1 corresponds to individuals with lower income and lower age, whereas Cluster C2 corresponds to individuals with higher income and higher age. If we look at the histograms of these attributes as illustrated in Figure 4-9, we see the number of cases is highest closest to the centroid of each cluster.

With this simple example, there is no need to use a data mining algorithm to identify the clusters — visual inspection can easily identify the clusters once the data is graphed. With advanced visualization

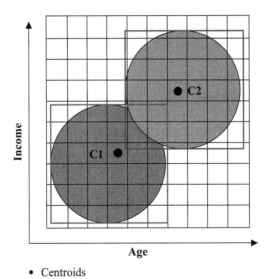

• Centroids

Figure 4-8 *Cluster centroids.*

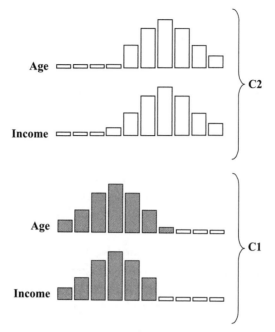

Figure 4-9 *Cluster histograms.*

techniques, it may also be possible to interpret clusters directly in three-dimensional space. However, when there are 10s, 100s, or 1,000s of attributes, it is not humanly possible to identify the clusters present in the data. This is where data mining comes in. Clustering algorithms automatically identify groups of cases into clusters. Humans can then inspect these clusters, looking either at the centroids themselves or at rules that define the clusters. For example, the rules for clusters C1 and C2 from the example in Figure 4-8 may look like

$$C1: 0 < \text{income} < 50{,}000 \text{ AND } 0 < \text{age} < 35$$

$$C2: 40 < \text{income} < 100{,}000 \text{ AND } 31 < \text{age } 57$$

Note that there is overlap between the regions defined by C1 and C2. Cases that fall into this overlapping region may actually be closer to one centroid than another, as determined by a distance measure. Sometimes a case may be equally close to multiple clusters, in which case the probability or confidence associated with the assignment to any one of these clusters may be equally low.

What constitutes similarity between cases depends on the type of attributes involved. When considering numerical values, such as income, it is quite easy to determine "closeness" since we can graph income values and compute the distance between them. For categorical values, such as marital status, determining similarity can be difficult. Whereas we could say *married* is far from *single*, it is less clear how much closer *divorced* is to *married* or *single*. Also consider colors. Is *green* closer to *red* or *blue*? If considering the colors scientifically, we could use their frequency or wavelength. However, in considering customer color choices, this is likely irrelevant. In this case, we may conclude that two cases are similar for attribute color only if they have the same color.

Some clustering algorithms produce hierarchies that characterize relationships among clusters. This can be useful when creating taxonomies for organizing documents or products, or trying to determine what clusters are most meaningful for a particular business problem.

JDM defines algorithm settings for k-means [MacQueen 1967]. However, there are many other clustering algorithms such as self-organizing maps [Kohonen 1995], orthogonal partitioning clustering [Milenova/Campos 2002], and hierarchical clustering.

4.7   Summary

In this chapter, we introduced the mining functions supported in the first release of JDM and mentioned some of the algorithms that can be used to support those functions, both those defined for the standard as well as some other popular algorithms. We discussed each mining function's capabilities and typical uses. We looked at the basic data requirements and formats of each mining function and how results may be interpreted.

There are other mining functions, not currently defined in JDM, that are useful in various situations. Examples include *time series analysis* [Chatfield 2004], to understand trends and cycles of numerical sequence-oriented data; *anomaly detection*, to identify unusual cases based on patterns identified to be normal; and *feature extraction*, to determine higher level attributes or features as linear combinations of the original attributes. In Chapter 18, we discuss some of the new features, like these, being considered for JDM 2.0.

For additional information on mining functions, see [Berry/Linoff 2004] [Witten/Frank 2005]. In the next chapter, we look at the overall strategy adopted for JDM, of which these mining functions form a part.

References

[Agrawal/Srikant 1994] Rakesh Agrawal, Ramakrishnan Srikant, "Fast Algorithms for Mining Association Rules," *Proceedings of the 20th VLDB Conference*, Santiago, Chile, 1994.

[Anderberg 1973] M. R. Anderberg, *Cluster Analysis for Applications*, New York, Academic Press Inc., 1973.

[Antonie/Zaiane 2002] Maria-Luiza Antonie, Osmar R. Zaiane, "Text Document Categorization by Term Association." In *IEEE International Conference on Data Mining*, pages 19–26, December 2002. http://www.cs.ualberta.ca/~zaiane/postscript/icdm02-1.pdf.

[Berry/Linoff 2004] M. Berry, G. Linoff, *Data Mining Techniques for Marketing, Sales, and Customer Relationship Management*, New York, John Wiley & Sons, Inc., 2004.

[Chatfield 2004] Chris Chatfield, *The Analysis of Time Series: An Introduction*, Boca Raton, FL, CRC Press, 2004.

[DEI 2005] Dipartimento di Elettronica e Informazione, Politecnico Di Milano, http://www.elet.polimi.it/upload/matteucc/Clustering/tutorial_html.

[Kohonen 1995] T. Kohonen, *Self-organizing Maps*, 2nd ed., Berlin, Springer-Verlag, 1995.

[Li+ 2001] Wenmin Li, Jiawei Han, Jian Pei, "CMAR: Accurate and Efficient Classification Based on Multiple Class-Association Rules." In *IEEE International Conference on Data Mining*, 2001. http://www-faculty.cs.uiuc.edu/~hanj/pdf/cmar01.pdf.

[Lui+ 1998] Bing Liu, Wynne Hsu, Yiming Ma, "Integrating Classification and Association Rule Mining." In *Knowledge Discovery and Data Mining*, pages 80–86, 1998. http://www.dsi.unive.it/~dm/liu98integrating.pdf.

[Lui+ 1998] Huan Liu, Hiroshi Motoda, *Feature Extraction Construction and Selection: A Data Mining Perspective*, Boston, Kluwer Academic Publishers, 1998.

[MacQueen 1967] J. B. MacQueen "Some Methods for Classification and Analysis of Multivariate Observations, *Proceedings of 5th Berkeley Symposium on Mathematical Statistics and Probability*, Berkeley, University of California Press, 1:281–297, 1967.

[Margineantu+ 2005] Dragos Margineantu, Stephen Bay, Philip Chan, Terran Lane, "International Workshop on Data Mining Methods for Anomaly Detection," Workshop Notes, Chicago, SIGKDD, 2005.

[Milenova/Campos 2002] Boriana Milenova, Marcos Campos, *O-Cluster: Scalable Clustering of Large High Dimensional Datasets*, Oracle Corporation, 2002, http://www.oracle.com/technology/products/bi/odm/pdf/o_cluster_algorithm.pdf.

[Pyle 1999] Dorian Pyle, *Data Preparation for Data Mining*, San Francisco, Morgan Kaufmann, 1999.

[StatSci-GLM 2006] Generalized Linear Models Introduction, StatSci.org, http://www.statsci.org/glm/intro.html.

[Wang+ 2005] Wei Wang, Jiong Yang, *Mining Sequential Patterns from Large Datasets,* Kluwer International Series on Advances in Database Systems, New York, Springer, vol. 28, 2005.

[Wikipedia 2005] http://en.wikipedia.org/wiki/Minimum_description_length.

[Witten/Frank 2005] Ian H. Witten, Eibe Frank, *Data Mining: Practical Machine Learning Tools and Techniques,* 2nd ed., San Francisco, Morgan Kaufmann, 2005.

Chapter

5

JDM Strategy

Strategy without tactics is the slowest route to victory.
Tactics without strategy is the noise before defeat.

—Sun Tzu (c. 400–430 B.C.), Chinese military strategist

The term *strategy* can be defined as "a long term plan of action designed to achieve a particular goal" [Wikipedia 2005]. The term *tactic* can be defined as "a method or action for accomplishing an end" [GBC 2005]. This chapter characterizes the strategic decisions made for the Java Data Mining (JDM) standard. In addition, some of the rationale for those strategies is provided. The overall goal in the case of JDM is to make data mining accessible to Java developers and Java-based applications. The JDM strategy is introduced in this chapter using 10 strategic objectives. To heed the warning in the chapter-opening quotation, we also highlight corresponding JDM tactics.

To understand the context of the JDM strategy, an understanding of standards in general and data mining standards in particular is beneficial. Hence, this chapter discusses the role of standards and motivations for creating them. The benefits that data mining standards offer the advanced analytics community are discussed. Later, in Chapter 17, the evolution of several data mining standards will be explored.

5.1   What Is the JDM Strategy?

Historically, data mining has been the domain of statisticians and data analysts. Sophisticated businesses often developed proprietary algorithms or implemented published algorithms by hiring experts with advanced degrees in statistics and machine learning. As data mining technology evolved, commercial tools entered the market, providing more general purpose tools that could be used by these same experts. However, a technology that can explain and predict behavior and outcomes, as well as automatically categorize and derive hidden associations among objects, should be more readily available to enhance applications. Although commercial tools go far toward making the raw technology more accessible, it is still difficult for many businesses to reap the benefits of data mining.

For example, many data mining tools provide complex graphical interfaces for performing data mining. This often results in the problem of how to deploy the results to business processes or applications. To address this problem, data mining vendors produced proprietary application programming interfaces (APIs) to their products to enable programmatic control. These APIs ranged from using traditional programming languages like C [Kernighan+ 2005] and Java [Weka 2005], to proprietary interpreted languages [Darwin 2005]. As discussed later in this chapter, the diversity in interfaces comes at a cost to vendors, developers, and businesses.

The JDM interfaces are defined as a pure Java specification, in which either client, server, or both can be implemented purely in Java. However, JDM also allows vendors to implement the system behind the Java interface specification in any implementation technology or programming language. This enables vendors with established products to wrap their products with the JDM interface.

JDM began and remains an open, pure Java, multivendor standard. An *open standard* can be defined as being

publicly available specifications for achieving a specific task. By allowing anyone to use the standard, [open standards] increase compatibility between various hardware and software components since anyone with the technical know-how and the necessary equipment to implement solutions can build something that works together with those of other vendors. [Wikipedia 2006a]

Here are 10 strategic objectives for JDM.

Strategic Objective 1: Address a large developer community

To gain mainstream adoption, it is important to attract the attention of a large and appropriate audience. It is easy for good designs to fade into obscurity for targeting too small of an audience or the wrong audience. The JDM standard is more likely to take root and grow by providing an established community of application developers programmatic access to data mining functionality, enabling them to extract knowledge and insight from data.

As of 2006, it is estimated there are millions of Java developers worldwide. Java™ and J2EE are natural choices for application development. With Java's powerful language concepts and J2EE's distributed application framework, Java offers a major application development framework as used in research and industry. Tactically, Java is a natural choice of language.

Strategic Objective 2: Be a standard interface

Proprietary interfaces rarely stand the test of time. The products that provide them or the companies that create them may come and go. Developing applications on such interfaces can be risky. Some *de facto* standards[1] arise because of extensive adoption in the marketplace. For better or worse, de facto standards normally reflect the perspective of the organization or company that defined them. Standards developed by multiple vendors and consumers are likely to address a broader set of needs. Standards provide a host of others benefits, as detailed later in this chapter, not least of which is to give consumers a greater sense of the maturity of the technology they are using. By providing a standard interface, technologies such as data mining can be more confidently deployed in business processes and applications.

Tactically, the Java Community Process (JCP) [JCP 2005] is the natural choice for a standards body through which to become a standard interface for Java.

---

1   *De facto* standards are those that are widely used and recognized by the industry as being standards as opposed to being approved by a standards organization [Webopedia 2006] [BellevueLinux 2006] such as Microsoft Word and Adobe PostScript.

Strategic Objective 3: Have broad acceptance among vendors and consumers

All too often, a standards effort can become dominated by technologists enamored with the technical details of a problem and vendors limited to focusing on the specific features they support, rather than on ease of use or what the consumer needs. Involving both consumers and vendors in the standards process helps to provide balance to the resulting work. The JCP encourages participation from multiple vendors and consumers to ensure that Java language extensions meet a wide range of needs. This and other aspects of the JCP, as discussed in Section 17.2, give potential users greater confidence in the resulting standard.

Tactically, we chose to involve multiple vendors and potential consumers to ensure the standard reflects the capabilities and practices common in data mining tools, as well as the needs of industry. For example, the JSR-73 expert group consisted of leading corporate and individual members from both data mining vendors and technology consumers, with Oracle as specification lead [JSR-73 2006].[2]

Strategic Objective 4: Be extensible

As in any healthy field, the number of data mining techniques and algorithms continues to expand. Variations on traditional algorithms are introduced to improve performance, quality, or ease of use. As such, no standard is ever complete. New requirements or capabilities are constantly evolving. Any of the proceedings from SIGKDD [SIGKDD 2005] give testament to the research supporting advancements in data mining.

To remain relevant, a standard must provide sufficient common functionality, yet enable vendors to enhance and grow that functionality in advance of the standards process itself. Having a framework through which new mining capabilities can be readily added makes it practical for vendors to implement the standard, yet provide their customers the same level of service and capabilities those customers are accustomed to.

Tactically, we designed JDM to be an easily extensible framework consisting of a small core set of interfaces from which JDM standard and vendor-proprietary interfaces can inherit to provide new capabilities (e.g., functions and algorithms) while keeping the same overall

---

2   See [JSR-73 2006] for a complete list of expert group members.

structure and feel of the API. This framework enables vendors to use the core of the standard while reflecting a product's unique capabilities. This framework also enables application developers to learn a standard set of interfaces yet easily leverage vendor extensions since they adhere to a common design. This framework is discussed further in Chapter 8.

Strategic Objective 5: Start small and grow in functionality

The field of data mining includes a wide variety of techniques. Some are mature and well-established in both tools and practice. For example, classification and regression have been long implemented using decision tree algorithms such as C4.5 [Quinlan 1993] and CART [Breiman+ 1984], and other algorithms including naïve bayes and neural networks [Mitchell 1997]. Newer algorithms such as support vector machine (SVM) [Christianini/Shawe-Taylor 2000] have also gained significant acceptance in both tools and applications. Other techniques are more experimental and evolving, or still proprietary. As the breadth of data mining is quite encompassing, it is important to focus initially on a set of techniques commonly available with well-known applications.

To enable a data mining standard to come to fruition, it is important to constrain its scope and focus on a core set of capabilities, while defining a framework within which new capabilities can be readily added. Tactically, we provide an initial set of mining functions and algorithms that can solve a wide range of problems and expand over time as demand dictates.

Strategic Objective 6: Simplify data mining for novices while allowing control for experts

As we have noted, data mining has traditionally been the domain of experts. Although there are still many aspects of the data mining problem space that require in-depth understanding of both the problem and solution, such as data preparation and domain-dependent knowledge, much can be done to simplify the data mining process, including automatic algorithm selection, data preparation, and settings tuning. This automation gives vendors the opportunity to add value to their products beyond algorithms. Yet at the same time, experts want to be able to exert control over all aspects of the modeling process.

Tactically, we provide an API that allows vendors to automate much of the data mining process such that both novice and expert data miners can obtain desired results. By distinguishing mining functions from mining algorithms, JDM simplifies the mining process for novices, while allowing experts complete control. Mining functions allow users to specify *what* they want to accomplish, e.g., classify these cases into two categories, or cluster these cases into *n* clusters. Novice data miners who are not familiar with the details of data mining can rely on the vendor to choose a specific algorithm. In addition, many of the settings that control the mining function or algorithm behavior allow a *system determined* setting that instructs the data mining engine to make an intelligent selection, perhaps based on the nature of the data presented. JDM also allows for automated data preparation to further support the novice user. On the other hand, expert data miners, familiar with the details of data mining, can select the specific algorithm or specify detailed settings. Expert data miners can prepare their data explicitly and instruct the data mining engine not to further transform their data.

Strategic Objective 7: Recognize conformance limitations for vendor implementations

Like the field of data mining itself, data mining software vendors support a wide range of data mining techniques. In some cases, vendors may specialize in a particular technique like neural networks, or in a small set of techniques such as classification and regression, providing a variety of algorithms. As such, it is important to create a standard that is flexible enough to allow vendors with different focuses to implement and comply with the standard.

Tactically, we reduce barriers to entry for vendors to support the standard by making conformance *a la cart*; that is, the standard is naturally segmented into logical units, which can be easily supported independent of others. Simply, this means that JDM is organized into packages specific to different types of functionality that vendors can optionally choose to support. Of course, there is a relatively small core set of packages that must be supported, yet vendors can select to implement a narrow subset of functionality, for example, only the classification mining function with the decision tree algorithm. Other vendors may choose to implement only interfaces at the mining function level, leaving out any algorithm details. This flexibility makes the JDM standard much more accessible to niche vendors.

Strategic Objective 8: Support requirements of real, industrial applications

A major impetus to businesses using data mining is how to derive value or operationalize their data mining results in business applications and processes. Deploying data mining results can involve moving the data mining models from the lab into the field, or publishing the results in reports or through dashboards. The complexity of applications often requires the ability to transport data mining objects and related information between machines.

Sophisticated graphical user interfaces (GUIs) for performing data mining can be feature rich with algorithms, transformations, and support for model building, test, and scoring. However, GUIs are often not enough to deploy data mining solutions in applications and throughout a business.

Tactically, we enable applications to exchange objects using export and import interfaces, to save mining objects to files, and to share settings and results, including models, between vendor implementations. The ability to transport data mining objects from one environment to another is often key in a distributed application environment. For example, where models are built in one system but applied to data in another, an XML representation of mining objects is highly valuable. Adopting a common XML Schema representation for JDM objects facilitates interchange among vendors, as discussed in Chapter 10.

Strategic Objective 9: Appeal to vendors and architects in other development domains

Implementing and conforming to a standard can be a major undertaking. If the data mining engine (DME) must be modified or enhanced to support a standard interface, vendors are more inclined to adopt that standard if it can reach a broader audience.

Tactically, we enable data mining in a Service Oriented Architecture (SOA) by defining a web services interface that maps closely with the Java API. This allows application designers and developers to freely move between Java and web services, especially within the same vendor implementation.

Strategic Objective 10: Leverage other data mining standards

Much effort has gone into standardizing various aspects of data mining. Some vendors and consumers are already familiar with some of these standards and may have already implemented systems and applications using them. Where possible, leverage existing data mining standards to achieve a greater degree of interoperability and avoid impedance mismatch between standards.

Tactically, we include the notion of import and export of objects conforming to PMML and CWM, as well as provide a conscious mapping of capabilities among data mining standards where possible and appropriate.

These are the strategic objectives for JDM. Next, we explore some of the basic premises for standards.

5.2   Role of Standards

Although data mining in the form of artificial intelligence, machine learning, and various statistical techniques has been around for many decades, only within the past 5 years have data mining standards taken hold—a proof point for the maturing of the field and its pervasiveness in the marketplace. This section explores the motivations for creating a standard and what standards enable for realizing the Java Data Mining strategy.

5.2.1   Why Create a Standard?

Standards exist in nearly every aspect of life. In the physical world, we have standards for phone jacks, electrical sockets, railroads, and bathroom fixtures, to name a few. We feel and experience how these standards make life much easier and products less expensive. Consider electrical sockets: Anyone who has traveled to a foreign country using a different electrical socket standard can readily understand the benefits of standards.

In the nonphysical world, we have standards for Internet communication protocols, SQL, and programming languages. Those who have used software and hardware products from multiple vendors also appreciate the benefits of standards, or at least the problems introduced by lack of standards.

The Java programming language is a specific case of a standard that benefits its user community. In particular, the Java Data Mining standard provides a common framework for exploring and developing applications using data mining. Developers are able to learn a single development framework and apply it in many situations, across applications, and across vendor-provided tool sets. A standard and consistently designed API also makes data mining more accessible to developers. Companies using data mining can choose from multiple, competing products while ensuring that their developers need not retool to a completely different way of developing applications. Companies can select products more on the merits of their capabilities than on what product their developers currently use or are familiar with. Moreover, applications solving business problems can take advantage of the capabilities of multiple data mining products more easily since the interface is standard. The risks associated with using a proprietary API such as vendor longevity or costly application rewrites due to changing vendors are greatly reduced. With a standard API, applications no longer need to be completely rewritten to adapt to a different vendor's interface.

As noted earlier, standards normally involve input from many diverse individuals and companies. *De facto* standards may reflect a marketplace consensus—sometimes resulting from a monopoly-like reign in an industry. However, open standards, like the Java Community Process, have the benefit of providing interfaces that can meet a broader set of needs due to input from participants with a broader range of experience and needs. Drawing on both vendors and consumers helps ensure a standard is both implementable and usable.

Innovation also benefits from standards; small enterprises including start-ups can join the big players on a level playing field provided by an open standards forum. Further, vendors can compete on features and performance, instead of on the interface. Customers do not have to feel they are taking as much of a risk adopting a small vendor's solution since they will be developing against a standard interface. Just as it is a benefit for customers to be able to change vendors more easily, it is also a benefit to vendors because a customer may be more willing to change vendors when competing on price or level of functionality.

The existence of standards also frees vendors from having to reinvent the wheel. Instead of expending resources to design alternative APIs, vendors can apply engineering resources to enhancing functionality and performance.

When some of the best minds come together to design a standard, often the whole is greater than the sum of the parts. That is, new ideas arise that make the standard better than any one vendor could have done independently.

5.2.2 What Do Data Mining Standards Enable?

The evolution of data mining standards speaks to the maturing of the market and the technology. By standardizing model representations, as is done via the Predictive Model Markup Language (PMML) [DMG-PMML 2006], users have greater potential to interchange models among different vendor data mining systems. By standardizing the mining operations, their input parameters, and output results, as is done via JDM, users have greater potential to develop more portable applications, as well as interchange settings and mining objects among vendors. Moreover, developers of advanced analytic applications can learn a single paradigm and leverage that across vendors. Applications that leverage multiple vendor mining systems are greatly simplified since a common framework can be used to invoke functionality in each mining system.

Extensible data mining standards such as JDM also provide a framework for integrating proprietary, new, or evolving algorithms and mining functions. Vendors can provide the needed delta functionality while reusing definitions, objects, and common functionality of the underlying framework.

As noted, the JDM standard enables more flexible application architectures, which provide application developers and businesses greater choice in how they address data mining solutions. These include:

- Avoiding vendor lock-in
- Multivendor solutions
- Best of breed interoperability

With most software purchases that involve extensive application development, business management is concerned with vendor lock-in. That is, after investing much time, resources, and money into a project using a vendor's proprietary interface, if the software supporting a key piece of that solution needs to be changed, this will require rewriting much of the application. Such a cost makes management afraid to choose certain solutions or to undertake a particular project until standard solutions are available. This places smaller vendors at a disadvantage due to concerns of longevity, but also larger vendors for fear of being held hostage to price increases. Figure 5-1 depicts the objective to enable an application using JDM with Vendor 1 to be able to write the application in such a way that the user can switch to Vendor 2 without significant modification to the application.

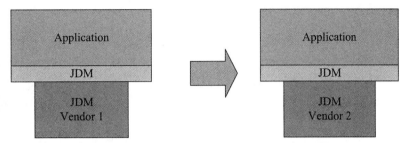

Figure 5-1 *Avoiding vendor lock-in.*

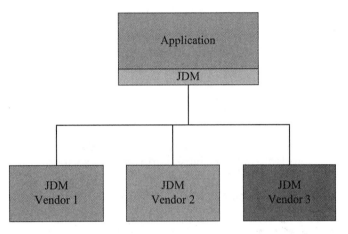

Figure 5-2 *Multivendor solutions.*

Apart from the negative aspects of vendor lock-in, a standard can also make new and innovative applications possible, leveraging the best features from a set of vendor tools. As illustrated in Figure 5-2, the same application, or application user, can choose which vendor features to use. Meanwhile, the application is using a common API to interact with each of the systems. (Chapter 13 introduces an example with code for such an application.)

Another variant of the multivendor solution involves possibly distributed applications where mining objects are exchanged between applications and among vendor products. The example depicted in Figure 5-3 illustrates a build application that uses Vendor 1 to build models. These models may be exported and then imported into other applications, such as a visualization application or an apply application, often referred to as a *scoring engine.*

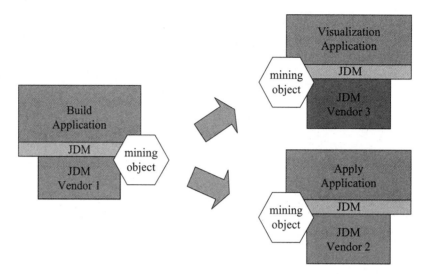

Figure 5-3 *Best of breed interoperability.*

Vendor 3 provides highly sophisticated graphical visualization of models that are displayed through a custom visualization application, while Vendor 2 provides a highly performant scoring engine that the apply application uses.

5.3 Summary

The JDM strategy revolves around making data mining more accessible to the masses of Java and web services developers. Making JDM a standard and working through an established standards organization reassures businesses in the strength and maturity of the data mining market. This chapter explored several strategic objectives and tactical approaches the expert group had for JDM, as well as the role of standards for meeting these objectives.

References

[Breiman+ 1984] Leo Breiman, J. H. Friedman, R. A. Olshen, C. J. Stone, *Classification and Regression Trees*, New York, Chapman & Hall, 1984.

[BellevueLinux 2006] http://www.bellevuelinux.org/de_facto_standard.html.

[Christianini/Shawe-Taylor 2000] N. Cristianini, J. Shawe-Taylor, *An Introduction to Support Vector Machines*, Cambridge, UK, Cambridge University Press, 2000.

[CWM 2005] http://www.omg.org/technology/cwm.

[Darwin 2005] http://www.oracle.com/technology/documentation/darwin.html.

[DMG-PMML 2006] http://www.dmg.org.

[GBC 2005] Government of British Columbia, http://www.for.gov.bc.ca/tasb/legsregs/fpc/fpcguide/defoliat/gloss.htm.

[ISO 2005] http://www.iso.org/iso/en/ISOOnline.frontpage.

[JCP 2005] http://www.jcp.org.

[JSR-73 2006] http://jcp.org/en/jsr/detail?id=73.

[Kernighan+ 2005] Brian W. Kernighan, Dennis Ritchie, Dennis M. Ritchie, *The C Programming Language*, 2nd ed., Upper Saddle River, NJ, Prentice Hall, 2005.

[Kimball/Ross 2002] R. Kimball, M. Ross, *The Data Warehouse Toolkit: The Complete Guide to Dimensional Modeling*, New York, John Wiley & Sons, 2002.

[OMG 2001] Common Warehouse Metadata (CWM) Specification, Object Management Group (OMG), http://www.omg.org/cgi-bin/apps/doc?ad/01-02-01.pdf, Version 1.0, February 2, 2001.

[OMG 2005] http://www.omg.org.

[Phonniah 2001] Paulraj Ponniah, *Data Warehousing Fundamentals: A Comprehensive Guide for IT Professionals*, New York, John Wiley & Sons, 2001.

[Pyle 1999] D. Pyle, *Data Preparation for DataMining*, San Francisco, Morgan Kaufmann, 1999.

[Quinlan 1993] R. Quinlan, *C4.5: Programs for Machine Learning*, San Mateo, CA, Morgan Kaufmann, 1993.

[SAS 2005] http://www.sas.com/technologies/analytics/datamining/miner/factsheet.pdf.

[SIGKDD 2005] *Proceedings of the Eleventh ACM SIGKDD International Conference on Knowledge Discovery and Data Mining*, ACM Press, 2005.

[SUN 2005] www.jcp.org.

[Wikipedia 2005] http://en.wikipedia.org/wiki/Strategy.

[Wikipedia 2006a] http://en.wikipedia.org/wiki/Open_standard.

[Webopedia 2006] http://www.webopedia.com/TERM/D/de_facto_standard.htm.

[Weka 2005] http://www.cs.waikato.ac.nz/ml/weka.

Chapter

6

Getting Started

The secret of getting ahead is getting started.

—Mark Twain (1835–1910)

As with any technology, the challenge to gaining proficiency is not being afraid to venture into the unknown. As Mark Twain noted, "the secret of getting ahead is getting started," and a strategy to get ahead with data mining is to start with small problems and datasets, learn some basic techniques and processes, and keep practicing. This chapter introduces a small code example to give the reader a feel for the Java Data Mining (JDM) application programming interface (API) in the context of a specific business problem before going into more detailed examples in Parts II and III of this book. The business problem we address involves response modeling, as discussed in Chapter 2, for a fictitious company DMWIZZ and their product *Gizmos*. Rather than dive right into the code, this chapter follows the CRISP-DM data mining process by first discussing the business understanding, data understanding, and data preparation phases. Code is shown for modeling, and evaluation and deployment are discussed. Note that each process phase is not explored in depth, but enough to give the reader a feel for the phase.

6.1 Business Understanding

The business objective of company DMWhizz is to increase the response rate for its latest campaign for a new product, *Gizmos*. DMWhizz has run many such campaigns, so from an operational standpoint, there is little risk associated with this project. However, this is the first time DMWhizz is employing data mining to try to increase the response rate over previous efforts. Historically, DMWhizz has obtained a 3 percent response rate from such campaigns, which they viewed as better than the norm in the retail industry. DMWhizz will be satisfied with anything over a 4 percent response rate, a 33 percent increase. They typically send a campaign to 400,000 of their customers, chosen at random. As such, they get about 12,000 responses. With the introduction of data mining, DMWhizz expects at least 16,000 responses if sent to 400,000 customers, a 33 percent increase.

The business has a base of 1 million existing customers to potentially send an offer to. Although Gizmos is a new product, it is related to several other less-featured products, so DMWhizz can use historical sales information of customers who have bought these other products.

DMWhizz knows that this data mining solution requires known outcomes to build predictive models, in this case, which customers actually purchased Gizmos. As such they factor into their plan conducting a small-scale, trial campaign to collect data on which customers actually purchased Gizmos. From this trial campaign, data mining models can be built to predict which of the remaining customers and prospects are likely to purchase Gizmos.

Specifically, DMWhizz takes a 2 percent random sample of the 1 million potential customers for Gizmos, totaling 20,000. They mail the offer to these customers and record which customers purchased the item. Based on previous campaigns, they expect a 3 percent response rate, or 600 customers purchasing Gizmos. This data, with known outcomes both positive and negative, serves as the basis for the modeling process.

Technically speaking, this is a classification problem in data mining. DMWhizz is as yet unfamiliar with the quality and character of the data; they expect to try several types of classification algorithms and to select the one that provides the best *lift*. Lift essentially indicates how well the model performs at predicting a particular outcome instead of randomly selecting cases, in this instance *customers,* to include in the campaign. The concept of lift is explored in more detail in Section 7.1.6.

The database of 1 million customers and prospects includes demographic data such as age, income, marital status, and household size. There is also previous customer purchase data for three related products: *Tads, Zads,* and *Fads,* which indicate whether the customer purchased these items or not. The *target* attribute, what is to be predicted, is called *response.* The *response* attribute contains a "1" if the customer responded to the Gizmos campaign, and "0" if not.

6.2 Data Understanding

DMWhizz's database administrators (DBAs) obtain the data and provide it to the data miner to begin data exploration. Three tables are obtained: *CUSTOMER, PURCHASES,* and *PRODUCT.* As illustrated in Figure 6-1, a customer can have many purchases, and a product can be purchased many times.

The CUSTOMER table contains many attributes, some of which will not be useful for mining. For example, the customer's name is not useful in predicting who will respond in general. A rule such as "all people named Smith buy Gizmos" likely does not hold, or even if it did hold in the build dataset, it will not *generalize* to other datasets or the broader customer base. Similarly, the attribute *street address* typically will not generalize (e.g, "people on Prospect Street buy Gizmos"). However, attributes like city, state, or zip code may prove useful as perhaps customers in Boston find Gizmos more appealing than customers in San Francisco. *Age* is the age of the registered customers determined from their birth date relative to the current year. *Gender, income, education level, occupation, years at residence,* and *household size* are as reported on the latest warranty registration card returned by the customer, or were purchased

Figure 6-1 *Entity-Relationship diagram of tables.*

through a third-party data provider. The following attributes will be included in the CUSTOMER table:

CUSTOMER

id

name

address

city

state

zip

age

gender

income

education

occupation

years_at_residence

household_size

The PURCHASE table contains past purchases of products for each customer. There is a unique transaction identifier for each separate purchase by a customer and a given transaction may have included one or more products. The PURCHASE table also records how many of a given item were purchased in the transaction.

PURCHASE

customer_id

transaction_id

product_id

quantity_sold

The PRODUCT table contains a list of products sold by DMWhizz, identified by a specific product identifier, and being sold for a specific price.

PRODUCT

product_id

product_name

product_price

6.3   **Data Preparation**

DMWhiz has clean data due to a data warehousing initiative they undertook the previous quarter. However, data can be acquired for specific tables without requiring the creation of a data warehouse. Clean data not only simplifies the data mining effort, but can also yield superior results.

Being satisfied with the quality of the data, the next step for data preparation involves joining the data tables into a single table that can be used for mining. In the PURCHASES table, the data is represented in *transactional* format. This means that each item purchased is captured in a separate row or record in the table. As noted above, there is an identifier that associates a set of purchases to a given transaction (purchase instance), and another identifier that identifies the customer. We are interested in transforming this into a table where a record indicates whether a customer previously purchased a Tads, Zads, or Fads. Because JDM 1.1 does not address specific transformations, an easy way to accomplish this is to use the database query language SQL [SQL 2003] via JDBC [JDBC 2006], or SQLJ [SQLJ 2003], which enables writing SQL statements in Java code as though they were ordinary embedded SQL, translating such statements into JDBC invocations. Examples of executing SQL through JDBC are given in Chapters 12 and 13.

We can define a view to provide the data in the desired format:

```
CREATE VIEW PURCHASES_v AS
SELECT customer_id,
    max(decode(product_name, 'Tads', 1, 0)) AS purchased_tads,[1]
    max(decode(product_name, 'Zads', 1, 0)) AS purchased_zads,
    max(decode(product_name, 'Fads', 1, 0)) AS purchased_fads
FROM PURCHASES AS pu, PRODUCTS AS pr
WHERE pu.product_id = pr.product_id
GROUP BY customer_id;
```

---

[1]   The standard SQL syntax for decode can be expressed as
```
CASE product_name
    WHEN 'Tads' THEN 1
    ELSE 0
END
```
We use the Oracle SQL decode to simplify the example.

The original data in PURCHASES is depicted in Table 6-1. The transformed data in PURCHASES_V, depicted in Table 6-2, contains new columns derived from the transactional format PURCHASES table. We used the PRODUCT table, depicted in Table 6-3, to look up the product ID by product name.

Table 6-1 *Original PURCHASES table data, example*

Customer_id	Transaction_id	Product_id	Quantity
1	1	1	1
1	2	2	2
1	3	3	5
2	1	1	3
2	2	4	7
3	1	3	1
3	2	4	2
4	1	2	6
5	1	1	4
5	2	3	3

Table 6-2 *Transformed PURCHASES_V view data, example*

Customer_id	Purchased_tads	Purchased_zads	Purchased_fads
1	1	1	1
2	1	0	0
4	0	1	0
5	1	0	1
3	0	0	1

Table 6-3 *Transformed PRODUCTS table data, example*

Product_id	Product_name	Product_price
1	Tads	30
2	Zads	20
3	Fads	10
4	Rads	40

The table GIZMOS_RESULTS, depicted in Table 6-4, records which customers in the trial campaign responded and placed an order for Gizmos.

Table 6-4 *Table GIZMOS_RESULTS from trial campaign*

Customer_id	Response
1	1
2	0
3	0
4	1

The SQL statement in the following code creates a view called CUSTOMER_RESPONSE, which produces a data mining-ready table based on the CUSTOMER and PURCHASES_V table.

```
CREATE VIEW CUSTOMER_RESPONSE as
SELECT id, name, address, city, state, zip, age, gender,
       income, education, occupation, years_at_residence,
       purchased_tads, purchased_zads, purchased_fads, household_size,
       response
from CUSTOMER c, PURCHASES_V p, GIZMOS_RESULTS g
where c.id = p.customer_id
and c.id = g.customer_id
```

We are now ready to begin building models using this data.

6.4 Modeling

For modeling, we select the technique we will use for mining the data. As noted above, DMWhizz will try several algorithms, each possibly with different settings to obtain better results. However, to get a model built quickly, and to see how well the data mining engine (DME) can do using default settings, we leave the selection of algorithm and any detailed settings to the DME. This can serve as a baseline model against which we can measure other models.

The DMWhizz data miner will likely want to do some additional data preparation once the initial results are obtained. For this initial model building exercise, DMWhizz relies on the DME to prepare the data automatically. Note that not all data mining tools support this capability and some tools may require algorithm-specific data preparation.

In the modeling phase, we first build, and then test the model. To be able to test, we need a test dataset, that is, one taken from the original data and used to determine how well the model performs on data it has not seen before. Since our data is randomly ordered, we will take the first 70 percent of records for the build dataset, called CUSTOMER_BUILD, and the remaining 30 percent for the test dataset, called CUSTOMER_TEST.

6.4.1   Build

For model building, there are a couple of JDM artifacts to be aware of. First, JDM requires a connection to the DME to perform mining. This is illustrated in the following code. JDM requires the instantiation of a factory object to create a connection. Factory objects also play a major role in working with JDM overall. See Chapter 8 for a discussion of JDM factories.

```
import javax.datamining.resource.ConnectionFactory;
import javax.datamining.resource.Connection;
import javax.datamining.resource.ConnectionSpec;

Hashtable env = new Hashtable();
env.put( Context.INITIAL_CONTEXT_FACTORY,
        "com.myCompany.javax.datamining.resource.initialContextFactoryImpl" );
env.put( Context.PROVIDER_URL, "http://myHost:myPort/myService" );
env.put( Context.SECURITY_PRINCIPAL, "user" );
env.put( Context.SECURITY_CREDENTIALS, "password" );
InitialContext jndiContext = new javax.naming.InitialContext( env );

// Perform JNDI lookup to obtain the connection factory
ConnectionFactory jdmCFactory = (ConnectionFactory)
        jndiContext.lookup("java:comp/env/jdm/MyServer");

// Create a data mining server connection
ConnectionSpec svrConnSpec = (ConnectionSpec) jdmCFactory.getConnectionSpec();
svrConnSpec.setName( "jdm_user" );
svrConnSpec.setPassword( "jdm_password" );
svrConnSpec.setURI( "serverURI" );
Connection dmeConn =
(Connection) jdmCFactory.getConnection( svrConnSpec );
```

Now that we have a connection, *dmeConn*, we can proceed to set up the model building task. The task requires defining the data using a PhysicalDataSet object. This object is saved to the DME for subsequent reference by name. See Chapter 8 for more details on JDM persistence. We then create the object that contains the classification settings, namely, the parameters that instruct the DME what type of model to build. Initially, DMWhizz will rely on the DME to decide the type of model to build, so we only need to specify the target, in this case, *response*.

We then create a build task object, specifying the input build data, the settings, and the name we want to give the resulting model. After saving that object, we execute it and check the resulting status. Upon success, we can retrieve the model if desired.

We can inspect the model that was produced to see which algorithm the DME chose. In the variable *algorithm*, the value is the mining algorithm "decisiontree," meaning a decision tree, which

```
// Create the physical representation of the data
PhysicalDataSetFactory pdsFactory = (PhysicalDataSetFactory)
        dmeConn.getFactory ("javax.datamining.data.PhysicalDataSet");
PhysicalDataSet pd = pdsFactory.create( "CUSTOMER_BUILD", true );
dmeConn.saveObject( "customer_build", pd, REPLACE);

// Create and save a settings object to be used for a classification model
ClassificationSettingsFactory csFactory = (ClassificationSettingsFactory)
 dmeConn.getFactory(
        "javax.datamining.supervised.classification.ClassificationSettings" );
ClassificationSettings settings = csFactory.create();
settings.setTargetAttributeName( "RESPONSE" );
dmeConn.saveObject( "response_settings", settings, REPLACE);

// Create the build task and verify the task before execution
BuildTaskFactory btFactory = (BuildTaskFactory)
 dmeConn.getFactory( "javax.datamining.task.BuildTask" );
BuildTask buildTask =
 btFactory.create( "customer_build", "response_settings", "resp_model_1" );
dmeConn.saveObject( "response_build_task", buildTask, REPLACE );

// Execute the task and block until finished
ExecutionHandle handle = dmeConn.execute( "response_build_task" );
handle.waitForCompletion( Integer.MAX_VALUE ); // wait until done

// Access the model if model was successfully built
ExecutionStatus status = handle.getLatestStatus();
if( ExecutionState.success.equals( status.getState() ) ) {
   ClassificationModel model = (ClassificationModel)
        dmeConn.retrieveObject( "resp_model_1", NamedObject.model );
   ClassificationSettings settings =
        (ClassificationSettings) model.getEffectiveSettings ();
   MiningAlgorithm algorithm = settings.getMiningAlgorithm();
}
```

produces rules; this was chosen by the DME, as the default algorithm. Now that we have a model, we need to understand how well it predicts whether a customer will respond to the campaign.

6.4.2   Test

For model testing, we use the CUSTOMER_TEST dataset. As the code below indicates, we first create a physical dataset object from the CUSTOMER_TEST data, and then create a classification test task which specifies the test dataset, the previously built model, called *response_model*, and the name of the test results. We accept the default set of tests performed by the DME, which includes computing a confusion matrix, lift, and ROC. After executing the task, we can examine the lift to understand how well the model performs over a random selection of customers.

```
// Create the physical representation of the input data for apply
PhysicalDataSetFactory pdsFactory = (PhysicalDataSetFactory)
        dmeConn.getFactory( "javax.datamining.data.PhysicalDataSet" );
PhysicalDataSet testInputData = pdsFactory.create( "CUSTOMER_TEST", true );
dmeConn.saveObject( "cust_response_test", testInputData, REPLACE );

// Create a task to run test operation
ClassificationTestTaskFactory cttFactory = (ClassificationTestTaskFactory)
        dmeConn.getFactory
        ( "javax.datamining.supervised.classification.ClassificationTestTask" );
ClassificationTestTask testTask = cttFactory.create(
"cust_response_test", "resp_model_1", "resp_model_1_test_result" );

// Enable computation of confusion matrix as the result of test
testTask.computeMetric(ClassificationTestMetricOption.confusionMatrix);
dmeConn.saveObject( "response_test_task_1", testTask, false );

// Execute the task asynchronously, but wait until done
ExecutionHandle execHandle = dmeConn.execute( "response_test_task_1" );
execHandle.waitForCompletion( WAIT_FOR_COMPLETION );

// Retrieve the test metrics
ClassificationTestMetrics testMetrics = (ClassificationTestMetrics)
dmeConn.retrieveObject( "resp_model_1_test_result",
        NamedObject.testMetrics );
Double accuracy = testMetrics.getAccuracy();
Lift lift = testMetrics.getLift();
Double cumulativeLift = lift.getCumulativeLift (4);
```

From this default model, the cumulative lift for the test dataset at 40 percent is .6, meaning that the model was able to predict 60 percent of the likely responders from only 40 percent of the data. The DMWhizz data miner may decide to specify other algorithms besides the decision tree that the DME selected, change some of the decision tree algorithm settings, or prepare the data differently to see if a better lift can be achieved. If another model produced a higher lift for 40 percent of the customers, perhaps 0.7, the data miner would likely choose that model. If another model produced the lift of 0.6 at 35 percent of the customers, DMWhizz may choose to send the campaign to fewer customers while maintaining the same number of likely responses.

We now move on to the evaluation phase of the process.

6.5   Evaluation

In the evaluation phase, we are interested in understanding how well the model meets the business objectives. We see from the test results of the model produced above that the lift is .6. How does this meet our business objectives? Out of 1 million customers, historically we know that 3 percent, or 30,000, should respond. The lift results tells us that by contacting the *right* 400,000 customers (or 40 percent of the 1 million customer base), DMWhizz can get 60 percent of the likely responders, or 18,000 (60 percent of 30,000). This is a response rate of 4.5 percent.

Given that DMWhizz's original requirement was to increase the response rate to 4 percent, the expected 4.5 percent provided by data mining yields a comfortable margin. As a result, DMWhizz decides to use this model to score the remaining 980,000 customers and proceed with the campaign.

6.6   Deployment

In the evaluation phase, DMWhizz found that the model meets the objective and can be used to complete the campaign. Since we have already contacted 20,000 of the 1 million customers for our sample campaign, we apply the model to the remaining 980,000 customer cases and send a mailing to the top 40 percent of customers predicted to respond to the campaign. We use the code below to score these customers in batch, that is, all at once, and produce a separate table that includes the customer identifier and the probability that the customer will respond. All the cases are ordered by their probability in descending order.

To apply the model, we first create a physical dataset object from the CUSTOMER_APPLY table. The CUSTOMER_APPLY table contains the same predictors as the CUSTOMER_RESPONSE table, but does not contain the target attribute 'response' since that is what we are predicting. We then create the object that indicates the results we are interested in, namely, the customer ID, and the probability that the customer will respond (response = 1). We then create the apply task specifying the apply dataset, the model, the apply settings, and the location for the apply result, namely, the scores. After executing the task, we have a dataset with all the customers scored.

```
// Create the physical representation of the input data
PhysicalDataSetFactory pdsFactory = (PhysicalDataSetFactory)
     dmeConn.getFactory( "javax.datamining.data.PhysicalDataSet" );
PhysicalDataSet applyInputData =
     pdsFactory.create( "CUSTOMER_APPLY", PhysicalDataSet.IMPORT_META_DATA );
dmeConn.saveObject( "customer_apply", applyInputData, REPLACE );

// Create the output specification of apply
ClassificationApplySettingsFactory casFactory =
(ClassificationApplySettingsFactory) dmeConn.getFactory
( "javax.datamining.supervised.classification.ClassificationApplySettings" );
ClassificationApplySettings applySettings = casFactory.create();

java.util.Map sourceDestMap = new java.util.HashMap();
// Output column containing the customer id
sourceDestMap.put( "customer_id", "ID" );
applySettings.setSourceDestinationMap( sourceDestMap );
// Output column for the probability of response = 1
applySettings.mapClass (ClassificationApplyContent.probability,
                    "probability" );
dmeConn.saveObject( "response_apply_settings", applySettings, REPLACE );

// Create a task for apply with dataset
DataSetApplyTaskFactory datFactory = (DataSetApplyTaskFactory)
     dmeConn.getFactory( "javax.datamining.task.apply.DataSetApplyTask" );
DataSetApplyTask applyTask =
       datFactory.create( "customer_apply", "resp_model_1",
       "response_apply_settings", "response_scores" );
dmeConn.saveObject( "response_apply_task", applyTask, REPLACE );

// Execute the apply task
ExecutionHandle execHandle = dmeConn.execute( "responseApplyTask" );
execHandle.waitForCompletion( Connection.WAIT_FOR_COMPLETION );
```

Now, we order the cases so that we can skim off the top 40 percent (392,000) of likely responders. The following SQL orders the cases.

```
SELECT customer_id
from RESPONSE_SCORES
order by probability
```

With this result, we proceed with the mailing and await the actual customer responses. It will be important to compare actual responses with those predicted to determine how accurate the model was in practice. This type of feedback is key to determine if the introduction of data mining indeed met the business objectives.

As part of deployment, the data miner produces a report summarizing the steps necessary to introduce data mining to the campaign process and the details of building and evaluating the models.

6.7   Summary

This chapter introduced the JDM API using a response modeling business problem. We followed the phases of the CRISP-DM methodology to illustrate where the API applies, putting the use of the API in the context of not only solving a data mining problem, but leveraging its results. We saw how the notion of lift could be used to assess the quality of a model and how it can impact the selection of a final model or strategy. There are other techniques for assessing model quality, such as a *confusion matrix* and *receiver operating characteristics* (ROC), which will be introduced in Chapter 7.

References

[JDBC 2006] http://java.sun.com/products/jdbc.

[SQL 2003] ISO/IEC 9075–2:2003, *Information technology–Database language–SQL–Part 2: Foundation (SQL/Foundation)*, International Standards Organization, 2003.

[SQLJ 2003] ISO/IEC 9075–2:2003, *Information technology–Database languages–SQL–Part 10: Object Language Bindings (SQL/OLB)*, International Standards Organization, 2003.

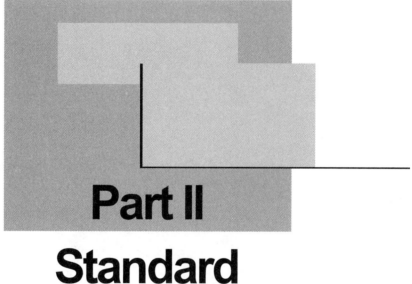

Part II

Standard

Part II focuses on the JDM standard itself, describing the conceptual view and overall design. We target not only the Java API, but also the XML Schema for JDM objects and data mining web services.

Chapter

7

Java Data Mining Concepts

*The intension of a complex concept may be defined
in terms of more primitive concepts.*

—Aristotle

Data mining has its origins in conventional artificial intelligence, machine learning, statistics, and database technologies, so it has much of its terminology and concepts derived from these technologies. This chapter further introduces data mining concepts for those new to data mining, and will familiarize data mining experts with JDM-specific data mining terminology and capabilities. Part I discussed various business problems and the type of data mining functions that can be used to solve these problems. An overview of general data mining concepts relevant to Java Data Mining (JDM) also was given. This chapter details and expands those concepts associated with each mining function and algorithm by example. Although we discuss higher-level details of each algorithm to give some intuition about how each algorithm works, a detailed discussion of data mining algorithms is beyond the scope of this book.

This chapter explores data mining concepts in financial services by using a set of business problems faced by a hypothetical consumer bank called ABCBank. ABCBank provides banking and financial services for individuals and corporate businesses. It has branch offices throughout the country. In addition it has online banking services for its customers. ABCBank offers products such as bank accounts for checking, savings, and certificates, and many types of credit cards, loans, and other financial services. ABCBank has a diverse customer base, distributed nationally. Customer demographics vary widely in income levels, education and professional qualifications, ethnic backgrounds, age groups, and family status. As Dale Terrell, president of BankOne Information Services Company, states, "Data mining is a key to providing not only more information but deeper information" on customers. Refer to [Johnston 1996] for other comments on the use of data mining in the banking industry.

Each section of this chapter introduces a business problem faced by ABCBank, its solution, and the concepts associated with the related mining function as discussed in Chapter 4. While developing a solution for the problem, we discuss the concepts related to the data mining technique used to solve it. We follow a common description pattern for each problem, starting with a problem definition, solution approach, data description, available settings for tuning the solution, and an overview of relevant algorithms. For supervised functions, we also describe how to evaluate a model's performance, and apply a model to obtain prediction results. For unsupervised functions, we describe model content and how to use models to solve the problem.

7.1   Classification Problem

7.1.1   Problem Definition: How to Reduce Customer Attrition?

ABCBank is losing customers to its competitors and wants to gain a better understanding of the type of customers who are closing their accounts. ABCBank also wants to be proactive in retaining existing customers by taking appropriate measures to improve customer satisfaction. This is commonly known as the *customer attrition* problem in the financial services industry. Refer to [Hu 2005] for a thorough study on banking attrition analysis.

7.1.2   Solution Approach: Predict Customers Who Are Likely to Attrite

ABCBank can use customer data collected in its transactional and analytical databases to find the patterns associated with customers likely, or unlikely, to attrite. Using the data mining *classification* function, ABCBank can predict customers who are likely to attrite and understand the characteristics, or *profiles*, of such customers. Gaining a better understanding of customer behavior enables ABCBank to develop business plans to retain customers.

Classification is used to assign cases, such as customers, to discrete values, called *classes* or *categories*, of the target attribute. The *target* is the attribute whose values are predicted using data mining. In this problem, the target is the attribute *attrite* with two possible values: *Attriter* and *Non-attriter*. When referring to the model build dataset, the value *Attriter* indicates that the customer closed all accounts, and *Non-attriter* indicates the customer has at least one account at ABCBank. When referring to the prediction in the model apply dataset, the value *Attriter* indicates that the customer is *likely* to attrite and *Non-attriter* indicates that the customer is *not likely* to attrite. The prediction is often associated with a probability indicating how likely the customer is to attrite. When a target attribute has only two possible values, the problem is referred to as a *binary classification* problem. When a target attribute has more than two possible values, the problem is known as a *multiclass classification* problem.

7.1.3 Data Specification: CUSTOMERS Dataset

As noted in Chapter 3, an important step in any data mining project is to collect related data from enterprise data sources. Identifying which attributes should be used for data mining is one of the challenges faced by the data miner and relies on appropriate domain knowledge of the data. In this example, we introduce a subset of possible customer attributes as listed in Table 7-1. In real-world scenarios, there may be hundreds or even thousands of customer attributes available in enterprise databases.

Table 7-1 lists *physical attribute* details of the CUSTOMERS dataset, which include *name*, *data type*, and *description*. The attribute name refers to either a column name of a database table or a field name of a flat file. The attribute data type refers to the allowed type of values for that attribute. JDM defines *integer*, *double*, and *string* data types, which are commonly used data types for mining. JDM conformance rules allow a vendor to add more data types if required. Attribute description can be used to explain the meaning of the attribute or describe the allowed values. In general, physical data characteristics are captured by database metadata.

Table 7-1 *Customers Table physical attribute details*

Attribute name	Data type	Attribute description
CUST_ID	INTEGER	Unique customer identifier
NAME	STRING	Name of the customer
ADDRESS	STRING	Address of the customer
CITY	STRING	City of residence
COUNTY	STRING	County
STATE	STRING	State
EDU	STRING	Educational level, e.g., diploma, bachelor's, master's, Ph.D.
MAR_STATUS	STRING	Marital status, e.g., married, single, widowed, divorced
OCCUPATION	STRING	Occupation of the customer, e.g., clerical, manager, sales, etc.
INCOME	DOUBLE	Annual income in thousands of dollars
ETHNIC_GROUP	STRING	Ethnic group
AGE	DOUBLE	Age
CAP_GAIN	DOUBLE	Current capital gains or losses
SAV_BALANCE	DOUBLE	Average monthly savings balance
CHECK_BALANCE	DOUBLE	Average monthly checking balance
RETIRE_BALANCE	DOUBLE	Current retirement account balance
MORTGAGE_AMOUNT	DOUBLE	Current mortgage/home loan balance
NAT_COUNTRY	STRING	Native country
CREDIT_RISK	STRING	Relative credit risk, e.g., high, medium, low
ATTRITE	STRING	The target attribute indicating whether a customer will attrite or not. Values include "attriter" and "non-attriter."

Users may also specify *logical attribute* characteristics specific to data mining. For example, physical attribute names in the table or file can be cryptic, such as, *HHSIZE* means *household size* representing the number of people living as one family. Users can map physical names to logical names to be more descriptive and hence easier to understand. Logical data characteristics also include the specification of data mining *attribute type, attribute usage type,* and *data preparation type* to indicate how these attributes should be interpreted in data mining operations. Table 7-2 lists the logical data specification details for the CUSTOMERS dataset shown in Table 7-1.

The *attribute type* indicates the attribute data characteristics, such as whether the attribute should be treated as *numerical, categorical,* or *ordinal. Numerical attributes* are those whose values should be treated as continuous numbers. *Categorical attributes* are those where attribute

Table 7-2 *Customers Table logical data specification*

Attribute name	Logical name	Attribute type	Usage type	Preparation
CUST_ID	Customer Id		Inactive	
NAME	Name		Inactive	
ADDRESS	Address		Inactive	
CITY	City	Categorical	Active	Prepared
COUNTY	County	Categorical	Active	Prepared
STATE	State	Categorical	Active	Prepared
EDU	Education	Categorical	Active	Prepared
MAR_STATUS	Marital Status	Categorical	Active	Prepared
OCCU	Occupation	Categorical	Active	Prepared
INCOME	Annual Income Level	Numerical	Active	Not prepared
ETHNIC_GRP	Ethnic Group	Categorical	Active	Prepared
AGE	Age	Numerical	Active	Not prepared
CAP_GAIN	Capital Gains	Numerical	Active	Not prepared
SAV_BALANCE	Avg. Savings Balance	Numerical	Active	Not prepared
CHECK_BALANCE	Avg. Checking Balance	Numerical	Active	Not prepared
RETIRE_BALANCE	Retirement Balance	Numerical	Active	Not prepared
MORTGAGE_AMOUNT	Home Loan Balance	Numerical	Active	Not prepared
NAT_COUNTRY	Native Country	Categorical	Active	Prepared
CREDIT_RISK	Credit Risk	Ordinal	Active	Prepared
ATTRITE	Attrite	Target		

values correspond to discrete, nominal categories. *Ordinal attributes* are also those with discrete values, but their order is significant. In Table 7-2, the *attribute type* column specifies attributes such as *city, county, state, education, and marital status* as categorical attributes. The attribute *capital gains* is a numerical attribute as it has continuous data values, such as $12,500.94. The attribute *credit risk* is an ordinal attribute as it has *high, medium, or low* as ordered relative values.

The *attribute usage type* specifies whether an attribute is *active*—should be used as input to mining; *inactive*—excluded from mining; or *supplementary*—brought forward with the input values but not used explicitly for mining. In Table 7-2, the *usage type* column specifies attributes *customer id, name*, and *address* as *inactive* because these attributes are identifiers or will not generalize to predict if a customer is an attriter. All other attributes are *active*, and used as input for data mining. In this example, we have not included supplementary attributes. However, consider a derived attribute computed as the *capital gains* divided by the *square of age,* called *ageCapitalGainRatio*. From the user perspective, if the derived attribute *ageCapitalGainRatio* appears in a model rule, it may be difficult to interpret the underlying values as it relates to the business. In such a case, the model can reference *supplementary attributes*, for example, *age* and *capital gain*. Although these supplementary attributes are not directly used in the model build, they can be presented in model details to facilitate rule understanding using the corresponding values of *age* and *capital gain*.

In addition to usual ETL[1] operations used for loading and transforming data, data mining can involve algorithm-specific data preparation. Such data preparation includes transformations such as binning and normalization as introduced in Section 3.2. One may choose to prepare data manually to leverage domain-specific knowledge or to fine-tune data to improve results. The *data preparation type* is used to indicate if data is manually prepared. In Table 7-2, the *preparation* column lists which attributes are already *prepared* for model building. For more details about data preparations refer to [Pyle 1999].

---

1   Extraction Transformation and Loading (ETL) is the process of extracting data from their operational data sources or external data sources, transforming the data, which includes cleansing, aggregation, summarization, and integration; and other transformations, and loading the data into a data mart or data warehouse.

7.1.4   Specify Settings: Fine-Tune the Solution to the Problem

After exploring attribute values in the CUSTOMERS dataset, the data miner found some oddities in the data. The *capital gains* attribute has some extreme values that are out of range from the general population. Figure 7-1 illustrates the distribution of capital gains values in the data. Note that there are very few customers who have capital gains greater than $1,000,000; in this example such values are treated as *outliers*. Outliers are the values of a given attribute that are unusual compared to the rest of that attribute's data values. For example, if customers have capital gains over 1 million dollars, these values could skew mining results involving the attribute *capital gains* and should be treated as discussed in Section 3.2.

In this example, the *capital gains* attribute has a valid range of $2,000 to $1,000,000 based on the value distribution, shown in Figure 7-1. In JDM, we use *outlier identification* settings to specify the valid range, or *interval*, to identify outliers for the model building process. Some data mining engines (DMEs) automatically identify and treat outliers as part of the model building process. JDM allows data miners to specify an *outlier treatment option* per attribute to inform algorithms how to treat outliers in the build data. The *outlier treatment* specifies whether attribute outlier values are treated *asMissing* (should be handled as missing values) or *asIs* (should be handled as the original values). Based on the problem requirements and vendor-specific algorithm implementations, data miners can either explicitly choose the outlier treatment or leave it to the DME.

In assessing the data, the data miner noticed that the *state* attribute has some invalid entries. All ABCBank customers who are

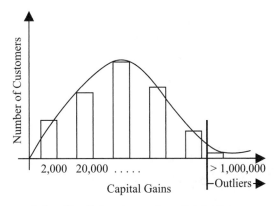

Figure 7-1   *Capital gains value distribution.*

U.S. residents must have the state value as a two-letter abbreviation of one of the 50 states or the District of Columbia. To indicate valid attribute values to the model build, a *category set* can be specified in the logical data specification. The *category set* characterizes the values found in a categorical attribute. In this example, the category set for the state attribute contains values {AL, AK, AS, AZ, ..., WY}. The state values that are not in this *set* will be considered as invalid values during the model build, and may be treated as missing or terminate execution.

Our CUSTOMERS dataset has a disproportionate number of *Non-attriters*: 20 percent of the cases are *Attriters*, and 80 percent are *Non-attriters*. To build an unbiased model, the data miner balances the input dataset to contain an equal number of cases with each target value using stratified sampling. In JDM, *prior probabilities* are used to represent the original distribution of attribute values. The prior probabilities should be specified when the original target value distribution is changed, so that the algorithm can consider them appropriately. However, not all algorithms support prior probability specification, so you will need to consult a given tool's documentation.

ABCBank management informed the data miner that it is more expensive when an *attriter* is misclassified, that is, predicted as a *Non-attriter*. This is because losing an existing customer and acquiring a new customer costs much more than trying to retain an existing customer. For this, JDM allows the specification of a *cost matrix* to specify *costs* associated with possible *false predictions*. A cost matrix is an $N \times N$ table that defines the cost associated with incorrect predictions, where N is the number of possible target values. In this example, the data miner specifies a cost matrix indicating that predicting a customer would not attrite when in fact he would is three times costlier than predicting the customer would attrite when he actually would not. The cost matrix for this problem is illustrated in Figure 7-2.

		Predicted	
		Attriter	**Non-attriter**
Actual	Attriter	0 (TP)	$150 (FN)
	Non-attriter	$50 (FP)	0 (TN)

Figure 7-2 *Cost matrix table.*

In this example, we are more interested to know about the customers who are likely to attrite, so the *Attriter* value is considered the *positive target value*—the value we are interested in predicting. As we will see in Section 7.1.6, the positive target value is necessary when computing lift and the ROC test metric. The *Non-attriter* value is considered the negative target value. This allows us to use the terminology *false positive* and *false negative*. A *false positive* (*FP*) occurs when a case is known to have the negative target value, but the model predicts the positive target value. A *false negative* (*FN*) occurs when a case is known to have a positive target value, but the model predicts the negative target value. The *true positives* are the cases where the predicted and actual positive target values are in agreement, and *true negatives* are the cases where the predicted and actual negative target values are in agreement. In Figure 7-2 note that the false negative cost is $150 and the false positive is $50 and all *diagonal* elements always have cost "O," because there is no cost for correct predictions.

7.1.5 Select algorithm: Find the Best Fit Algorithm

Since JDM defines algorithm selection as an optional step, most data mining tools provide a default or preselected algorithm for each mining function. Some data mining tools automate finding the most appropriate algorithm and its settings based on the data and user-specified problem characteristics. If the data miner does not specify the algorithm to be used, the JDM implementation chooses the algorithm.

If the JDM implementation does not select the algorithm automatically, or the data miner wants control over the algorithm settings, the user can explicitly select the algorithm and specify its settings. Selection of the right algorithm and settings benefits from data mining expertise, knowledge of the available algorithms, and often experimentation to determine which algorithm best fits the problem. Data miners will often try different algorithms and settings, and inspect the resulting models and test results to select the best algorithm and settings. This section provides a high-level overview of the algorithms supported by JDM for classification problems: *decision tree, naïve bayes (NB), support vector machine (SVM)*, and *feed forward neural networks*. For more detailed descriptions of these algorithms, refer to [Jiawei+ 2001] [Witten/Frank 2005].

Decision Tree

The decision tree algorithm is one of the most popular algorithms because it is easy to understand how it makes predictions. A decision tree produces rules that not only explain how or why a prediction was made, but are also useful in segmenting a population, that is, showing which groupings of cases produce a certain outcome. Decision tree is widely used for classification, and some implementations also support regression. In this section, we give an overview of the decision tree algorithm and discuss concepts behind its settings as defined in JDM.

Overview

Decision tree models are a lot like playing the game 20 Questions [20QNET], where a player asks a series of questions of a person concealing the name of an object. These questions allow the player to keep narrowing the space of possible objects. When the space is sufficiently constrained, a guess can be made about the name of the object. In playing 20 Questions, we rely on a vast range of experience acquired over many years to know which questions to ask and what the likely outcome is. With decision trees, an algorithm looks over a constrained set of experience, that is, the dataset. It then determines which questions can be asked to produce the right answer, that is, classify each case correctly.

In this example, let us assume the input dataset has only three *active* attributes from the CUSTOMERS dataset introduced in Section 7.1.3: *age, capital gains,* and *average savings account balance* and 10 customer cases. Each case has a known target value as shown in Table 7-3. Note that 5 out of 10 customers attrite, hence there is a 50 percent chance that a randomly selected customer will attrite. Using the attribute details in this dataset, a decision tree algorithm can learn data patterns and build a tree as shown in Figure 7-3.

In a decision tree, each node-split is based on an attribute condition that partitions or splits the data. In this example, the tree root node, node-1, shown in Figure 7-3, represents all 10 customers in the dataset. From these 10 customer cases the algorithm learns that customers whose *age* is greater than 36 are likely to attrite. So node-1 splits data into node-2 and node-3 based on the customer's *age.* Node-3 further splits its data into node-4 and node-5 based on the customer's *savings account balance.*

Each tree node has an associated rule that predicts the target value with a certain *confidence* and *support.* The *confidence* value is a measure of likelihood that the tree node will correctly predict the target value.

Table 7-3   *Customer attrition build data*

Customer id	Age	Capital gain	Average saving account balance	Attrite
1	41	$4,500	$11,500	Attriter
2	35	$15,000	$3,000	Non-attriter
3	26	$3,400	$21,500	Attriter
4	37	$6,100	$36,000	Attriter
5	32	$14,500	$7,000	Non-attriter
6	40	$2,500	$15,000	Attriter
7	30	$11,000	$6,000	Non-attriter
8	21	$4,100	$2,000	Non-attriter
9	28	$10,000	$5,500	Non-attriter
10	27	$7,500	$31,500	Attriter

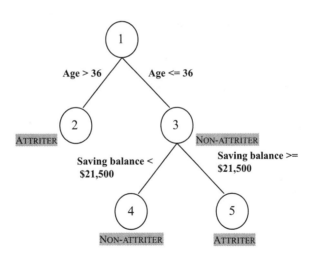

Figure 7-3   *Decision tree for customer attrition.*

Confidence is the ratio between the cases with correct predictions in the node and the total number of cases assigned to that node. The *support* value is a measure of how many cases were assigned to that node from the build dataset. Support can be expressed as a count or the ratio between the number of cases in the node and the total number of cases in the build dataset.

Table 7-4 *Tree node details table*

Node	Rule	Prediction	#Cases	Confidence	Support
1		Attriter	10	5/10 = 0.5	5/10 = 0.5
2	Age > 36	Attriter	3	3/3 = 1.0	3/10 = 0.3
3	Age <= 36	Non-attriter	7	5/7 = 0.7	7/10 = 0.7
4	Age <= 36 and Sav. Bal < 21,500	Non-attriter	5	5/5 = 1.0	5/10 = 0.5
5	Age <= 36 and Sav. Bal >= 21,500	Attriter	2	2/2 = 1.0	2/10 = 0.2

Table 7-4 lists tree node details, such as node ID, rule, prediction, the number of cases that belong to the node, and the *confidence* and *support* of the rule. For example, node-2 has three cases (1, 4, and 6) that satisfy the predicate *age* > 36 and all of them are attriters, hence this node's confidence value is 3/3 = 1, or 100 percent. However, only 3 out of 10 cases support the rule defined by node-2, hence the support value is 3/10 = 0.3. As node-2 has a confidence value of 1, it is called a *pure node* and no further splits can be made. Node-3 can be split further because its confidence value is less than 1, that is, 5/7 = 0.71, and confidence can be improved by using the *average savings balance* attribute as shown in Table 7-4. In this tree, nodes 2, 4, and 5 are called *leaf nodes*, because they do not have any child nodes.

Algorithm Settings

Algorithm settings allow users to exert finer control over the algorithm to attain better results during the build process. Decision tree models can be extremely accurate on the build data if allowed to *overfit* the build data. This occurs by allowing the algorithm to build deeper trees with rules specific to even individual cases. Hence, overfit models give very good accuracy with the build data, but do not generalize well on new data, resulting in decreased predictive accuracy.

To avoid overfitting, users can apply stopping criteria and pruning techniques. Algorithms typically iterate over the build data, learning the patterns that exist in the data or making finer distinctions. Some algorithms could continue this iteration practically indefinitely. As such, algorithms often provide *stopping criteria*, which tell the algorithm when to stop building the model. In the case of a decision tree algorithm, stopping criteria are used to avoid model overfitting and control tree size. Decision tree stopping criteria include *maximum depth* of the tree to avoid deep trees with too many predicates, minimum leaf node size to avoid tree nodes with low support, *maximum confidence* to avoid pure nodes, and *minimum decrease in impurity* to avoid node splits that gain only minimal increase in predictive accuracy of the prediction. Users can specify one or more of these stopping criteria, and the tree will grow until the first stopping criteria is met.

Pruning is the process of removing the less significant tree nodes, for example, those with insufficient support. There are two types of pruning: *pre-pruning* and *post-pruning*. Pre-pruning avoids insignificant node splits while building the tree by measuring the goodness of the split. Post-pruning removes the insignificant nodes after building a *fully grown* tree. Different measures called tree homogeneity metrics are used to define the goodness of a node split, such as *gini, entropy, mean absolute deviation, mean square error*, and *misclassification ratio. Tree homogeneity metrics* are also known as *information gain*. Refer to [Han/ Kamber 2006] for more details about the tree homogeneity metrics.

Naïve Bayes

The naïve bayes algorithm is one of the fastest classification algorithms. It produces results comparable to other algorithms, often outperforming other classification algorithms. Naïve bayes works well with large volumes of data.

Overview

Naive bayes is based on *Bayes Theorem* [Han/Kamber 2006] and assumes that the predictor attributes are *conditionally independent*[2] [Wikipedia-CI 2006] of each other with respect to the target attribute. This assumption significantly reduces the number of computations required to predict a target value and hence the *naïve bayes* algorithm performs well with large volumes of data.

The naïve bayes algorithm involves computing the probability of each target and predictor attribute value combination. To control the number of such combinations, attributes that have either continuous values or a high number of distinct values are typically binned. Refer to Section 3.2 for more detailed discussion on binning. In this example, to simplify the description of the naïve bayes algorithm, consider two attributes *age* and *savings balance* from the CUSTOMERS (Table 7-3) dataset. These attributes are binned to have two binned

---

2   Two events *A* and *B* are conditionally independent given a third event *C* precisely if the occurrence or non-occurrence of *A* and *B* are independent events in their conditional probability distribution given *C*. In other words, $\Pr (A \cap B|C) = \Pr(A|C)\,\Pr(B|C)$.

values to further simplify this discussion. For *age*, bin-1 contains values less than or equal to 35 and bin-2 contains the values greater than 35. For *savings balance*, bin-1 contains values less than or equal to $20,000 and bin-2 contains values greater than $20,000. In JDM, a naïve bayes algorithm computes the probabilities of a target value for a given attribute value using the cases in the build dataset. In this example, we have two attributes with two binned values for a binary target.

Listing 7-1 shows the list of eight possible probabilities that are computed as part of the naïve bayes model build. Using these probability values, the naïve bayes algorithm computes the most probable target value for a given new case. In this example, for a new customer whose age = 25 and savings balance = $13,300, the probability of being an *Attriter* and *Non-Attriter* is computed as shown in Listing 7-2. Note that in Listing 7-2 P(*Attriter*) and P(*Non-Attriter*) are *prior-probabilities* of the target values that are specified as input to the model build. For this new customer case, the probability of being a *Non-attriter* (*0.31*) is more than that of an *Attriter* (*0.03*) and hence the model predicts this customer as a *Non-attriter*. For a more detailed discussion on naïve bayes and bayesian classification refer to [Han/Kamber 2006].

Algorithm Settings

In JDM, a naïve bayes algorithm has two settings, *singleton threshold*, and *pairwise threshold*, that are used to define which predictor attribute values or predictor-target value pairs should be ignored.

Listing 7-1   *Naïve bayes algorithm computation of probabilities using build data*

```
Probability of age < 35 when the customer is Attriter
  P( age < 35 / Attriter ) = 2/6 = 0.33
Probability of age < 35 when the customer is Non-attriter
  P( age < 35 / Non-attriter ) = 4/6 = 0.64

Probability of age > 35 when the customer is Attriter
  P( age > 35 / Attriter ) = 3/4 = 0.75
Probability of age > 35 when the customer is Non-attriter
  P( age > 35 / Non-attriter ) = 1/4 = 0.25

Probability of savings balance (SB) < 20000 when the customer is Attriter
  P( SB < 20000 / Attriter ) = 3/7 = 0.43
Probability of savings balance (SB) < 20000 when the customer is Non-attriter
  P( SB < 20000 / Non-attriter ) = 4/7 = 0.57

Probability of savings balance (SB) > 20000 when the customer is Attriter
  P( SB > 20000 / Attriter ) = 3/3 = 1.00
Probability of savings balance (SB) > 20000 when the customer is Non-attriter
  P( SB > 20000 / Non-attriter ) = 0/3 = 0.00
```

Listing 7-2 *Naïve bayes algorithm computing probability for a new case*

```
Probability that customer is attriter given age = 35 and
savings balance (SB) = $13,300
  P(Attriter / age=25 and SB = $13,300) =
   P(age < 35/Attriter) X P(SB < $20000/Attriter) X P(Attriter) =
        0.33          X            0.43           X      0.2      = 0.03

Probability that customers is Non-attriter given age = 35 and
savings balance = $13,300
  P(Non-attriter / age=25 and SB = $13,300) =
   P(age < 35/Non-attriter) X P(SB < $20000/Non-attriter) X P(Non-attriter) =
        0.67              X            0.57               X       0.8        = 0.31
```

When a naïve bayes model is built, a given value of a predictor attribute is ignored unless there are enough occurrences of that value. The frequency of occurrences in the build data must equal or exceed the fraction specified by the singleton threshold. For example, when a singleton threshold of 0.001 is specified and *age* = *15* occurred only 10 times out of 100,000 cases, then age = 15 is ignored because $(10/100000 = 0.0001) < 0.001$.

Similarly, a pair of values between a predictor and target attribute is ignored unless there are enough occurrences of that pair in the build data. The frequency of occurrences in the build data must equal or exceed the fraction specified by the pairwise threshold. For example, when a pairwise threshold of 0.01 is specified and the pair *age* = *25* and target value *Attriter* occurred 2,000 times out of 100,000 cases, then age = 25 is used by the model because $(2000/100000 = 0.02) > 0.01$.

Support Vector Machine

The support vector machine (SVM) algorithm is one of the most popular, relatively new supervised algorithms. SVM is proven to give highly accurate results in complex classification problems, such as gene expression analysis in which the number of known cases is small but the number of attributes can be quite large [Brown+ 2000]. SVM is gaining greater acceptance in solving traditional data mining problems [DM Methods Poll 2006], including being a preferred alternative to neural networks.

Overview

The SVM algorithm creates a *hyperplane* that separates target values with a *maximum-margin*. A *hyperplane* is the plane that divides a space into two spaces. For example, in two-dimensional space, as

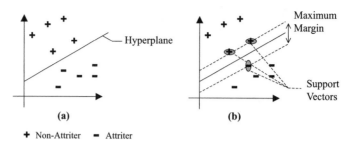

+ Non-Attriter ▬ Attriter

Figure 7-4 *Support vector machine: (a) two-dimensional hyperplane, (b) with support vectors.*

shown in Figure 7-4(a), the line that divides the target values *Attriter* and *Non-attriter* is called a *hyperplane*. A *hyperplane* exists as a complex equation that divides the space using N attribute dimensions, where N is the number of predictor attributes. To understand the concept of *support vectors* we look at two-dimensional space. In Figure 7-4(b), the *hyperplane* that classifies *Attriters* from *Non-attriters* and those data points that the margin pushes up against are called *support vectors*. Margin is the minimal distance between the data points and the *hyperplane* that divides *Attriters* and *Non-attriters*.

SVM allows the selection of a *kernel* function. Kernel functions morph data into high-dimensional vector space and look for relations in such space. Many kernel functions have been introduced in the data mining community. JDM includes *kLinear, kGaussian, hypertangent, polynomial, and sigmoid.* For more details about the SVM and kernel functions refer to [Cristianini/Shawe-Taylor 2000].

Feed Forward Neural Networks

Multilayer feed-forward neural networks with a back propagation learning algorithm are one of the most popular neural network techniques used for supervised learning. Despite the fact that neural networks often take longer to build than other algorithms and they do not provide interpretable results, they are popular for their predictive accuracy and high tolerance to noisy data.

Overview

A *neural network* is an interconnected group of *simulated neurons* that represent a computational model for information processing. A *simulated neuron* is a mathematical model that can take one or more inputs to produce one output. The output is calculated by multiplying each input by a corresponding *weight*, and combining them to produce an ouput, which may be subject to an *activation function*. An activation function effectively is a transformation on the output, which includes the specification of a *threshold* above which the output is 1, otherwise zero. Figure 7-5(a) illustrates a neuron that takes $x1$, $x2$, and $x3$ input value and $w1$, $w2$, and $w3$ as input weights to produce output value y.

Back propagation is the most common neural network learning algorithm. It learns by iteratively processing the build data, comparing the network's prediction for each case with the actual known target value from the *validation data*.[3] For each case, the weights are updated in the opposite direction, so as to minimize the error between the network's prediction and actual target value.

Figure 7-5(b) illustrates a *back propagation neural network* that consists of three types of layers: *input, hidden,* and *output*. The input layer will have a number of neurons equal to the number of input attributes, the output layer will have a number of neurons equal to number of target values. The number of hidden layers and number of neurons in each hidden layer can be determined by the algorithm or specified by the data miner explicitly. In general, the addition of a hidden layer can allow the network to learn more complex patterns, but it can also adversely affect model build and apply performance. For each neural layer, JDM allows specifying an *activation function* that computes the activation state of each neuron

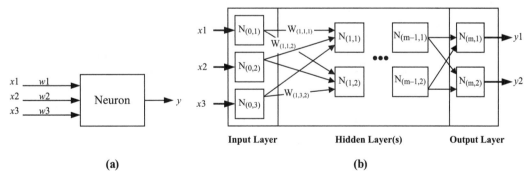

(a)   (b)

Figure 7-5 *Neural networks: (a) Neuron representation, (b) back propagation neural networks.*

3   Validation data is a kind of test data used during model building, which the algorithm may automatically create by partitioning the build data. Validation data allows the algorithm to determine how well the model is learning the patterns in the data. JDM allows users to provide an evaluation dataset explicitly in a build task, if desired.

in that layer. For more details about neural networks refer to [Han/ Kamber 2006].

7.1.6 Evaluate Model Quality: Compute Classification Test Metrics

It is important to evaluate the quality of supervised models before using them to make predictions in a production system. As discussed in Chapter 3, to test supervised models, the historical data is split into two datasets, one for building the model, the other for testing it. Test dataset cases are typically not used to build a model, in order to give a true assessment of a model's predictive accuracy.

JDM supports four types of popular test metrics for classification models: *prediction accuracy, confusion matrix, receiver operating characteristics (ROC),* and *lift.* These metrics are computed by comparing predicted and actual target values. This section discusses these test metrics in the context of the ABCBank's customer attrition problem.

In the customer attrition problem, assume that the test dataset has 1,000 cases and the classification model predicted 910 cases correctly, 90 cases incorrectly. The accuracy of the model on this dataset is 910/1,000 = 0.91 or 91 percent.

Consider that out of 910 correct predictions 750 customers are non-attriters and the remaining 160 are attriters. Out of 90 wrong predictions 60 are predicted as *Attriters* when they are actually *Non-attriters* and 30 are predicted as *Non-attriters* when they are actually *Attriters.* This is illustrated in Figure 7-6. To represent this, we use a matrix called a *confusion matrix.* A *confusion matrix* is a two-dimensional, N × N table that indicates the number of correct and incorrect predictions a classification model made on specific test data, where N represents the number of target attribute values. It is called a confusion matrix because it points out where the model gets *confused,* that is, makes incorrect predictions.

		Predicted	
		Attriter	**Non-attriter**
Actual	**Attriter**	160	30 (FN)
	Non-attriter	60 (FP)	750

Figure 7-6 *Confusion matrix.*

The structure of this table looks similar to the cost matrix that was illustrated in Figure 7-2, but the confusion matrix cells have the model's incorrect and correct prediction counts. If we consider *Attriter* as the positive target value, *false-positive* (*FP*) prediction count is 60, and the *false-negative* (*FN*) prediction count is 30.

Although the confusion matrix measures misclassification of target values, in our example, false-negatives are three times costlier than the false-positives. To assess model quality from a business perspective, we need to measure cost in addition to accuracy. The total cost of false predictions is $3 \times 30 + 1 \times 60 = 150$. If with a different model you get 40 false-positives and 40 false-negatives, then the overall accuracy is better, however total cost is more at $3 \times 40 + 1 \times 40 = 160$. If a cost matrix is specified, it is important to consider cost values to measure the performance and select the model with the least cost value.

Receiver operating characteristics (*ROC*) is another way to compare classification model quality. An *ROC* graph places the false positive rate on the X-axis and true positive rate on the Y-axis as shown in Figure 7-7. Here, the *false positive rate* is the ratio of the number of false positives and the total number of actual negatives. Similarly, the *true positive rate* is the ratio of the number of true positives and the total number of actual positives.

To plot the ROC graph, the test task determines the false positive and true positive rates at different *probability thresholds*. Here, the probability threshold is the level above which a probability of the predicted positive target value is considered a positive prediction. Different probability threshold values result in different false positive rates and true positive rates. For example, when the *Attriter* prediction probability is 0.4 and the probability threshold is set to 0.3, the customer is predicted as an *Attriter*. Whereas if the probability threshold is 0.5, the customer is predicted as a *Non-attriter* as illustrated in Figure 7-7(a).

Figure 7-7(b) illustrates the ROC curves of two classification models that are plotted at different probability thresholds. These models perform better at different false positive rates; for example, at a false positive rate of 0.1, Model B has better true positives than Model A. However, at 0.3 and above the false positive rate of Model A outperformed that of Model B. Based on the accepted false positive rate, users can select the model and its probability threshold. The *area under the ROC curve* is another measure of overall performance of a classification model. The higher the area under the ROC curve, generally, the better the model performance.

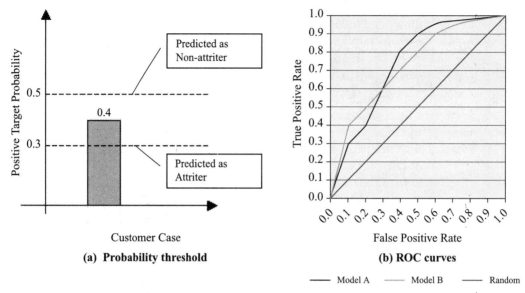

Figure 7-7   *Receiver operating characteristics.*

In the ROC graph, the point (0,1) is the perfect classifier[4]: it classifies all positive cases and negative cases correctly. It is (0,1) because the false positive rate is 0 (none), and the true positive rate is 1 (all). The point (0,0) represents a classifier that predicts all cases to be negative, while the point (1,1) corresponds to a classifier that predicts every case to be positive. Point (1,0) is the classifier that is incorrect for all classifications.

Lift and *cumulative gain* are also popular metrics to assess the effectiveness of a classification model. *Lift* is the ratio between the results obtained using the classification model and a random selection. *Cumulative gain* is the percentage of positive responses determined by the model across quantiles of the data. Cases are typically divided into 10 or 100 quantiles against which the lift and cumulative gain is reported, as illustrated later in Table 7.5. The lift chart and cumulative gains charts are often used as visual aids for assessing model performance. An understanding of how cumulative lift and cumulative gains are computed helps in understanding the cumulative lift and cumulative gains charts illustrated in Figure 7-8.

---

4   A classification model is also referred to as a classifier since it classifies cases among the possible target values.

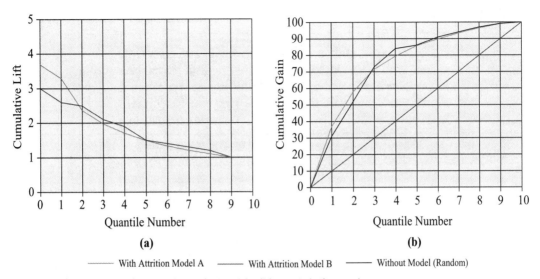

Figure 7-8 *Lift charts: (a) Cumulative lift, (b) cumulative gain.*

Following are the typical high-level steps used to compute cumulative lift and gain values:

- Compute the positive target value probability for all test dataset cases.
- Sort cases in descending order of the positive target value probability.
- Split the sorted test dataset cases into *n* groups, also known as *quantiles*.
- Compute lift for each quantile – the ratio of the cumulative number of positive targets and cumulative number of positive targets that can be found at random.
- Compute the cumulative gain for each quantile – the ratio of cumulative predicted number of positive targets using the model and total number of positive targets in the test dataset.

Table 7-5 details lift and cumulative gain calculations for our customer dataset example. Each row of this table represents a quantile that has 100 customer cases. In the test dataset, there are 1,000 cases, of which 190 are known to be attriters. Hence, picking a random customer from this dataset, we have a 19 percent probability that the customer is an attriter.

Table 7-5 *Lift computations table*

Quantile number	Number of customers likely to attrite	Cumulative number of customers likely to attrite	Cumulative quantile lift	Cumulative gain
1	70	70	70/19 = 3.684	70/190 = 36.8%
2	40	110	110/38 = 3.289	110/190 = 57.9%
3	25	135	135/57 = 2.368	135/190 = 71.5%
4	15	150	150/76 = 1.974	150/190 = 79.4%
5	12	162	162/95 = 1.705	162/190 = 85.7%
6	8	170	170/114 = 1.491	170/190 = 89.8%
7	7	177	177/133 = 1.331	177/190 = 93.4%
8	5	183	183/152 = 1.204	183/190 = 96.5%
9	5	188	188/171 = 1.099	188/190 = 99.0%
10	3	190	190/190 = 1.000	190/190 = 100%

Using the classification model, the first quantile contains the top 100 customers that are predicted to be attriters. Comparing the prediction against the known actual values, we find that the algorithm was correct for 70 of these 100 customers. Therefore, the lift for the first quantile is 70/19 = 3.684, where 70 is the number of attriters found using the classification model and 19 is the number of customers that would have been found given a random selection of customers.

Similarly, the cumulative gain value for this first quantile is the percentage of the attriters in this quantile, that is, 70/190 = 0.368. In Table 7-5, observe that the cumulative quantile lift values gradually decrease, because the addition of each quantile includes fewer probable cases, and the last quantile has lift value 1 because it includes all 1,000 cases. Cumulative gain values gradually increase, because the addition of each quantile increases the proportion of attriters, and the last quantile has cumulative gain of 100 percent because it includes all 1,000 cases.

In this example, suppose that ABCBank wants to launch a customer retention campaign with a limited budget that can retain at least 50 percent of the attriters. Here, the user can select the 200 customers in the first two quantiles whose cumulative gain is 57.9 percent and has a lift of 3.289.

Let us say there are two attrition models, *Model A* and *Model B*, that are built using different algorithms or with different settings using the same algorithm. Figure 7-8 illustrates the cumulative lift and cumulative gains charts plotted for these models to compare the results. Note that Model A outperforms Model B in the first two quantiles; however, Model B outperforms from the third quantile onward. A user can pick Model A when the budget allows for at most 20 percent of customers, otherwise the user can pick Model B if more than 20 percent of customers are budgeted.

7.1.7 Apply Model: Obtain Prediction Results

After evaluating model performance using the test data, the user selects the best model for the problem and applies it to predict target values for an apply dataset. As noted for decision tree, some algorithms may use a subset of the input attributes in the final model. This sub-set of attributes is called the *model signature*, and it can be retrieved from the model to determine which attributes are required to apply the model.

In this section, we take the simple decision tree model discussed in Section 7.1.5 to illustrate the model apply operation. This model has three input attributes: *age, capital gain, and average savings balance* as shown in Table 7-3 and the model uses only two of these, *age* and *average savings balance*, as shown in Figure 7-9. These two attributes form the model signature. Consequently, to use this model, the apply dataset for this model needs only contain cases with *age* and *average savings balance* attribute values. Consider an apply dataset that has two customer cases for customers Jones and Smith as shown in Table 7-6 to understand the apply process.

Figure 7-9 illustrates how the decision tree model predicts if these customers are attriters. *Jones* is older than 36, so from the root node he is assigned to node-2 that predicts him as an *attriter*. *Smith* is younger than 36, so he is assigned to node-3 and node-3 further splits

Table 7-6 *Customer apply table*

Id	Customer name	Address	City	State	Zip code	Age	Average saving account balance
A1	Jones	10 Main St.	Boston	MA	02101	41	$11,500
A2	Smith	120 Beacon St.	Buffalo	NY	14201	35	$3000

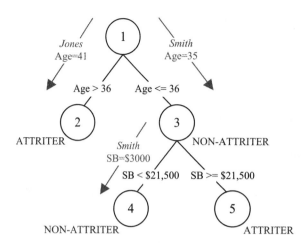

Figure 7-9 *Apply decision tree to predict customer type.*

based on average savings balance (SB). Because Smith's average savings balance is less than $21,500, he is assigned to node-4, which predicts him as a *Non-attriter*.

The classification apply operation enables generating prediction results with various types of content such as the *predicted category*—the target value predicted by the model; *probability*—the probability that the prediction is correct according to the model; *cost*—the cost associated with the model's prediction (cost is computed only when cost matrix is specified); and *node-id*—node or rule identifier used to make the prediction (this is applicable *only* for models such as decision tree that can provide a tree node or rule use for the prediction). In JDM the apply prediction results can be presented in various forms, such as the top prediction details, top-n or bottom-n predictions, probabilities associated with all target values, and the probability of predicting a specified target value(s). Selection of the prediction results depends on the problem requirements and the type of information a user wants to see. In this example, we produce the top prediction value and its corresponding probability and cost to identify the *attriters*.

Even though applying a model to a dataset is common, predictions and probabilities will likely change when customer attributes change. For example, when a customer calls a bank to transfer a large sum from his savings account to another bank, the call center application can display a precomputed prediction that the customer is likely to attrite. This would have been based on the customer's previous account balance. With the funds transfer, this may change the model's prediction for this customer. As such, it is useful to rescore customers in real-time based on current data. This can be achieved using the JDM *single record apply* capability, designed to provide real-time response. Refer to [Middlemiss 2001] for an actual banking industry use case involving real-time scoring.

7.2   Regression Problem

7.2.1   Problem Definition: How to Reduce Processing Time of Residential Real-Estate Appraisals?

ABCBank wants to supplement the conventional real-estate appraisal process by automated property evaluation to the current system. Its objective is to reduce the processing time of home mortgage-based loans and improve the customer experience. Refer to [Rossini 2000] for a thorough study on real-estate value prediction.

7.2.2   Solution Approach: Property Value Prediction Using Regression

ABCBank has accumulated data for the past year on real-estate appraisal values for loans they process. In addition to appraisal values, ABCBank acquired the real-estate details such as *year built, home size, features,* and *location details*. Using the data mining *regression* function, the bank can predict the property value, based on recent trends and sales data. Depending on the confidence associated with the prediction, where confidence refers to the width of the interval around the prediction, the bank may heavily rely on the predicted value in making a loan decision, which can reduce appraisal evaluation time significantly. As real-estate value is a continuous number, the regression function is the right technique to use. Refer to Section 4.3 for an introduction of the regression function.

7.2.3   Data Specification: REAL_ESTATE_APPRAISALS Dataset

Concepts of physical and logical data specifications discussed in Section 7.1.3 are the same for all data mining techniques. So in this section we will not repeat the concepts covered earlier; instead we illustrate the selected attributes for this problem and their logical characteristics in Table 7-7. This table includes predictor attributes

Table 7-7 *Real-estate appraisal data*

Attribute name	Logical name	Attribute type	Usage type	Preparation
LOAN_ID	Loan Id		Inactive	
CITY	City	Categorical	Active	Prepared
COUNTY	County	Categorical	Active	Prepared
STATE	State	Categorical	Active	Prepared
HOME_SIZE	Size of the home in sq. ft	Numerical	Active	Not prepared
YEAR_BUILT	Year home was built	Numerical	Active	Not prepared
LAND_SIZE	Total land size in sq. ft	Numerical	Active	Not prepared
NUM_ROOMS	Number of rooms	Numerical	Active	Not prepared
NUM_GARAGES	Number of garages	Numerical	Active	Not prepared
POOL_TYPE	Type of pool (none, inground, above ground)	Categorical	Active	Prepared
SCHOOLS	Number of schools	Categorical	Active	Prepared
NUM_MALLS	Number of nearby malls	Numerical	Active	Not prepared
CRIME RATE	City crime rate	Numerical	Active	Not prepared
SCHOOL RATING	Avg. school ratings	Numerical	Active	Not prepared
APPRAISAL_VALUE	Home appraisal value	Numerical	Target	

such as city, county, state, house size, year built, land size, number of rooms, garages, pool type, number of schools, school rating, number of nearby malls, crime rate, and the target appraisal value.

7.2.4 Select Algorithm: Find the Best Fit Algorithm

The algorithms discussed for classification in Section 7.2.1 can also be used for regression. However, among them, support vector machine (SVM), feed forward neural networks, and decision tree algorithms are commonly used. There are other regression algorithms, such as *linear regression* and *generalized linear models* (GLM) that are not currently included among the JDM supervised algorithms. Regression model quality depends on data characteristics, algorithm choice, and settings to find the most appropriate algorithm, or rely on selection performed by the data mining engine.

7.2.5   Evaluate Model Quality: Compute Regression Test Metrics

In regression models, quality is measured by computing the cumulative errors when comparing predicted values against known values. Generally, the lower the cumulative error the better the model performance. There are many mathematical metrics that can be used to quantify error, such as *root mean squared (RMS)* error, *mean absolute error*, and *R-squared* error. Table 7-8 illustrates the computation of some of these metrics by taking three cases. To compute the mean absolute error, we take the ratio between the sum of the absolute value of prediction errors and number of predictions. To compute the root mean squared error, we first compute the mean of the prediction error squares, then take the square root.

There is another metric called the R-squared value, which measures the relative predictive power of a model. R-squared is a descriptive measure between 0 and 1. The closer it is to 1, the greater the accuracy of the regression model. When R squared equals 1, the regression makes perfect predictions. For more details about these regression model evaluation metrics refer to [Witten/Frank 2005].

7.2.6   Apply Model: Obtain Prediction Results

After finding a regression model with minimum error, we apply that model to new data to make predictions. The model signature, as discussed for classification in Section 7.2.1, is also applicable for regression. The apply data must provide all the attributes in the model's signature. Of course, attribute values for some cases may be missing and most models can function normally in the presence of some missing values. The regression apply operation can produce contents such as *predicted value* (model predicted target value) and

Table 7-8 *Regression test metrics*

Promotion ID	Predicted value	Actual value	Prediction error (predicted (p) − actual (a))
1	$950,000	$900,000	$50,000
2	$725,000	$745,000	−$20,000
3	$1,050,000	$970,000	$70,000
Mean Absolute Error $(50{,}000 + 20{,}000 + 70{,}000)/3$			$46,667
Root Mean Squared Error $\sqrt{50{,}000^2 + 20{,}000^2 + 70{,}000^2/3}$			$50,990

confidence (confidence associated with the model's prediction). Typically *confidence* values are either represented as a value between 0 and 1 or as a percentage value between 0 and 100; 0 being the lowest confidence and 1 being the highest confidence. Unlike classification that can produce multiple-target values and associated probabilities, regression produces a single target value and associated confidence because target is a continuous value.

7.3 Attribute Importance

7.3.1 Problem Definition: How to Find Important Customer Attributes

ABCBank has collected hundreds of attributes of its customers, and the user wants to understand which attributes most greatly affect customer attrition. Using ranking of attributes by importance, the user can recommend that high ranking attributes be cleaned more carefully. The user may also select a top *n* subset of these attributes to include in model building. This might not only reduce the time required to build a model and score, but also might improve model accuracy.

7.3.2 Solution Approach: Rank Attributes According to Predictive Value

JDM defines the *attribute importance* function that can measure the predictive power of each attribute in predicting a target and produces a list of attributes ranked by their relative importance. Using this function, analysts can select the attributes that are important to predicting attrition. As noted above, the attribute importance function helps to automate the selection of attributes for predicting target attribute values.

7.3.3 Data Specification, Fine-Tune Settings, and Algorithm Selection

We use the same dataset as discussed in Section 7.1.3 for the classification problem. The data specification for attribute importance is the same as for classification.

JDM does not specify any algorithm settings for attribute importance. However, several algorithms can be used to support this mining function such as *minimum description length* [Wikipedia 2005] and even *decision tree*. Decision trees inherently select the best attributes for branching in the tree and normally include far fewer attributes in the resulting model than originally input.

JDM allows a model's signature to contain attribute importance rankings that result as a by-product of model building. After a model is built, the user can determine the relative importance of the attributes as determined by the specific algorithm. Since different independent attribute importance algorithms can produce significantly different results, having access to the importance assigned by the algorithm is more accurate.

7.3.4   Use Model Details: Explore Attribute Importance Values

An attribute importance model produces relative importance values by which attributes are ranked. In this example, Table 7-9 lists the

Table 7-9   *Attribute importance values*

Attribute name	Importance	Rank
Education	0.46	1
Occupation	0.40	2
Age	0.36	3
Marital Status	0.34	4
Avg. Savings Balance	0.31	5
Home loan balance	0.27	6
Annual Income	0.22	7
Retirement Balance	0.16	8
Avg. Checking Balance	0.10	9
Capital Gain	0.09	10
City	0.06	11
Ethnic Group	0.02	12
Native Country	−0.03	13
County	−0.06	14
State	−0.11	15

attributes sorted by their importance values and assigns ranks to each attribute based on its importance value. In JDM, selecting attributes can be based on a percentage of attributes, number of attributes, or importance value threshold. For example, if a user gives the importance threshold as 0.0, then *native country, county,* and *state* attributes will be filtered from the returned set of attributes, because they have negative importance values. Typically, attributes with negative importance values may adversely impact model quality. However, the interpretation of the importance values depends on the implementation.

7.4 Association Rules Problem

7.4.1 Problem Definition: How to Identify Cross-Sell Products for Customers

Part of ABCBank's strategy for customer retention and increased profits is to cross-sell products to existing customers. When customers have multiple products with the same bank, they are less likely to attrite, if for no other reason than the effort and complexity involved in switching to another bank. As a result, ABCBank wants to understand which set of products are normally purchased by customers, so that ABCBank can recommend appropriate cross-sell products to customers missing products in that set. Refer to [DeBlasio 2001] for a real-world cross-sell scenario in the banking industry.

7.4.2 Solution Approach: Discover Product Associations from Customer Data

ABCBank has customer data, which includes the products or services each customer purchased along with some usage characteristics, for example, average checking account balance. Using this data, ABCBank wants to identify product associations, such as if a customer has a single account with the bank, or in what other accounts or financial services might that customer be interested.

Product associations are discovered and measured by learning product purchase patterns from the historical purchase data. For example, an association model may identify a rule indicating that a customer with an average annual checking account between $3,000 and $5,000 and savings account greater than $15,000 is likely to open a certificate of deposit.

7.4.3 Data Specification: CUSTOMERS and Their Product Purchase Data

In this example, to explain the association concepts, we consider five customers and three product purchase details out of possibly millions of customers. Table 7-10 illustrates the data for these five customer accounts, where each case is represented as multiple records (rows). A case here corresponds to the set of products the customer uses and a value indicating average annual balance range. For example, Customer 1 has three records that represent three products used and his monthly average balance range. This type of data format is known as *multirecord case* or *transactional format*, where the *Customer Id* column is the case identifier, the *attribute name* column represents the product name, and the value column contains the average annual balance range.

7.4.4 Fine-Tune Settings: Filter Rules Based on Rule Quality Metrics

In practice, business data can have thousands of products and millions of product transactions. As a result, an association model can derive a large number of rules. Rule quality thresholds are used

Table 7-10 *Customer product transactions*

Customer ID	Attribute Name	Amount Range
1	Checking Account	$2,000 to $5,000
1	Savings Account	$10,000 to $15,000
1	Certificate Account	$2,500 to $15,000
2	Savings Account	$10,000 to $15,000
2	Certificate Account	$2,500 to $15,000
3	Checking Account	$2,000 to $5,000
3	Savings Account	$10,000 to $15,000
4	Checking Account	$10,000 to $15,000
4	Money Market Account	$5,000 to $10,000
5	Savings Account	$10,000 to $15,000
5	Certificate Account	$2,500 to $15,000

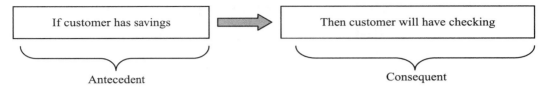

Figure 7-10 *Association rule.*

to limit the number of rules, and hence reduce model size, allowing users to focus on a more relevant subset of possible rules.

Rule quality can be specified using one or more metrics, such as *support, confidence,* and *lift.* Figure 7-10 shows the rule *"If customers have a savings account, then they have a checking account"* derived from the data in the Table 7-10. A rule consists of a condition part, called the *antecedent,* and a result part, called the *consequent.* Using this example we illustrate the rule quality metrics. Figure 7-11 shows two sets, the first represents the cases that conform to the antecedent and the second represents the cases that conform to the consequent. The intersection of these two sets represents the cases that conform to both antecedent and consequent, that is, the rule.

The *support* of a rule is the ratio of cases that match the rule when compared to the total number of records in the dataset. In this example, there are two customers, 1 and 3, that conform to the rule out of five customers, so support for this rule is $2/5 = 0.4$.

The *confidence* of a rule is the ratio of the number of records that include all items in the rule to the number of records that include all items in the antecedent part of the rule. In this example, there are four customers, 1, 2, 3, and 5, that match the antecedent portion of the rule,

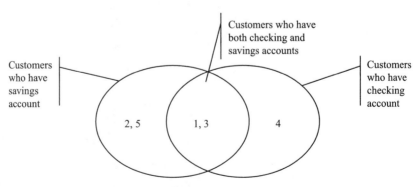

Figure 7-11 *Associations.*

so the confidence is $2/4 = 0.5$. Confidence is directional; when we invert the rule, for example, "*If a customer has a checking account, then they have a savings account,*" we will get a different confidence value. For the inverted rule, there are only three customers, 1, 3, and 4, that satisfy antecedent, so the confidence value of this rule is $2/3 = 0.67$. Note that the inverted rule has greater confidence than the original.

The *lift* is the ratio between the rule confidence and its *expected* confidence. *Expected confidence* is the frequency of the consequent in the data. Lift measures how much more likely the consequent is when an antecedent happens. In this example, there are three customers, 1, 3 and 4, that have a checking account, so the expected confidence is $3/5 = 0.6$. Hence *lift* for this rule is $0.4/0.6 = 0.66$.

In addition to the rule quality metrics, JDM allows users to specify taxonomy per attribute (Section 4.5), and settings that include the maximum number of rules in the model and inclusion or exclusion of model items. Section 9.7 will discuss more about these setting when we discuss the API usage.

7.4.5 Use Model Content: Explore Rules From the Model

An association model primarily contains the association rules and their support, confidence, and lift details. Even with the model rule quality thresholds, this model may contain a large number of rules based on the number of items and the relationships among these items. To explore the rules, users often need a filter and to order the rules to get an interesting or manageable subset. To this end, JDM provides rule filtering capabilities.

Filtering criteria may include rule support, confidence, and lift thresholds; inclusion or exclusion of the specified items from the rule or specific rule components, that is, antecedent and consequent; and rule or rule component length. Section 9.7 will discuss more about the various types of filtering criteria using JDM.

7.5   Clustering Problem

7.5.1   Problem Definition: How to Understand Customer Behavior and Needs

ABCBank has thousands of customers whose profiles and needs widely differ from each other. ABCBank wants to understand customer segments to design new products and personalize campaigns to increase revenues and market share. Refer to [Dragoon 2005] for more details about customer segmentation.

7.5.2 Solution Approach: Find Clusters of Similar Customers

Using ABCBank's customer data such as profiles, products owned, and product usage, a clustering model can be built that identifies customer segments. Each cluster in the model represents a customer segment, that is, customers with similar characteristics. By understanding the characteristics of the customers in each segment, ABCBank can gain greater insight into product design and achieve more focused campaigns.

7.5.3 Data Specification and Settings

In this example, we use the CUSTOMERS dataset discussed in Section 7.1 for finding the natural groupings of the customers based on customer attribute values. Attributes used for segmentation may vary from those used for classification. For example, you may omit the target attribute *attrite* or add customer product purchase indicators. Section 4.6 introduced the concepts of clustering and clusters, and Section 12.3 will include a more detailed discussion on customer segmentation.

Clustering techniques vary in their approach to find clusters, for example, partitioning-based, hierarchical, density-based, and grid-based algorithms. For more details on these techniques, refer to [Han/Kamber 2006]. JDM defines a clustering mining function and one of the popular partitioning-based clustering algorithms called *k*-means.

Partitioning based algorithms, such as *k*-means, typically require users to specify the desired number of partitions, or clusters, *k*. The algorithm then finds the clusters that have high intra-cluster similarity but low inter-cluster similarity. The *k*-means algorithm randomly selects *k* cases to serve as the seeds for the clusters. It then measures the distance from each case to each cluster's centroid and assigns the case to the "nearest" cluster. New cluster centroids are computed based on all the cases assigned to each centroid, and the process repeats.

To illustrate clustering concepts, we take a dataset with ten customer cases of two attributes, *age* and *income*, listed in Table 7-11(a). In clustering, one of the challenges is how to measure similarity between cases. For example, numerical attributes may be in different scales and categorical attributes may have discrete values, perhaps

Table 7-11 *Customers' (a) original attribute values and (b) normalized attribute values*

Customer	Age	Income
C1	70	55,000
C2	17	30,000
C3	30	25,000
C4	65	45,000
C5	27	60,000
C6	35	1,30,000
C7	45	1,20,000
C8	20	5,000
C9	15	6,000
C10	25	45,000

(a)

Normalize

Customer	Age	Income
C1	0.182	0.32
C2	0	0.008
C3	0.091	0
C4	0.545	0.92
C5	0.364	1
C6	0.218	0.44
C7	0.909	0.32
C8	0.273	0.16
C9	0.036	0.2
C10	1	0.4

(b)

with no clear notion of one value being close to another. To address numerical attributes, the values can be normalized, as discussed in Section 3.2, to bring numerical attributes to the same scale. After normalizing the data in our example using min-max normalization, the values of *age* and *income* are brought to the same scale — values between 0 and 1. To address categorical attributes for a distance-based algorithm like k-means, the attributes are exploded, as discussed in Section 3.2. This converts the categorical attributes into multiple attributes with numerical values.

Since our example is in two dimensions (attributes), we can easily graph the clusters, as illustrated in Figure 7-12, and visually identify the customer clusters. However, clustering problems can involve hundreds or even thousands of attributes, requiring alternative analysis and visualization techniques [Keahey 1999].

When two cases are compared, we can use distance or similarity. Both distance and similarity can be computed by first comparing pairs of attribute values and then aggregating the results to arrive at a final comparison measure between the two cases. To this end, JDM defines commonly used *aggregation functions*, such as euclidian distance, and *attribute comparison functions*, such as absolute difference or similarity matrix. Using a similarity matrix for categorical attributes, JDM allows the user to specify explicit similarity values for categorical attributes using a *similarity* matrix. For example, if *credit_risk* is a categorical attribute with values *high, medium,* and *low,*

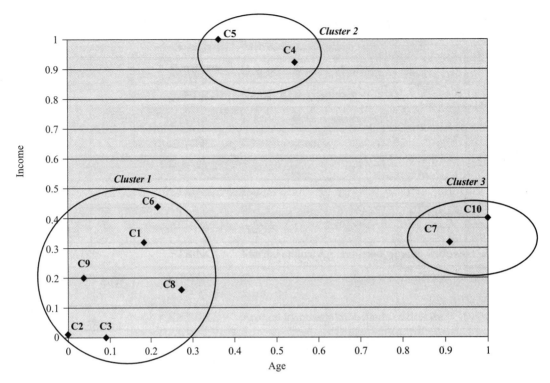

Figure 7-12 *Customer clusters.*

Table 7-12 *Similarity matrix for credit-risk attribute*

	High	Medium	Low
High	1	0.5	0
Medium	0.5	1	0.25
Low	0	0.25	1

a similarity matrix can be expressed, as shown in Table 7-12. Here, the diagonal values have similarity value 0 indicating that there is no "distance" between two high values. Nondiagonal values can be set as appropriate.

7.5.4 Use Model Details: Explore Clusters

Each cluster in a clustering model can have associated attribute statistics and a rule that describes the cluster. Figure 7-13 illustrates

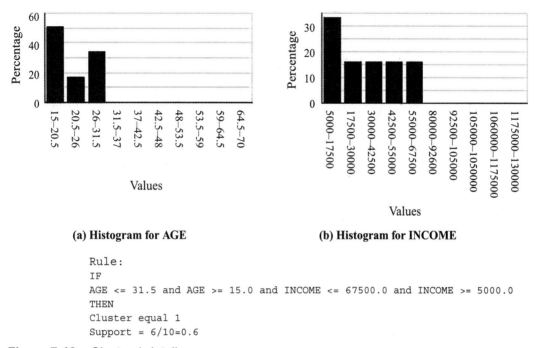

(a) Histogram for AGE   **(b) Histogram for INCOME**

```
Rule:
IF
AGE <= 31.5 and AGE >= 15.0 and INCOME <= 67500.0 and INCOME >= 5000.0
THEN
Cluster equal 1
Support = 6/10=0.6
```

Figure 7-13 *Cluster 1 details.*

the attribute histograms and the rule of Cluster 1. Users can visually inspect the attribute value distributions in each cluster to understand how they differ. In this case Cluster 1 can be described as *customers whose age is between 15 and 31.5 and whose income is between $5,000 and $67,500.*

7.5.5 Apply Clustering Model: Assign New Cases to the Clusters

A clustering model can be applied to the original cases or new cases to assign each case a cluster ID. Clustering apply also computes the probability that the case belongs to the cluster, and the distance of the case from the centroid of the cluster to assess how well each case fits a given cluster. Like classification, JDM supports assigning the top cluster, mapping the top or bottom clusters for each case, and per cluster probabilities.

7.6   Summary

This chapter illustrated various JDM concepts related to data specifications, classification, regression, attribute importance, association rules, and clustering functions. We saw that data specifications are divided into physical and logical specifications to facilitate reusability. Model build settings provide function-specific settings and algorithm settings that are used to tune the models for problem-specific requirements. JDM provides test metrics for supervised models to understand model quality. JDM supports model apply for supervised and clustering models, providing control over the output values. JDM defines algorithm settings for decision tree, support vector machine, naïve bayes, feed forward neural networks, and k-means algorithm settings. In the next chapter we explore how these concepts are mapped to Java classes and interfaces in JDM.

References

[Brown+ 2000] M. P. Brown, W. N. Grundy, D. Lin, N. Cristianini, C. W. Sugnet, T. S. Furey, M. Ares Jr., D. Haussler, "Knowledge-Based Analysis of Microarray Gene Expression Data by Using Support Vector Machines," *Proc Natl Acad Sci USA*, 97:262–7.

[Cluster Tutorial 2006] See http://www.elet.polimi.it/upload/matteucc/Clustering/tutorial_html/index.html.

[Cristianini/Shawe-Taylor 2000] Nello Cristianini, John Shawe-Taylor, *An Introduction to Support Vector Machines and Other Kernel-based Learning Methods*, Cambridge, UK: Cambridge University Press, 2000.

[DeBlasio 2001] Agnes DeBlasio, "Data Mining Application Helps BB&T Increase Cross-Sell Ratio, Bank Systems & Technology," http://www.banktech.com/features/showArticle.jhtml?articleID=14701565.

[DM Methods Poll 2006] "Latest KDnuggets Poll Results on Usage of Data Mining Methods," http://www.kdnuggets.com/polls/2006/data_mining_methods.htm.

[Dragoon 2005] Alice Dragoon, "How to Do Customer Segmentation Right?" *CIO Magazine*, October 2005, http://www.cio.com/archive/100105/cus_segment.html.

[Han/Kamber 2006] Jiawei Han, Micheline Kamber, *Data Mining, Second Edition: Concepts and Techniques*, San Francisco, Morgan Kaufmann, 2006.

[Hu 2005] Xiaohua Hu, "A Data Mining Approach for Retailing Bank Customer Attrition Analysis," Springer Science+Business Media B.V., formerly Kluwer Academic Publishers B.V., vol. 22, no. 1, http://www.springerlink.com/(maecq445vroxvm33fwowiyua)/app/home/contribution.asp?referrer=parent&backto=issue,5,6;journal,7,74;linkingpublicationresults,1:100236,1.

[Johnston 1996] Stuart J. Johnston, "How to Get a Better Return on Data?" http://www.informationweek.com/596/96bank.htm.

[Keahey 1999] T. Alan Keahey, "Visualization of High-Dimensional Clusters Using Nonlinear Magnification," Los Alamos National Laboratory, MS B287, http://www.ccs.lanl.gov/ccs1/projects/Viz/pdfs/99-spie.pdf.

[Middlemiss 2001] Jim Middlemiss, "Bank of Montreal Aims to Score with Clients Using Data Mining Product," *Bank Systems & Technology*, http://www.banktech.com/showArticle.jhtml?articleID=14701805.

[Pyle 1999] Dorian Pyle, "Data Preparation for Data Mining," San Francisco, Morgan Kaufmann, 1999.

[Rossini 2000] Peter Rossini, "Using Expert Systems and Artificial Intelligence for Real Estate Forecasting," Sixth Annual Pacific-Rim Real Estate Society Conference, Sydney, Australia, January 24–27, 2000, http://www.unisanet.unisa.edu.au/staff/peterrossini/Documents/Using%20Artificial%20Intelligence%20for%20Real%20Estate%20-Forecasting.pdf.

[20QNET] http://www.20q.net.

[Wikipedia-CI 2006] http://en.wikipedia.org/wiki/Conditionally_independent.

[Witten/Frank 2005] Ian H. Witten, Eibe Frank, *Data Mining: Practical Machine Learning Tools and Techniques*, San Francisco, Morgan Kaufmann, 2005.

Chapter

8

Design of the JDM API

*Perfection (in design) is achieved not when there is nothing more to add,
but rather when there is nothing more to take away.*

—Antoine de Saint-Exupéry

Designing a vendor-neutral standard application programming interface (API) involves many constructive altercations to find a common ground where all participants can agree on the standard. Despite being widely used across many industries to solve business problems, there previously was no data mining standard for Java that allowed applications to include data mining solutions that are portable across multiple data mining engines (DMEs). With the advent of the Java Data Mining (JDM) standard, application developers can more easily use portable data mining functionality.

One of the challenges in designing a standard data mining API is that DME capabilities differ significantly from one another. Even though many of the data mining techniques and algorithms are public and standardized, vendors differentiate themselves by improving performance, automating settings selection, or specializing algorithms for a particular domain or need.

In addition, not all vendors implement or expose the same level of DME capabilities. JDM is designed to be flexible to adapt for any vendor that supports at least one data mining function. Moreover, JDM enables applications to discover DME capabilities at runtime. This feature is particularly useful for the development of vendor-neutral data mining tools or solutions.

To reduce the complexity of the implementation and integration of data mining solutions, DMEs are providing advanced automation for data preparation, attribute selection, algorithm selection, and automated tuning of algorithm settings. This simplifies data mining for novice users, allowing them to quickly reach a solution. The expert group designed JDM to be flexible for defining both auto-mated data mining processes and highly customized solutions involving problem-specific settings by expert users.

This chapter discusses some of the design decisions made for JDM. Readers will also become familiar with the JDM object model, packages, and objects. This chapter uses Unified Modeling Lan-guage [OMG_UML 2006] notation for class diagrams and package diagrams.

8.1   Object Modeling of Data Mining Concepts

This section explores the JDM object model for representing the data mining concepts discussed in Chapter 7: data specifications, the set-tings used for data mining techniques and algorithms, function level model contents, algorithm level model details, test metrics for supervised models, and model apply. The JDM object model enables developing data mining solutions using Java and Web services inter-faces.

Figure 8-1 depicts the class diagram of mining objects in JDM—a mining object in JDM is the prime object that can be saved with a name to the mining object repository (MOR) via the DME. Applica-tions can then retrieve mining objects by name from the MOR across application executions. JDM divides mining objects into data specifi-cation, settings, model, test metrics, and task objects. The gray boxes in Figure 8-1 highlight the mining object categories *Data Specification Objects and Settings Objects*. The *MiningObject* interface encapsulates the common characteristics of these objects, such as name, descrip-tion, object identifier, and the mining object type. We now explore each mining object category in detail.

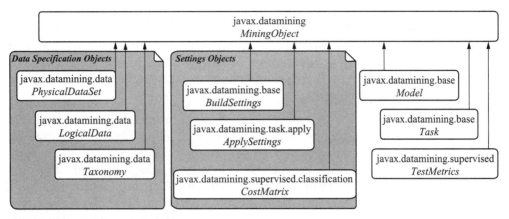

Figure 8-1 *JDM mining objects.*

8.1.1   Data Specification Objects

Data specification objects are used to describe the input data for mining. It is important for the DME to know data attribute characteristics so data can be mined effectively. For example, in the CUSTOMERS dataset, as discussed in Section 7.1.3, the attribute *Marital Status* might have numerical values such as 1, 2, 3, 4 to represent *unmarried, married, divorced,* and *widowed,* respectively. Here, the DME needs to know this is a categorical attribute as opposed to a numerical one.

JDM defines physical and logical data objects to encapsulate input data details common across all mining functions. The *PhysicalDataSet* object captures the physical data characteristics, such as data location, physical attribute names, data types, and what role the attributes play. The *LogicalData* object specifies how to interpret the data. It captures logical data characteristics, such as whether an attribute is categorical/numerical/ordinal, prepared/unprepared, and what are the valid values. Separating logical data from physical data allows applications to manage them independently and map multiple *PhysicalDataSet* objects to a single *LogicalData* object and vice versa, thereby allowing reuse of both physical and logical specifications across mining operations and activities. For example, in a production system, the physical data may change weekly such that each dataset has a different table name, yet the way to interpret those attributes logically remains the same. In this case, the data miner maps multiple physical dataset objects with one logical data object. Alternatively, during the modeling phase, a data miner may have physical data that does not change until the solution is deployed; however, the analyst changes the logical data to experiment with various ways to interpret the logical characteristics of attributes, in this case one physical dataset object with multiple logical data objects.

Figure 8-2 depicts the class diagram of the physical and logical data-related objects and their relationships (objects with gray backgrounds are enumerations). A *PhysicalDataSet* can have zero or more physical attributes. This allows specifying only the dataset URI without any physical attribute details and results in accepting default characteristics for each physical attribute. Users can specify physical attributes for a physical dataset to indicate per attribute data type and role. In JDM the allowed data types and roles are represented as the enumerations *AttributeDataType* and *Physical-AttributeRole*. The *AttributeDataType* has the enumerated values *double type, integer type, string type,* and *unknown type.* The *Physical-AttributeRole* defines the special roles some attributes may play in the dataset. For example, the *case id* role is used to specify the attribute that uniquely identifies each case in the dataset.

For the transactional data that was discussed in Section 7.4.3, attributes and values are stored in multiple-records where the

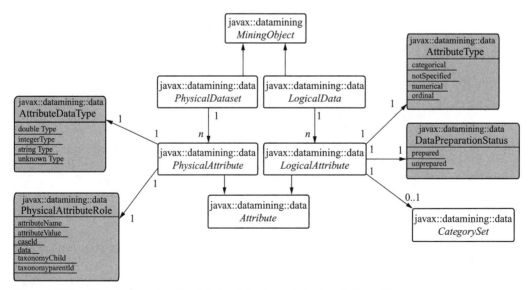

Figure 8-2 *Physical and logical data objects and their relationship.*

attribute name role can be specified to indicate the column in the dataset that has the attribute names and the *attribute value* role can be specified to indicate the column that has the attribute values. In addition to *PhysicalDataSet,* JDM defines *PhysicalDataRecord* to represent a single record that contains the *PhysicalAttributes* and associated attribute values for a single case. A *PhysicalDataRecord* instance is used to apply a model on a single case. Section 9.4.6 will discuss more about the single record apply.

For each physical attribute, there can be an associated logical attribute specified in the logical data. In a *LogicalAttribute* object, users can specify a list of values for a categorical attribute using a *CategorySet* object. For example, one can specify the values {1, 2, 3, 4} as the set of valid values for the *Marital Status* attribute and map those values to unmarried, married, divorced, and widowed, respectively.

Section 4.5 introduced the concept of taxonomy as used by the association function. We consider a *taxonomy* a data specification object since it captures characteristics of the data used for model building.

JDM supports taxonomy representations as either external tables or as native objects. Figure 8-3 depicts the taxonomy objects and their relationships. *Taxonomy* is an abstract interface that generalizes the two interfaces *TaxonomyTable* and *TaxonomyObject*. A *TaxonomyTable* object maps to an existing dataset containing the taxonomy data. This design allows applications to maintain the taxonomy separately from JDM and use the taxonomy in other environments where table access via SQL may be necessary. A *TaxonomyObject* interface is used to create the taxonomy using the JDM API. JDM provides full support for describing taxonomies as objects when the sole use of the taxonomy is for mining with a DME.

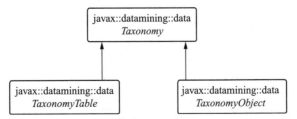

Figure 8-3   *Taxonomy interfaces.*

8.1.2   Settings Objects

Model building and model apply involve the specification of various settings. JDM allows vendor-specific defaults for settings that users can use or override. Default values are assigned as part of settings object creation and applications can retrieve the vendor-specified default values using various *get* methods. This section discusses the settings objects available to control the build and apply process.

Build Settings

To build models, users specify settings at the mining function level, and optionally at the algorithm level. A mining function can be supported by multiple algorithms, similarly, the same algorithm can support multiple mining functions. For example, a classification function can use any of the algorithms such as naïve bayes, decision tree, support vector machine, or neural networks. However, many of these algorithms can also support the regression function. From a design perspective, separating function settings from algorithm settings reduces redundant specification of algorithm settings per function, but also provides more flexibility to allow users to specify function-level settings only.

Figure 8-4 depicts the build settings—related objects and their relationships. Here, the *BuildSettings* object is used for function-level settings and the *AlgorithmSettings* object is used for algorithm-level

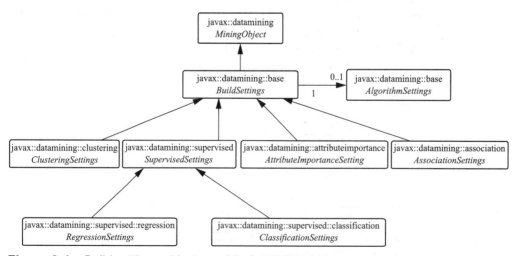

Figure 8-4   *Build settings objects and their relationships.*

settings. Note that *BuildSettings* has a "*has a*" relationship with *AlgorithmSettings*. As mining functions are broadly divided into supervised and unsupervised functions, the *SupervisedSettings* base interface is used to represent all the supervised functions. For example, classification is a supervised type function, so *ClassificationSettings* inherits from *SupervisedSettings*. There are no common settings for unsupervised functions, because these functions are significantly different from each other. As a result, the settings for unsupervised mining functions directly inherit from *BuildSettings*. For example, clustering is an unsupervised type function, so *ClusteringSettings* inherit from *BuildSettings*.

Figure 8-5 depicts the objects related to algorithm settings. Since algorithms are used in the context of a function, *AlgorithmSettings* are always used as part of a *BuildSettings* object. *AlgorithmSettings* is the base interface for all algorithm settings. *SupervisedAlgorithmSettings* is the base interface for algorithms supporting supervised functions. For example, the decision tree algorithm is used for supervised functions so *TreeSettings* inherits from *SupervisedAlgorithmSettings*. Although many algorithms that can support classification and regression accept the same settings, some algorithms, such as support vector machine (SVM), differ enough to warrant their own interfaces.

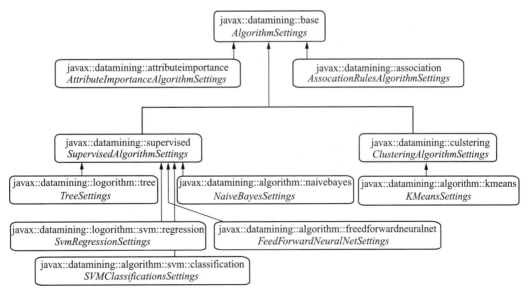

Figure 8-5 *Algorithm settings objects and their relationships.*

Each algorithm settings object is used to define algorithm-specific parameters. For example, a *TreeSettings* object is used to specify decision tree algorithm—specific settings such as maximum depth of the tree and maximum number of splits.

Cost Matrix

Section 7.1.4 discussed the use of a cost matrix for classification, where a cost matrix is used to represent the costs associated with incorrect predictions from a classification model. Since the cost matrix supplements the build settings of a classification model, JDM considers this object as one of the classification-specific settings objects.

JDM defines a cost matrix as a named mining object that can be managed separately by users and easily updated for model rebuilding. A cost matrix can be specified for model build, apply, or test operations depending on the capabilities of the particular JDM implementation.

Figure 8-6 depicts the cost matrix object and its related objects. Note that *CostMatrix* inherits from the *CategoryMatrix*, which represents any matrix that uses target values (a.k.a. categories) as row and column header values. The *CategorySet* object, which is referenced by the *CategoryMatrix*, contains the category values that are used to represent the matrix row and column values.

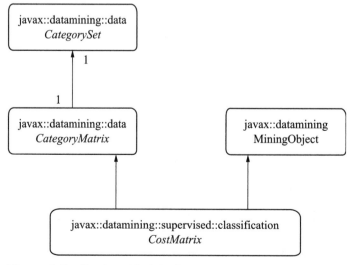

Figure 8-6 *Cost matrix interfaces.*

Apply Settings

JDM apply settings were designed to provide flexibility in defining the results from model apply. Section 3.3.2 introduced the model apply operation. In general, all supervised models and some unsupervised models such as clustering can be applied to produce apply results—a table or view in a database or a file in a file system.

Apply settings specify the desired contents in the *apply output data*. The specific content varies by mining function, hence JDM defines function-specific apply settings interfaces. Figure 8-7 depicts various apply settings interfaces and their relationships. The *ApplySettings* is the base interface that defines the common settings across all function-level apply settings. *ClassificationApplySettings, RegressionApplySettings,* and *ClusteringApplySettings* interfaces specify the settings for applying classification, regression, and clustering models, respectively.

Apply for a classification model computes the target value and corresponding probability for each case of the specified *apply input data*. Normally, the target value with highest probability is considered the top prediction. However, the probability is not always the best measure to find the top prediction. If the cost matrix is specified for model build or apply, the *cost* values are computed in addition to probability. We may want to select the target value that has the least cost as the top prediction.

For example, in the customer attrition problem discussed in Section 7.1, the target attribute *attrite* can have one of two possible target values *Attriter* or *Non-Attriter*. Note that the model cannot predict attrition with 100 percent probability for each case. In this example, let us say the model predicted that a customer is 30 percent likely to attrite, meaning 70 percent unlikely to attrite. As such, the value *Non-attriter* is selected as the top prediction since it has the

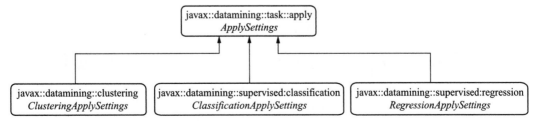

Figure 8-7 *Apply settings objects.*

highest probability. The first row of Figure 8-8(a) depicts this case. However, if we use the cost matrix in Figure 8-8(b), the *cost of predicting a Non-attriter value* is computed as the cost the business incurs when the actual value is *Attriter* and vice versa. If this cost matrix is applied for the same customer case, the cost of predicting *Attriter* is $30 and *Non-attriter* is $45 as shown in the second row of Figure 8-8(a). Since we are choosing the lowest cost prediction, the model predicts this same customer as an *Attriter* ($30 < $45).

Figure 8-9 shows the apply content options for each function that supports apply using the JDM enumerations *ClassificationApplyContent, RegressionApplyContent,* and *ClusteringApplyContent.*

For classification models, JDM defines four possible contents— *predicted category, probability, cost,* and *node ID.* The *predicted category* results in the predicted target value in the apply output, similarly *probability* and *cost* contents result in the probability or cost corresponding to the predicted target value. The *node id* content is specific to rules-based models such as decision tree that use a specific tree node or rule for making a prediction. When node id content is specified, the node id that produced the prediction is provided in the apply result. Node id is useful to show why a given prediction was made.

	Attriter	Non-Attriter	Top Prediction
Probability	0.30	0.70	Non-Attriter
Cost	0.7 × $50 = $30	0.3 × $150 = $45	Attriter

(a)

		Predicted	
		Attriter	Non-Attriter
Actual	**Attriter**	0 (TP)	$150 (FN)
	Non-Attriter	$50 (FP)	0 (TN)

(b)

Figure 8-8   *Prediction Costs. (a) Computation of costs based on the (b) specified cost matrix.*

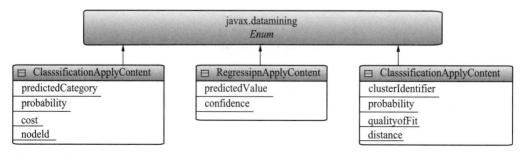

Figure 8-9   *Apply contents.*

For regression models, JDM defines two possible contents: *predicted value* and *confidence*. Unlike classification, *regression* predicts a continuous value. It provides a *confidence level* associated with the *predicted value* indicating the prediction quality. Generally, the more narrow the confidence band, the more accurate the prediction. Confidence values are represented as a percentage value or as a value between 0 and 1, where 1 is the highest confidence and 0 the lowest. For more details about confidence, refer to [Wikipedia-Confidence 2006].

For clustering models, JDM defines four possible contents: *cluster identifier, probability, quality-of-fit,* and *distance*. The clustering apply operation computes one or more of these contents for each case and cluster combination. For example, when a clustering model has three clusters, the apply operation can compute the probability, quality-of-fit, and distance for each case with respect to each of the three clusters. The cluster probability is a measure of the degree of confidence by which a case belongs to a given cluster. The quality-of-fit indicates how well a case fits the cluster. The distance indicates how "far" a given case is from the cluster centroid.

Sections 9.4, 9.5, and 9.8 detail the use of these contents in apply settings.

8.1.3   Models

A model object contains a compact representation of the knowledge contained in the build data, providing details at the function and algorithm level, as well as the build settings used to create the model. *Model* is the base interface for all types of models. In JDM, each mining function has an associated model object. A model may also contain algorithm-specific representations implemented through the base interface *ModelDetail*, which encapsulates algorithm-specific details. For example, a model that is built using *ClassificationSettings* with the decision tree algorithm has an instance of *ClassificationModel* with *TreeModelDetail*. Here, the *ClassificationModel* instance provides content that is common across all classification algorithms, such as the attributes used by the model build, the target attribute used, and the settings used to build the model. *TreeModelDetail* provides the model details specific to the decision tree algorithm, such as the list of tree nodes, their hierarchical structure, and node details like predicted target and probability.

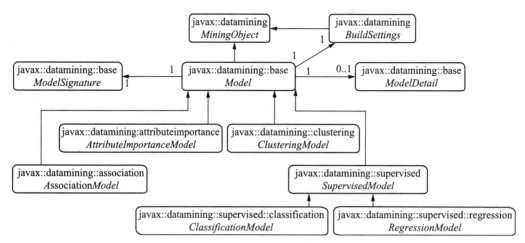

Figure 8-10   *Model objects and their relationships.*

Figure 8-10 depicts the class diagram of the model-related objects. Each model has an associated *BuildSettings* object. A model may have an associated *ModelDetail* object. The *ModelSignature* object provides details of the attributes needed to apply the model. *ModelSignature* is defined as a separate object because it can be used as input to validate the attributes of the datasets supplied to the apply and test operations. For example, the decision tree model discussed in Section 7.1 uses *Age* and *Savings Account Balance* as predictors and hence these attributes are considered part of the model signature. When applying this model, these attributes should be provided. In addition, *ModelSignature* can be used to create a default instance of *PhysicalDataRecord* that can be used for record apply—as used for real-time scoring. Refer to *PhysicalDataRecordFactory* interfaces in [JDM11 2006] for more details about the *PhysicalDataRecord* create options.

8.1.4   Test Metrics

The quality of supervised models is evaluated by generating metrics based on comparing predicted target values with actual target values. These metrics provide valuable insight into how a model performs relative to test data, as well as how a model compares with other models.

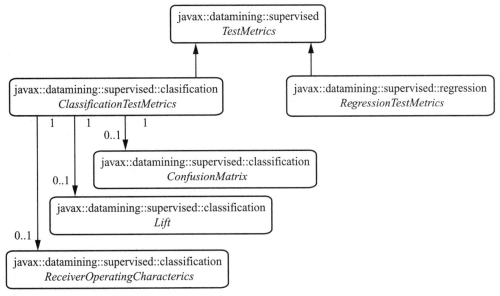

Figure 8-11   *Test metrics objects.*

Figure 8-11 depicts the class diagram of the test metrics object relationships. There are two types of test metrics: one for classification and one for regression. *TestMetrics* is the base interface. *ClassificationTestMetrics* contains the subobjects *ConfusionMatrix*, *Lift*, and *ReceiverOperatingCharacterics*. The *RegressionTestMetrics* object contains the various error metrics mentioned in Section 7.2.5. JDM defines test metrics as a mining object that can be saved with a name by the DME. This allows applications to manage test metrics independently from the models or data that produced them and to compare test metrics across models and over time.

8.1.5 Tasks

JDM defines a *Task* object to support the JDM operations for model build, test, apply, compute statistics, as well as import and export. Tasks can be executed synchronously or asynchronously in the DME. In general, data mining operations can be long running, for example, when scoring millions of records or building models using compute-intensive algorithms. Applications can execute such long running operations asynchronously to avoid blocking the application. The *Task* object encapsulates the specification of input and output objects required to execute tasks in the DME. For example, the *BuildTask* object is used to build a mining model and takes data specifications, build settings, and the output model name, among others, as arguments.

Figure 8-12 depicts the JDM task-related objects. For each operation, we define a specialized task object. *TestTask* is the common superinterface for testing supervised model quality. *ClassificationTestTask* is used to test classification models and *RegressionTestTask* is used to test regression models.

The *ApplyTask* object is used for the apply operation. The *DataSetApplyTask* is used to perform apply on a dataset with many cases, whereas the *RecordApplyTask* is used to perform the apply operation for single case, enabling real-time scoring. From a design perspective, JDM places apply functionality in a separate package to enable conformance for DMEs as scoring engines.

The *ComputeStatisticsTask object* is used to compute the attribute univariate statistics that are discussed in Section 3.1.2. This task takes as input physical data and an optional logical data and produces per attribute univariate statistics. The logical data attribute types can influence the type of univariate statistics computed by the DME.

ExportTask and *ImportTask* objects are used to perform mining object import to and export from a DME. These tasks are particularly useful to export models and settings from a data mining solution development system and import them to a production environment.

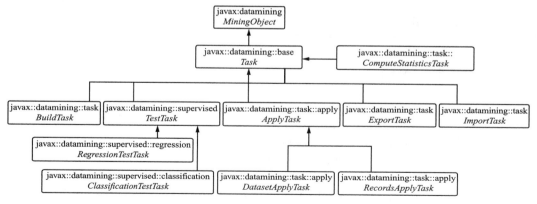

Figure 8-12 *Task objects and their relationships.*

When a task is executed asynchronously, JDM provides ways to retrieve task execution information from the DME using an *ExecutionHandle* object, which is returned to the client application. Using an *ExecutionHandle* object, applications can monitor and control task execution by using status retrieval and terminate methods. The same task cannot be executed more than once concurrently to avoid naming conflicts for the resulting objects. Once a task has completed, or terminated, it can be re-executed. However, the user needs to remove any created objects prior to re-execution to avoid naming conflicts.

8.2 Modular Packages

In JDM, we use Java packages to group collections of related classes or interfaces with similar data mining functionality. Careful package design ensures that an API is easy to understand, adopt, extend, maintain, and reuse. One of the challenges in defining a standard Java Data Mining API is that not all vendors will support all functions, algorithms, or features. Java packages provide an effective way to modularize the API by mining functions and algorithms so that vendors can choose the packages that they want to implement.

Figure 8-13 depicts the package diagram and the relationships between various JDM packages. The gray boxes highlight the package categories in JDM. Core packages contain classes with the required API functionality. The mining function level packages are organized one package per function. Similarly, algorithm level packages are organized as one package per algorithm. Note that there are two types of algorithm level packages: algorithm settings and model details. Vendors who do not explicitly define algorithms can ignore the implementation of either or both of these packages. According to the JDM conformance requirements, a vendor can selectively choose which mining functions and algorithms to implement. To be compliant with JDM, the core packages and at least one mining function must be supported by the vendor product. For applications to discover what a particular vendor supports, JDM provides an API to discover DME capabilities. This API is discussed in Section 8.8.

Based on the object relationships in the various packages, Java packages will have implicit relationships; these dependencies are

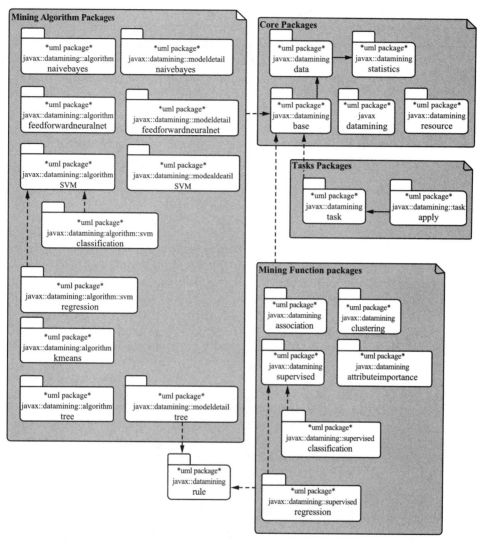

Figure 8-13 *JDM package dependency diagram.*

shown as dotted arrows in Figure 8-13. For example, decision tree model details package *javax.datamining.modeldetail.tree* depends on the *javax.datamining.rule* package.

8.3 Connection Architecture

Most vendors offer the DME as a server component, where client applications make an explicit connection to communicate with the DME. For example, some database vendors offer data mining capabilities where the DME is embedded in the database. Non-database vendors provide the DME as a middle tier component that accesses data from databases and file systems. How applications connect to a DME depends on a vendor's implementation choices. To isolate vendor-specific dependencies, JDM uses a vendor-neutral connector architecture that allows applications to connect to a DME with interoperable code. Using the Java Naming and Directory Interface (JNDI) and the factory method pattern, JDM isolates the vendor-specific connection implementation. This section discusses the details of the connection interfaces.

ConnectionFactory is the factory object that can create a *Connection* object. The *ConnectionFactory* object has three overloaded *getConnection* methods. Each method supports a different type of DME connection configuration. The *getConnection(ConnectionSpec)* method, allows users to specify the DME location and authentication details in a *ConnectionSpec* object to obtain a connection. In this approach, the application must provide a *ConnectionSpec* object each time it wants to obtain a connection. This would be suitable for applications where a user must log into the DME with credentials to do a mining operation.

The *getConnection(javax.resource.cci.Connection)* method connects to DMEs that support the *J2EE Connector Architecture* (JCA). In this case, applications can use a DME's JCA connection and supply it to the *getConnection* method to obtain a JDM Connection object. This approach is suitable for DMEs that provide JCA-based connections.

The third method, *getConnection( )*, does not take any inputs from the application. The *ConnectionFactory* holds the DME connection details and creates a *Connection* object. This approach is suitable for applications where the user does not need to provide DME details to perform mining. Vendor products can support all three methods; however, at least one of the *getConnection* methods must be supported.

Figure 8-14 illustrates how a vendor, XYZ, might implement connection-related interfaces using the factory method pattern. Here, the *ConnectionFactory* interface provides *getConnection* methods to create a *Connection* object. Note that the *XYZConnectionFactory* implements *Serializable* and *Referenceable* interfaces in addition to the *ConnectionFactory* interface. This enables the connection factory object to register with a JNDI service, and applications can look up the JNDI server to obtain the connection factory object in a

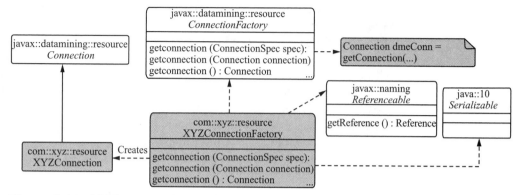

Figure 8-14 *XYZ vendors ConnectionFactory implementation details.*

vendor-neutral way. Once the application gets access to the vendor-specific *ConnectionFactory,* here the *XYZConnectionFactory* object, it can instantiate a vendor-specific implementation of the *Connection* object, that is, *XYZConnection*. This vendor-neutral DME connection framework enables an application to interact with multiple DME implementations.

8.4   Object Factories

In JDM, objects are defined as Java interfaces except for enumeration and exception classes. A vendor must implement the JDM interfaces to provide an implementation. All object factories inherit from a common interface called *Factory.* Factory is defined as a *marker interface,* that is an interface with no methods to distinguish the factory objects from the other API objects. An application uses JDM object factories, which are obtained through the Connection, to instantiate mining objects. The *Connection* object serves as an *abstract factory* that can create factory objects for any vendor-provided JDM interface object. The *getFactory* method in *Connection* takes an object's class name as input and creates an associated factory object. For example, to create a *PhysicalDataSetFactory* instance, users invoke *getFactory("javax.datamining.data.PhysicalDataSet")*. The abstract factory pattern nicely hides the details of how the factory object is created by the vendor-specific implementation.

Figure 8-15 depicts how a client application can create a vendor-neutral object factory using the abstract factory pattern.

Note that the client application uses the vendor-specific *Connection* instance to create a vendor-specific object factory. This enables applications to connect to multiple vendor DMEs when developing a data mining solution.

After the application creates an object factory using the connection, it creates JDM objects using *create* methods provided in the factory object. For example, to create a *PhysicalDataSet* object, users invoke the create method in the *PhysicalDataSetFactory* object. Figure 8-16 depicts *PhysicalDataSetFactory*-related objects. All other JDM objects follow the same pattern to create JDM objects.

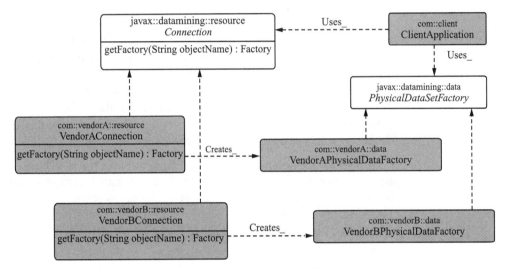

Figure 8-15 *ObjectsFactory creation using Connection.*

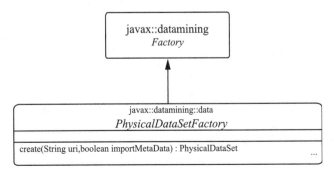

Figure 8-16 *PhysicalDataSetFactory.*

8.5 Uniform Resource Identifiers for Datasets

Input data, in the form of build, test, or apply datasets, for data mining can come in a wide variety of formats and locations. Structured data for data mining often comes from databases as tables or views, but may also reside in a flat files in a file system in formats like CSV, Excel file, etc. To support various formats and locations, JDM defines a data location as a simple Uniform Resource Identifier (URI) string. JDM recommends using a URI string in conformance with the specification defined by *RFC 2396: Uniform Resource Identifiers (URI): Generic Syntax,* amended by *RFC 2732: Format for Literal IPv6 Addresses in URLs.*

For vendors who support data mining in the database, where the database itself acts as the DME, users can specify the URI for data as a table or view name, since the connection already authenticates and connects the user to a database schema. Most database vendors support schemas within the database and remote database links; in those cases they can use *schemaName.tableName* to identify tables or views in other schemas. If a schema name is not specified, the data is considered to be in the user's local schema.

For vendors who support data mining outside the database, but mine data accessing from the database, users can leverage a JDBC URL as the URI specification. Section 16.2.5 gives some examples of these URIs. For vendors who support file input, users can leverage the file URI, for example, *file:///C:/DMData.*

8.6 Enumerated Types

JDM uses type-safe enumerated types to define the possible values for arguments and settings. For example, to list the possible values of mining functions, JDM uses the *javax.datamining.MiningFunction* enumerated type. *MiningFunction* defines the following enumerated values that can be used in the API: *association, attributeImportance, classification, clustering, regression.*

Enumerations are defined as classes to provide standard implementation for enumerations and also to be able to easily migrate to the J2SE 5.0 *Enum* classes. Since JDM 1.0 and 1.1 must be compatible with J2SE 1.4 and above, JDM does not use the J2SE 5.0 Enum and other new language features. Instead, it defines a JDM-specific Enum class that is compatible with J2SE 5.0.

Figure 8-17 illustrates the JDM Enum class diagram. Here *javax.datamining.Enum* is an abstract base class for all the enumerations defined in JDM. The Enum class has methods *name( )*, *equals( )*, and *compareTo( )*. The *name( )* method is used to retrieve the name of the enumeration. The *Enum* class overrides the *Object.equals(obj)* method and does the comparison of this enumerated value with the provided enumerated value. It returns *true* when both are equal; otherwise it returns false. The *compareTo(obj)* method compares this enumerated value with the provided enumerated value, it returns 0 when both the objects have same enumerated value. For more details about these methods refer to [JDM11 2006].

Figure 8-17 also illustrates some JDM enumerations: *MiningFunction, MiningTask,* and *MiningAlgorithm.* These enumeration classes have methods: *values( )*, *valueOf(name),* and *addExtension(name).* For *MiningFunction* the *values( )* method returns an array of *MiningFunction* enumerations. The *valueOf(name)* method returns the *Mining-Function* associated with the supplied name.

The method *addExtension(name)* is used to add vendor-specific extensions to the JDM standard enumeration type. For example, it can be used to add a vendor-specific mining function, say *feature extraction* by calling *addExtension("featureExtraction").* This method adds *feature-Extraction* as a *MiningFunction* at the end of the JDM standard enumeration values. The *addExtension* method gives vendors the ability to add new enumeration values to the existing standard *Enum* class at runtime.

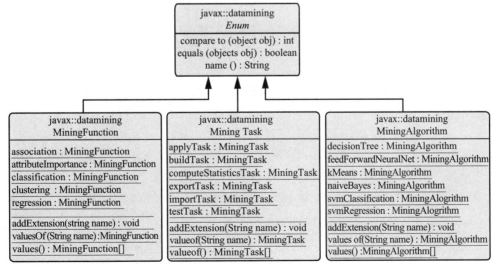

Figure 8-17 *JDM enumeration classes.*

8.7 Exceptions

An *exception* is an event that occurs during the execution of a program that disrupts the normal flow of instructions. Java provides checked and unchecked exceptions. For checked exceptions, where the application can take appropriate actions for anticipated errors, JDM provides the *javax.datamining.JDMException* as the base class that inherits from the standard Java exception. JDM provides subclasses of *JDMException* to allow specialized exception handling in applications.

Unchecked exceptions result from unanticipated application execution failure and may require stopping the application. For unchecked exceptions, vendors may choose among several options: throw standard Java *RuntimeException* objects, wrap these exceptions as appropriate in *JDMException* or *JDMRuntimeException* objects, or throw the specific JDM subclass of a Java runtime exception.

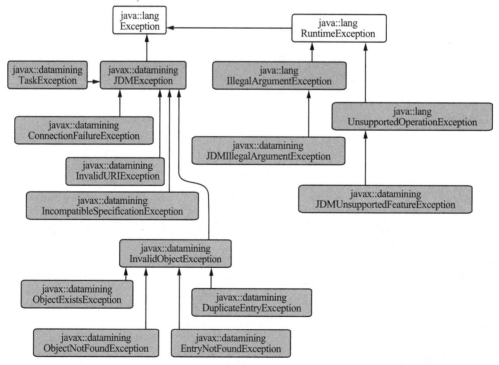

Figure 8-18 *JDM exception classes.*

To keep the number of *JDMException* and *RuntimeException* subclasses relatively small, yet provide meaningful feedback to applications and developers, JDM defines standard exception messages and error codes to support code portability. Vendors can embed their specific error codes within the JDM exception-related classes, as well as wrap other Java exceptions, as appropriate.

Figure 8-18 depicts the exceptions defined in the JDM API. Here you can see JDM defines several specialized checked exceptions and unchecked exceptions, also known as *Runtime exceptions*. All checked exceptions inherit from the generic *JDMException* to enable applications to catch either a generic exception or a specialized exception. Table 8-1 details when these exceptions will be thrown in the JDM API.

Table 8-1 *JDM exceptions*

Exception	Description
ConnectionFailureException	Thrown when the API client fails to connect to the DME. For example, it is thrown either by the *getConnection* method of *ConnectionFactory* or any method in *Connection* that is used for communicating with the DME.
InvalidURIException	Thrown when the user-supplied URI does not conform to the vendor-supported format or the dataset specified by the URI is not accessible.
IncompatibleSpecificationException	Thrown when a method receives incompatible attributes. For example, *LogicalAttribute.setCategorySet* method throws this exception when a *CategorySet* object with *string* values is specified for a *numerical* type attribute.
InvalidObjectException	Thrown when the given object is invalid. This exception is a common superclass for further specialized exceptions, such as *ObjectExistsException* that is thrown by the *Connection.saveObject* method when the specified object name already exists in the DME. The *ObjectNotFoundException* is thrown when the specified object does not exist in the DME. The *DuplicateEntryException* is thrown when a duplicate entry is added to an object; for example, a *LogicalData* object must have unique names for its attribute. If a user adds a duplicate named logical attribute, this exception is thrown. The *EntryNotFoundException* is thrown by a method invocation for the entry that does not exist in the object; for example, *LogicalData.getAttribute (attrName)* throws this exception when the specified *attributeName* does not exist in the *LogicalData* object.

Table 8-1 *JDM exceptions (continued)*

Exception	Description
TaskException	Thrown when there is failure in task execution or execution status retrieval methods.
JDMIllegalArgumentException	Thrown when the given method arguments are not valid. For example, when the user gives a mining object name longer than the supported name length, this exception is thrown.
JDMUnsupportedException	Thrown when the application calls the methods that are not supported by a JDM implementation. For example, if a JDM implementation does not support the cost matrix capability for a classification function, the cost matrix–related methods would throw this exception.

8.8 Discovering DME Capabilities

Since not all vendors support all mining algorithms and functions, the JDM standard provides vendors the flexibility to adopt the standard without expanding their basic set of mining functions or algorithms. However, having a standard that allows flexible feature implementation poses challenges for writing interoperable application code. To mitigate this, JDM provides the ability to discover DME capabilities at runtime by defining a list of capabilities using enumeration classes. For example, the capabilities of *Connection* are enumerated using the *ConnectionCapabilities* enum. The *ConnectionFactory* and *Connection* objects provide *supportCapabilities* methods to discover DME capabilities.

DME capabilities are broadly divided into three major types: *infrastructure capabilities, function and algorithm capabilities,* and *task capabilities*. Infrastructure capabilities include, for example, whether the DME supports synchronous and asynchronous execution of the tasks, the types of mining objects supported by the DME, and the persistence options supported for mining objects by the DME. Function capabilities include, for example, whether the *CostMatrix* is supported for *Classification*. Algorithm capabilities include, for example, whether *tree node statistics* output is supported by the decision tree algorithm implementation.

Applications can check function and algorithm capabilities supported by a DME before using them, especially if application designers want to run such applications across multiple vendor DME implementations. To this end, the factory object associated with each function and algorithm typically provides one or more *supportsCapability* methods to discover DME capabilities. For example, to discover the capabilities of a decision tree implementation, invoke the *supportCapability(TreeCapability)* method in the *TreeSettingsFactory* object. Here, *TreeCapability* is the enumeration that lists the decision tree capabilities supported by a DME.

Applications can also check the task capabilities supported by a DME. Specifically, applications can discover whether a particular task is supported for a specific function, algorithm, or for a function and algorithm pair, for example whether the apply task is supported for the k-means algorithm of the clustering function. JDM also defines optional capabilities at each task level, for example, whether the *BuildTask* supports specification of validation data that is used as part of the model build operation.

8.9   Summary

The JDM standard defines Java interfaces to enable application designers and developers to develop comprehensive data mining solutions that are also portable across multiple DMEs. JDM objects are primarily divided into data specification, settings, model, task and test metrics. For each mining function and algorithm, we define separate packages, which also contain related objects. Since vendors will not typically implement all JDM features, conformance to the standard is *a la carte*, allowing a vendor to choose among a subset of features. JDM provides the ability to explore the capabilities of a DME at runtime to implement portable code.

References

[Gamma+ 1994] Erich Gamma, Richard Helm, Ralph Johnson, John Vlissides, *Design Patterns: Elements of Reusable Object-Oriented Software*, Reading, MA, Addison-Wesley Professional Computing Series, 1994.

[JDM11 2006] Java Data Mining 1.1 specification and API Java documentation, http://jcp.org/aboutJava/communityprocess/mrel/jsr073.

[JDMSpec] JDM 1.0 Standard Specification, http://www.jcp.org/aboutJava/communityprocess/final/jsr073/index.html.

[Wikipedia-Confidence 2006] http://en.wikipedia.org/wiki/Confidence_Interval.

[OMG_UML 2006] Unified Modeling Language, http://www.uml.org.

Chapter

9

Using the JDM API

*Data mining has become a must-have element of enterprise analytics.
However, there are many obstacles to broaden inclusion of data
mining in everyday operational business intelligence (BI).*

—From a Seth Grimes article *Intelligent Enterprise Magazine* [IEM, 2004]

One of the obstacles to operationalizing data mining in a *business intelligence* (BI) solution is not having a standard framework or effective application programming interface (API). JDM addresses this obstacle by defining a standard API to enable data mining functionality in BI solutions. This chapter focuses on how to use the JDM API to develop vendor-neutral data mining solutions.

We extend the discussion of JDM object design in Chapter 8 with details of object methods and their use. Further, we provide code samples for the problems discussed in Chapter 7 to explain function-specific and algorithm-specific JDM interfaces. Part III carries this one step further by providing more detailed code examples to develop various data mining solutions and tools. This chapter is important to understand JDM at the code level.

Although core JDM interfaces are used irrespective of the data mining problem type, other JDM interfaces are very much tied to the specific data mining problem. This chapter begins with the details of the JDM core API functionality, such as connecting to the

DME, exploring the DME metadata and capabilities, creating and maintaining object factories, and using JDM enumerations, data specifications, and base settings interfaces. Later in this chapter, we explain the use of function level interfaces with code examples.

In JDM, *javax.datamining* is the base package. All JDM interfaces and classes are declared either in this package or its subpackages. In this chapter, we refer to the JDM packages, interfaces, and classes using relative path names. For example, the interface *javax.datamining. base.Model* is referred to as *base.Model*.

9.1 Connection Interfaces

Connecting to the data mining engine (DME) is the first step in a JDM application to establish communication between the API and the DME. The DME connection-related interfaces are declared under the *resource* package. A brief description of these interfaces is provided in Table 9-1.

Table 9-1 *javax.datamining.resource package interfaces and classes*

Interfaces	
ConnectionFactory	*Used to create a DME Connection using one of the getConnection methods.*
ConnectionSpec	*Used to specify DME location, authentication, and locale information.*
Connection	*Used to communicate with the DME. In addition, it provides methods to create object factories, manage objects, and execute mining tasks.*
ConnectionMetaData	*Provides DME metadata, such as DME and JDM version information.*
Classes	
ConnectionCapability	*Enumeration of the various DME connection capabilities.*
PersistenceOption	*Enumeration of persistence options of named objects.*

In the previous chapter, Section 8.3 briefly introduced different ways to establish a DME connection using three different *getConnection* methods declared in the *resource.ConnectionFactory* interface. In this section, we extend that discussion with the comprehensive details about all the connection-related interfaces, their methods, and their use.

9.1.1 Using the *ConnectionFactory* Interface

The *resource.ConnectionFactory* interface implementation is DME-specific, because each DME may differ in the way it establishes a connection to the DME. To write a DME-independent application, JDM recommends that the *ConnectionFactory* object implement the *javax.naming.Referenceable* and *javax.io.Serializable* interfaces, so that it can be registered with a JNDI directory. The DME-specific connection factory must be created and preregistered with the JNDI directory such that a JDM application can look up a vendor's connection factory object. Listing 9-1 illustrates how to get the JDM connection factory from a JNDI registry. In this example, the *ConnectionFactory* object is registered with the name "*MyConnFactory*" under the directory "*java:comp/env/jdm*".

Listing 9-1 *Lookup ConnectionFactory object from JNDI*

```
1. //Lookup ConnectionFactory
2. javax.datamining.resource.ConnectionFactory connFactory =
3. (ConnectionFactory) jndiContext.lookup("java:comp/env/jdm/MyConnFactory");
```

In practice, simple Java applications (non-J2EE) may not have a JNDI directory in their application architecture. In those cases, the vendor-specific *ConnectionFactory* class can be used. For example, the Oracle implementation of JDM has the *oracle.dmt.jdm.resource.Ora-ConnectionFactory* class that implements the JDM standard *ConnectionFactory* interface. Listing 9-2 illustrates the creation of the *ConnectionFactory* object when JNDI is not available. In this example, when the *DMEVendor* attribute is *Oracle*, it uses an Oracle-specific constructor; when it is *KXEN*, it uses a KXEN-specific constructor. Note that only *ConnectionFactory* creation requires vendor-specific code; the rest of a JDM application can be implemented in a vendor-neutral approach. Chapter 13 illustrates more examples of *ConnectionFactory* creation in specific tool and application scenarios.

Listing 9-2 *Create ConnectionFactory based on the type of the DME*

```
1. javax.datamining.resource.ConnectionFactory connFactory = null;
2. //Based on the DME Vendor create the ConnectionFactory
3. if(DMEVendor == "Oracle")
4. connFactory = new oracle.dmt.jdm.OraConnectionFactory();
5. else if (DMEVendor == "KXEN")
6. connFactory = new com.kxen.kxJDMImpl.ConnectionFactoryImpl();
7. else if . . .
```

After getting the *ConnectionFactory* object, the DME *Connection* can be created using one of the *getConnection* methods. Table 9-2 lists all the methods in the *ConnectionFactory* interface. The *getConnection()* method that takes no arguments is used when the *ConnectionFactory* maintains the DME location and authentication details. In this case, no connection specification is required to get the DME *Connection* from the *ConnectionFactory*. The *ConnectionSpec* interface is used to specify the connection details, such as the location of the DME, user name, password, and client locale information. Table 9-3 lists all the methods declared in the *ConnectionSpec* interface.

Method *getConnectionSpec()* in the *ConnectionFactory* is used to get the *ConnectionSpec* of the DME. If *ConnectionSpec* is not pre-specified in the *ConnectionFactory*, the method *getConnectionSpec* returns an empty *ConnectionSpec* object and the application can set appropriate DME details using its *set* methods, as shown in Table 9-3. In this example, the method *getConnection(ConnectionSpec)* is used to get a *Connection*. Listing 9-3 shows the code example for this case. In line 2, method *supportsCapability* is used to ensure that the JDM implementation supports the *ConnectionSpec* approach to get a connection before using this method. JDM-compliant implementations can support one or more of the *getConnection* methods.

Method *getConnection(javax.connector.cci.Connection)* is used to create a DME connection using the *J2EE Connector Architecture* (JCA) JSR-16. The JCA is generally used by J2EE tools vendors and system integrators to create resource adapters that support access to *enterprise information systems* (EISs). These EISs can then be plugged into any J2EE product [J2EE Tutorial 2006]. If a DME vendor supports a JCA-compliant connection interface, it can use the *getConnection* method that creates a wrapper JDM-compliant connection using the specified *javax.resource.cci.Connection*.

Table 9-2 *javax.datamining.resource.ConnectionFactory interface*

Method	Description
getConnection()	*Used to get the connection in container managed scenarios.*
getConnection(ConnectionSpec)	*Used to get the connection with the caller specified connection details.*
getConnection(javax.resource.cci.Connection)	*Used to get the connection using the J2EE Connector API client connection.*

Table 9-2 *(continued)*

Method	Description
getConnectionSpec()	*Used to get the ConnectionSpec object if it is already specified in the getConnection method. If it is not specified, this method returns a newly created ConnectionSpec instance.*
supportsCapability(ConnectionCapability)	*Used to find the connection capabilities of the DME. Returns true if the specified capability is supported.*

Table 9-3 *javax.datamining.resource.ConnectionSpec interface*

Method	Description
set/getURI(String)	*Used to set and get the location of the DME with which the API will interact.*
set/getUsername(String)	*Used to set and get the user name used to connect to the DME.*
set/getPassword(String)	*Used to set and get the password used to connect to the DME.*
set/getLocale(Locale)	*Used to get the locale information of the client so that the DME can use language-specific settings and error messages.*

Listing 9-3 *Get the Connection using ConnectionSpec*

```
1.   //If getConnection(ConnectionSpec) supported by the DME
2.   if(connFactory.supportsCapability(ConnectionCapability.connectionSpec)) {
3.     //Get the empty connection spec from the factory
4.     ConnectionSpec connSpec = connFactory.getConnectionSpec();
5.     //Specify the connection details
6.     connSpec.setURI("DMELocation");
7.     connSpec.setUsername("user");
8.     connSpec.setPassword("passwd");
9.     //Get the DME Connection
10.    Connection dmeConn = connFactory.getConnection(connSpec);
11. }
```

9.1.2 Using the Connection Interface

The JDM *resource.Connection* interface provides methods to create and manage mining objects, execute mining tasks, and explore the capabilities of the DME. Table 9-4 lists all the methods in the *Connection* interface. In this table, the *Connection* interface methods are categorized as core and non-core. Users of the JDM API need to be familiar with the core methods. Core methods are subdivided into object management, task execution, and other core methods. Non-core methods are subdivided among supports capability, metadata, object listing, and load methods. All of the core and most of the non-core methods are required to be supported by the JDM implementations. In this section, we discuss the use of the core methods. For more details about these methods, refer to the Java API document provided by the JDM 1.1 specification [JDM11 2006].

Table 9-4   *javax.datamining.resource.ConnectionFactory interface*

Core Object Management Methods	*Description*
getFactory(className):Factory	*Used to create the object factory for the specified object types.*
saveObject(objName, MiningObject, replaceFlag)	*Used to save mining objects in the DME with the specified name. The replaceFlag indicates whether the existing object with the same name should be replaced.*
setDescription(objName, NamedObject, desc)	*Used to set the description of the object with the specified name and type. The mining object type is specified using the Named-Object enumeration of all named JDM objects.*
getDescription(objName, NamedObject):String	*Used to retrieve the description of the mining object by its name and type.*
removeObject(objName, NamedObject):String	*Used to remove the mining objects from the DME by its name and type.*
retrieveObject(objName, NamedObject):MiningObject	*Used to retrieve the mining objects from the DME by its name and type.*
doesObjectExist(objName, NamedObject):boolean	*Returns true when the specified mining object exists in the DME.*
renameObject(oldObjName, newObjName, NamedObject)	*Renames the mining object with the specified name.*
Core Task Execution Methods	*Description*
execute(Task, Long timeOut): ExecutionStatus	*Executes the task synchronously and returns after task completion. This method returns the status of the execution using the javax.datamining.ExecutionStatus object. If the task does not complete by the specified timeOut in seconds, it will be terminated and the method returns with the terminated ExecutionStatus.*

Table 9-4 *(continued)*

Core Task Execution Methods	*Description*
execute(taskName):ExecutionHandle	*Executes the task asynchronously. It returns after submitting the task for execution in the DME. This method returns an ExecutionHandle to the caller, so that applications can track task execution.*
getLastExecutionHandle(taskName): ExecutionHandle	*A task can be executed multiple times. Using this method, the last execution handle can be retrieved to track the latest execution of the specified task.*
Other Core methods	*Description*
getLocale()	*Returns the locale specified at the time of Connection creation.*
setLocale(Locale)	*Overrides the locale specified at the ConnectionFactory object.*
close()	*Closes and releases all the resources used by the DME Connection. Applications should call this method when finished with a JDM connection. Any non-persistent objects created using this connection will not be usable once the connection is closed.*
Support capabilities methods	*Description*
getSupportedFunctions(): MiningFunction[]	*Returns the list of mining functions supported by the connected DME.*
getSupportedAlgorithms (MiningFunction):Algorithm[]	*Returns the list of mining algorithms supported for the specified mining function by the connected DME.*
getNamedObjects (PersistenceOption):NamedObject[]	*Returns the list of named objects that supports the specified persistence option.*
supportsCapability (MiningFunction, Mining-Algorithm, MiningTask):boolean	*Returns true if the specified combinations of mining function, algorithm, and task are supported.*
supportsCapability (NamedObject, Persistence-Option):boolean	*Returns true if the specified named object supports the specified persistence option.*
Metadata methods	*Description*
getConnectionMetaData(): ConnectionMetaData	*Returns the resource.ConnectionMetaData object containing the DME and JDM version information.*
getMaxNameLength(): int	*Returns the maximum length of the name supported for the named object by the DME. Not all DMEs have the same name limit.*
getMaxDescriptionLength(): int	*Returns the maximum description length supported for the named objects by the DME.*

Table 9-4 *(continued)*

Object list methods	Description
getObjectNames(NamedObject): Collection	*Returns the object names of the specified named object type. If the object type is not specified, it lists all the object names.*
getObjectNames(createdAfter, createdBefore, NamedObject):Collection	*Returns the object names in the specified type and time range.*
getObjectNames(createdAfter, createdBefore, NamedObject, minorType):Collection	*Returns the object names that match the query criteria for time range, named object type, and a minor type. Minor type is used to further filter names. For example, using MiningFunction as minor type, one can list function-specific build settings object names, such as classification settings names.*
getModelNames(MiningFunction, MiningAlgorithm, createdAfter, createdBefore):Collection	*Returns the collection of model names with the specified mining function and/or algorithm in the specified time range.*
getCreationDate(objName, Named Object):Date	*Returns the creation date of the specified object.*
retrieveObjects(NamedObject): Collection	*Retrieves the mining objects with the specified named object type.*
retrieveObjects(createdAfter, created-Before, NamedObject): Collection	*Retrieves the mining objects with the specified named object type and the time range.*
retrieveObjects(createdAfter, createdBefore, NamedObject, minorType): Collection	*Retrieves the mining objects that match the query criteria for time range, named object type and a minor type.*
retrieveModelObjects(Mining-Function, MiningAlgorithm, created-After, createdBefore): Collection	*Retrieves the models with the specified mining function, algorithm and time range.*
Load methods	**Description**
requestDataLoad(dataURI)	*Some DMEs require explicit data loading before using the data for mining. This method is used to load the data.*
requestDataUnload(dataURI)	*Used to unload the data.*
getLoadedData(): String[]	*Lists all the loaded data.*
requestModelLoad(modelName)	*Some DMEs require explicit loading of the model before using it for applying and exploring. This method is used to load the model.*
requestModelUnload(modelName)	*Used to unload the model.*
getLoadedModels(): String[]	*Lists all the models loaded into the DME.*

Listing 9-4 gives the JDM code example that builds a classification model for the customer attrition problem discussed in Section 7.1. The *CustomerAttrition* class (line 6) builds a classification model called the *attrition_model* using customers in CUSTOMERS_BUILD_DATA as input data and the default classification settings. This class has four methods: *init, input, run*, and *output*. The *init* method (line 29) creates the DME connection and the object factories. The *input* method (line 41) creates and saves input object(s). The *run* method (line 49) executes the task(s) and returns *true* if the tasks are successfully completed; otherwise it returns *false*. The *output* method (line 60) retrieves the output object(s). Lastly, the *reset* method (line 65) removes the output object(s) to reset the DME environment. In this chapter, we use the *CustomerAttrition* Java class to illustrate the code for the JDM core API and the classification-specific API. Listing 9-4 illustrates the use of the *Connection* interface core methods.

The *init* method omits *Connection* creation code since it was introduced in Section 9.1.1, but illustrates using *Connection.getFactory* to create factory objects for the *PhysicalDataSet, ClassificationSettings* input objects, and the *BuildTask* object. The *input* method instantiates and saves input objects, as shown in lines 41 to 46. Objects are created using the corresponding factory's *create* method, and saved using the *Connection.saveObject* method. The *saveObject* method takes a boolean flag *replaceExistingObject* as an argument to control whether to replace an existing object with the new one. In the example, this flag is set to *true* to replace an existing object with the same name. Based on application requirements, this flag can be set to *false*; in this case, when there is an object name conflict the *saveObject* method throws *ObjectExistsException*.

The *run* method creates a *BuildTask* object using the *BuildTaskFactory.create* method (line 50). This method takes the names of the input objects as arguments to create a task, namely, *attritionBuildData, attritionBuildSettings*, and the name of the output object: *attritionModel*. The *Connection.execute* method (line 53) executes the build task synchronously; the next section details task execution and monitoring. The *output* method uses the *Connection.retrieveObject* method to get the model from the DME.

Listing 9-4   *CustomerAttrition example class that illustrates the use of the Connection interface core methods*

```
1. import javax.datamining.data.*;
2. import javax.datamining.supervised.classification.*;
3. import javax.datamining.task.*;
```

```
4. import javax.datamining.resource.*;
5. /** This class build a classification model with default settings */
6. public class CustomerAttrition {
7. //Data members
8. static ConnectionFactory connFactory = null;
9. static Connection dmeConn = null;
10. static PhysicalDataSetFactory pdsFactory = null;
11. static PhysicalAttributeFactory paFactory = null;
12. static ClassificationSettingsFactory clsFactory = null;
13. static BuildTaskFactory btkFactory = null;

14. //Main method
15. public static void main(String args[]) throws Exception {
16. CustomerAttrition attrition_model = new CustomerAttrition();
17. try { attrition_model.reset() } catch(Exception anyCleanupFailures) {}//Ignore
18. try {
19.   attrition_model.init(); //Create object factories
20.   attrition_model.input(); //Create input objects
21.   if( attrition_model.run() ) //Execute model build task
22.     attrition_model.output(); //Retrieve the model
23. } catch(Exception anyFailures) { anyFailures.printStackTrace();
24. } finally { if(dmeConn != null) dmeConn.close(); //Close connection
25. }
26. }

27. //Create object factories using the DME connection
28. public void init() throws JDMException {
29.   //Create DME connection as shown in Listing 9.1 or 9.2
30.   // . . .
31.   //Create object factories for the objects in this example
32.   pdsFactory = (PhysicalDataSetFactory)dmeConn.getFactory(
33.   "javax.datamining.data.PhysicalDataSet");
34.   clsFactory = (ClassificationSettingsFactory)dmeConn.getFactory(
35.   "javax.datamining.supervised.classification.ClassificationSettings");
36.   btkFactory = (BuildTaskFactory)dmeConn.getFactory(
37.   "javax.datamining.task.BuildTask");
38. }

39. //Create and save input objects for build task
40. public void input() throws JDMException {
41.   PhysicalDataSet pds = pdsFactory.create( "CUSTOMERS_BUILD_DATA", false );
42.   ClassificationSettings cls = clsFactory.create();
43.   cls.setTargetAttributeName("Attrition");
44.   boolean replaceExistingObject = true;
45.   dmeConn.saveObject( "attrition_build_data", pds, replaceExistingObject );
46.   dmeConn.saveObject( "attrition_build_settings", cls, replaceExistingObject );
47. }

48. //Create build task and execute it to build model
49. public boolean run() throws JDMException {
50. BuildTask btk = btkFactory.create( "attrition_build_data",
51. "attrition_build_settings", "attrition_model" );
52. Long timeOut=null;//Run until completion
```

```
53. ExecutionStatus status = dmeConn.execute( btk, timeOut );
54. if( ExecutionState.success.equals( status.getState() ) )
55.   return true;
56. else
57.   return false;
58. }

59. //Retrieve built model
60. public void output() throws JDMException {
61.   ClassificationModel clsModel = (ClassificationModel)dmeConn.retrieveObject(
62. "attrition_model", NamedObject.model );
63. }
64. //Remove the model to be able to reexecute this example
65. public void reset() throws JDMException {
66.   dmeConn.removeObject("attrition_model", NamedObject.model );
67. }
```

9.1.3 Executing Mining Operations

The *Connection* interface has two *execute* methods, one used for synchronous task execution and another used for asynchronous task execution. Listing 9-4 uses the synchronous execution in the *run* method: *Connection.execute(Task, timeOut)* (line 53). This method returns the status of task execution only after the task finishes execution in the DME. In line 52, the *timeOut* argument value is specified as *null* to indicate that the code will block until the task finishes execution, ending in either success or failure. However, one can specify a maximum task duration in seconds. If task execution is not completed by the specified *timeOut* period, it will be terminated and the *execute* method returns, putting the task in a terminated state. Often, synchronous execution will be used for short running tasks, such as a record apply task where the apply results can be obtained in real-time.

Listing 9-5 shows the asynchronous version of this example using the *attritionBuildTask* and the method *Connection.execute(taskName)* (line 5). This method takes the name of a task saved in the DME (line 4) before invoking the *execute* method. This method returns an *ExecutionHandle* object that is used to monitor the task execution in the DME. To get task execution status, the application uses the *getLatestStatus* method (line 7). Table 9-5 and Table 9-6 list the methods of the *ExecutionHandle* and *ExecutionStatus* interfaces, respectively. Applications either can wait for the completion of an asynchronous task using the *ExecutionHandle.waitForCompletion* method (line 10) or can check the status as needed using the *ExecutionHandle.getLatestStatus*

Listing 9-5 *Asynchronous execution of the task and monitoring of task execution*

```
1.  public boolean run() throws JDMException {
2.     BuildTask btk = btkFactory.create( "attritionBuildData",
3.                            "attritionBuildSettings", "attrition_model" );
4.     dmeConn.saveObject("attrition_build_task", btk, true);
5.     ExecutionHandle btkExecHandle = dmeConn.execute("attrition_build_task");
6.     //Get the status of the execution
7.     ExecutionStatus btkExecStatus = btkExecHandle.getLatestStatus();
8.     System.out.println(btkExecStatus.getState());
9.     int waitUntilCompletion=0;
10.    ExecutionStatus status = btkExecHandle.waitForCompletion(waitUntilCompletion);
11.    if( ExecutionState.success.equals( status.getState() ) )
12.        return true;
13.    else
14.        return false;
15. }
```

---

method. Both methods return an *ExecutionStatus* object that is used to get the *execution state* using the *getState* method. Figure 9-1 shows the possible state transitions for task execution. When a task is executed, it starts in the *submitted* state to indicate that the task is successfully submitted to the DME for execution. Based on the DME implementation, the task execution can be queued or executed immediately. When the task begins execution, it enters the *executing* state and remains there until completion. When execution successfully completes, the execution status enters the *success* state, otherwise it enters the *error* state. Using the *ExecutionHandle.terminate* method, a task can be terminated when it is in either the *submitted* or *executing* states. When the *terminate* method is invoked, the task enters the *terminating* state, and after successful termination, it enters the *terminated* state.

The *ExecutionStatus* object encapsulates execution state entry time, and any description or warnings associated with the state. A JDM implementation can add implementation-specific states, for example, a *queued* state between the *submitted* and *executing* states, etc.

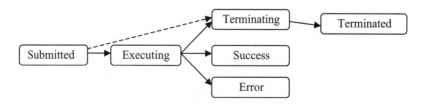

Figure 9-1 *Task execution state transition.*

Table 9-5 *javax.datamining.ExecutionHandle interface*

Methods	Description
getLatestStatus(): ExecutionStatus	Returns the latest ExecutionStatus for the task.
waitForCompletion(int timeoutIn-Seconds): ExecutionStatus	Waits synchronously for the specified time until the task associated with the handle completes, either successfully, in error, or as a result of termination.
getStatus(fromTimestamp): java.util.Collection	Returns a collection containing a time-ordered set of Execution-Status instances since the specified timestamp.
terminate(): ExecutionStatus	Issues an asynchronous termination request for the executing task.
getStartTime(): java.util.Date	Returns the timestamp when task execution began.
getDurationInSeconds(): java.lang.Integer	Returns the duration of execution for the associated task in seconds.
containsWarning(): boolean	Returns true if there were any warnings during the execution.
getWarnings():ExecutionStatus[]	Returns an array of ExecutionStatus objects that contain warnings.

Table 9-6 *javax.datamining.ExecutionStatus interface*

Methods	Description
getState(): returns ExecutionState	Returns the ExecutionState of the task at a point in time.
getTimestamp(): returns java.util.Date	Returns the timestamp of when a given ExecutionStatus instance was created.
getDescription(): returns String	Used to set the description of the object with the specified name and type. Mining object type is specified using the Named Object enumeration of named JDM objects.
containsWarning(): returns boolean	Returns true if there is a warning reported in this Execution-Status instance.

9.1.4 Exploring Mining Capabilities

The *Connection* interface provides methods to explore the capabilities of the DME, such as what functions, algorithms, and tasks are supported. Listing 9-6 adds the validation of supported capabilities to the *init* method for the *CustomerAttrition* class. Line 5 uses the *Connection.supportsCapability(MiningFunction, MiningAlgorithm, MiningTask)* method to validate whether the DME supports the classification function and build task. Because we are not using any algorithm in Listing 9-4, the *MiningAlgorithm* argument is specified as null.

Listing 9-6 *Explore DME-supported capabilities*

```
1. public void init() throws JDMException {
2.   //Create DME connection as shown in Listing 9.1 or 9.2
3.   . . .
4.   //validate required capabilities to execute this program
5.   boolean capabilitiesExist =
     dmeConn.supportsCapability(MiningFunction.classification, null, MiningTask. build);
6.   if(!capabilitiesExist) //If required capabilities doesn't exist throw exception
7.   . . .
8.   //Create object factories for the objects in this example
9.   . . .
10.}
```

Recall that Table 9-4 lists all support capabilities methods in the *Connection* interface for your reference. These methods can be used by applications to validate a DME's capabilities before actually using them to ensure application portability across JDM implementations. Application designers determine how to check capabilities. For example, an application can check all capabilities required immediately after connecting to the DME, or can check capabilities just before using them.

9.1.5   Finding DME and JDM Version Information

Applications may need to find DME and JDM version information to use capabilities based on a vendor product version. JDM supports the retrieval of this information using the *Connection.getConnectionMetaData* method. This method returns an object called *resource.ConnectionMetaData* that encapsulates DME and JDM version information. Table 9-7 lists the methods in *resource.ConnectionMetaData*.

Table 9-7   *javax.datamining.recorce.ConnectionMetaData interface*

Methods	*Description*
getVersion(): String	*Returns the version of the JDM standard is supported by the connected DME.*
getProviderVersion(): String	*Returns the version of the connected DME. It is typically the provider's product version.*
getProviderName(): String	*Returns the JDM implementation product/provider name.*

Table 9-7   *(continued)*

Methods	Description
getMajorVersion(): int	*Returns the major version number. For the JDM1.1, it must be 1.*
getMinorVersion(): int	*Returns the minor version number. For the JDM1.1, it must be 1.*

9.1.6   Object List Methods

The *Connection* interface defines methods to list the objects available to the DME and stored in the mining object repository (MOR). These methods allow applications to explore the contents of the DME and MOR. Table 9-4 shows the object list methods. Applications use these methods—along with different filtering criteria, such as object type, creation dates, etc.—to get either the names of the objects or the objects themselves.

9.1.7   Model and data load methods

The *Connection* interface defines optional *load* methods that are used to pre-load data and models to the DME. In general, explicit loading is not required, however some DME implementations provide an explicit option to load model and/or data to cache them in memory for better performance.

9.2   Using JDM Enumerations

Section 8.6 discussed the design of JDM Enum classes. In this section, we explore methods of the common abstract superclass for JDM enumerations (*javax.datamining.Enum*) and methods of the enumeration classes.

Table 9-8 shows the *MiningFunction* enumerated values and the instance methods declared in the base *Enum* class and the static members declared in the *MiningFunction* enumeration class. Note that *MiningFunction* defines the enumerated values as static data members that can be referenced with the class name. For example, *MiningFunction.classification* can be used to specify the classification mining function.

The *javax.datamining.Enum* class provides common methods implementations for *name*, *equals*, and *compareTo*; these are described in Table 9-8. The *MiningFunction* class provides enumeration-specific method implementations, such as *values*, *valueOf* and *addExtension* methods as described in Table 9-8.

Table 9-8 *javax.datamining.MiningFunction enum*

javax.datamining.MiningFunction *extends javax.datamining.Enum*	
Data Members	
static MiningFunction *association;*	
static MiningFunction *attributeImportance;*	
static MiningFunction *classification;*	
static MiningFunction *clustering;*	
static MiningFunction *regression;*	
Enum instance Methods	*Description*
name(): String	*Returns the name of the enumeration value.*
Equals(java.lang.Object obj):boolean	*Performs a shallow comparison to check if the enumeration is the same as the specified enumeration.*
compareTo(java.lang.Object obj): int	*Compares this object with the specified object for order. Returns the difference between this object and the compared object. Returns 0 if the two objects are the same object, otherwise returns a non-zero number*
MiningFunction static methods	*Description*
static values(): MiningFunction[]	*Returns a list of all the defined MiningFunction enumerations.*
static valueOf(String name): MiningFunction	*Returns an instance of MiningFunction corresponding to the specified name.*
static addExtension(java.lang.String name): void	*Adds a vendor extension name to MiningFunction.*

9.3 Using Data Specification Interfaces

The *javax.datamining.data* package contains all the data specification-related interfaces. Table 9-9 lists the object interfaces and enumerations under this package used to specify physical and logical data specifications. This package also contains the object factory interfaces, which are not listed in this table. In subsequent sections of this chapter factory interfaces will not be included, because they are similar in structure. For example, the *PhysicalDataSet* interface has an associated object factory called *PhysicalDataSetFactory*; similarly, other objects have associated factories in the respective packages.

Table 9-9 *javax.datamining.MiningFunction enumerations*

javax.datamining.data *package*	
Physical data specification related interfaces	
PhysicalDataSet	*A PhysicalDataSet instance describes data for mining. It encapsulates data location and access information. It can have a set of physical attributes that describe the physical nature of the data, such as attribute name, data type, and role.*
PhysicalAttribute	*A PhysicalAttribute instance describes an attribute of a physical data source.*
PhysicalDataRecord	*A PhysicalDataRecord instance represents a set of attribute name-value pairs and enables singleton record scoring. Users can set specific values for PhysicalAttribute instances.*
Logical data specification related interfaces	
LogicalData	*A LogicalData instance is a set of logical attributes that describes the logical nature of the data used as input for model building.*
LogicalAttribute	*A LogicalAttribute instance describes the data to be used as input to data mining operations. As such, a logical attribute references additional metadata that characterizes the attribute as either categorical or numerical.*
CategorySet	*A CategorySet instance specifies a set of categorical values that constitute a categorical attribute, cost matrix, or confusion matrix. Each category exists at an index from 0 to $N-1$, where N is the cardinality of the set. To have NULL be a valid value, it must be explicitly assigned or use the default property of "valid". To have NULL as a missing value, it must be explicitly identified as "missing" using the CategoryProperty enumeration.*
Data related enumerations	
AttributeDataType	*AttributeDataType enumerates the JDM data types: integer, double, and string.*
PhysicalAttributeRole	*A role defines how an algorithm or mining operation will interpret the values of an attribute. PhysicalAttributeRole enumerations include case id, transactional data attribute roles, and taxonomy-related attribute roles.*
AttributeType	*AttributeType enumerates the options for indicating how an attribute is to be interpreted by mining algorithms. For example, an attribute whose values are integers may be treated as categorical instead of the default numerical.*
DataPreparationStatus	*DataPreparationStatus enumerates the data preprocessing options for an attribute: either prepared or unprepared. For example, to indicate that the attribute needs no further preprocessing steps, the user can specify the attribute as prepared.*
CategoryProperty	*CategoryProperty enumerates the types of categorical attribute values, i.e., categories. For example, it can be used to specify whether the attribute NULL values are treated as valid, invalid, missing, or error.*

Recall that in Listing 9-4 we use the simple data specifications, where the data location is specified and all vendor defaults for the data specification are accepted. However, in practice data specifications involve the specification of attribute roles, attribute types, data preparation requirements, and attribute usage types that we discussed in Section 7.1.

Listing 9-7 extends the code in Listing 9-4 with additional data specifications such as the physical data that specifies the *case id* role for the *cust_id* attribute, logical data that specifies the valid values, and data preparation status for *marital status*. The *init* and *input* methods in Listing 9-7 create *PhysicalAttribute*, *LogicalData*, *CategorySet*, and *LogicalAttribute* objects to specify these additional settings. Lines 10 to 17 create the object factories associated with these objects. Lines 22 and 23 create the physical attribute object for the *cust_id* attribute, which has the integer data type and a role of *case id* to uniquely identify each customer case. Line 26 creates the *LogicalData* object and line 27 creates the *LogicalAttribute* object that specifies the name as *Marital Status* and attribute type as *categorical*.

The DME uses the implementation-specific defaults for the attributes that don't have an associated logical attribute. In this simple example, only the *marital status* attribute has a logical specification; however, in practice more or all attributes may have logical specifications. Lines 30 to 35 show the category set creation that specifies the valid values of the *marital status* attribute: married, single, divorced, and widowed. A category set is an optional logical specification for categorical attributes to inform the model build operation of valid, missing, and invalid category values. When there is no category set specification, algorithms use the JDM implementation defaults to identify missing values. For example, *null* values are typically interpreted as missing. Unless otherwise specified, all values of an attribute are typically considered valid.

In this example, the logical data object is saved with name *attrition_logical_data* and is associated with the build settings object using the *setLogicalDataName* method as shown in line 42. In the build task, the physical dataset attributes can be explicitly mapped to the logical data attributes as shown in lines 49 to 51. This mapping allows the build operation to know which logical attribute specifications are associated with which physical attribute. If not explicitly mapped, attribute name equivalence is used to associate physical attributes to logical attributes.

Listing 9-7   *Specify PhysicalDataSet and LogicalData for the input dataset*

```
1.   static PhysicalAttributeFactory paFactory = null;
2.   static LogicalDataFactory ldFactory = null;
3.   static LogicalAttributeFactory laFactory = null;
4.   static CategorySetFactory csFactory = null;
5.
6.   public static void init() throws JDMException {
7.     //Create DME connection other object factories as shown in Listing 9.4
8.     //. . .
9.     //Create object factories for the new objects not specified in listing 9.4
10.    paFactory = (PhysicalAttributeFactory)dmeConn.getFactory(
11.            "javax.datamining.data.PhysicalAttribute");
12.    ldFactory = (LogicalDataFactory)dmeConn.getFactory(
13.            "javax.datamining.data.LogicalData");
14.    laFactory = (LogicalAttributeFactory)dmeConn.getFactory(
15.            "javax.datamining.data.LogicalAttribute");
16.    csFactory = (CategorySetFactory)dmeConn.getFactory(
17.            "javax.datamining.data.CategorySet");
18.  }
19.  //Create input objects
20.  public static void input() throws JDMException {
21.    . . .
22.    PhysicalAttribute paCustID = paFactory.create(
23.     "cust_id", AttributeDataType.integerType, PhysicalAttributeRole.caseId);
24.    pds.addAttribute(paCustID);
25.
26.    LogicalData ld = ldFactory.create( );
27.    LogicalAttribute la = laFactory.create("Marital Status",
28.    AttributeType.categorical);
29.    //Create categoryset
30.    CategorySet cs = csFactory.create(AttributeDataType.stringType);
31.    cs.addCategory("Married", CategoryProperty.valid);
32.    cs.addCategory("Single", CategoryProperty.valid);
33.    cs.addCategory("Divorced", CategoryProperty.valid);
34.    cs.addCategory("Widowed", CategoryProperty.valid);
35.    //Set category set and data preparation status
36.    la.setCategorySet(cs);
37.    la.setDataPreparationStatus(DataPreparationStatus.prepared);
38.    //Add logical attribute
39.    ld.addAttribute(la);
40.    boolean replaceExistingObject = true;
41.    dmeConn.saveObject("attrition_logical_data", ld, replaceExistingObject);
42.    cls.setLogicalDataName("attrition_build_logical_data");
43.    . . .
44.  }
45.  //Create build task and execute it to build model
46.  public boolean run() throws JDMException {
47.    BuildTask btk = btkFactory.create( "attrition_build_data",
48.    "attritionBuildSettings", "attrition_model" );
49.    HashMap pdaLdaMap = new HashMap();
50.    pdaLdaMap.put("mar_status", "Marital Status");
51.    btk.setBuildDataMap(pdaLdaMap);
52.    . . .
53.  }
```

9.4   Using Classification Interfaces

The *javax.datamining.supervised.classification* package contains classification function interfaces, such as *ClassificationSettings*, *Classification-Model*, *ClassifiationApplySettings*, *ClassificationTestMetrics*, etc. This section illustrates the use of the classification interfaces and methods by extending the *CustomerAttrition* example in Listing 9-4, which illustrated a simple classification model build using DME default settings. In this section, we extend this code to illustrate advanced classification settings, algorithm settings, model contents, and model evaluation. We also provide code to apply the model to identify customers likely to attrite, in line with the customer attrition problem discussed in Section 7.1.

9.4.1   Classification Settings

The *ClassificationSettings* interface allows us to specify outliers, prior probabilities, a cost matrix, and various types of classification algorithms. Table 9-10 lists the methods of the *ClassificationSettings*, *SupervisedSettings*, and *BuildSettings* interfaces. *BuildSettings* is the base interface for all function level settings that provide common methods across all mining functions. *SupervisedSettings* inherits from *BuildSettings* to specify supervised function-specific settings, such as the target attribute name. *ClassificationSettings* inherits from *SupervisedSettings* to specify classification-specific settings.

Listing 9-8 illustrates the use of the classification settings methods to specify outliers and a cost matrix. Lines 5 and 6 show the specification of outliers for the *capital gains* attribute using the *setOutlierIdentification* and *setOutlierTreatment* methods of the *BuildSettings*. The outlier identification is used to set the valid value range for *capital gains* ($2,000 to $1,000,000). The outlier treatment option is used to specify how algorithms must treat outliers; in this example, outliers are treated as missing values. Lines 8 to 12 show the creation and setting of the prior probabilities for the *Attrite* target attribute values; *Attriters* are 20 percent and *Non-attriters* are 80 percent in the original dataset. Lines 14 to 24 show the creation of the cost matrix discussed in Section 7.1.4. The *CostMatrixFactory.create* method creates the default cost matrix using a given *CategorySet* object, with a cost value "1" for all nondiagonal cells and value "0" for all diagonal cells of the matrix. Using the *CostMatrix.setCellValue* method, an application can override the default cost values. In this example, as shown in lines 20 and 21, cost value is set to $150 for a false negative and $50 for a false positive. Recall that the cost matrix can be reused across algorithms since it is a named object. In this example, we named the cost matrix *attrition_cost_matrix* and set it as input to the model build using the *ClassificationSettings.setCostMatrixName* method.

Table 9-10 *javax.datamining.supervised.classification.ClassificationSettings interfaces*

supervised.classification.ClassificationSettings *extends supervised.SupervisedSettings*	
Methods	*Description*
set/getPriorProbabilitiesMap(attrName, priorsMap)	*Used to set/get the map of prior probabilities between attribute values and their prior probabilities per attribute.*
usePriors(boolean usePriors)	*Control the use of priors for the target attribute.*
set/getCostMatrixName(costMatrixName)	*Used to set/get the name of a cost matrix that measures the cost of incorrect predictions.*
supervised.SupervisedSettings *extends base.BuildSettings*	
Methods	*Description*
set/getTargetAttributeName(attributeName)	*Used to set/get the target attribute by its name to be used for supervised learning.*
Base.BuildSettings *extends MiningObject*	
Methods	*Description*
set/getLogicalDataName (java.lang.String name)	*Used to set/get the logical data to reference a named LogicalData object.*
set/getOutlierIdentification(logicalAttr-Name, Interval bounds)	*Used to set/get the range of non-outliers values.*
set/getOutlierTreatment (java.lang.String logicalAttrName, OutlierTreatment treatment)	*Used to set/get the outlier treatment for numerical attributes.*
set/getUsage(java.lang.String logicalAttr-Name, LogicalAttributeUsage usage)	*Used to set/get the use of the specified logical attribute.*
set/getAlgorithmSettings (AlgorithmSettings)	*Used to set/get the algorithm settings to be associated with the build settings.*
set/getDesiredExecutionTimeInMinutes (int minutes)	*Used to set/get the desired execution time specified by the user, if any.*
set/getWeight (java.lang.String logicalAttrName, double weight)	*Used to set/get the weight of the specified logical attribute by name.*

Table 9-10 *javax.datamining.supervised.classification.ClassificationSettings interfaces (continued)*

Methods	Description
set/getWeightAttribute(java.lang.String logicalAttrName)	*Used to set/get the name of the attribute that contains case (record) weights.*
verify():VerificationReport	*Verifies if the settings are valid to some degree of correctness as specified by the vendor.*

Listing 9-8 *ClassificationSettings use*

```
1.   public static void input() throws JDMException {
2.      . . .
3.      cls.setLogicalDataName("attritionBuildLogicalData");
4.      //Capital Gain attribute outlier settings
5.      cls.setOutlierIdentification("capital_gain", 2000—20000);//TODO How to create
        interval object
6.      cls.setOutlierTreatment("capital_gain", OutlierTreatment.asMissing);
7.      //Attrition prior probabilities settings
8.      Map attritionPriors = new HashMap();
9.      attritionPriors.put("Attriter", new Double(20.0));//Attrter
10.     attritionPriors.put("Non-attriter", new Double(80.0));//Non-attriter
11.     //Set Prior Probabilities
12.     cls.setPriorProbabilitiesMap("Attrite", attritionPriors);
13.     //Create cost matrix
14.     CostMatrixFactory cmFactory = (CostMatrixFactory)dmeConn.getFactory(
15.       "javax.datamining.supervised.classification.CostMatrix");
16.     CategorySet csAttrition = csFactory.create(AttributeDataType.stringType);
17.     csAttrition.addCategory("Attriters", CategoryProperty.valid);
18.     csAttrition.addCategory("Non-attriters", CategoryProperty.valid);
19.     CostMatrix cm = cmFactory.create(csAttrition);
20.     cm.setCellValue("Attriters", "Non-attriters", 150);
21.     cm.setCellValue("Non-attriters", "Attriters", 50);
22.     dmeConn.saveObject("attrition_cost_matrix", cm, true);
23.     //Set cost matrix
24.     cls.setCostMatrixName("attrition_cost_mMatrix");
25.     dmeConn.saveObject( "attrition_build_settings", cls, replaceExistingObject );
26.  }
```

9.4.2 Algorithm Settings

The specification of algorithm settings is optional for JDM applications. When it is not specified, the DME will select the algorithm, using either a default algorithm or intelligent selection based on the nature of the data. However, in vendor implementations that support algorithms, users can specify algorithm settings to control the choice of algorithm as well as to fine-tune the resulting model.

The *BuildSettings.setAlgorithmSettings* method is used to specify algorithm settings. JDM defines the algorithm settings interfaces under the *javax.datamining.algorithm* package. Table 9-11 shows the list of classification algorithm interfaces supported by JDM.

In Listing 9-9, we illustrate the creation of a simple decision tree algorithm settings object, which specifies the maximum allowed depth of the tree as 10, minimum node size as 5, and the tree homogeneity metric as *gini*, as shown in lines 6 to 12. Refer to the JDM API documentation [JDM11 2006] for a complete listing of available algorithm settings methods.

Table 9-11 *javax.datamining.algorithm interfaces for classification function*

javax.datamining.algorithm *package*	
Decision Tree: javax.datamining.algorithm.tree package	
TreeSettings	*A TreeSettings object encapsulates decision tree algorithm-specific settings, such as maximum tree depth, minimum node size, homogenity metric, etc.*
TreeHomogeneityMetric	*TreeHomogeneityMetric enumerates the various types of goodness measures of a split.*
TreeSelectionMethod	*TreeSelectionMethod enumerates the types of methodologies used for choosing the best tree along the pruning path.*
Naïve Bayes: javax.datamining.algorithm.naivebase	
NaiveBayesSettings	*A NaiveBayesSettings object encapsulates naïve bayes algorithm-specific settings, such as singleton and pairwise thresholds.*
Support Vector Machine (SVM): javax.datamining.algorithm.svm.classification	
SVMClassification-Settings	*A SVMClassificationSettings object encapsulates Support Vector Machine (SVM) algorithm-specific settings used for classification function, such as type of kernal function, complexity factor, etc.*
Feed Forward NeuralNet: javax.datamining.algorithm.feedforwardneuralnet	
FeedForwardNeural-NetSettings	*A FeedForwardNeuralNetSettings object captures the parameters associated with a neural network algorithm, such as the type of learning algorithm, hidden neural layers, maximum number of iterations, etc.*
NeuralLayer	*A NeuralLayer object captures the parameters required to describe a layer in a neural network model, such as activation function, number of nodes, bias, etc.*
Backpropagation	*A Backpropagation object specifies the parameters used by the backpropagation learning algorithm, such as learning rate, momentum, etc.*
ActivationFunction	*The enumeration ActivationFunction indicates the type of activation function used by the neural layer.*

Listing 9-9 *Specification of decision tree algorithm settings*

```
1.  public static void input() throws JDMException {
2.     . . .
3.     PhysicalDataSet pds = pdsFactory.create("customers", false);
4.     ClassificationSettings cls = clsFactory.create();
5.     cls.setTargetAttributeName("Attrite");
6.     TreeSettingsFactory treeFactory = (TreeSettingsFactory)dmeConn.getFactory(
7.     "javax.datamining.algorithm.tree.TreeSettings");
8.     TreeSettings treeSettings = treeFactory.create();
9.     treeSettings.setBuildHomogeneityMetric(TreeHomogeneityMetric.gini);
10.    treeSettings.setMaxDepth(10);
11.    treeSettings.setMinNodeSize(5, SizeUnit.percentage);
12.    cls.setAlgorithmSettings(treeSettings);
13.    . . .
14. }
```

9.4.3 Model Contents

After the successful build of the *attrition_model* it can be retrieved from the DME to explore its contents. Table 9-12 lists the methods of the *ClassificationModel*, *SupervisedModel*, and *Model* interfaces. The inheritance hierarchy of the *ClassificationModel* is similar to that of the classification settings discussed in Section 9.4.1. The *Model* interface is the base interface for all types of models. It provides the methods to retrieve model metadata and basic contents. As shown in Table 9-12, *Model* has methods for getting the model signature, algorithm-specific model details, build settings specified by the user, the actual build settings used by the algorithm, the model build time duration, and version information.

The *SupervisedModel* interface is common for all supervised models, providing the target attribute name used to build the model. The *ClassificationModel* interface contains methods to retrieve the target category set, a flag to indicate whether a cost matrix was used by the model, and the classification error if computed by the model. Listing 9-10 shows the output method that retrieves the *attrition_model* and some of the model metadata and algorithm-specific model details. JDM defines algorithm-specific model detail interfaces as shown in Table 9-13.

Listing 9-10 in lines 5 to 12 shows the model signature retrieval using the *Model.getSignature()* method that returns the *data.ModelSignature* object. The model signature contains a collection of *data.SignatureAttribute* objects that represent the actual attributes used for model build. Line 14 shows how to get the mining algorithm from the model, and lines 16 to 58 show the retrieval of model details

Table 9-12 *javax.datamining.supervised.classificaton.ClassificationModel interfaces*

supervised.classification.ClassificationModel *extends supervised.SupervisedModel*	
Methods	*Description*
getTargetCategorySet():CategorySet	*Returns the set of target categories used in the model.*
wasCostMatrixUsed(): boolean	*Returns true if a cost matrix was specified and used to build the model.*
GetClassificationError(): double	*Returns the percentage, expressed between 0 and 100, of the incorrect predictions made by the model.*

supervised.SupervisedModel *extends base.Model*	
Methods	*Description*
getTargetAttributeName(): String	*Returns the name of the LogicalAttribute that is the target.*

base.Model *extends MiningObject*	
Methods	*Description*
getMiningFunction(): MiningFunction	*Returns the type of the mining function used to build the model.*
getMiningAlgorithm(): MiningAlgorithm	*Returns the type of the mining algorithm used to build the model.*
getSignature(): ModelSignature	*Returns the model signature, i.e., the set of required inputs for applying the model, or as was used for building the model.*
getModelDetail(): ModelDetail	*Returns the algorithm-specific model detail for this model.*
getAttributeStatistics(): AttributeStatisticsSet	*Returns the set of attribute statistics from the build data computed with this model.*
getBuildDuration(): Integer	*Returns the time in seconds that was taken to build the model.*
getBuildSettings(): BuildSettings	*Returns the build settings used to build the model, as specified by the user.*
getEffectiveBuildSettings(): BuildSettings	*Returns the build settings that were actually used by the DME (with systemDefault and systemDetermined replaced with actual values).*
getUniqueIdentifier(): String	*Returns a string that can be used to uniquely reference the JDM model.*
getTaskIdentifier(): String	*Returns the identifier of the task used to build or import the model.*

Table 9-12 *javax.datamining.supervised.classificaton.ClassificationModel interfaces (continued)*

Methods	Description
getApplicationName(): String	*Returns the name of the application that generated this model.*
getVersion(): String	*Returns the JDM version by which the model was built.*
getMajorVersion(): String	*Returns the major version of JDM by which the model was built.*
getMinorVersion(): String	*Returns the minor version of JDM by which the model was built.*
getProviderName(): String	*Returns the name of the JDM provider, i.e., the vendor, that built the model.*
getProviderVersion(): String	*Returns the version number of the JDM system provided by a vendor that was used to build the model.*

produced by different classification algorithms. Lines 16 to 26 show retrieval of the *TreeModelDetail* object that encapsulates the decision tree nodes; using its methods, applications can display the decision tree. The *TreeNode* encapsulates a node's prediction value, the number of cases per node, the rule associated with the node, and the node's child and parent node references.

In this example, we retrieve the first level node details. Lines 27 to 37 show retrieval of the *NaiveBayesModelDetail* object that encapsulates the target probability and pair probability details. We retrieve the target probability associated with the target *attrite* attribute value *Attriter*, pair probabilities associated with the *capital gains* values, and the attrite value *Non-attriter*. Using these details applications can show the target and attribute value correlations. Lines 37 to 43 show the retrieval of the *SVMClassificationModelDetail* object that encapsulates coefficients associated with the attribute and target value pairs. In line 40, we retrieve the coefficients associated with the *capital gains* attribute values and the *attrite* value *Attriter*. Lines 45 and 46 show the retrieval of the *NeuralNetworkModelDetail* object that encapsulates the details of the weights associated with the neurons. In lines 47 to 58, we retrieve the weights associated with each layer and the parent and child neuron possible combinations.

Listing 9-10   *Exploring model contents*

```
1. //Retrieve built model
2. public void output() throws JDMException {
3.    ClassificationModel clsModel = (ClassificationModel)dmeConn.retrieveObject(
4.      "attrition_model", NamedObject.model );
5.    //Print attributes actually used by this model i.e., model signature
6.    ModelSignature signature= clsModel.getSignature();
7.    Collection signatureAttrs = signature.getAttributes();
8.    Iterator signatureAttrsIterator = signatureAttrs.iterator();
9.    while(signatureAttrsIterator.hasNext()) {
10.       SignatureAttribute attr = (SignatureAttribute)signatureAttrsIterator.next();
11.       System.out.println(attr.getName() + " " + attr.getAttributeType().name());
12.    }
13.    //Get algorithm used by the model
14.    MiningAlgorithm algorithm = clsModel.getMiningAlgorithm();
15.    //Cast model details appropriately based on algorithm
16.    if(MiningAlgorithm.decisionTree.equals(algorithm)) {
17.    TreeModelDetail modelDetails = (TreeModelDetail)clsModel.getModelDetail();
18.    TreeNode rootNode = modelDetails.getRootNode();
19.    boolean hasNodes = true;
20.    TreeNode[] firstLevelNodes = rootNode.getChildren();
21.    for(int i=0; i < firstLevelNodes.length; i++) {
22.       System.out.println("Nodes Prediction: " +
23.         firstLevelNodes[i].getPrediction().toString());
24.       System.out.println("Number of cases: " + firstLevelNodes[i].getCaseCount());
25.       System.out.println("Node Rule: " + firstLevelNodes[i].getRule().toString());
26.    }
27.    } else if(MiningAlgorithm.naiveBayes.equals(algorithm)) {
28.    NaiveBayesModelDetail modelDetails =
29.      (NaiveBayesModelDetail)clsModel.getModelDetail();
30.    Map pairProbabilities =
         modelDetails.getPairProbabilities("capital_gain", "Atttriter");
31.    double targetProbability = modelDetails.getTargetProbability("Attriter");
32.    System.out.println("Target Probability of the attrition value 'Attriter': " +
33.       targetProbability);
34.    System.out.println(
35.    "Pair Probabilities of the capital gains values and attrition value 'Attriter': "
36.         + pairProbabilities.toString());
37.    } else if(MiningAlgorithm.svmClassification.equals(algorithm)) {
38.    SVMClassificationModelDetail modelDetails =
39.      (SVMClassificationModelDetail)clsModel.getModelDetail();
40.    Map attributeCoefficients =
         modelDetails.getCoefficients( "Attriter", "capital_gain");
41.    System.out.println(
42.    "Capital gain attribute coefficient values when the attrition value 'Attriter': " +
43.         attributeCoefficients.toString());
44.    } else if(MiningAlgorithm.feedForwardNeuralNet.equals(algorithm)) {
45.    NeuralNetworkModelDetail modelDetails =
46.       (NeuralNetworkModelDetail)clsModel.getModelDetail();
47.    int[] layerIds = modelDetails.getLayerIdentifiers();
```

```
48.  for(int i=0; i < (layerIds.length-1); i++) {
49.    int[] parentNeuronIds = modelDetails.getNeuronIdentifiers(layerIds[i]);
50.    int[] childNeuronIds = modelDetails.getNeuronIdentifiers(layerIds[i+1]);
51.    int parentLayerId = layerIds[i];
52.    for(int j=0; j < parentNeuronIds.length; j++) {
53.      for(int k=0; k < childNeuronIds.length; k++) {
54.      System.out.println("Wight for the parent layer " + parentLayerId +
55.      ", parent neuron id " + parentNeuronIds[j] +
56.      ", child neuron id " + childNeuronIds[k] + " is " +
57.      modelDetails.getWeight(parentLayerId, parentNeuronIds[j], childNeuronIds[k]));
58.  }}}}
59.}
```

Table 9-13 *javax.datamining.modeldetails interfaces for classification function*

javax.datamining.modeldetails *package*	
Decision Tree: *javax.datamining.modeldetails.tree package*	
TreeModel	*TreeModelDetail contains details of a tree model, such as, tree structure, nodes and rule associated with each node.*
TreeNode	*A TreeNode characterizes a partition of a multidimensional dataset.*
Naïve Bayes: *javax.datamining.algorithm.naivebayes*	
NaiveBayesModelDetail	*NaiveBayesModelDetail contains the counts of the occurrences of each target value, and counts of the co-occurrences of predictor values with target values.*
Support Vector Machine (SVM): *javax.datamining.algorithm.svm.classification*	
SVMModelDetail	*SVMModelDetail is the superinterface for classification and regression SVM model details.*
SVMClassificationModelDetail	*An SVMModelDetail contains details of the SVM classification model. SVM model details contain the support vector details, such as number of bounded and unbounded vectors, coefficients associated with the target attribute value and predictor attribute value pairs.*
SVMRegressionModelDetail	*An SVMModelDetail contains details of the SVM regression model. Similar to SVM classification regression model detail contains the support vector details. The difference is SVM regression contains coefficients associated with the predictor attributes and their values as target is continuous number in case of regression.*
Feed Forward NeuralNet: *javax.datamining.algorithm.feedforwardneuralnet*	
NeuralNetworkModelDetail	*NeuralNetworkModelDetail captures the detailed representation of a fully connected, multilayer, feed-forward neural network model.*

9.4.4   Test Metrics for Model Evaluation

This section introduces interfaces and methods used to compute and retrieve classification test metrics using JDM. Table 9-14 lists the classification test metrics-related interfaces. JDM provides two types of tasks for computing test metrics for supervised functions: *supervised.TestTask* and *supervised.TestMetricsTask*. The *TestTask* requires a supervised model and test data, whereas the *TestMetricsTask* interface uses apply output data that includes actual and predicted target values. In this example, we use *ClassificationTestTask* and illustrate how the *TestMetricsTask* interface is used for the regression example shown later in Section 9.5.

Listing 9-11 shows the code that extends the *CustomerAttrition* class with the *attrition_model* evaluation. Recall that section 7.1.6 illustrates classification test metrics such as accuracy, error, confusion matrix, lift, and receiver operating characteristics (ROC). Listing 9-11 shows the computation and retrieval of the classification test metrics. Lines 15 to 22 show the creation and execution of the *attritionTestTask* that computes the test metrics of the *attrition_model* using the CUSTOMERS_TEST_DATA. Lines 27 to 29 show the retrieval of the *attrition_test_metrics* object that was created by the test

Table 9-14 *Classification test metrics-related interfaces*

javax.datamining.supervised.classification *package*	
ClassificationTestTask	*A ClassificationTestTask is used for testing a classification model to measure the model quality on test data.*
ClassificationTestMetrics	*A ClassificationTestMetrics encapsulates classification test metrics such as confusion matrix, lift, and ROC. It provides get methods to retrieve these metrics.*
ConfusionMatrix	*A ConfusionMatrix specifies the statistics of the correct predictions and errors.*
Lift	*A Lift specifies the results of the lift computation. It contains the lift, target denisity details for each quantile. Using this object, one can plot the lift charts that are described in Chapter 7.*
ReceiverOperatingCharacteristics	*A ReceiverOperatingCharacteristics specifies the result of receiver operating characteristic computation. It contains the false and true positive rates at various probability thresholds. Using this object, one can plot the ROC charts described in Chapter 7.*
ClassificationTestMetricsTask	*A ClassificationTestMetricsTask is a mining task used to compute test metrics given an apply output data.*

task. Lines 31 to 35 show how to get the *confusion matrix* object from the test metrics and retrieve *model prediction accuracy, prediction error,* and the *number of predictions* for the specified actual and predicted target values. Using these data, applications can construct a visual representation of the confusion matrix as was shown in Table 7-6. Lines 37 to 44 show how to get the *lift* object from the test metrics and retrieve cumulative lift and gain values that can be used to plot cumulative lift and gain charts as was shown in Figure 7-6. Lines 47 to 57 show how to get the ROC object from the test metrics and retrieve true and false positive rates at various threshold points to plot the ROC graph as was shown in Figure 7-7.

Listing 9-11   *Classification test metrics computation*

```
1. . . .
2. public class CustomerAttrition {
3. . . .
4. //Create and save input objects for build task
5. public void input() throws JDMException {
6.           . . .
7.     //After creating build task input objects, create test task input objects
8.     PhysicalDataSet pdsTest = pdsFactory.create( "CUSTOMERS_TEST_DATA", false );
9.     dmeConn.saveObject( "attrition_test_data", pdsTest, replaceExistingObject );
10.    }

11. //Create test task and execute it to compute test metrics
12. public boolean run() throws JDMException {
13.        . . .
14.    //After successful completion of the build task create and execute test task
15.    ClassificationTestTaskFactory csTestTaskFactory =
16.     (ClassificationTestTaskFactory)dmeConn.getFactory(
17.       "javax.datamining.supervised.classification.ClassificationTestTask");
18.    ClassificationTestTask csTestTask =
19.     csTestTaskFactory.create(
20.       "attritionTestData","attrition_model","attrition_testMetrics");
21.    dmeConn.saveObject("attrition_test_task", csTestTask, replaceExistingObject);
22.    ExcutionStatus testTaskStatus = dmeConn.execute("attrition_test_task", timeOut);
60.    if(ExecutionState.success.equals(testTaskStatus.getState()))
61.      return true;
62.    else
63.      return false;
23.    }

24. //Retrieve test metrics
25. public void output() throws JDMException {
26.        . . .
27.    ClassificationTestMetrics clsTestMetrics =
```

```
28.    (ClassificationTestMetrics)dmeConn.retrieveObject(
29.        "attrition_test_metrics", NamedObject.testMetrics);
30. //Get model accuracy and confusion matrix details such as false prediction counts
31. ConfusionMatrix cfMatrix = clsTestMetrics.getConfusionMatrix();
32. double accuracy = cfMatrix.getAccuracy();
33. double error = cfMatrix.getError();
34. long falseNegatives = getNumberOfPredictions("Attriter", "Non-attriter");
35. long falsePositives = getNumberOfPredictions("Non-attriter", "Attriter");
36. //Get Lift object and cumulative lift and gain values to plot charts
37. Lift lift = clsTestMetrics.getLift();
38. double[] cumulativeLifts = new double[10];
39. double[] cumulativeGains = new double[10];
40. for(int quantile=1, index=0; qunatile <=10; quantile++, index++) {
41.   cumulativeLifts[index] = lift.getCumulativeLift(quantile);
42.   cumulativeGains[index] =
43.     (double)lift.getCumulativePositiveCase(quantile)/(double)lift.getTotalCases();
44. }
45. //Get ROC object and retrieve true and false positive rates
46. //at various probability thresholds
47. ReceiverOperativeCurve roc = clsTestMetrics.getROC();
48. int numberOfThresholdPoints = roc.getNumberOfThresholdCandidates();
49. double[] thresholds = new double[numberOfThresholdPoints];
50. double[] truePositiveRates = new double[numberOfThresholdPoints];
51. double[] falsePositiveRates = new double[numberOfThresholdPoints];
52. for(int threshold=1, index=0; threshold <= numberOfThresholdPoints;
53.     threshold++, index++) {
54.     thresholds[index] = roc.getProbabilityThreshold(threshold);
55.     truePositiveRates[index] = roc.getHitRate(threshold);
56.     falsePositiveRates[index] = roc.getFalseAlarmRate(threshold);
57. }
58. }
```

9.4.5 Applying a Model to Data in Batch

After evaluating model performance, we often apply a model to new data to predict target attribute values. JDM provides options for applications to specify the content of apply output data according to their requirements. In this section, we explore the interfaces related to *batch apply* for classification models. Batch apply refers to applying a model to cases stored in a database table or flat file.

Table 9-15 lists the interfaces related to the apply operation including classification apply-specific interfaces. The *task.apply* package declares common interfaces used for model apply. The *supervised. classification* package declares classification-specific apply settings interfaces and an enumeration of classification-specific apply output contents, such as *predicted category, probability, cost,* and *node id.*

Table 9-15 *Classification apply – related interfaces*

Javax.datamining.task.apply *package*	
ApplySettings	An *ApplySettings* object captures a specification that describes the output of an apply task.
ApplyTask	An *ApplyTask* object captures the task of applying a mining model to data that matches the model signature.
DataSetApplyTask	A *DataSetApplyTask* object captures the task of applying a mining model to a dataset with multiple records.
Javax.datamining.supervised.classification *package*	
ClassificationApplySettings	A *ClassificationApplySettings* object prescribes the output of an apply task specific to a classification model.
ClassificationApplyContent	*ClassificationApplyContent* enumerates the types of value to appear in the apply output of a classification model.

The predicted category content is the predicted value of the target attribute. In our example, it can be the values *Attriter* or *Non-attriter*. The probability content provides the probability associated with the model's predictions for a given target class value. The cost content is the cost associated with the model's predictions based on the specified cost matrix. The node id is specific to decision tree models, where it shows the node that was used for the prediction. Using this node id, applications can retrieve the node details, such as rule, associated with the prediction.

Listing 9-12 extends the *CustomerAttrition* example class to show model apply to predict *attrite* values for customers in the CUSTOMERS_APPLY_DATA. Lines 9 to 10 show the creation of the physical dataset object that represents the input apply data. Lines 12 to 15 show the creation of the empty classification apply settings object using the object factory *create* method. Lines 16 to 23 show how to use the *ClassificationApplySettings.mapTopPrediction* method to specify the apply output contents with the top prediction details. The *ClassificationApplySettings* provides four types of map methods that applications can choose to describe the apply output data. The *mapTopPrediction* method is used when the application is mainly interested in the prediction value with the highest probability. Using the *ClassificationApplyContent* enumeration, a user can choose the type of content desired in the apply output table.

Listing 9-12 *Applying classification model to compute predictions*

```
1. . . .
2. public class CustomerAttrition {
3. . . .
4. //Create and save input objects for build task
5. public void input() throws JDMException {
6.       . . .
7. //Create apply task input objects
8.    //Create apply PhysicalDataSet
9.  PhysicalDataSet pdsApply = pdsFactory.create("CUSTOMERS_APPLY_DATA", false);
10. dmeConn.saveObject("attrition_apply_data", pds, replaceExistingObject);
11.    //Create apply settings
12. ClassificationApplySettingFactory csApplyFactory =
13.   (ClassificationApplySettingFactory)dmeConn.getFactory(
14.    "javax.datamining.supervised.classification.ClassificationApplySetting");
15. ClassificationApplySettings csApplySettings = csApplyFactory.create();
16.    //Top prediction, probability and cost output
17. csApplySettings.mapTopPrediction(ClassificationApplyContent.predictedCategory,

18.    "PredictedAttrition");
19. csApplySettings.mapTopPrediction(ClassificationApplyContent.probabity,
20.    "Probability");
21. csApplySettings.mapTopPrediction(ClassificationApplyContent.cost,
22.    "Cost");
23.  //Specify carry forward attributes from the input dataset (source) to
24.  //output dataset (destination)
25. Map sourceDestinationMap = new HashMap();
26. sourceDestinationMap.put("CUST_ID", "CustomerId");
27. csApplySettings.setSourceDestinationMap(sourceDestinationMap);
28. //Save apply settings object
29. dmeConn.saveObject( "attrition_apply_settings",
30.     csApplySettings, replaceExistingObject );
31. }

32. //Create test task and execute it to compute test metrics
33. public boolean run() throws JDMException {
34.       . . .
35.  //After successful completion of the test task create and execute apply task
36.  DataSetApplyTaskFactory csApplyTaskFactory =
37.    (DataSetApplyTaskFactory)dmeConn.getFactory(
38.      "javax.datamining.task.apply. DataSetApplyTask");
39.  DataSetApplyTask csApplyTask =
40.    csApplyTaskFactory.create(
41.      "attrition_apply_data","attrition_apply_settings",
42.      "attrition_model","attrition_top_prediction_apply_output");
43.  dmeConn.saveObject( "attritionApplyTask", csApplyTask, replaceExistingObject );
44.  ExecutionStatus testTaskStatus = dmeConn.execute("attrition_apply_task", timeOut);
45.  if( ExecutionState.success.equals(testTaskStatus.getState() ) )
46.    return true;
47.  else
48.    return false;
49. }
```

```
50. //Retrieve test metrics
51. public void output() throws JDMException {
52.   . . . .
53.   //Access apply output data that will have following columns:
54.   // Customer Id, PredictedAttrition, Probability, Cost
55.   // . . . Use JDBC if the output is a table in the database . . .
56.
57.   // . . . Use java.io if the output is a data file . . .
58. }
```

In this example, top predicted category, probability, and cost contents are specified to be computed by the apply task. In Table 9-16, we describe the map methods of the *ClassificationApplySettings* interface. For classification, JDM defines methods: *mapTopPrediction*—maps apply contents to the top prediction, *mapByRank*—maps apply contents for the predictions ordered by their probability rank, *mapByCategory*—maps apply contents by the target value, and *mapPredictions*—maps apply contents for all possible predictions. These map methods enable specifying various types of apply output contents that will be produced in the apply output results. However, an apply settings object can only specify contents from a single map method. If a user calls multiple map methods, only the last map method's contents will be stored with the apply settings object. For example, when a user invokes *mapTopPrediction* and *mapByRank* methods in sequence, then the *mapByRank* overrides the *mapTopPrediction* contents and the apply settings will have only the contents specified by the *mapByRank* method calls.

Table 9-16 *Classification apply settings methods*

supervised.classification.ClassificationApplySettings *extends task.apply.ApplySetting*	
Methods	*Description*
mapTopPrediction(ClassificationApplyContent content, String destPhysAttrName)	*Used to specify top prediction apply contents for the apply task. After completion of the task, the apply output data will have the specified apply contents associated with the top prediction. For example, when a user calls the following method, the apply task will compute the top prediction value and populate the* top-Prediction *column with the computed prediction value.* mapTopPrediction(ClassificationApplyContent.predicted-Category,"topPrediction")

Table 9-16   *(continued)*

mapByRank(ClassificationApplyContent content, String[] destPhysAttrNameArray, boolean fromTop)	*Used to specify prediction rank based apply contents for the apply task. The number of ranks and their order depends on the size of the* destPhysAttrNameArray *and* fromTop *boolean value. For example, when a user calls the following method the apply task will compute the top two predictions and populate the columns* Rank_1 *and* Rank_2 *with the prediction values. A user can call this method multiple times with different apply contents to obtain additional information.* mapByRank(ClassificationApplyContent.predicted-Category, new String[] { "Rank_1", "Rank_2" }, true)

mapByCategory(
ClassificationApplyContent content,
Object categoryValue,
String destinationAttrName)
	Used to specify prediction category, i.e., target value, apply contents for the apply task. A user can obtain the category set from the model using the ClassificationModel.getCategory-Set() *method and can call this method for each target value. For example, when a user calls the following methods, the apply task computes the probabilities associated with the target values* Attriter *and* Non-attriter *and populates the probability values in the specified columns i.e.,* Attriter_probability *and* NonAttriter_Probability.
	
	mapByCategory(ClassificationApplyContent.probability,"Yes", "Yes_Probability");
	
	mapByCategory(ClassificationApplyContent.probability,"No", "No_Probability");

mapPredictions(
ClassificationApplyContent content,
String baseDestPhysAttrName)
	Used to specify all possible predictions for the apply task. When this method is used, the apply output data will have apply contents for all possible target values. The base attribute name specified by the user is used to generate column names in the apply output data. For example, when a user calls the following methods where the input model has two possible predicted categories i.e., { Attriter, Non-attriter *}, it creates apply output data that has columns* PredictedVlaue_1, PredictedVlaue_2, Probability_1, Probability_2. *The column* Probability_1 *will have the probability value associated with the predicted value in column* PredictedValue_1. *Similarly, column* Probability_2 *will have the probability value associated with the predicted value in column* PredictedValue_2.
	
	mapPredictions(ClassificationApplyContent.predicted-Category, "PredictedValue");
	
	mapPredictions(ClassificationApplyContent.probability, "Probability");

9.4.6 Applying a Model to a Single Record—Real-Time Scoring

JDM supports a single record apply operation to enable real-time performance for interactive applications such as those used for online retail or in support of call center representatives. Listing 9-13 shows the code that computes the likelihood (probability) of a customer to attrite for the given customer profile. In this example, the *getCustomerAttritionProbability* method takes the customer profile record as input and returns the probability that the customer will attrite. Lines 9 to 26 show the initial setup required to execute a record apply task. This setup involves creating the apply settings object and using the *mapByCategory* method to specify having the probability for the attrite value *Attriter* in the apply output. This step further involves creating a *RecordApplyTask* object. Subsequent invocations will reuse the task and settings objects. The customer profile is set using the *setInputRecord* as shown in line 27. Line 29 shows the synchronous execution of the record apply task. After the completion of the *RecordApplyTask*, we can retrieve the output record using the *getOutputRecord* method and further retrieve the probability value using the *PhysicalDataRecord.getValue* method as shown in line 31.

Listing 9-13 *Single record apply operation (real-time scoring)*

```
1. . . .
2. public class CustomerAttrition {
3. . . .
4. RecordApplyTask csRecordApplyTask = null;
5. //Create and save input objects for build task
6. public double getCustomerAttritionProbability(PhysicalDataRecord customerProfile)
7. throws JDMException {
8.   //When first time called setup all input setting and create record apply task
9.   if(csRecordApplyTask == null) {
10.    //Create input objects for the apply task
11.    ClassificationApplySettingFactory csApplyFactory =
12.      (ClassificationApplySettingFactory)dmeConn.getFactory(
13.        "javax.datamining.supervised.classification.ClassificationApplySetting");
14.    ClassificationApplySettings csApplySettings = csApplyFactory.create();
15.      //Use mapByCategory to get probability associated with the attriter value
16.    csApplySettings.mapByCategory(ClassificationApplyContent.probabity,
17.      "Attriter", "Probability");
18.    dmeConn.saveObject("category_attrition_apply_settings", csApplySettings,
19.      replaceExistingObject);
20.    RecordApplyTaskFactory csRecordApplyTaskFactory =
21.      (RecordApplyTaskFactory)dmeConn.getFactory(
22.        "javax.datamining.task.apply.RecordApplyTask");
23.    csRecordApplyTask =
```

```
24.        csApplyTaskFactory.create(
25.          customerProfile, "attrition_model", "attritionApplySettings");
26.      } else {
27.        csRecordApplyTask.setInputRecord(customerProfile);
28.      }
29.  dmeConn.execute(csRecordApplyTask, timeOut);
30.  PhysicalDataRecord outputRecord = csRecordApplyTask.getOutputRecord();
31.  return ((Number)outputRecord.getValue("Probability")).doubleValue();
32. }
```

9.5   Using Regression Interfaces

The *javax.datamining.supervised.regression* package contains regression function interfaces, such as *RegressionSettings*, *RegressionModel*, *RegressionApplySettings*, *RegressionTestMetrics*, etc. Regression interfaces are similar to classification interfaces in many ways. The main difference, however, is that *regression* predicts continuous values, whereas classification predicts discrete values. Hence, regression does not accept objects for cost matrix, target category set, or prior probabilities. All JDM-specified algorithms discussed for the classification can also be used for regression. However, in the case of the support vector machine (SVM) algorithm, due to variations between regression and classification JDM explicitly defines an algorithm settings interface called *SVMRegressionSettings*. This section illustrates the use of the regression-related interfaces by taking the prediction of the real-estate appraisal value example that was discussed in Section 7.2.

Table 9-17 lists all the regression-specific interface method details. Note that *RegressionSettings* doesn't have any regression-specific build settings. Even though there are no regression-specific settings, this interface is defined to be consistent with other build settings for future extensions. These setting do, however, inform the *BuildTask* object to build a regression model when executed. A *RegressionModel* object can return the *R-squared* error if the regression model validates the model either on the build data itself or using the validate data specified at build time. The *RegressionApplySettings* has only one *map* method through which a user can specify the desired apply content in the apply output table. The *RegressionApplyContent* allows users to specify content for the *predicted value* and the *prediction confidence*. The *RegressionTestMetrics* interface defines the get methods for various types of regression error measures that were discussed in Section 7.2.5. By extending the generic *supervised.TestMetricsTask*, the *RegressionTestMetricsTask* computes test metrics using an apply output table instead of a regression model.

Table 9-17   *Regression-related interfaces*

supervised.regression.RegressionSettings *extends supervised.SupervisedSettings*	
Methods	*Description*
None	

supervised.regression.RegressionModel *extends supervised.SupervisedModel*	
Methods	*Description*
getRSquared	*Returns the proportional reduction in the variability of the target associated with the predicted target values.*

supervised.regression.RegressionApplySettings *extends supervised.ApplySettings*	
Methods	*Description*
map(RegressionApplyContent content, String destPhysAttrName)	*Maps the specified generated value for the prediction to a destination attribute.*

supervised.regression.RegressionTestMetricsTask *extends supervised.TestMetrics*	
Methods	*Description*
None	

supervised.TestMetricsTask *extends task.Task*	
Methods	*Description*
set/getActualTargetAttrName(String)	*Used to set/get the attribute name of the actual targets in the apply output data.*
set/getApplyOutputDataName(String)	*Used to set/get the name of the apply output data.*
set/getPredictedTargetAttrName(String)	*Used to set/get the attribute name of the predicted targets in the apply output data.*
set/getPredictionRankingAttrName(String)	*Used to set/get the attribute name of the ranking factors for the predictions in the apply output data.*
set/getTestMetricsName(String)	*Used to set/get the name of the test metrics to be created as the result of test metrics task.*

supervised.RegressionTestMetrics *extends supervised.TestMetrics*	
Methods	*Description*
getMeanAbsoluteError():java.lang.Double	*Returns the mean absolute error of predictions.*
getMeanActualValue():java.lang.Double	*Returns the mean (i.e., average) actual target value.*
getMeanPredictedValue():java.lang.Double	*Returns the mean predicted target value.*

Table 9-17 *(continued)*

Methods	*Description*
getRMSError():java.lang.Double	*Returns the root mean sum of squared errors of predictions.*
getRSquared():java.lang.Double	*Returns proportional reduction in the variability of the target associated with the predicted target values.*

Listing 9-14 shows the code that builds the *appraisal_model*, computes test metrics named *appraisal_test_metrics*, and then applies the model that outputs the APPRAISAL_APPLY_OUTPUT table with the *appraisal value* predictions. The *input* method in lines 27 to 38 shows the creation and saving of input objects for model build. Similar to classification settings, regression settings require specification of the target attribute name. Line 36 sets the *appraisal value* attribute as the target attribute. Execution of the build task is the same as for classification, as shown in lines 69 to 71. After successful execution of the build task, the test metrics task is used to compute the regression test metrics. Section 9.4.4 introduced the test task for classification. Similarly, the *RegressionTestTask* can be used to compute *RegressionTestMetrics* using the model and test data as input.

In contrast, JDM also defines a *TestMetricsTask* that takes the apply output data computed using the test data as input instead of the model. This approach may be useful for data miners who want to keep the apply output results on test data for some other reasons, such as to compute additional tests to visualize the results.

Lines 74 to 89 show application of the *appraisal_model* on the APPRAISAL_TEST_DATA that produces the APPRAISAL_TEST_APPLY_OUTPUT dataset. Lines 90 to 101 show the execution of the *RegressionTestMetricsTask* that takes the *appraisal_test_apply_output* physical dataset object. The actual and predicted target value columns are the inputs that are used to produce the *appraisal_test_metrics* object. Lines 104 to 109 show the execution of the apply task that produces the APPRAISAL_APPLY_OUTPUT data with the target predictions. Apply using either a dataset for batch scoring or a record for real-time scoring is similar to that of classification. Lines 127 to 139 show the retrieval of the regression model and the regression test metrics from the DME. The regression model also has contents, such as model signature, model details, model version, and model metadata. Using the get methods of *RegressionTestMetrics*, users can retrieve the various types of prediction error measures computed by the test task. Note that vendor implementations can return null values for metrics they do not support.

Listing 9-14 *Regression example code*

```
1. public class RealEstateAppraisal {
2. //Data members
3. . . .
4. static RegressionSettingsFactory rgrFactory = null;
5. static RegressionApplySettingsFactory rgrApplySettingsFactory = null;
6.
7. . . .
8. static RegressionTestMetricsTaskFactory rttkFactory = null;
9.
10. //Main method
11. public static void main(String args[]) throws Exception {
12.    try {
13.    //Create DME connection as shown in Listing 9.1 or 9.2
14.    // . . .
15.    input(); //Create input objects
16.    if( run() ) //Execute model build task
17.      output(); //Retrieve the model
18.    } catch(Exception anyFailures) {anyFailures.printStackTrace();
19.    } finally {if(dmeConn != null) dmeConn.close(); //Close connection
20.    }
21. }
22.
23. //Create and save input objects
24. public static void input() throws JDMException {
25.    //Create Input object factories
26.      . . .
27.    rgrFactory = (RegressionSettingsFactory)dmeConn.getFactory(
28.    "javax.datamining.supervised.classification.RegressionSettings");
29.    rgrApplySettingsFactory = (RegressionApplySettingsFactory)dmeConn.getFactory(
30.    "javax.datamining.supervised.classification.RegressionApplySettings");
31.
32.    boolean replaceObject = true;
33.    //Input objects for building appraisal_model using appraisal_build_data dataset
34.    PhysicalDataSet pdsBuild = pdsFactory.create("appraisal_build_data", false );
35.    RegressionSettings regrSettings = rgrFactory.create();
36.    regrSettings.setTargetAttributeName("APPRAISAL_VALUE");
37.    dmeConn.saveObject("appraisal_build_data", pdsBuild, replaceObject);
38.    dmeConn.saveObject("appraisal_builds_settings", regrSettings, replaceObject);
39.
40.    //Input objects for testing appraisal_model using APPRAISAL_TEST_DATA dataset
41.    PhysicalDataSet pdsTest = pdsFactory.create("APPRAISAL_TEST_DATA", false );
42.    dmeConn.saveObject("appraisal_test_data", pdsTest, replaceExistingObject );
43.
44.    //Input objects for applying appraisal_model for appraisal_apply_data dataset
45.    PhysicalDataSet pdsApply = pdsFactory.create("appraisal_apply_data", false);
46.    dmeConn.saveObject( "appraisal_apply_data", pdsTest, replaceExistingObject );
47.    RegressionApplySettings regApplySettings = rgrApplySettingsFactory.create();
```

```
48.     //Save predicted value in the predicted_appraisal_value column
49.   regApplySettings.map(RegressionApplyContent.predictedValue,
50.                 "predicted_appraisal_value");
51.     //Carry forward loan id column
52.   Map sourceDestMap = new HashMap();
53.   sourceDestMap.put("loan_id","loan_id");
54.   dmeConn.saveObject( "appraisal_apply_settings", regApplySettings, true );
55. }
56.
57. //Create and execute tasks
58. public boolean run() throws JDMException {
59.     //Create task object factories
60.   btkFactory = (BuildTaskFactory)dmeConn.getFactory(
61.   "javax.datamining.task.BuildTask");
62.   atkFactory = (DataSetApplyTaskFactory)dmeConn.getFactory(
63.   "javax.datamining.task.apply.DataSetApplyTask");
64.   rttkFactory = (RegressionTestMetricsTaskFactory)dmeConn.getFactory(
65.       "javax.datamining.supervised.regrssion.RegressionTestMetricsTask");
66.   //Run until completion when timeout is set to null
67.   Long timeOut = null;
68.   //Create and run build task
69.   BuildTask btk = btkFactory.create( "appraisalBuildData",
70.                 "appraisal_build_settings", "appraisal_model" );
71.   ExecutionStatus buildStatus = dmeConn.execute( btk, timeOut );
72.   //If Build task is successful run test metrics task
73.   if( ExecutionState.success.equals( buildStatus.getState())) {
74.   //Apply on test data that produces the predicted appraisal value
75.   //along with the actual appraisal value from the test dataset
76.   RegressionApplySettings regTestApplySettings = rgrApplySettingsFactory.create();
77.     //Save predicted value in the predicted_appraisal_value column
78.   regTestApplySettings.map(RegressionApplyContent.predictedValue,
79.       "predicted_appraisal_value");
80.     //Carry forward actual appraisal_value column and loan id column
81.   Map sourceDestinationMap = new HashMap();
82.   sourceDestinationMap.put("loan_id","loan_id");
83.   sourceDestinationMap.put("appraisal_value","actual_appraisal_value");
84.   regTestApplySettings.setSourceDestinationMap(sourceDestinationMap);
85.   dmeConn.saveObject("appraisal_test_apply_settings", regTestApplySettings, true );
86.   DataSetApplyTask testApplyTask =
87.     atkFactory.create("appraisalTestData","appraisal_model",
88.       "appraisal_test_apply_settings", "APPRAISAL_TEST_APPLY_OUTPUT");
89.   ExecutionStatus testApplyStatus = dmeConn.execute( testApplyTask, timeOut);
90.   //If the apply task on test data is successful then run test metrics task
91.   if(ExecutionState.success.equals(testApplyStatus.getState())) {
92.   //Create Physical dataset for the test metrics task using the apply output data
93.   PhysicalDataSet pdsTestApply = pdsFactory.create(
94.             "APPRAISAL_TEST_APPLY_OUTPUT", false);
95.   dmeConn.saveObject("appraisal_test_apply_output", pdsTestApply, true);
96.
97.     //Regression Test Metrics task
98.   RegressionTestMetricsTask rttk = rttkFactory.create(
99.       "appraisal_test_apply_output", "actual_appraisal_value",
```

```
100.       "predicted_appraisal_value", "appraisal_test_metrics");
101.   ExecutionStatus testStatus = dmeConn.execute( rttk, timeOut );
102.   //If the test data is successful then run test metrics task
103.   if( ExecutionState.success.equals(testStatus.getState() ) ) {
104.   DataSetApplyTask applyTask =
105.    atkFactory.create( "appraisal_apply_data", "appraisal_model",
106.         "appraisal_test_apply_settings", "APPRAISAL_APPLY_OUTPUT" );
107.   ExecutionStatus applyStatus = dmeConn.execute( applyTask, timeOut );
108.   //If the apply task on test data is successful then run test metrics task
109.   if( ExecutionState.success.equals(applyStatus.getState() ) )
110.     return true;
111.   else
112.     return false;
113.   } else {
114.   System.out.println("Failed due to: " + testStatus.getDescription());
115.     return false;
116.   }} else {
117.   System.out.println("Failed due to: " + testApplyStatus.getDescription());
118.     return false;
119.   }}
120.   else {
121.       System.out.println("Failed due to: " + buildStatus.getDescription());
122.       return false;
123. }}
124.
125. //Retrieve built model and test metrics
126. public void output() throws JDMException {
127.   //Retrieve regression model
128.   RegressionModel regModel = (RegressionModel)dmeConn.retrieveObject(
129.   "appraisal_model", NamedObject.model );
130.   //Similar to classification model can retreive model signature and
131.   //details as shown in Listing 9.4.2
132.   . . .
133.   //Retrieve regression test metrics
134.   RegressionTestMetrics regTestMetrics =
135.    (RegressionTestMetrics)dmeConn.retrieveObject(
136.       "appraisal_test_metrics", NamedObject.testMetrics );
137.   System.out.println(regTestMetrics.getMeanAbsoluteError());
138.   System.out.println(regTestMetrics.getRMSError());
139.   System.out.println(regTestMetrics.getRSquared());
140. }}
```

9.6 Using Attribute Importance Interfaces

The *javax.datamining.attributeimportance* package contains attribute importance function-specific interfaces, such as *AttributeImportance-Settings* and *AttributeImportanceModel*. Table 9-18 lists the methods of these interfaces. Attribute importance interfaces are designed to support finding important attributes for both supervised and unsupervised mining functions. If the target attribute name is specified using

Table 9-18 *Attribute importance–related interfaces*

attributeimportance.AttributeImportanceSettings *extends base.BuildSettings*	
Methods	*Description*
set/getMaxAttributeCount(int maxCount)	*Used to set/get the maximum number of attributes to be included in the resulting model.*
set/getTargetAttributeName(String)	*Used to set/get the target attribute for supervised attribute importance.*
isSupervised():boolean	*Returns true if a target attribute has been set.*
attributeimportance.AttributeImportanceModel *extends base.Model*	
Methods	*Description*
getAttributesByPercentage(double percent, SortOrder ordering):Collection	*Returns a collection of attributes whose rank is within the specified percentage of the entire attributes.*
getAttributesByRank(int lowerRank, int upperRank):Collection	*Returns a collection of attributes whose rank is within the specified range.*
getAttributesByRank(SortOrder ordering): Collection	*Returns a collection of all attributes in the specified order.*
getMaxRank():int	*Returns the rank number of the least important attribute.*
getAttributeCount():int	*Returns the number of attributes ranked in the model.*

AttributeImportanceSettings.setTargetAttributeName(String), the DME will build a supervised attribute importance model. In this case, the model ranks the attributes according to their ability to predict the specified target attribute. The DME will build an unsupervised model if a target attribute is not specified. In this case, the model ranks attributes according to their contribution to the desired unsupervised model.

Listing 9-15 shows the code that builds an attribute importance model for the CUSTOMERS dataset to find the importance of predictor attributes used for predicting the *attrite* target attribute. Lines 28 and 29 show the creation of an *AttributeImportanceSettings* object and sets the target attribute to *attrite*.

In some domains, data may have thousands of attributes. For example, in gene analysis, thousands of gene types can be collected to find their effect on a particular disease; each type can be included as an attribute in the dataset. To reduce the size of the attribute importance model by filtering the attributes at the time of model building, users can specify the maximum number of attributes using the *AttributeImportanceSettings.setMaxAttributeCount(int)* method. In addition, after building the model, applications can filter the set of attributes further, either by the percentage of the important attributes using *AttributeImportanceModel.getAttributesByPercentage(double, Sort Order)* method, or by attribute rank range using the *AttributeImportanceModel.getAttributesByRank(int lowerRank, int upperRank)* method. Lines 55 to 69 show the retrieval of the *ai_model* that ranks the importance of the predictor attributes. The *get* methods of this model return the collection of *SignatureAttribute* objects that encapsulates the attribute details, such as name, type, data type, rank, and importance value. Lines 64 to 67 show the signature attribute usage.

Listing 9-15 *Select important attributes for building attrition_Model*

```
1.    public class SelectImportantAttributes {
2.    //Data members
3.    . . .
4.    static AttributeImportanceSettingsFactory aiSettingsFactory = null;
5.    . . .
6.    //Main method
7.    public static void main(String args[]) throws Exception {
8.      try {
9.      //Create DME connection as shown in Listing 9.1 or 9.2
10.     // . . .
11.       input(); //Create input objects
12.       if( run() ) //Execute model build task
13.         output(); //Retrieve the model
14.     } catch(Exception anyFailures) { anyFailures.printStackTrace();
15.     } finally { if(dmeConn != null) dmeConn.close(); //Close connection
16.   }}
17.
18.    //Create and save input objects
19.    public static void input() throws JDMException {
20.     //Create Input object factories
21.     . . .
22.     aiSettingsFactory = (AttributeImportanceSettingsFactory)dmeConn.getFactory(
23.     "javax.datamining.attributeimportance.AttributeImportanceSettings");
24.
25.     boolean replaceObject = true;
26.     //Input objects for building appraisal_model using appraisal_build_data dataset
27.     PhysicalDataSet pdsBuild = pdsFactory.create( "customers", false );
28.     AttributeImportanceSettings aiSettings = aiSettingsFactory.create();
29.     aiSettings.setTargetAttributeName("attrite");
30.     dmeConn.saveObject( "ai_build_data", pdsBuild, replaceObject);
31. dmeConn.saveObject( "ai_builds_settings", aiSettings, replaceObject);
32. }
33.
```

```
34.    //Create and execute tasks
35.    public boolean run() throws JDMException {
36.      //Create task object factories
37.      btkFactory = (BuildTaskFactory)dmeConn.getFactory(
38.      "javax.datamining.task.BuildTask");
39.      //Run until completion when timeout is set to null
40.      Long timeOut = null;
41.      //Create and run build task
42.      BuildTask btk = btkFactory.create("ai_build_data",
43.                      "ai_build_settings", "ai_model");
44.      ExecutionStatus buildStatus = dmeConn.execute( btk, timeOut );
45.      //If Build task is successful run test metrics task
46.      if( ExecutionState.success.equals( buildStatus.getState() ) )
47.         return true;
48.       else
49.         return false;
50.     }
51.
52.    //Retrieve built model and test metrics
53.    public void output() throws JDMException {
54.      //Retrieve regression model
55.      AttributeImportanceModel ai_model =
56.      (AttributeImportanceModel)dmeConn.retrieveObject("ai_model",NamedObject.model);
57.      //List attributes in the descending order of importance and display rank and
58.      //importance value
59.      Collection impAttrs = ai_model.getAttributesByRank(SortOrder.descending);
60.      Iterator impAttrsIterator = impAttrs.iterator();
61.      SignatureAttribute attr = null;
62.      System.out.println("AttributeName    Rank    Importance Value");
63.      while(impAttrsIterator.hasNext()) {
64.       attr = (SignatureAttribute)impAttrsIterator.next();
65.       String attrName = attr.getName();
66.       int rank = attr.getRank();
67.       double importanceValue = attr.getImportanceValue();
68.        System.out.println(attrName + " " + rank + " " + importanceValue);
69.     }
70. }}
```

9.7 Using Association Interfaces

The *javax.datamining.association* package contains *association* function interfaces, such as *AssociationSettings, AssociationModel, AssociationRule, RulesFilter,* etc. JDM defines interfaces to build the association model and retrieve the contents of the model. The *AssociationSettings* interface provides the model settings to control model contents by filtering criteria such as minimum rule support, confidence, maximum rule length, and items to be included or excluded. The *AssociationModel* interface provides methods to retrieve model contents, such as rules, items, and itemsets, using different types of filters.

Note that JDM does not have any algorithm-specific model details defined for the association function since the model contents are considered general enough for most algorithms. Table 9-19 shows the list of association-related interfaces and their methods.

Table 9-19 *Association-related interfaces*

association.AssociationSettings *extends base.BuildSettings*	
Methods	*Description*
get/add/removeItem (Object item, boolean included))	*Used to get/add/remove an item from/to the list of items to be excluded from (if included flag is false) or included in (if true) the frequent itemset building.*
get/add/removeItems (Object[] items, boolean included))	*Used to get/add/remove an items from/to the list of items to be excluded when building the frequent itemsets (if included flag is false), or included when building the frequent itemsets (if true).*
set/getMinSupport(double support)	*Used to set/get the minimum support allowed for any generated rule.*
set/getMinConfidence (double confidence)	*Used to set/get the minimum confidence allowed for any generated rule.*
set/getMaxNumberRules(int maxRules)	*Used to set/get the maximum number of rules to be included in the model.*
set/getMaxRuleLength(int maxLength)	*Used to set/get the maximum number of items in a rule.*
set/getMaxRuleComponentLength (int maxLength, boolean isAntecedent)	*Used to set/get the maximum number of items in a rule component. The isAntecedent boolean flag is used to indicate the antecedent (if* true*) or consequent (if* false*)*
set/getTaxonomyName (String attributeName, String taxonomyName)	*Used to set/get the name of the Taxonomy object to be used for the specified attribute.*
association.AssociationModel *extends base.Model*	
Methods	*Description*
getAverageTransactionSize():Double	*Returns the average number of items in the transactions in the build data used when building the model.*
getItems():Collection	*Returns a collection of all items used to build the model that can be used to sequentially fetch items that occur in at least one rule in the model.*
getItemsets():Collection	*Returns a collection of all itemsets found that can be used to sequentially fetch the itemsets that occur in at least one rule in the model.*

Table 9-19 *(continued)*

Methods	Description
getItemsets(int itemsetSize): Collection	*Constructs and returns a collection of the itemsets of the specified size that allows sequential inspection of the generated itemsets of the given size.*
getMaxAbsoluteSupport(): int	*Returns the maximum support value of the rules contained in the model.*
getMinAbsoluteSupport(): int	*Returns the minimum support value of the rules contained in the model.*
getMaxConfidence(): Double	*Returns the maximum confidence value of the rules contained in the model.*
getMaxRuleLength(): int	*Returns the largest rule length in terms of the number of items.*
getMaxTransactionSize(): int	*Returns the number of items in the largest transaction in the build data used when building the model.*
getMinConfidence(): Double	*Returns the minimum confidence value of the rules contained in the model.*
getNumberOfItems(): int	*Returns the number of distinct items in the build data used when building the model.*
getNumberOfItemsets(): int	*Returns the number of itemsets whose support values are equal to or exceed the support threshold specified in the AssociationRulesSettings used when building the model.*
getNumberOfTransactions(): long	*Returns the number of transactions used to build the model.*
getRules(): Collection	*Constructs and returns a collection of all rules in the model that allows sequential inspection of the generated rules.*
getRules(RulesFilter filter): Collection	*Constructs and returns a collection of model rules as filtered by the specified filter.*

association.AssociationRule	
Methods	**Description**
getAbsoluteSupport(): int	*Returns the support for the given association rule in terms of absolute count of transactions supporting this rule.*
getAntecedent(): Itemset	*Returns the antecedent of the association rule.*
getConsequent (): Itemset	*Returns the consequent of the association rule.*
getSupport (): double	*Returns the support for the given association as a percentage of the total number of transactions. The percentage is a number between 0 and 100, denoted as (0,100] where 100 is included.*

Table 9-19   *Association-related interfaces (continued)*

Methods	*Description*
getConfidence(): double	*Returns the confidence for the given association rule as the total number of transactions with antecedent and consequent divided by the number of transactions with the antecedent as a percentage. The percentage is a number between 0 and 100, denoted as (0,100] where 100 is included.*
getLift(): double	*Returns the lift for the given association rule defined as the number of transactions with the confidence of the rule divided by the number of transactions with the consequent.*
getLength(): int	*Returns the number of items in the rule, which includes both antecedent and consequent itemsets.*

association.RuleFilter

Methods	*Description*
set/getItems(Object[] itemArray, RuleComponentOption componentOption, boolean included)	*Used to set/get the items to be included in the specified component of the rules to be selected.*
set/getMaxNumberOfRules (int maxRules)	*Used to set/get the maximum number of rules for the result.*
set/getOrderingCondition (RuleProperty[] orderByArray, SortOrder[] sortOrderArray)	*Used to set/get the ordering condition for the rules after they are filtered.*
set/getRange(RuleProperty type, double minValue, double maxValue)	*Used to set/get the range of the specified rule property. Rule property can be antecedent, consequent or both.*
set/getThreshold (RuleProperty property, ComparisonOperator compOp, double thresholdValue)	*Used to set/get the threshold value with a comparison operator. Rule property can be antecedent, consequent or both. ComparisonOperator enumerates various operators, such as =, <, >, <=, >=, != etc.*
set/getOrderingCondition (RuleProperty[] orderByArray, SortOrder[] sortOrderArray)	*Used to set/get the ordering condition for the rules after they are filtered.*

Listing 9-16 shows the building of an association model that finds the products that are sold together based on customer purchase data. Lines 27 to 35 show the creation of a physical dataset object using a transactional format table. Lines 37 to 41 show the creation of association settings that specify the minimum support, confidence, maximum length, and maximum number of rules. Lines 49 to 61 show the execution of the build task, which is similar to other models. Lines 67 to 104 show retrieving the model and its contents using different filters and displaying the rules. The *association.RulesFilter* interface provides multiple filtering and sorting capabilities for selecting subsets of model rules. Typically, association models contain a large number of rules (tens or hundreds of thousands). Consequently, applications need a powerful and flexible filtering mechanism to obtain the rules of interest. Lines 72 to 79 show the creation of the rules filter to obtain rules with support and confidence greater than 0.5 and to order those rules in descending order of the confidence and support. Lines 81 to 85 show another type of rules filter used to obtain rules with antecedent item "savings account" and consequent item "certificate account." Lines 87 and 88 show rules retrieval that satisfies these two filtering criteria. Lines 87 to 105 show how to display the retrieved rules; this highlights several *AssociationRule* interface methods.

Listing 9-16 *Build Association model to discover product associations*

```
1. public class CrossSellProducts {
2.    //Data members
3.    . . .
4.    static AssociationSettingsFactory arSettingsFactory = null;
5.    . . .
6.    //Main method
7.    public static void main(String args[]) throws Exception {
8.      try {
9.      //Create DME connection as shown in Listing 9.1 or 9.2
10.     // . . .
11.      input(); //Create input objects
12.      if( run() ) //Execute model build task
13.        output(); //Retrieve the model
14.      } catch(Exception anyFailures) { anyFailures.printStackTrace();
15.      } finally { if(dmeConn != null) dmeConn.close(); //Close connection
16.    }}
17.
18.    //Create and save input objects
19.    public static void input() throws JDMException {
20.      //Create Input object factories
21.      . . .
22.      arSettingsFactory = (AssociationSettingsFactory)dmeConn.getFactory(
23.      "javax.datamining.association.AssociationSettings");
24.
25.      boolean replaceObject = true;
26.      //Input objects for building appraisal_model using appraisal_build_data dataset
27.      PhysicalDataSet pdsBuild = pdsFactory.create( "product_transactions", false );
28.      PhysicalAttribute[] transactionalAttrs = new PhysicalAttribute[3];
29.      transactionalAttrs[0] = psFactory.create("CustomerId",
30.               AttributeDataType.integerType, PhysicalAttributeRole.caseId);
```

```
31.    transactionalAttrs[1] = psFactory.create("Product Name",
32.                AttributeDataType.stringType, PhysicalAttributeRole.attributeName);
33.    transactionalAttrs[2] = psFactory.create("Amount Range",
34.                AttributeDataType.stringType, PhysicalAttributeRole.attributeValue);
35.    pdsBuild.addAttributes(transactionalAttrs);
36.
37.    AssociationSettings arSettings = arSettingsFactory.create();
38.    arSettings.setMinConfidence(0.2);
39.    arSettings.setMinSupport(0.2);
40.    arSettings.setMaxRuleLength(10);
41.    arSettings.setMaxNumberOfRules(100000);
42.    dmeConn.saveObject( "ar_build_data", pdsBuild, replaceObject);
43.    dmeConn.saveObject( "ar_build_settings", arSettings, replaceObject);
44. }
45.
46. //Create and execute tasks
47. public boolean run() throws JDMException {
48.    //Create task object factories
49.    btkFactory = (BuildTaskFactory)dmeConn.getFactory(
50.    "javax.datamining.task.BuildTask");
51.    //Run until completion when timeout is set to null
52.    Long timeOut = null;
53.    //Create and run build task
54.    BuildTask btk = btkFactory.create( "ar_build_data",
55.                "ar_build_settings", "ar_model" );
56.    ExecutionStatus buildStatus = dmeConn.execute( btk, timeOut );
57.    //If Build task is successful run test metrics task
58.    if( ExecutionState.success.equals( buildStatus.getState() ) )
59.      return true;
60.    else
61.      return false;
62. }
63.
64. //Retrieve built model and test metrics
65. public void output() throws JDMException {
66.    //Retrieve regression model
67.    AssociationModel arModel =
68.      (AssociationModel)dmeConn.retrieveObject("ar_model",NamedObject.model);
69.    //Create a rules filter object that filters the rules that have specified range of
70.    //support and confidence. In addition filter can specify the sort order of the
71.    //rules.
72.    RulesFilterFactory rulesFilterFactory = dmeConn.getFactory(
73.      "javax.datamining.association.RulesFilter");
74.    RulesFilter filterByConfidenceSupport = rulesFilterFactory.create();
75.    filterByConfidenceSupport.setRange(RuleProperty.confidence, 0.5, 1.0);
76.    filterByConfidenceSupport.setRange(RuleProperty.support, 0.5, 1.0);
77.    filterByConfidenceSupport.setOrderingCondition(
78.    new RuleProperty[] { RuleProperty.confidence, RuleProperty.support },
79.    new SortOrder[]    { SortOrder.descending,    SortOrder.descending } );
80.    //Create another filter that filters by items in antecedent and consequent
```

```
81.   RulesFilter filterByItems = filterByItems.create();
82.   filterByItems.setItems(new Object[] { "Savings Account" },
83.       RuleComponentOption.antecedent, true );
84.   filterByItems.setItems(new Object[] { "Certificate Account" },
85.       RuleComponentOption.consequent, true );
86.   //Get filtered rules
87.   Collection rulesByConfidenceSupport = arModel.getRules(filterByConfidence Support);
88.   Collection rulesByItems = arModel.getRules(filterByItems);
89.   //Iterate and display rules by items
90.   Iterator rulesByItemsIterator = rulesByItems.iterator();
91.   while(rulesByItemsIterator.hasNext()) {
92.    AssociationRule arRule = (AssociationRule)rulesByItemsIterator.next();
93.    ItemSet arRule.getItemSet();
94.    ItemSet antecedentItemSet = arRule.getAntecedent();
95.    ItemSet consequentItemSet = arRule.getConsequent();
96.    Object[] antecedentItems = antecedentItemSet.getItems();
97.    Object[] consequentItems = consequentItemSet.getItems();
98.   //Display rule contents
99.   System.out.print("\n Rule-" + arRule.getRuleIdentifier() + ": IF");
100.     for(int i=0; i < antecedentItems.length; i++)
101.    System.out.print(antecedentItems[i].toString() + " ");
102.   System.out.print(" THEN ");
103.       for(int j=0; j < consequentItems.length; j++)
104.    System.out.print(consequentItems[j].toString() + " ");
105. }} }
```

9.8 Using Clustering Interfaces

The *javax.datamining.clustering* package contains clustering function interfaces, such as *ClusteringSettings*, *ClusteringModel*, *Cluster*, and *ClusteringApplySettings*. Table 9-20 shows the clustering-related interface methods. *ClusteringSettings* provides various set methods for users to select the aggregation function, attribute comparison function, maximum number of model clusters, maximum and minimum size of clusters allowed, etc. As a descriptive model, a clustering model allows users to examine its contents. The *ClusteringModel* interface provides methods to retrieve clusters, rules, and if it is a hierarchical cluster model, the hierarchical structure. Table 9-20 shows the list of methods in *ClusteringModel*.

The *Cluster* interface provides methods to retrieve cluster-specific details such as cluster id, name, attribute statistics, and number of cases that substantiate the cluster. For hierarchical cluster models, users can retrieve the cluster children, parent, and ancestors. Similar to supervised models, clustering models can be applied to assign apply data cases to the most closely matching cluster. The *Clustering ApplySettings* object provides several *map* methods, as shown in

Table 9-20, to specify apply output contents. Similar to classification, clustering apply has methods: *mapTopCluster*—maps apply contents to the top cluster, *mapByRank*—maps apply contents to the clusters by the specified rank, *mapByClusterIdentifier*—maps apply contents to the specified clusters, and *mapClusters*—maps apply contents to all clusters.

Table 9-20 *Clustering-related interfaces*

clustering.ClusteringSettings *extends base.BuildSettings*	
Methods	*Description*
set/getAggregationFunction(AggregationFunction function)	*Used to set/get the aggregation function to be used.*
set/getAttributeComparison-Function(String logicalAttribute-Name,AttributeComparisonFunction function)	*Used to set/get the attribute comparison function to be used.*
set/getMaxNumberOfClusters(int maxClusters)	*Used to set/get the maximum number of clusters allowed in the model.*
set/getMinClusterCaseCount(long minCaseCount)	*Used to set/get the minimum number of cases allowed per cluster.*
set/getMaxLevels(int numberOfLevels)	*Used to set/get the maximum level, or hierarchy depth, for hierarchical clustering.*
set/getSimilarityMatrix(String logicalAttributeName, SimilarityMatrix matrix)	*Used to set/get the similarity values to be used for the specified attribute. The SimilarityMatrix represents the similarity values between attribute values.*
clustering.ClusteringModel *extends base.Model*	
Methods	*Description*
getClusters(): Collection	*Returns the collection of Cluster objects in the clustering model.*
getLeafClusters(): Collection	*Returns the collection of leaf Cluster objects in the clustering model.*
getNumberOfClusters(): int	*Returns the number of clusters in the model.*
getCluster(int identifier): Cluster	*Returns the Cluster object in the model with the specified identifier.*
getNumberOfLevels(): int	*Returns the number of levels in the ClusteringModel.*
getRootClusters(): Collection	*Returns a collection of the root clusters of the Clustering-Model.*
getRules(): Collection	*Returns a collection of the rules from the clustering model.*

Table 9-20   *(continued)*

Methods	Description
getSimilarity(int clusterIdentifier1, int clusterIdentifier2): Double	*Returns the similarity of two clusters represented as a value between 0 and 1.*
hasProperty(ClusteringModelProperty property): boolean	*Returns true if the specified property is supported by the clustering model. ClusteringModelProperty is an enumeration of properties, such as centroid, hierarchy, cluster rules, attribute statistics etc.*

clustering.Cluster

Methods	Description
getClusterId(): int	*Returns the cluster identifier.*
getCaseCount(): long	*Returns the number of cases from the build data assigned to the cluster during the model build, inclusive of children counts.*
getName(): String	*Returns the name of the cluster designated by the clustering algorithm.*
getStatistics(): AttributeStatisticsSet	*Returns the AttributeStatisticsSet object that characterizes the cases assigned to the cluster.*
getRule(): Rule	*Returns the cluster rule.*
getCentroidCoordinate (java.lang.String numericalAttribute-Name): Double	*Returns the center point of the specified numerical attribute for the cluster.*
getCentroidCoordinate (java.lang.String categoricalAttribute-Name, java.lang.Object category): java.lang.Double	*Returns the center point of the specified categorical attribute for a specific category value for the cluster.*
getSupport(): double	*Returns the support defined as a percentage of cases assigned to this cluster relative to the total number of cases in the build data.*
getLevel(): int	*Returns the level in the clustering hierarchy associated with the Cluster object.*
getAncestors(): Cluster[]	*Returns the ancestors of the cluster.*
getChildren(): Cluster[]	*Returns an array of Cluster objects that are children of the cluster node.*
getParent(): Cluster	*Returns the parent of the cluster.*
getSplitPredicate(): Predicate	*Returns a Predicate object that stores information on how cases are assigned to the cluster node's children.*

Table 9-20 *Clustering-related interfaces (continued)*

Methods	Description
isLeaf(): boolean	*Returns true if the cluster is a leaf node in a hierarchical clustering model and false if it is an internal node.*
isRoot(): boolean	*Returns true if the cluster is a root node in a hierarchical clustering model and false if it is an internal node.*

clustering.ClusteringApplySettings *extends task.apply.ApplySettings*

Methods	Description
mapTopCluster(ClusteringApplyContent content, String destPhysAttrName)	*Maps the cluster with the highest prediction metric to appear in the apply output under the specified attribute name. After task completion, apply output data contains the specified apply contents associated with the top cluster. For example, when a user calls the following method, the apply task will compute the top prediction value and populate* topPrediction *column with the computed prediction value.* mapTopCluster (ClusteringApplyContent.clusterIdentifier,"topCluster")
mapByRank(ClusteringApplyContent content, String[] destPhysAttrNameArray, boolean fromTop)	*Maps the specified generated values for the predictions with the specified ranks to an array of destination attributes. Used to specify the prediction rank based apply contents for the apply task. The number and order of ranks depends on the size of the* destPhysAttrNameArray *and* fromTop *boolean value. For example, when a user calls the following method, the apply task will compute the top two clusters and populate columns* Top_1_Cluster *and* Top_2_Cluster *with the appropriate cluster ids. A user can call this method multiple times with different types of apply contents to obtain additional information.* mapByRank(ClusteringApplyContent.clusterIdentifier, new String[] { "Top_1_Cluster", "Top_2_Cluster" }, true)
mapByClusterIdentifier(ClusteringApplyContent content, int clusterIdentifier, String destinationAttrName)	*Maps the specified content value for the specified cluster identifier to the named destination attribute. For example, when a user calls the following methods, the apply task will compute the probabilities associated with clusters 1 and 2 and populate the probability values in the specified columns i.e., cluster_1_probability and cluster_2_probability.* mapByClusterIdentifier (ClusteringApplyContent. probability, "1", "Cluster_1_Probability"); mapByClusterIdentifier (ClusteringApplyContent. probability, "2", "Cluster_2_Probability");

Table 9-20   *(continued)*

mapClusters(
  ClusteringApplyContent content,
  String baseDestPhysAttrName)
	Maps all clusters in the model and the specified content value to a set of named destination attributes. When this method is used, the apply output data will have apply contents for all the leaf clusters. The base attribute name specified by the user will be used to generate the columns in the apply output data. For example, when a user calls the following methods where the input model has four leaf clusters i.e.,{ 1, 2, ,3 ,4 }, the apply task creates apply output data with columns ClusterId_1, ClusterId_2, ClusterId_3, ClusterId_4, Probability_1, Probability_2, Probability_3, Probability_4. The column Probability_1 has the probability value associated with the cluster id value in column ClusterId_1. Similarly, the other columns will have cluster ids and associated probabilities.

> mapClusters
>   (ClusteringApplyContent.clusterIdentifier,
>   "ClusterId");
>
> mapClusters
>   (ClusteringApplyContent..probability,
>   "Probability");

Listing 9-17 shows the code that illustrates the use of clustering interfaces for the customer segmentation problem discussed in Section 7.5. Lines 34 to 41 show the creation of the clustering settings object that specifies the aggregation function as *euclidean* and the attribute comparison function for age attribute as *absolute difference* in values. All other attributes use the DME's default attribute comparison function. In addition, the maximum number of clusters is specified as 50 and the cluster case count must be between 500 and 100,000 cases. Building this *segmentModel* is similar to building the other types of models, as shown from lines 69 to 71. Once the *segmentModel* is built, we apply this model to the apply input data to find the most probable cluster id using the *ClusterApplySettings.mapTopCluster* method. Lines 47 to 53 show the creation of the apply settings object and lines 74 to 79 show the execution of the dataset (batch) apply task. Similar to classification and regression, clustering models can also support real-time single record apply operations. Lines 95 to 119 show retrieving the clustering model and each cluster's details. In this example, we show retrieving the *age* attribute statistics details such as frequencies and how applications can obtain further cluster details from the model.

Listing 9-17 *Clustering example code*

```
1.  public class CustomerSegmentation {
2.    /Data members
3.    . . .
4.    static ClusteringSettingsFactory clusFactory = null;
5.    static ClusteringApplySettingsFactory clusApplySettingsFactory = null;
6.
7.    . . .
8.
9.    //Main method
10.    public static void main(String args[]) throws Exception {
11.      try {
12.      //Create DME connection as shown in Listing 9.1 or 9.2
13.      // . . .
14.          input(); //Create input objects
15.        if( run() ) //Execute model build and apply task
16.          output(); //Retrieve the model
17.      } catch(Exception anyFailures) { anyFailures.printStackTrace();
18.      } finally { if(dmeConn != null) dmeConn.close(); //Close connection
19.      }
20.    }
21.
22.    //Create and save input objects
23.    public static void input() throws JDMException {
24.      //Create Input object factories
25.      . . .
26.      clusSettingsFactory = (ClusteringSettingsFactory)dmeConn.getFactory(
27.      "javax.datamining.clustering.ClusteringSettings");
28.      clusApplySettingsFactory = (ClusteringApplySettingsFactory)dmeConn.getFactory(
29.      "javax.datamining.clustering.ClusteringApplySettings");
30.
31.      boolean replaceObject = true;
32.      //Input objects for building appraisal_model using appraisal_build_data dataset
33.      PhysicalDataSet pdsBuild = pdsFactory.create( "CUSTOMERS_BUILD_DATA ", false);
34.      ClusteringSettings cluSettings = cluSettingsFactory.create();
35.      cluSettings.setAggregationFunction(AggregationFunction.euclidean);
36.      cluSettings.setAttributeComparisonFunction("age"
37.          ,AttributeComparisonFunction.absDiff);
38.      cluSettings.setMaxNumberOfClusters(50);
39.      cluSettings.setMaxClusterCaseCount(100000);
40.      cluSettings.setMinClusterCaseCount(500);
41.      dmeConn.saveObject("segment_build_data", pdsBuild, replaceObject);
42.      dmeConn.saveObject("segment_builds_settings", cluSettings, replaceObject);
43.
44.      //Input objects for applying segmentModel for CUSTOMERS_APPLY_DATA dataset
45.      PhysicalDataSet pdsApply = pdsFactory.create("CUSTOMERS_APPLY_DATA", false);
46.      dmeConn.saveObject("segment_apply_data", pdsTest, replaceExistingObject);
47.      ClusteringApplySettings clusApplySettings = clusApplySettingsFactory.create();
48.        //Save predicted value in the predicted_appraisal_value column
49.      clusApplySettings.mapTopCluster(ClusteringApplyContent.clusteridentifier,
```

```
50.                     "segment_id");
51.       //Carry forward customer id column
52.       Map sourceDestMap = new HashMap();
53.       sourceDestMap.put("cust_id","Customer id");
54.       clusApplySettings.setSourceDestinationMap(sourceDestMap);
55.       dmeConn.saveObject( "segmentApplySettings", clusApplySettings, true);
56.     }
57.
58.     //Create and execute tasks
59.     public boolean run() throws JDMException {
60.       //Create task object factories
61.       btkFactory = (BuildTaskFactory)dmeConn.getFactory(
62.       "javax.datamining.task.BuildTask");
63.       atkFactory = (DataSetApplyTaskFactory)dmeConn.getFactory(
64.       "javax.datamining.task.apply.DataSetApplyTask");
65.
66.       //Run until completion when timeout is set to null
67.       Long timeOut = null;
68.       //Create and run build task
69.       BuildTask btk = btkFactory.create("segment_build_data",
70.                       "segment_build_settings", "segment_model");
71.       ExecutionStatus buildStatus = dmeConn.execute(btk, timeOut);
72.       //If Build task is successful run apply task
73.       if(ExecutionState.success.equals( buildStatus.getState())) {
74.       DataSetApplyTask applyTask =
75.         atkFactory.create( "segment_apply_data", "segment_model",
76.             "segment_apply_settings", "segment_apply_output");
77.       ExecutionStatus applyStatus = dmeConn.execute(applyTask, timeOut);
78.       //If the apply task on test data is successful then run test metrics task
79.       if( ExecutionState.success.equals(applyStatus.getState()))
80.       return true;
81.       else
82.       return false;
83.       } else {
84.       System.out.println("Failed due to: " + testApplyStatus.getDescription());
85.       return false;
86.       }}
87.       else {
88.          System.out.println("Failed due to: " + buildStatus.getDescription());
89.          return false;
90.     }}
91.
92.       //Retrieve built model and test metrics
93.       public void output() throws JDMException {
94.       //Retrieve regression model
95.       ClusteringModel clusModel = (ClusteringModel)dmeConn.retrieveObject(
96.       "segment_model", NamedObject.model );
97.       //Get clusters
98.       Collection clusters = clusModel.getLeafClusters();
99.       Iteraor clusterIterator = clusters.iterator();
100.       while(clusterIterator.hasNext()) {
```

```
101.        //Display cluster details
102.        Cluster c = (Cluster)clusterIterator.next();
103.        System.out.println("Cluster: " + c.getClusterId());
104.        System.out.println("Number of cases: " + c.getCaseCount());
105.        //Display age attribute details of the cluster
106.        Double centroidValue = c. getCentroidCoordinate("age");
107.        System.out.println("CentroidCoordinate for Age attribute: "
108.                + centroidValue.toString());
109.        AttributeStatisticsSet clusterAttrStatitics = c.getStatistics();
110.        UnivariateStatitics ageAttrStatistics =
111.                        clusterAttrStatitics.getStatistics("age");
112.    if(ageAttrStatistics != null) {
113.     System.out.println("Age attribute values distribution:");
114.     Object[] ageValues = ageAttrStatistics.getValues();
115.     long[] frequencies = ageAttrStatistics.getFrequencies();
116.     for(int i=0; i< ageValues.length; i++)
117.      System.out.println("Age:" + ageValues[I].toString() + " -> Frequency " +
118.          frequencies[i]);
119. }}}}
```

9.9 Summary

JDM provides a comprehensive API to build data mining solutions and tools. JDM provides an API to build, apply, test, and describe models. Vendors can easily extend the standard API to add more implementation-specific non-JDM standard functions, algorithms, and settings. The Connection interface provides methods for interacting with the DME, such as saving and exploring mining objects, and executing mining tasks. Data specification interfaces provide various types of data description capabilities and function and algorithm level settings specification. JDM supports specifying minimal settings for mining operations via simple object representations and DME defaults. JDM also supports highly customized settings with options for detailed DME control. For descriptive models, JDM provides the function and algorithm-specific model details that applications can retrieve and present to the user. For supervised and clustering models, the apply task can produce apply outputs for multi-record or single-record data, supporting batch and real-time applications, respectively. Test metrics can be computed to evaluate the quality of supervised models.

References

[JDM11 2006] Java Data Mining 1.1 specification and API Java documentation, http://jcp.org/aboutJava/communityprocess/mrel/jsr073

[J2EE Tutorial 2006] J2EE 1.4 Tutorial, http://java.sun.com/j2ee/1.4/docs/tutorial/doc

[IEM 2004] Data Mining for the Masses by Seth Grimes available at http://www.intelligententerprise.com/showArticle.jhtml?articleID=21400394

Chapter

10

XML Schema

We now have 80% of data living in the messy horror world of proprietary formats. If those 80% are taken over by XML, that's a big step forward.

—Alexander Jerusalem on the *XML Developers* mailing list

Extensible Markup Language (XML) is becoming the ubiquitous choice for data representation in a machine-readable format and for data exchange [W3CXML 2006]. An XML Schema provides mechanisms to define and describe the structure, content, and to some extent semantics of XML documents [W3CXML-SCHEMA 2006].

In Java Data Mining (JDM), we defined an XML Schema for JDM objects to complement the Java application programming interface (API) and provide a standards-based data model. JDM XML Schema definitions supported multiple uses, such as interchanging data mining objects among data mining engines (DMEs), defining Web services, storing data mining objects as XML documents, and integrating JDM implementations with non-Java applications. Readers of this chapter are expected to be familiar with XML and XML Schema concepts [Ray 2003].

This chapter provides an overview of the JDM Schema, the structure of JDM-compliant XML documents, JDM Schema complex types, use cases for XML Schema, and lastly, how the JDM Schema complements the Predictive Model Markup Language [DMG-PMML

2006]. Throughout this chapter, we refer to the *JDM XML Schema* as the *JDM Schema* and a *JDM XML document* as a *JDM document*.

10.1   Overview

Chapters 8 and 9 introduced various JDM objects. Most of these objects were defined as Java interfaces that define associated methods but no data members. The JDM standard uses an interface-based approach to provide data mining vendors greater flexibility when implementing JDM functionality. However, the lack of a standard data model causes interoperability issues for exchanging JDM objects between implementations. The JDM Schema fills this gap by defining a standard data model using XML for JDM objects. For example, the *javax.datamining.MiningObject* interface has a corresponding complex type called *MiningObject* that defines a data model, as shown in Listing 10-1. Note that each element and attribute defined in this complex type has a corresponding *get* method defined in the *javax.datamining.MiningObject* interface. Similarly, all other JDM API interfaces and classes have an associated JDM Schema type.

Listing 10-1   *JDM Schema MiningObject complexType*

```
<xsd:complexType name="MiningObject">
  <xsd:sequence>
    <xsd:element name="description" type="xsd:string" minOccurs="0"/>
  </xsd:sequence>
  <xsd:attribute name="name" type="xsd:string" use="optional"/>
  <xsd:attribute name="type" type="NamedObjectType" use="optional"/>
  <xsd:attribute name="creatorInfo" type="xsd:string" use="optional"/>
  <xsd:attribute name="creationDate" type="xsd:date" use="optional"/>
  <xsd:attribute name="objectIdentifier" type="xsd:string" use="optional"/>
</xsd:complexType>
```

10.2   Schema Elements

The JDM Schema's elements structure is fairly simple. Listing 10-2 illustrates the JDM Schema snippet that defines the element structure and related complex types. In Line 1, we specify the namespace used for the JDM Schema, *http://www.jsr-73.org/2004/JDMSchema*. This namespace includes the Java Specification Request (JSR) number and the release year of the standard to uniquely identify the major releases of the JDM Schema. For JDM maintenance releases, the namespace will not be changed, because the changes are limited to simple fixes. Currently, this JDM Schema is not hosted on the Internet at the specified namespace; applications have to access this schema by downloading it from [JDM11 2006]. Line 2 of Listing 10-2 shows the root element called *JDM*. The *JDM* element can have children as one *header* element (line 3) and multiple *object* elements (line 4). The *header*

Listing 10-2 *JDM Schema elements*

```
1. <xsd:schema xmlns:xsd="http://www.w3.org/2001/XMLSchema"
           xmlns="http://www.jsr-73.org/2004/JDMSchema"
           targetNamespace="http://www.jsr-73.org/2004/JDMSchema"
           elementFormDefault="qualified">
2.    <xsd:element name="JDM">
         <xsd:complexType>
           <xsd:sequence>
3.            <xsd:element name="header" type="Header"/>
4.            <xsd:element name="object" type="NamedObject" minOccurs="0"
                      maxOccurs="unbounded"/>
           </xsd:sequence>
5.         <xsd:attribute name="version" type="xsd:string" use="required"/>
         </xsd:complexType>
      </xsd:element>

6.   <xsd:complexType name="Header">
       <xsd:sequence>
         <xsd:element name="copyright" type="xsd:string" minOccurs="0"/>
         <xsd:element name="timestamp" type="xsd:date" minOccurs="0"/>
         <xsd:element name="applicationName" type="xsd:string" minOccurs="0"/>
         <xsd:element name="applicationVersion" type="xsd:string" minOccurs="0"/>
         <xsd:element name="description" type="xsd:string" minOccurs="0"/>
       </xsd:sequence>
     </xsd:complexType>

7. <xsd:complexType name="NamedObject">
      <xsd:sequence>
        <xsd:choice>
           <xsd:element name="task" type="Task"/>
           <xsd:element name="buildSettings" type="BuildSettings"/>
           <xsd:element name="model" type="Model"/>
           <xsd:element name="logicalData" type="LogicalData"/>
           <xsd:element name="physicalDataSet" type="PhysicalDataSet"/>
           <xsd:element name="testMetrics" type="TestMetrics"/>
           <xsd:element name="taxonomy" type="Taxonomy"/>
           <xsd:element name="costMatrix" type="CostMatrix"/>
           <xsd:element name="applySettings" type="ApplySettings"/>
        </xsd:choice>
      </xsd:sequence>
    </xsd:complexType>

    . . .  JDM complexTypes . . .
    </xsd:schema>
```

element is of type *Header* (line 6) and encapsulates the optional details. It provides human-readable information about the document, such as the application that created it, when it was created, document description, and copyright information.

The *object* element is of type *NamedObject* (line 7) and encapsulates one of the JDM named objects, such as task and build settings. One JDM element can encapsulate multiple *object* elements. There is a required *version* attribute (line 5) of the *JDM* element used to specify the JDM Schema version.

Listing 10-3 illustrates a JDM document that conforms to the JDM Schema's elements structure. This document encapsulates a *classification* build settings object using the decision tree algorithm. Note that the *buildSettings* element (line 4) uses *xsi:type="ClassificationSettings"* to indicate that it is a *ClassificationSettings* complex type. Similarly its child element *algorithmSettings* (line 5) uses *xsi:type="TreeSettings"* to indicate that it is a *TreeSettings* complex type.

Listing 10-3   *Example JDM document (Classification settings object with decision tree algorithm)*

```
    <?xml version="1.0"?>
1.  <JDM version="1.1"
        xmlns="http://www.jsr-73.org/2004/JDMSchema"
        xmlns:xsi="http://www.w3.org/2001/XMLSchema-instance" >
2.    <header>
        <copyright>Copyright (c) 2004, 2005, Oracle. All rights reserved.</copyright>
        <timestamp>2005-12-06</timestamp>
        <applicationName>XYZ Predictive Analytics</applicationName>
        <applicationVersion>10.2</applicationVersion >
        <description>Provides settings to build customer attrition model</description>
      </header>
3.    <object>
4.      <buildSettings xsi:type="ClassificationSettings"
            miningFunction="classification" targetAttributeName="customer_type">
5.        <algorithmSettings xsi:type="TreeSettings"
              miningAlgorithm="decisionTree" maxDepth="10" />
        </buildSettings>
      </object>
      </JDM>
```

10.3   Schema Types

JDM Schema types have a one-to-one mapping with the JDM API classes or interfaces. JDM Schema types use the same name of the associated Java classes or interfaces, and maintain the same object inheritance and relationships as in the API whenever possible. In addition, the JDM Schema follows JAX-RPC Java-XML data type mapping guidelines [JAXRPC-SPEC 2006]. For example, Figure 10-1 depicts the class diagram and schema diagram for the *PhysicalDataSet* related objects illustrating the similarity between the API and the schema. In the class diagram, the *PhysicalDataSet* interface inherits from the *Mining-Object* interface, similarly in the schema diagram, the *PhysicalDataSet-* complex type inherits from the *MiningObject* complex type. In the class diagram, *PhysicalDataSet* has a one-to-many relationship with *Physical-Attribute* and it may have an *AttributeStatisticsSet* that gives statistics details of the data. Similarly, the schema diagram shows that the *Physi-calDataSet* complex type can have a one-to-many relationship with the *PhysicalAttribute* type elements and it may have an *AttributeStatisticsSet* element. Maintaining these similarities between the JDM API and XML Schema simplifies the implementation of the marshalling and unmarshalling of Java objects to and from XML, and the developer who understands the API can easily understand the schema.

The rest of this section explores some of the complex types defined in the JDM Schema to illustrate how various JDM API objects discussed in previous chapters are mapped to the schema.

The task objects discussed in Section 8.1.5 have more flexible options in the JDM Schema than the API to reduce the number of server invocations to perform a mining operation. Consider the following example. The *BuildTask* is used to build a mining model using input such as the build data and build settings. The *javax.datamining.task.BuildTask* API

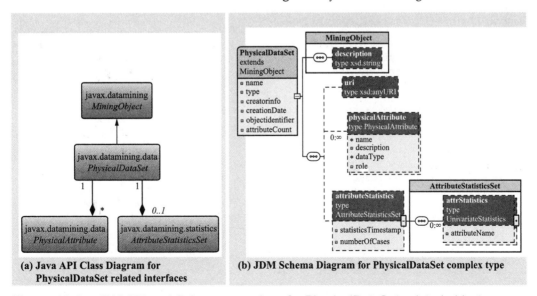

(a) Java API Class Diagram for PhysicalDataSet related interfaces

(b) JDM Schema Diagram for PhysicalDataSet complex type

Figure 10-1   *JDM API and Schema mappings for* PhysicalDataSet-*related objects.*

interface has *get* and *set* methods for specifying names of the input and output objects, as shown in Listing 10-4(a). Whereas in the JDM Schema, the *BuildTask* complex type gives applications the option of specifying either an object name or the object itself, as shown in Listing 10-4(b).

Listing 10-4(a) *javax.datamining.task.BuildTask interface*

```
1.  public interface BuildTask extends Task {
2.  public String getBuildDataName();
      public void setBuildDataName(String name) throws JDMException;
3.  public String getBuildSettingsName();
      public void setBuildSettingsName(String name) throws JDMException;
4.  public String getValidationDataName();
      public void setValidationDataName(String validationDataName) throws JDMException;
5.  public String getModelDescription();
      public void setModelDescription(String description);
6.  public Map getBuildDataMap();
      public void setBuildDataMap(Map buildDataMap) throws JDMException;
7.  public Map getValidationDataMap();
      public void setValidationDataMap(Map validationDataMap) throws JDMException;
8.  public String getModelName();
      public void setModelName(String name) throws JDMException;
9.  public String getInputModelName();
      public void setInputModelName(String modelName) throws JDMException;
10. public String getApplicationName();
      public void setApplicationName(String name);
    }
```

Listing 10-4(b) *BuildTask XML complex type*

```
1.  <xsd:complexType name="BuildTask">
    <xsd:complexContent>
    <xsd:extension base="Task">
     <xsd:sequence>
2.  <xsd:choice>
     <xsd:element name="buildDataName" type="xsd:string"/>
     <xsd:element name="buildData" type="PhysicalDataSet"/>
    </xsd:choice>
3.  <xsd:choice>
     <xsd:element name="buildSettingsName" type="xsd:string"/>
     <xsd:element name="buildSettings" type="BuildSettings"/>
    </xsd:choice>
4.  <xsd:choice>
     <xsd:element name="validationDataName" type="xsd:string" minOccurs="0"/>
     <xsd:element name="validationData" type="PhysicalDataSet" minOccurs="0"/>
    </xsd:choice>
5.  <xsd:element name="modelDescription" type="xsd:string" minOccurs="0"/>
6.  <xsd:element name="buildDataMap" type="LogicalAttrNameMap" minOccurs="0"
    maxOccurs="unbounded"/>
```

```
7. <xsd:element name="validationDataMap" type="AttributeNameMap" minOccurs="0"
   maxOccurs="unbounded"/>
 </xsd:sequence>
8. <xsd:attribute name="modelName" type="xsd:string" use="required"/>
9. <xsd:attribute name="inputModelName" type="xsd:string" use="optional"/>
10. <xsd:attribute name="applicationName" type="xsd:string" use="optional"/>
        </xsd:extension>
      </xsd:complexContent>
    </xsd:complexType>
```

In the API, task input objects are always referenced by name, so input objects must be saved and made available for task execution. Since the XML Schema gives the choice of specifying task input object contents, the task element can encapsulate all required inputs to execute the task with no object dependency. Applications using Web services can gain performance benefits by reducing the number of DME service calls; this can be accomplished by using a task with input objects instead of named references. However, with unnamed inputs, objects in the task cannot be reused by other tasks.

The JDM Schema maps the JDM matrix objects using a sparse representation. In the JDM API, there are three types of matrix objects: *cost matrix, confusion matrix,* and *similarity matrix.* For example, consider the simple cost matrix shown in Figure 10-2. Here the target attribute has two values: *Yes* and *No.* Note that the diagonal elements for a cost matrix are always zero, because there is no cost associated with the correct predictions. For nondiagonal elements, the default cost value is 1. Therefore, to create this cost matrix object, the user specifies only the nondiagonal element that has nondefault cost value 3. Listing 10-5(a) shows the XML document for this cost matrix; it first lists all the target values using the *category* element and then specifies the false-negative (FN) cell that has cost value 3. Because it is known that all diagonal elements have cost value 0 and unspecified nondiagonal elements have cost value 1, these elements do not have to be specified in the document.

		Predicted	
		Yes	No
Actual	Yes	0	3 (FN)
	No	1 (FP)	0

Figure 10-2 *Cost matrix table.*

Listing 10-5(b) illustrates the JDM Schema for the *CostMatrix* complex type. In line 2, we define the category elements of type *DataValueType* to list the target values in the cost matrix. The *DataValueType* is used to specify any target attribute value. The *CategoryMatrixElement* type (line 4) is used to define a cell of the matrix.

Listing 10-5(a)   *Cost Matrix XML document*

```
<JDM version="1.1"> <object>
 <costMatrix>
  <!--List of target values -->
  <category string="Yes">
  <category string="No">
  <!-- False Negative cost cell -->
  <costElement value="3">
   <predictedCategory string="No"/>
   <actualCategory string="Yes"/>
  </costElement>
 </object> </JDM>
```

Listing 10-5(b)   *CostMatrix complex type*

```
1. <xsd:complexType name="CostMatrix">
     <xsd:complexContent>
       <xsd:extension base="MiningObject">
         <xsd:sequence>
2.         <xsd:element name="category" type="DataValueType" minOccurs="2"
                         maxOccurs="unbounded"/>
3.         <xsd:element name="costElement" type="CategoryMatrixElement"
                         minOccurs="1" maxOccurs="unbounded"/>
         </xsd:sequence>
       </xsd:extension>
     </xsd:complexContent>
   </xsd:complexType>

4. <xsd:complexType name="CategoryMatrixElement">
     <xsd:sequence>
       <xsd:element name="predictedCategory" type="DataValueType"/>
       <xsd:element name="actualCategory" type="DataValueType"/>
     </xsd:sequence>
     <xsd:attribute name="value" type="xsd:double" use="required"/>
   </xsd:complexType>
```

The JDM API extensively uses enumerations to provide a type-safe list of values and the ability to extend standard enumeration values with vendor-specific extensions. Listing 10-6 shows the schema definitions for the *javax.datamining.MiningAlgorithm* enumeration class.

The *MiningAlgorithmStd* simple type (line 1) is used to specify the enumeration of JDM standard algorithms. The *MiningAlgorithm* simple type (line 2) is the union of values defined in *MiningAlgorithmStd,* and *EnumerationExtension.* JDM implementations can optionally define *EnumerationExtension* to add vendor specific enumeration values. The *EnumerationExtension* type (line 3) is a string type whose value starts with *"ext:".* For example, a vendor can add a new genetic algorithm to the *MiningAlgorithm* enumerations as *"ext:genetic"* using the *EnumerationExtension.*

Listing 10-6   *MiningAlgorithm enumeration*

```
1.<xsd:simpleType name="MiningAlgorithmStd">
    <xsd:restriction base="xsd:string">
     <xsd:enumeration value="svmClassification"/>
     <xsd:enumeration value="svmRegression"/>
     <xsd:enumeration value="decisionTree"/>
     <xsd:enumeration value="naiveBayes"/>
     <xsd:enumeration value="kMeans"/>
     <xsd:enumeration value="feedForwardNeuralNet"/>
   </xsd:restriction>
   </xsd:simpleType>

2. <xsd:simpleType name="MiningAlgorithm">
     <xsd:union memberTypes="MiningAlgorithmStd EnumerationExtension"/>
   </xsd:simpleType>

3. <xsd:simpleType name="EnumerationExtension">
   <xsd:restriction base="xsd:string">
     <xsd:pattern value="ext:\S.*"/>
   </xsd:restriction>
   </xsd:simpleType>
```

10.4   Using PMML with the JDM Schema

The Predictive Model Markup Language (PMML) is a data mining XML standard that defines the XML Schema for representing mining model contents and model details [DMG-PMML 2006]. Instead of redefining schema for model details, the JDM Schema defines only JDM-specific model details and allows vendors to specify PMML-compatible model contents as part of it.

Listing 10-7 illustrates a sample decision tree classification model XML document that is compatible with JDM and PMML 3.0 XML Schemas. Note that a JDM model element can encapsulate a PMML model, as shown in line 3.

Listing 10-7 *JDM and PMML compatible decision tree classification model XML document*

```
<?xml version="1.0"?>
1. <JDM version="1.1" xmlns="http://www.jsr-73.org/2004/JDMSchema"
   xmlns:xsi="http://www.w3.org/2001/XMLSchema-instance" >
   <header>
     <applicationName>XYZ Predictive Analytics</applicationName>
   </header>
2. <object>
     <model xsi:type="SupervisedModel" targetAttributeName="customer_type">
3.     <modelDetail format="PMML3.0">
       <PMML version="3.0" xmlns="http://www.dmg.org/PMML-3_0">
         <Header copyright="All rights reserved."/>
         <DataDictionary numberOfFields="3">
           <DataField name="ATTRITION" optype="categorical"/>
           <DataField name="AGE" optype="continuous"/>
           <DataField name="SAVINGS_BALANCE" optype="continuous"/>
         </DataDictionary>
         <TreeModel modelName="AttritionTreeModel" functionName="classification"
                 splitCharacteristic="binarySplit">
           <MiningSchema>
             <MiningField name="ATTRITION" usageType="predicted"/>
             <MiningField name="AGE" usageType="active"/>
             <MiningField name="SAVINGS_BALANCE" usageType="active"/>
           </MiningSchema>
           <Node id="1" score="0" recordCount="10">
             <True/>
             <ScoreDistribution value="No" recordCount="5"/>
             <ScoreDistribution value="Yes" recordCount="5"/>
             <Node id="2" score="Yes" recordCount="3">
               <SimplePredicate field="AGE" operator="greaterThan" value="36"/>
               <ScoreDistribution value="Yes" recordCount="3"/>
               <ScoreDistribution value="No" recordCount="0"/>
             </Node>
             <Node id="3" score="No" recordCount="7">
               <SimplePredicate field="AGE" operator="lessOrEqual" value="36"/>
               <ScoreDistribution value="Yes" recordCount="2"/>
               <ScoreDistribution value="No" recordCount="5"/>
                <Node id="4" score="No" recordCount="5">
                 <SimplePredicate field="SAVINGS_BALANCE" operator="lessThan" value="21500"/
                 <ScoreDistribution value="Yes" recordCount="0"/>
                 <ScoreDistribution value="No" recordCount="5"/>
               </Node>
               <Node id="5" score="Yes" recordCount="2">
                 <SimplePredicate field="SAVINGS_BALANCE"operator="greaterOrEqual"value="21500"/>
                   <ScoreDistribution value="Yes" recordCount="2"/>
                   <ScoreDistribution value="No" recordCount="0"/>
               </Node>
             </Node>
           </Node>
         </TreeModel>
       </PMML>
```

```
          </modelDetail>
        </model>
      </object>
    </JDM>
```

Listing 10-8 depicts the *Model* and *ModelDetail* complex types defined in the JDM Schema. Lines 1 to 6 illustrate the *Model* complex type that contains the JDM standard model metadata types, such as *signature, buildSettings, effectiveBuildSettings, attributeStatistics,* and *modelDetail,* that we discussed in Sections 8.1.3 and 9.4.3. Lines 7 to 9 illustrate the *ModelDetail* complex type that uses the *xsd:any* to allow any type of content as model detail (line 8). An optional *format* attribute can be specified using the enumerated values defined in the *ImportExportFormat* enumeration that defines some of the industry standard data mining formats, such as PMML. As a result, the JDM Schema allows specifying model details in any vendor-specific format. However, vendors can extend the JDM Schema to enforce specific formats such as PMML.

Listing 10-8 *XML Schema complex types for the mining model and model details*

```
1. <xsd:complexType name="Model">
   <xsd:complexContent>
     <xsd:extension base="MiningObject">
       <xsd:sequence>
2.       <xsd:element name="signature" type="ModelSignature" minOccurs="0"/>
       <xsd:choice>
3.         <xsd:element name="buildSettingsName" type="xsd:string"
                         minOccurs="0"/>
           <xsd:element name="buildSettings" type="BuildSettings" minOccurs="0"/>
       </xsd:choice>
4.       <xsd:element name="effectiveBuildSettings" type="BuildSettings"
                       minOccurs="0"/>
5.       <xsd:element name="attributeStatistics" type="AttributeStatisticsSet"
                       minOccurs="0"/>
6.       <xsd:element name="modelDetail" type="ModelDetail" minOccurs="0"/>
       </xsd:sequence>
       <xsd:attribute name="uniqueIdentifier" type="xsd:string" use="optional"/>
       <xsd:attribute name="version" type="xsd:string" use="optional"/>
       <xsd:attribute name="majorVersion" type="xsd:string" use="optional"/>
       <xsd:attribute name="minorVersion" type="xsd:string" use="optional"/>
       <xsd:attribute name="providerName" type="xsd:string" use="optional"/>
       <xsd:attribute name="providerVersion" type="xsd:string" use="optional"/>
       <xsd:attribute name="applicationName" type="xsd:string" use="optional"/>
       <xsd:attribute name="miningFunction" type="MiningFunction"
                       use="optional"/>
       <xsd:attribute name="miningAlgorithm" type="MiningAlgorithm"
                       use="optional"/>
```

```
            <xsd:attribute name="taskIdentifer" type="xsd:string" use="optional"/>
            <xsd:attribute name="buildDuration" type="xsd:int" use="optional"/>
        </xsd:extension>
      </xsd:complexContent>
   </xsd:complexType>

7.<xsd:complexType name="ModelDetail">
      <xsd:sequence>
8.      <xsd:any minOccurs="0"/>
      </xsd:sequence>
9.  <xsd:attribute name="format" type="ImportExportFormat" use="optional"/>
   </xsd:complexType>
```

10.5   Use Cases for JDM XML Schema and Documents

A well-designed data model defined using XML Schema can enable designers and developers to create innovative applications using compatible XML documents. For example, ebXML (Electronic Business using Extensible Markup Language) enabled enterprises to conduct various types of businesses over the Internet [ebXML 2006]. XML is widely used for anything from simple file representations, such as configuration files, to complex data model representations, such as those used at NASA [NASA-XML 2006]. Similarly, applications can use the JDM XML Schema in numerous ways. This section identifies a few use cases for the JDM Schema.

A primary purpose of the JDM Schema is to provide a standard, interchangeable data format for JDM objects among DMEs. For example, from a data mining model built by an analyst with a sample dataset in a local development environment, a user can export the model's logical data representation, build settings, and build task objects as JDM XML documents to a production environment. In the production environment, new models are built with production datasets using the analyst specified settings.

Via the JDM Schema, we define the data model for JDM Web services. JDM Web services use XML types defined in the JDM Schema to represent the Web service messages. For example, in support of real-time scoring, *RecordApplyTask* and *RecordElement* complex types are used to represent the *executeTask* message. Similarly, all other complex types defined in the JDM Schema are used to represent messages in the JDM Web services.

Even though the JDM standard does not require XML as a storage format for its mining objects in the mining repository, some implementations may choose to use a JDM XML Schema object representation. By using the JDM definition, designers and developers reduce data model design time, gain flexibility to store JDM objects in file systems or databases, and avoid any conversion from a proprietary format to standard JDM XML format when importing or exporting mining objects or using them in JDM Web services.

Other uses of JDM Schema include combining JDM XML Schema objects with XML process or workflow definition standards such as Business Process Execution Language (BPEL) [Wikipedia_BPEL 2006], and representing XML-based configuration files of a deployed mining solution.

10.6   Summary

The JDM XML Schema provides a comprehensive data model for JDM objects. It follows the same design principles and object model as the API to maintain consistency between the API and the schema. The JDM Schema provides the same level of extensibility as that of the API for JDM implementations to support vendor-specific extensions. Complex types defined in JDM Schema will be included in the JDM Web services definitions discussed in the next chapter.

References

[DMG-PMML 2006] http://www.dmg.org.

[JAXRPC-SPEC 2006] http://java.sun.com/webservices/jaxrpc/docs.html.

[JDM11 2006] http://www.jcp.org/en/jsr/detail?id=73.

[NASA-XML 2006] http://xml.nasa.gov.

[Ray 2003] Erik T. Ray, *Learning XML*, 2nd ed., Sebastopol, CA O'Reilly & Associates Inc., September 2003.

[W3CXML 2006] http://www.w3.org/XML.

[W3CXML-SCHEMA 2006] http://www.w3.org/XML/Schema.

[Wikipedia_BPEL 2006] http://en.wikipedia.org/wiki/BPEL.

Chapter

11

Web Services

Web Services will dominate deployment of new application solutions for Fortune 2000 companies.

—Gartner Analysts

Web services are evolving as the key technology that enables software application functionality as services, which can be discovered and used by other applications over a network. Users developing service-oriented applications and integrating existing applications are becoming increasingly interested in Web services. This results from the evolution of multiple standards, such as Simple Object Access Protocol (SOAP), Web Service Description Language (WSDL) that are unanimously supported by the software industry, and the increased availability of tools and software platforms, such as J2EE and .Net, that ease the development of Web service applications.

The Java Data Mining (JDM) standard defines Web services that complement the Java application programming interface (API). These vendor-neutral Web services fulfill the strategic objective of providing broad architectural choices for application architects to integrate data mining functionality. This chapter briefly explores Web services and service-oriented architecture (SOA) before going into a detailed discussion of JDM Web services (JDMWS) and how

JDM vendors can enable JDMWS using the JDM API and J2EE platform.

11.1   What Is a Web Service?

There are many industry definitions for Web services. The latest W3C Web Services Architecture document defines a Web service as follows:

> *A Web service is a software system designed to support interoperable machine-to-machine interaction over a network. It has an interface described in a machine-processable format (specifically WSDL). Other systems interact with the Web service in a manner prescribed by its description using SOAP-messages, typically conveyed using HTTP with an XML serialization in conjunction with other Web-related standards. [WS-ARCH 2006]*

Even though this definition may be difficult to understand at first, Web services are similar to real-world services. This section uses a fictitious pizza service, *Eat Fat Pizza* in New York City, to compare concepts and workings of Web services with those of real-world services.

Eat Fat Pizza offers custom pizzas to customers by delivery or pickup. It offers two delivery options: deliver by bike to avoid delays due to city traffic or by car if the customer is not within two miles of its location. Typically, customers make a phone call and inquire about the types of pizzas available, and then order the pizza, specifying toppings, drinks, etc. In response to a customer request, the *Eat Fat Pizza* service provider prepares and delivers the pizza according to the request. *Eat Fat Pizza* publishes its services in the local yellow pages, flyers, and advertisements.

Figure 11-1 illustrates the similarities between the workings of a pizza service and the workings of a Web service. When a customer calls, the pizza service provider gives the details of the services they offer. Similarly, in the case of a Web service, the provider gives the details of the services they offer using a machine interpretable XML document to the service requester. This XML document is written using the Web Service Description Language (WSDL, often pronounced as "Whiz-Dull"). WSDL describes the types of XML elements used and the contents of the service request and response messages, available service operations, message format, and service provider location details. After processing the provider's WSDL document, the requester knows which services are provided, and how to place a request to the provider.

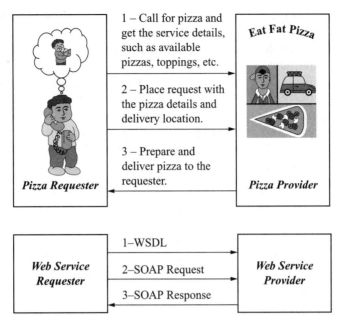

Figure 11-1 *Simple Web services comparison with a real-world pizza service.*

As with the pizza service, where the customer must provide required information such as type of pizza, toppings, and delivery location, a Web service requester also must provide required inputs for an operation to the provider so that it can process the requested service. Web services use the Simple Object Access Protocol (SOAP) standard for exchanging the XML messages between requester and provider. (SOAP is the industry accepted XML messaging standard for Web services; for details refer to [Haefel 2003].) The Web service requester sends a message using the SOAP protocol and the provider processes the request and responds with the appropriate SOAP response message as defined in the WSDL document. Because the requester has the provider's WSDL document, it knows what to expect for a response and the semantics of the response message for the specific request.

In the pizza service example, we assumed that the customer already knows the contact details of *Eat Fat Pizza*. If the customer doesn't know the local pizza services, then he typically searches in the yellow pages to find the list of pizza providers and selects one from which to order the pizza. Similarly, in the case of a Web service, the provider can also publish its services by registering the WSDL documents in Web service registries.

Figure 11-2 illustrates a Web services architecture with a *discovery service*, which finds the appropriate Web service(s) requested by the requester. When a requester sends a service request to a discovery service, the service finds the available provider service, which matches the request criteria and provides the WSDL associated with the provider to the requester. From the WSDL specification the requester understands the location of the provider and semantics for communicating with the provider and places SOAP requests as discussed in the simple Web services architecture above.

There are three types of discovery services: registry, index, and peer-to-peer (P2P). Registry services centrally control the registry of Web services, where a provider registers in the centrally managed registry so that it can be discovered by the requester. Index services do not centrally control the information, rather index services compile information about services and a requester can search there for appropriate services. P2P allows services to discover each other dynamically in a network. In P2P, a requester broadcasts service requirements; peers in the network that satisfy these requirements respond with the WSDL.

Universal Description, Discovery, and Integration (UDDI) is accepted as an industry standard for registry services. There are public Internet UDDI business registries in which one can register the provider Web services; thus any requester can find via the Internet the available providers for a service. The UDDI registry can be installed in a private network, so that requesters in the same network can find available providers.

WSDL, SOAP, and XML Schema are developed by the W3C standards group; for more details about these technologies refer to [W3C 2006]. The UDDI standard, other Web services standards such as the Business Process Execution Language (BPEL), WS-Security,

Figure 11-2 *Web services architecture with Discovery Service.*

WS-Reliability, Security Assertion Markup Language (SAML), and other XML-based e-commerce standards such as ebXML are developed by the OASIS standards group; for more details on these standards refer to [OASIS 2006]. The WS-I, a Web services interoperability organization, defines Web services usage recommendations based on real-world issues to promote interoperability between various software platforms; for more details refer to [WSI 2006]. JDMWS is compliant with WS-I Basic Profile 1.0.

11.2 Service-Oriented Architecture

With the advent of Web services and other XML standards, Service-Oriented Architecture (SOA) is gaining acceptance as an application architecture. SOA provides needed flexibility for ever-changing business requirements. SOA typically uses Web services as the base technology that enables legacy application functionality as services that can be orchestrated using standards such as the Business Process Execution Language (BPEL, often pronounced "bee-pel") to define business processes. BPEL is an XML-based business process design and execution standard language that is receiving wide adoption by applications to define and manage business processes. There are many commercial BPEL engines [BPEL-ENGINES 2006], which typically are used to design business processes using a graphical tool and deploy these processes to a BPEL engine. The BPEL engine executes the BPEL processes and provides graphical user interfaces for managing these deployed processes. For more details refer to [BPEL 2006].

Figure 11-3 illustrates the typical SOA layers. The bottom layer, Layer 1, represents the legacy systems and applications that evolved in an enterprise over time; these can come from a variety of sources including mainframe systems, open systems, prepackaged software like ERP, CRM applications, or homegrown applications. Layer 2 represents the components layer that uses container-based technologies such as Enterprise Java Beans (EJB) in J2EE. Typically this layer is built using components-based design patterns to define reusable components at a higher-level of abstraction than the detailed object level functionality. Layer 3 represents the services layer. A *service* can be a composite service that uses the functionality of multiple components. Layer 4 defines the business process flows using orchestration services such as BPEL. Layer 5 represents the presentation layers, such as portals, and dashboards. Layer 6 enables integration of services popularly known as the Enterprise Service Bus (ESB).

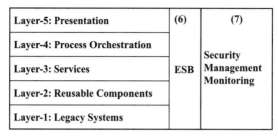

Figure 11-3 *SOA layered architecture.*

ESB provides an abstraction layer on top of enterprise messaging systems that are used for services integration. Layer 7 enables management and monitoring of the deployed services. Layers 6 and 7 provide common infrastructure capabilities that can be accessed by other layers and hence they are shown as vertical layers in Figure 11-3. For more details about SOA refer to [Erl 2005].

Enterprise level adoption of SOA has many challenges. These include complexities in changing monolithic legacy applications, fundamentally changing the IT organization's approach to software development, security of services, and performance overhead due to loose coupling of applications. Even though SOA has fundamental benefits, due to the complexities involved SOA projects often start small and evolve over time. SOA adoption will increase as more software applications and products provide out-of-the-box standards-based Web services, and tools evolve to simplify SOA application development and management. As data mining functionality is typically integrated with existing applications, adopting an SOA architecture with JDMWS will provide a flexible, reusable, and extensible integration strategy. Section 11.3.2 discusses a JDMWS use case of how JDMWS and SOA help integrate data mining functionality in an enterprise.

11.3 JDM Web Service

The JDM standard defines a Web service's interface (JDMWS) that uses the XML Schema discussed in Chapter 10 and provides functionality consistent with the JDM Java API. The concepts and object model discussed in Chapters 7 and 8 for the Java API are applicable for the JDMWS interface. However, unlike a Java API, Web services typically define a small number of operations with relatively large messages to reduce the number of service calls to be made. JDM Web services define 11 operations. This section gives an overview of JDMWS operations and provides an example of an SOA application integration scenario. The section also describes the details of the JDM WSDL and explains how JAX-RPC can be used to enable JDM Web services.

11.3.1 Overview of JDMWS Operations

The JDM Java API discussed in Chapter 9 defines mining classes and interfaces with many methods for designing and developing object-oriented applications. In contrast, JDMWS is designed to develop service-oriented applications and as such defines a small number of operations with large messages. The JDM standard maintains the interchangeable object model between the Java and Web Services API by defining a consistent data model using the JDM XML Schema discussed in Chapter 10. JDMWS operations are designed to be consistent with those of the Java API. This enables a JDM API interface provider to support JDMWS more easily. It also enables developers familiar with the Java API to understand the workings of JDMWS more readily.

JDMWS operations are categorized into three types: mining task execution and monitoring, mining object management, and capability discovery. Table 11-1 lists the JDMWS operations with signatures and a brief description of each operation. In this table, the simplified notations [in] and [out] are used to represent the service request message and response message. For detailed syntax of these operations, refer to [JDMWSDL 2006].

The JDMWS *executeTask* operation is similar to the *resouce.Connection.execute* method in the Java API. However, unlike the Java API where the application must save input objects before executing the task, JDMWS allows users to specify the contents of input objects as part of the mining task. This is an important distinction that allows applications to perform a complete mining operation with one JDMWS call. For example, in the Java API, before the model build task is executed, the task input objects (physical data, logical data, and build settings) must be saved. In JDMWS, on the other hand, users can specify the contents of all the input objects within the build task itself to submit a mining task for execution.

Table 11-1 *JDM Web service operations*

JDM Web service interfaces	
Task Execution and Monitoring operations	***Description***

executeTask (
    [in] task object or name
    [out] execution status)
	Used to execute the task in the DME synchronously or asynchronously. This operation takes either a task object or task name as input and returns the status of the task execution as output. When a task object is passed as input, it runs synchronously. When a task name is passed as input, it runs asynchronously.

getExecutionStatus (
    [in] task name
    [out] execution status)
	Used to get the status of a task submitted for execution asynchronously. This operation takes the task name as input and returns the latest execution status as output.

terminateTask (
    [in] task name
    [out] execution status)
	Used to terminate the task that is currently executing in the DME and returns the termination status of the task. If the task already completed by the time of this operation's invocation, this method throws an exception with a failure to terminate message.

Mining Object Management operations	***Description***

SaveObject (
    [in] object name
    [in] overwrite flag
    [in] verify flag
    [in] mining object details
    [out] verification report)
	Used to save input mining objects: physical data, logical data, build settings, apply settings, cost matrix, taxonomy, and task objects. When the overwrite flag is set to TRUE, this operation will overwrite the old object with the specified new object. When the verify flag is set to TRUE, this operation includes object verification before saving the mining object. If there are object verification issues, a verification report will be generated and returned to the requester. For example, when a model build task is saved with the verification flag set to TRUE and the specified input data for the build task doesn't exist in the DME, the verification report will be generated.

getObject (
    [in] object name
    [in] object type
    [out] mining object)
	Used to retrieve a mining object from the DME. By specifying the object name and type, the requester can retrieve the object with that name from the DME. If no object exists conforming to the request message, this operation responds with the 'object not found exception' message.

Table 11-1   *(continued)*

getSubObjects (
  [in] content type
  [in] object name
  [in] object type
  [out] subobjects)
	Instead of getting all the contents of an object, this operation is used to retrieve specific subobjects of mining object(s). This operation is useful when the requester is interested in specific details of the mining object. For example, an application that wants to process only the model signature *of a model can use this method by specifying content type as* modelSignature *and the object details. This saves network traffic and client processing time.*

listContents (
  [in] object filter
  [out] mining object header(s))
	Used to list mining object headers that satisfy the specified object filtering criteria. Mining object header contains the primitive details of the object, such as name, type, when it was created, etc. When there is no object with the specified criteria it responds with an object not found exception message.

removeObject (
  [in] object name
  [in] object type
  [out] object name
  [out] object type)
	Used to remove object from the DME. This operation returns the object name and type after successfully removing the specified object. If the object removal fails, this method responds with a failure message.

renameObject (
  [in] from name
  [in] to name
  [in] object type
  [out] from name
  [out] to name
  [out] object type)
	Used to rename the mining objects in the DME. This operation returns with the new and old object names and the object type as response message. When the object rename fails this method responds with the failure message.

verifyObject (
  [in] object name (or) object
  [in] object to be verified
  [out] verification report)
	Used to explicitly verify the provided object oe one that is already saved in the DME. When the object has valid contents this method responds with an empty verification report; otherwise it returns the error and warning messages embedded in the verification report.

DME Capabilities Discovery Operations	**Description**
getCapabilities ([out] capabilities report)	*Used to retrieve the list of capabilities of the DME as an XML report. The requester can process this capabilities report to discover the DME capabilities before placing a request.*

Similar to the Java API, JDMWS provides the ability to execute a task *synchronously* or *asynchronously* based on the *executeTask* request message. A task is executed *synchronously* when the request message contains the whole *task object*. When the request message has only the name of the task, it is executed asynchronously. With a named task object, the client can inquire about the status of the task execution by task name. Typically, short running operations such as *single record apply* are executed synchronously and long-running operations such as model building and batch apply are executed asynchronously.

In addition to the *executeTask* operation, there are two other task-related operations: *getExecutionStatus* and *terminateTask* that can be used to monitor and control the execution of tasks in a data mining engine (DME). The *getExecutionStatus* operation retrieves the status of tasks that are currently submitted for execution, executing or already completed. Since mining tasks can be long running, the *terminateTask* operation is used to terminate task execution in the DME.

Chapters 8 and 9 discussed various types of mining objects: physical data, logical data, build settings, task, model, apply settings, and test metrics. Similar to the Java API, JDMWS provides operations to manage these objects. Table 11-1 describes all the mining object management operations that are used to save, retrieve, remove, and rename mining objects.

The JDM standard allows vendors to provide a subset of the full standard capabilities, while allowing them to extend those capabilities. In the JDM API, appropriate *supports capability* methods are defined in *Factory* objects so that applications can discover DME capabilities at runtime. In the JDMWS, the *getCapabilities* operation is used to retrieve the list of capabilities supported by a DME as a single parsable XML document, which the requester can process to find the capabilities of the DME. This operation is useful to customize requests based on DME capabilities. For example, if the requester prefers using the support vector machine (SVM) algorithm for classification and also wants to be interoperable with DMEs that do not support SVM, it can have an internal rule such as "if the DME supports SVM then use it, otherwise use the default classification algorithm." The request can then be customized based on supported capabilities retrieved from the *getCapabilities* operation.

11.3.2   JDMWS Use Case

Chapter 7 described business problems for ABCBank and explained how data mining techniques can be used to solve those problems. This section extends the discussion by mapping these solutions to JDM Web services and SOA design principles.

ABCBank has an internal data mining lab (DM Lab) that is responsible for finding data mining solutions for given business problems. DM Lab has business analysts and data analysts that work together to define the mining attributes and data needed for the business problems and to define the model building process. DM Lab coordinates with the ABCBank information technology (IT) department to acquire the relevant data from various data sources for mining. DM Lab then communicates back to IT with the final results produced using the data. IT integrates the data mining results with the appropriate applications, so that company executives can view the results. Figure 11-4 depicts the high-level view of the current scheme of integrating data mining results with the production applications.

The current scheme is not efficient due to delays in delivering the data mining results to the organization's information consumers. Even though DM Lab generates accurate models, ABCBank is dissatisfied with the time it takes DM Lab to produce results and IT to incorporate those results into applications and reports. For example, for the customer attrition problem, the *attrition model* produces good results at DM Lab. However, by the time the model is deployed to the call center, some valuable customers have already left. In addition, ABCBank would like to expand the use of data

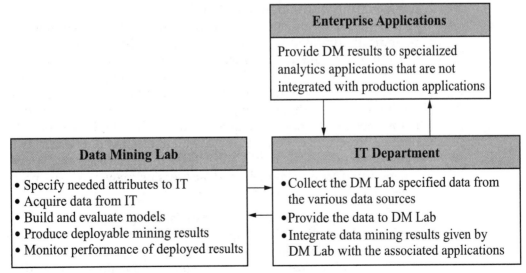

Figure 11-4 *ABCBank's current data mining model deployment process without using JDMWS.*

mining to many production applications. But the current process is not scalable for its needs because data analysts must maintain hundreds of models and produce results manually. Moreover, the IT group needs to integrate data mining results manually by deploying to the appropriate applications. In addition, ABCBank wants to be able to change DMEs used in the production environment and to have the ability to integrate with multiple DMEs. Due to legacy, their enterprise applications are written using multiple computer languages such as Java, C++, C, and COBOL.

From the perspective of ABCBank's business analysts, automating data mining processes and embedding the results with production applications will produce more fruitful results than the current limited integration. Embedding data mining results in the production applications will enable business executives of all levels to make more informed decisions using the latest data. In addition, ABCBank call-center representatives can interact with customers more effectively if the customer attrition likelihood, profitability, and appropriate cross-sell products are displayed along with the customer profile.

From the perspective of ABCBank's data analysts, to ensure the quality of the data mining results they would like to maintain control of the specification of model build settings such as algorithm and function level settings and the attributes to be used; they would also like to be able to add or remove attributes. Once the mining attributes and model build settings are specified for a specific problem, model quality can be maintained if the model is periodically updated with the new data, thereby learning new patterns. In the future, analysts would like to build a mining solution once for a problem and deploy the required settings to production applications. The automated processes should be able to rebuild the mining models with new data at the specified intervals. Over time, if the models do not meet quality thresholds, DM Lab must be notified to improve them. Automation enables the data analysts to manage many models easily, and allows them to focus on improving non-performing models and addressing new business problems.

From the perspective of ABCBank's IT department, the data mining and application integration architecture must be flexible enough to support both current and future applications. The IT department also must be able to run computationally intensive data mining operations in a separate machine without affecting production applications. To have the flexibility to change DMEs to avoid vendor lock-in and having to rewrite applications, IT prefers a standards-based solution.

Because the integration solution requires programming language and DME independence, as well as a low impact on existing production applications, JDM Web services with an SOA architecture fits well for these needs. Now, we detail changes to the process and application architecture to fulfill ABCBank's application integration needs. We also explain which JDMWS operations can be used to automate the data mining process using BPEL and which JDMWS operations can be used to get data mining results reflecting real-time changes.

Figure 11-5 depicts the new architecture and department responsibilities. In the proposed system, DM Lab finds the best performing model(s), provides the necessary settings to build models, and communicates results and quality thresholds to IT. IT integrates the proposed data mining solution in coordination with DM Lab using BPEL process designer tools and JDMWS. IT verifies the process and deploys it to the BPEL engine. Unlike the old integration where DM Lab was responsible for producing results every time data was updated, in the new process DM Lab needs only to define the initial model, and the model will be automatically rebuilt at specified intervals with new data. When a model is not producing results within the specified limits, DM Lab will be notified to improve the model.

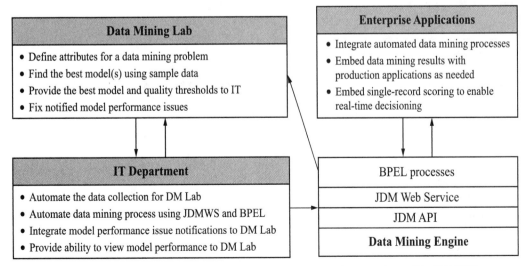

Figure 11-5 *ABCBank's proposed data mining process integration with JDMWS.*

The IT department builds the automated process using a BPEL process designer tool and deploys these processes using a BPEL engine in the production system. For more details about available BPEL tools and engines, refer to [BPEL-ENGINE 2006]. Figure 11-6 illustrates a BPEL process that builds a model using the initial model given by the DM Lab; this figure gives side-by-side the BPEL process flow and associated JDMWS calls. The left side flow shows the process definition along with each node description. The right side flow diagram shows the corresponding JDMWS call.

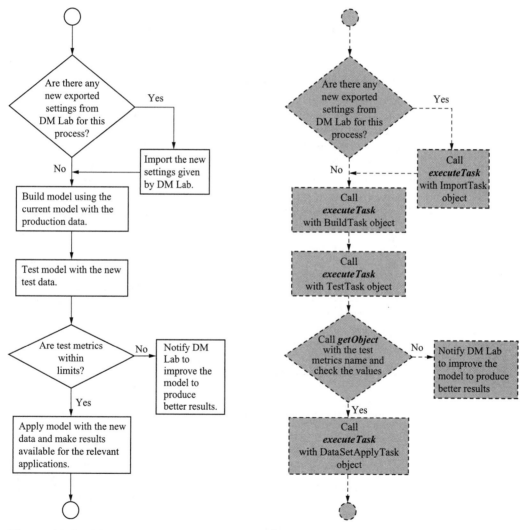

Figure 11-6 *BPEL process flow for automating DM process using JDMWS operations.*

This process begins by checking for any newly exported settings by DM Lab in their repository for the associated business problem. If settings exist, they are imported to the production system using the *executeTask* operation with the appropriate *ImportTask* message and the new imported settings are used to rebuild the production model with the latest data. Otherwise, the process continues and rebuilds the model with the current settings and the latest data available in the system. We assume that IT automated dataset creation, used up-to-date data collection for building, and automated testing and applying the model. This is typically done using data warehousing tools. The *executeTask* method is used to build, test, and apply the model in the subsequent steps of the process as shown in Figure 11-6.

Before the model is applied to produce the prediction results, an automated process will validate the test metrics with the DM Lab-specified quality limits. If the computed test metrics are within limits the apply operation will be performed; otherwise a notification will be sent to DM Lab to improve the model.

Another need for the new system is getting real-time predictions to production applications. Consider the case of a customer call center application where an attrition model discussed in Section 7.1 is used to display *customer attrition likelihood* along with the customer profile to the call center representative. The *attrition likelihood* measure is precomputed using batch apply with the existing customer profile. However, when a customer calls a representative and changes any of the attributes used to build the model, the *customer attrition likelihood* displayed is no longer valid because the batch apply does not reflect the recent changes. JDMWS record apply allows the application to dynamically re-score the customer based on the new customer data. Figure 11-7 shows the BPEL process used for record apply results when the attributes are changed in the application.

This process begins with the retrieval of the model's signature attributes, which are used to verify whether any of the signature attribute values have changed in the current application session. In the call center example, suppose the customer marital status is in the model signature. When a customer calls the representative and says that he was recently married and wants to add his wife as a joint owner of his account, the process identifies that a model signature attribute has changed and executes the record apply task with the updated customer profile. The *executeTask* operation takes the newly updated record as part of the record apply task and responds with

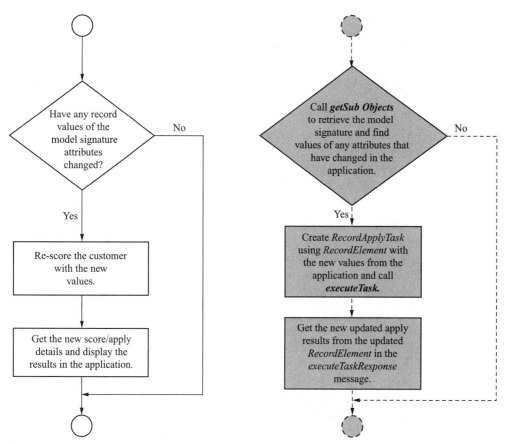

Figure 11-7 *BPEL process flow real-time record apply results using JDMWS operations.*

the updated prediction details for the customer. The application can display this result immediately.

11.3.3 JDM WSDL

This chapter so far has discussed JDMWS operations and presented a use case where JDMWS and SOA can be used to solve data mining process integration problems. This section introduces the JDM WSDL specification. An understanding of JDM WSDL contents is important when developing applications using JDMWS.

The JDM standard defines the WSDL specification for data mining Web services that is conformant with WSDL 1.1 specifications.

Figure 11-8 depicts a representation of JDM WSDL contents from Oracle JDeveloper [JDEV 2006]. The first column in the figure, *Services*, shows that JDM WSDL contains a service called *DataMiningService* with one port called *IDataMiningPort* to which a service requester can communicate. The second column, *Bindings*, shows the details of the operation binding, message formats, and protocols to which *IDataMiningPort* is binded. The third column, *PortTypes*, defines the operations and the messages used in those operations. The last column, *Messages*, shows the list of defined messages.

Listing 11-1 illustrates the structure and contents of JDM WSDL [JDM-WSDL 2006]. This listing shows the WSDL's seven important elements — *types, import, message, portType, operations, binding,* and *service* — that are under the common parent element *definitions*. The *definitions* element (line 2) has a *name* attribute to define the name of the WSDL document; the *targetNameSpace* attribute refers to the JDM Web services namespace *http://www.jsr-73.org/2004/webservices* that defines the types and elements specific to the JDMWS. The namespace is different from the JDM Schema namespace to

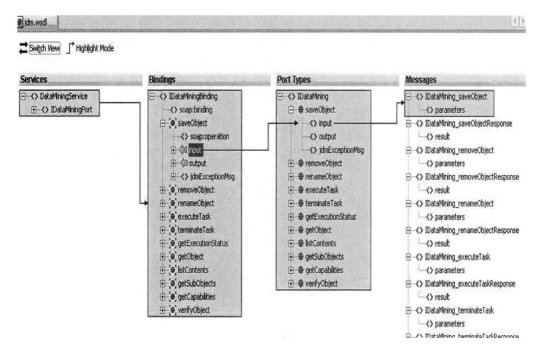

Figure 11-8   *JDM WSDL view from Oracle JDeveloper 10.1.3 WSDL Viewer.*

differentiate JDM Schema elements from the Web services–specific elements. One of the reasons for splitting JDM Schema elements from JDMWS is that JDM Schema elements can be used outside Web services. (Note that these namespace URLs host neither JDM Schema nor WSDL files. To get JDM Schema and WSDL files, download the specification bundle from [JDM11 2006].)

The *types* element (line 8) declares the JDM Web services–specific complex types and elements, *xsd:import* (line 12) is used to import the JDM Schema types and elements that are used to define Web services–specific types and elements. JDM WSDL follows the naming pattern of using operation name for the associated complex types, elements, and message names. For example, the *saveObject* operation's input and outputs are represented using *saveObjectElement* (line 28) and *saveObjectResponseElement* (line 29); these elements are of types *saveObject* (line 14) and *saveObjectResponse* (line 22), and the associated message names are *IDataMining_saveObject* (line 34) and *IDataMining_saveObjectResponse* message (line 44). Because these operation-related elements are defined at different parts of the WSDL document, the use of the operation name simplifies their identification in the WSDL document. For all messages the *IDataMining_* prefix is used, so that when the JDMWS messages are mixed with other Web services, the prefix identifies that the message is related to data mining. These naming conventions are introduced to ease reading of the WSDL documents and to get proper names for the interfaces created from the WSDL by the code generators, such as WSDL-to-Java, WSDL-to-C#. These mappings in the JAX-RPC context are discussed further in Section 11.4.

The *portType* element defines the list of operations provided by the Web service and defines the input, output, and fault messages associated with the operations. For example, the *saveObject* operation (line 42) element has sub-elements *input* (line 43), *output* (line 44), and *fault* (line 45) used to define operation inputs, outputs, and exception messages.

The *binding* element defines the protocol bindings for the message format and transport protocol. JDMWS follows the WS-I Basic Profile 1.0 guidelines and uses the SOAP binding (line 50) with *document* style (line 51) with *literal* content (line 55) for all the operations. For more details about the message formats and WS-I Basic Profile 1.0 refer to [Haefel 2003].

Listing 11-1   *JDM WSDL structure*

```
1.   <?xml version="1.0" encoding="UTF-8"?>
2.   <definitions name="DataMiningService"
3.     targetNamespace="http://www.jsr-73.org/2004/webservices"
4.     xmlns:jdmws="http://www.jsr-73.org/2004/webservices"
5.     xmlns="http://schemas.xmlsoap.org/wsdl/"
6.     xmlns:xsd="http://www.w3.org/2001/XMLSchema"
7.     xmlns:soap="http://schemas.xmlsoap.org/wsdl/soap/">
8.   <types>
9.     <xsd:schema targetNamespace="http://www.jsr-73.org/2004/webservices"
10.      xmlns:xsi="http://www.w3.org/2001/XMLSchema-instance"
11.      xmlns:jdm="http://www.jsr-73.org/2004/JDMSchema">
12.    <xsd:import namespace="http://www.jsr-73.org/2004/JDMSchema"
13.      schemaLocation="jdm.xsd"/>
14.    <xsd:complexType name="saveObject">
15.      <xsd:sequence>
16.        <xsd:element name="object" type="jdm:MiningObject"/>
17.      </xsd:sequence>
18.      <xsd:attribute name="objectName" type="xsd:string" use="required"/>
19.      <xsd:attribute name="overwrite" type="xsd:boolean" use="optional"/>
20.      <xsd:attribute name="verify" type="xsd:boolean" use="optional"/>
21.    </xsd:complexType>
22.    <xsd:complexType name="saveObjectResponse">
23.      <xsd:sequence>
24.        <xsd:element name="report" type="jdm:VerificationReport" minOccurs="0"/>
25.      </xsd:sequence>
26.    </xsd:complexType>
27.    .. .. .. ..
28.    <xsd:element name="saveObjectElement" type="jdmws:saveObject"/>
29.    <xsd:element name="saveObjectResponseElement"
30.      type="jdmws:saveObjectResponse"/>
31.    .. .. .. ..
32.    </xsd:schema>
33.  </types>
34.  <message name="IDataMining_saveObject">
35.    <part name="parameters" element="jdmws:saveObjectElement"/>
36.  </message>
37.  <message name="IDataMining_saveObjectResponse">
38.    <part name="result" element="jdmws:saveObjectResponseElement"/>
39.  </message>
40.  .. .. .. ..
41.  <portType name="IDataMining">
42.    <operation name="saveObject">
43.      <input message="jdmws:IDataMining_saveObject"/>
44.      <output message="jdmws:IDataMining_saveObjectResponse"/>
45.      <fault name="jdmExceptionMsg" message="jdmws:IDataMining_exception"/>
46.    </operation>
47.    .. .. .. ..
48.  </portType>
49.  <binding name="IDataMiningBinding" type="jdmws:IDataMining">
50.    <soap:binding transport="http://schemas.xmlsoap.org/soap/http"
```

```
51.       style="document"/>
52.    <operation name="saveObject">
53.      <soap:operation style="document" soapAction=""/>
54.      <input>
55.        <soap:body use="literal"/>
56.      </input>
57.      <output>
58.        <soap:body use="literal"/>
59.      </output>
60.      <fault name="jdmExceptionMsg">
61.        <soap:fault name="jdmExceptionMsg" use="literal"/>
62.      </fault>
63.    </operation>
64.    .. .. .. ..
65.  </binding>
66.  <service name="DataMiningService">
67.    <port name="IDataMiningPort" binding="jdmws:IDataMiningBinding">
68.      <soap:address location="http://www.jsr-73.org/2004/web services/
         DataMiningService"/>
69.    </port>
70.  </service>
71.  </definitions>
```

11.3.4 Data Exchange and Security in JDMWS

JDMWS does not define standards for large input and output data exchange between the data mining service provider and requester. Data mining processes often involve large input and output datasets, on the order of gigabytes, which are not efficiently sent through Web services protocols. This is a problem for any Web service that needs to process large volumes of data, and it is expected that users of JDMWS will leverage existing protocols, standards, and mechanisms to achieve vendor-neutral data exchange. In this release, JDM assumes that the requester provides the data input and output location details to the JDMWS provider and the provider has appropriate privileges and mechanisms for data exchange.

JDMWS intentionally does not define the DME connection details specification as part of the operation payload. This is because Web services security details are typically handled as part of the SOAP headers and JDMWS assumes that security is dealt with separately as part of the overall Web services framework.

11.4   Enabling JDM Web Services Using JAX-RPC

One of the objectives of defining JDMWS as part of the JDM Standard is to maintain a consistent API for both Java and Web services applications, thereby allowing them to share the same JDM implementation. JAX-RPC provides an easy way to wrap the JDM API implementation as JDMWS. Figure 11-9 illustrates the higher-level implementation architecture of the JDMWS using JAX-RPC and JDM API. JAX-RPC provides tools to generate the wrapper Java objects for the types defined in JDM WSDL and XML Schema.

This section gives a brief overview of JAX-RPC, and explains how to build JDMWS using JAX-RPC. In particular, this discussion will benefit Java developers who want their applications to communicate with an existing JDMWS implementation.

11.4.1   Overview of JAX-RPC

JAX-RPC is the Java API for XML-based Remote Procedure Call (RPC) defined under JSR-101 and included as part of J2EE 1.4. JAX-RPC API is used to develop Java-based portable Web services using WSDL-to-Java and Java-to-WSDL standard mappings. The JAX-RPC runtime system automates the conversion of Java method calls and objects to appropriate SOAP request and response messages in a Web services environment.

Figure 11-10 illustrates the high-level steps involved in a JAX-RPC runtime system. In this figure, the functionalities shown in gray boxes are handled by the JAX-RPC runtime—the user does not have to write any code for these functions. When a Web services Java client invokes a service provider operation, the JAX-RPC runtime

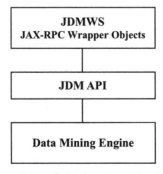

Figure 11-9   *JDMWS higher-level implementation architecture.*

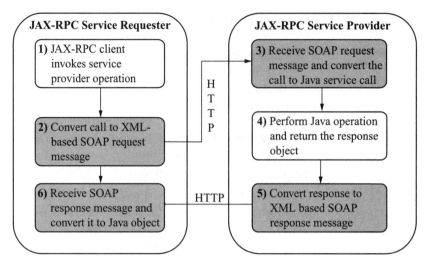

Figure 11-10   *JAX-RPC runtime.*

converts this call to the XML-based SOAP protocol–compliant request message and sends this message to the remote service provider using HTTP protocol as shown in steps 1 and 2. Once the service provider receives this message, it converts the SOAP request message to the appropriate Java service method call as shown in step 3. After the completion of the Java method execution by the service provider, the method's return parameter is converted to the appropriate SOAP response message and sent to the requester over HTTP protocol, as shown in steps 4 and 5 in Figure 11-10. The service requester receives the response message and converts it to the appropriate Java object that can be used by the Java client program as a regular method return parameter. For more details on JAX-RPC, refer to [Haefel 2003] and [JAX-RPC 2006].

11.4.2   Building JDMWS Using JAX-RPC

This section describes how to use JAX-RPC to build a JDM Web service that can be portable across multiple JDM vendor implementations. The JDM API defines Java interfaces; hence there are no data members defined in the API. As a result, it is not feasible to directly map the JAX-RPC from the JDM standard API to JDM Schema and WSDL definitions. However, as the JDM Schema maps to the JDM API object structure, by using JAX-RPC tools one can easily implement JDMWS. The following steps describe how to build a JDMWS.

Step 1: Convert JDM WSDL and JDM Schema to Java Objects

Typically, JAX-RPC runtime provides the WSDL-to-Java tool; one can use this tool to convert the JDM WSDL to JDM objects. As JDM WSDL imports the JDM Schema, the WSDL-to-Java tool converts all the JDM Schema elements to the associated JAX-RPC compatible objects. Figure 11-11 illustrates the typical Java files generated by a WSDL-to-Java tool. Because JDM uses different namespaces for schema and Web services, generated files will have associated packages. For example, all JDM Schema–related Java classes will be generated under the jdmws.schema package and all Web services–related Java classes will be generated under the jdmws. webservices package.

Step 2: Implement the *PortType* Interface

The next step to building the JDMWS is to implement the Java remote interface generated by the WSDL-to-Java tool. This interface can use either a wrapper on the JDM API (to be portable across JDM standard–compatible DMEs) or a DME-specific implementation. Because the JDM API maps to the Web services objects, JDMWS is easier to implement using the JDM API. For example, Listing 11-2

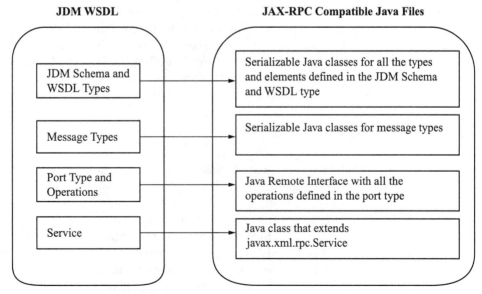

Figure 11-11 *WSDL-to-Java mapping.*

shows the *executeTask* operation defined under the *portType* element and has an associated Java method signature as shown in Listing 11-3. Note that this interface method is not taking input parameters using JDM API objects. Instead it is taking the mapping objects in the *jdmws.webservices* package generated by the JAX-RPC WSDL-to-Java tool, because the JAX-RPC runtime automates the object serialization and deserialization for these objects. The implementation of the *executeTask* method uses the JDM API *Connection.execute* method and returns the *ExecutionTaskResponse* by wrapping *ExecutionStatus* in the JDM API.

Listing 11-2   *executeTask WSDL portType operation*

```
1. <operation name="executeTask">
2.   <input message="jdmws:IDataMining_executeTask"/>
3.   <output message="jdmws:IDataMining_executeTaskResponse"/>
4.   <fault name="jdmExceptionMsg" message="jdmws:IDataMining_exception"/>
5. </operation>
```

Listing 11-3   *JDM WSDL structure*

```
public jdmws.webservices.ExecuteTaskResponse executeTask(
  jdmws.webservices.ExecuteTask parameters )
throws java.rmi.RemoteException
```

Step 3: Deploy the Service

Based on the JAX-RPC runtime, define the deployment profile and deploy as a service. For more details about the JAX-RPC deployment refer to [Haefel 2003] and [JAXRPC 2006]. The JAX-RPC is one of the most popular frameworks for enabling JDMWS and interacting with JDM implementations. However, developers can choose any other framework, such as .Net [.Net 2006], to enable JDMWS.

11.5   Summary

JDMWS provides the functionality consistent with the JDM Java API and increases the breadth of options available to application architects for integrating data mining functionality with existing applications. JDMWS fits well with the requirements of SOA and enables enterprises to adopt more flexible and standards-based data mining integration. JDMWS defines the WSDL document that describes the standard JDM Web services operations and messages. JDMWS can be enabled either by wrapping existing JDM implementations using JAX-RPC or by using any vendor-specific implementation. As Web services technologies evolve, JDMWS will take a primary role in the JDM standard to support vendor-neutral data mining application development.

References

[BPEL 2006] http://en.wikipedia.org/wiki/BPEL.

[BPEL-ENGINES 2006] http://en.wikipedia.org/wiki/List_of_BPEL_ engines.

[Erl 2005] Thomas Erl, *Service-Oriented Architecture (SOA): Concepts, Technology, and Design*, Service-Oriented Computing Series, Upper Saddle River, NJ, Prentice Hall, 2005.

[Haefel 2003] Richard Monson-Haefel, *J2EE Web Services*, Boston, Addison-Wesley, 2003.

[JAVA-RMI 2006] http://java.sun.com/products/jdk/rmi.

[JAX-RPC 2006] http://java.sun.com/webservices/jaxrpc/index.jsp.

[JDEV 2006] http://www.oracle.com/technology/products/jdev/index. html.

[JDM-WSDL 2006] http://www.jcp.org/en/jsr/detail?id=73.

[.Net 2006] http://en.wikipedia.org/wiki/.NET_Framework.

[MS-DCOM 2006] http://msdn.microsoft.com/library/en-us/dndcom/ html/msdn_dcomtec.asp.

[OASIS 2006] http://www.oasis-open.org.

[OMG-CORBA 2006] http://www.omg.org/gettingstarted/corbafaq.htm.

[WS-ARCH 2006] http://www.w3.org/TR/ws-arch.

[W3C 2006] http://www.w3c.org.

[WS-I 2006] http://www.ws-i.org.

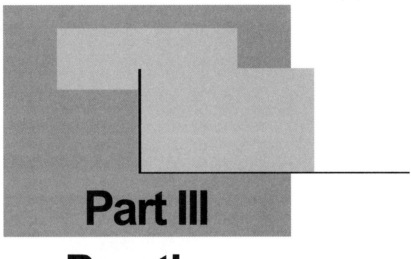

Part III
Practice

Chapter

12

Practical Problem Solving

In theory, there is no difference between theory and practice.
But, in practice, there is.

—Jan L. A. van de Snepscheut (1953–1994),
computer scientist and educator

It is one thing to use a well-defined process, such as CRISP-DM presented in Chapter 3, to define a business problem and data mining solution. However, it's quite another, as a developer, to implement that solution to realize business value and return on investment. In theory, a well-defined and thorough process should lead us more readily to success. In practice, we need concrete examples and guidance to ensure this.

This chapter presents several business scenarios, proposes an application design to solve the problems faced in each scenario, and provides Java code implementing the solution. This gives Java architects and programmers a starting point for writing applications using each of the major functionalities available in Java Data Mining (JDM). We focus not only on the specific tasks concerning data mining, such as building a model and deploying it, but also the operations that must be used to realize data mining solutions in a real environment. We complement this programmatic exercise with some considerations about the practical problems to be solved, and the skills needed to solve them.

Each scenario is associated with its business environment, the main actors involved in the process, and the specifications leading to the actual Java implementation. When needed, the scenario itself is broken down into operations or tasks.

12.1 Business Scenario 1: Targeted Marketing Campaign

As discussed in Chapter 2, there are many potential applications of data mining in customer relationship management (CRM). For example, response modeling can be used to determine whether a customer will respond positively to a campaign: often, the offer is made via a marketing campaign that can be a mass e-mailing, paper brochure, or call center solicitation to propose a new product to consumers. We have selected a scenario in this domain to illustrate the classification mining function. The scenario description follows.

The company High End Widgets (HEW) sells high-tech appliances to wealthy individuals. Because it is a very dynamic environment, HEW must perform marketing campaigns to its base of a million customers to present their new offers. On average, the company offers two new products every month. So, currently, all HEW customers are contacted twice a month. The HEW marketing department has been asked to reduce the cost of mailing campaigns as well as to reduce the number of mails per customer, because some of these customers are now complaining about the number of mails they receive from HEW—customer fatigue. The current response rate of each campaign is about 2 percent, which means that roughly 2 percent of the people contacted through these campaigns actually buy products.

Because these mailings are done twice a month, the HEW marketing department has decided to develop a specific application to target the consumers to contact. In marketing, this is called *targeting* or *campaign optimization*. This application will be realized in Java and will be used by a campaign manager. The following section describes the specifications of this application example.

12.1.1 Campaign Specifications

To both reduce the number of mails and avoid contacting customers not interested by the new offers, HEW has decided to focus its marketing campaigns using *starter* campaigns. A starter is a first wave of mails sent to a *sample* of the population, say 5,000 prospects, to collect responses. The starter campaign informs HEW which customers actually bought the products following the mailing, and can be used in conjunction with other customer information to produce a build dataset. The build dataset contains demographic data such as age, marital status, and zip code, or behavioral data such as aggregate values on previously purchased products per product category. These attributes serve as predictors and will be associated with a binary target to represent whether or not the person selected in the sample has bought the product. From the build dataset, HEW can produce a classification model for generating a probability that customers not selected for the starter campaign will buy the product. Combining this probability with the mailing cost structure, such as the per-item cost, and the profit generated when the customer buys the product, allows minimizing the number of mails sent for a predicted profit.

In this scenario, there are three actors: the campaign manager, the information technology (IT) department, and the contact agency. For each marketing campaign, the HEW marketing department nominates a campaign manager who will use the proposed predictive application. This campaign manager will be in contact with the HEW IT department in charge of database administration tasks, such as performing data extracts as requested by the campaign manager. The third actor is the contact agency (TCA), which is an external organization used by HEW to conduct the mailings: TCA must be provided with lists of names and addresses to be contacted for starter campaigns, collect the responses of the contacted persons, and return these responses to the campaign manager. TCA will also be used to contact the list of prospective customers, which will be provided in the same format as for the starter campaign.

The following is a step-by-step outline of the targeting campaign scenario process:

- HEW marketing department nominates a campaign manager.
- The campaign manager creates a new campaign in the application and defines campaign contents (such as the message of the mail) outside of the application.
- The campaign manager asks for a database extract showing all active customers, and specifies the information that must be associated with these prospects, such as demographic or behavioral data (also not done in the application). This data

extract is provided as a logical view or a physical table in the operational marketing database (OMDB).

- The campaign manager uses the application to sample customers from this extract for the starter campaign. The first version of the application permits selection of a simple random sample; however, subsequent versions will implement more sophisticated sampling strategies. Because the sampling technique may vary, sampling is not directly performed by the IT department. The sample is provided as a table in the OMDB that contains columns: customer name, customer address, and response, which will be filled later by values indicating *Responded* or *Did-not-respond*. In this example, HEW's customers are offered a single product, so the value *Responded* means that the customer purchased the proposed product. More complex situations can be met when mailing catalogs in which consumers choose possibly several products.

- HEW IT sends this extract to TCA as a text file.

- Some weeks later, HEW IT loads the customer prospect responses obtained by TCA in the OMDB.

- The campaign manager uses the application to produce a build dataset, to build classification models, and to forecast the expected profit of a large-scale campaign associated with a specific cost structure. The cost structure is composed of fixed costs, the unitary cost per mail, and the profit generated when the customer buys the product. Using this cost structure, the application optimizes the number of mails sent to maximize expected profit. It then reports this profit for each model built.

- The campaign manager uses the application to select the most effective model and uses this model to generate the prospective customers list for the large-scale mailing. This list will be stored in an OMDB table. The application reports the number of actual mails to be sent, the expected profit, and the expected number of respondents.

- HEW IT sends this prospective customers list to TCA as a file.

- Some weeks later, HEW IT loads the "response" values associated with the customers in the OMDB table.

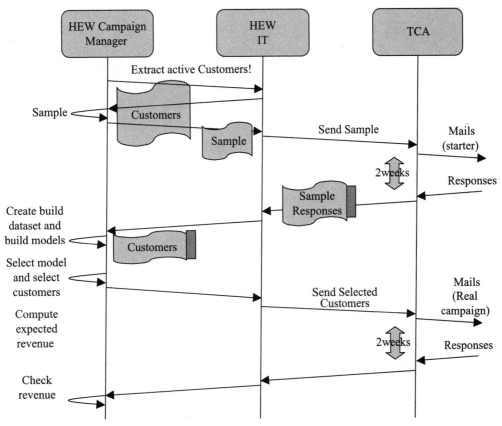

Figure 12-1   *Targeting campaign scenario.*

- The campaign manager uses the application to assess model accuracy by comparing expected and actual profit and predicted and actual number of respondents.

This process is illustrated in Figure 12-1.

12.1.2   Design of the "Campaign Optimization" Object

Here you are, a Java programmer, hired to implement this application. You are in charge of implementing the business layer of this project. Some other team members will be in charge of the user interface layer or the infrastructure layer such as the business layer persistence.

After a first look at the specifications, you know you will need two things: (1) Java Database Connectivity (JDBC) for some direct data manipulation, such as sampling, or merging of tables and (2) JDM to create a classification model for each campaign.

For simplicity, we will implement all services of the business layer in a single class called *CampaignOptimizer*. (This may not be the best design choice, but we wanted to focus on the implementation of the application.)

Because this chapter presents a lot of Java code, some naming conventions for variable names have been adopted:

- Input arguments are prefixed with *i*.
- Output arguments are prefixed with *o*.
- Member variables of objects are prefixed with *m*.
- Local variables are prefixed with *l*.

12.1.3   Code Examples

This section details the code of the *CampaignOptimizer* class that follows the steps described earlier.

The constructor creates a new campaign optimization object with a name and a creation date. Because our object must deal with some basic data manipulations as well as data mining operations, we provide it with two valid connections (JDBC and JDM). This is reflected in the following code:

```
1.   public CampaignOptimizer(String iName,
2.                            java.sql.Connection iJDBCConnection,
3.                            Connection iJDMConnection) {
4.       mName = iName;
5.       mCreationDate = Calendar.getInstance().getTime();
6.       mJDBCConnection = iJDBCConnection;
7.       mJDMConnection = iJDMConnection;
8.   }
```

The name of a *CampaignOptimizer* can be used by the persistence layer to save and retrieve *CampaignOptimizer* objects from repositories.

The next step involves sampling customers for the starter campaign, using a simple random sample as defined earlier for the first implementation of our application.

The first method collects the sampling parameters such as the data table name, name of columns to be used as mining attributes, the name of the customer identifier column, and the percentage of records to be kept in the sampled dataset. Some sanity checks can be performed when collecting parameters, for example, verifying that the input table and identified column names exist. These are identified as "TODO" items. The code reads as follows:

```
1.  public void defineSamplingParameters(String iInputTableName,
2.                          Collection iColumnNames,
3.                          String iIdentifierColumnName,
4.                          double iPercentage,
5.                      String iOutputTableName) throws SQLException {
6.      mInputTableName = iInputTableName;
7.      mColumnNames = iColumnNames;
8.      mPercentage = iPercentage;
9.      mIdentifierColumnName = iIdentifierColumnName;
10.     mOutputTableName = iOutputTableName;
11.     //TODO: add test about presence of the input table.
12.     //TODO: add tests about the existence of columns
13.     //TODO: add test about absence of the output table.
14.     mCurrentState = CampaignOptimizerState.SAMPLE_SELECTING;
15. }
```

The next method uses the JDBC connection to generate an SQL statement to produce the sample. In the following code, we assume that the customer identifier is an integer to allow SQL code that could be used on any database. When the remainder of dividing the customer identifier by 100 is below the sample percentage provided, we add that record to the sample. This approach has limitations, but it can work reasonably well if the customer identifiers' last two digits are uniformly distributed. Most of the commercial databases now provide specific SQL extensions to perform random sampling, such as the SAMPLE statement for Oracle,[1] but these extensions are not yet standardized.

The output table is generated with a column called RESPONSE filled with NULL values. This column will later be filled by the IT department with actual customer responses obtained from the starter campaign; these will be used as the target values to build a

---

[1]   The Oracle sample clause can be used as follows:
`SELECT * FROM tablename SAMPLE (20) SEED (4)`
In this example, a sample containing about 20 percent of the records in "tablename" will be returned. A "seed" value can be provided to ensure either the same sample is returned or a different sample is returned upon subsequent invocations.

classification model. Once the output table is created, the number of customers selected in this table is reported. This is reflected in the following code:

```
1.   public void exportSample() throws SQLException {
2.       // 1- Prepare the SQL statement and execute it
3.       String lSQLQuery = "create table " +mOutputTableName +" as select ";
4.       lSQLQuery += mIdentifierColumnName;
5.       for (Iterator lColNamesIter = mColumnNames.iterator();
            lColNamesIter.hasNext();) {
6.           String lColName = (String) lColNamesIter.next();
7.           lSQLQuery += ", " + lColName;
8.       }
9.       lSQLQuery += ", cast(NULL as INT) as RESPONSE";
10.      lSQLQuery += " from " + mInputTableName;
11.      lSQLQuery +=
             " WHERE (mod(" + mIdentifierColumnName + ", 100)) < " + mRatio;
12.      Statement lStatement = mJDBCConnection.createStatement();
13.      lStatement.executeQuery(lSQLQuery);
14.      // 2- Now determine the exported number of records
15.      String lSQLCountQuery = " select count(*) from " + mOutputTableName;
16.      Statement lStatementCount = mJDBCConnection.createStatement();
17.      ResultSet lResultSetCount =
             lStatementCount.executeQuery(lSQLCountQuery);
18.      lResultSetCount.next();
19.      mSamplingCount = lResultSetCount.getInt(1);
20.      report("SamplingCount: " + mSamplingCount);
21.      mExportDate = Calendar.getInstance().getTime();
22.      mCurrentState = CampaignOptimizerState.SAMPLE_SELECTED;
23.  }
```

For example, if you have requested to extract two columns, NAME and EMAIL, and a sample of 5 percent of the customer table called CUSTOMERS for which the primary identifier is a column called CUSTOMER_ID, the generated select statement follows:

```
create table STARTER_CUSTOMERS as
   select CUSTOMER_ID, NAME, EMAIL, cast(NULL as INT) as RESPONSE
   from CUSTOMERS
   where (mod(CUSTOMER_ID, 100)) < 5;
```

It is expected, in this specific scenario, that some period of time will elapse between the previous operation and when TCA returns the actual responses to the IT department for loading into the OMDB. The RESPONSE column contains a "1" if the customer responded positively to the mail by buying the product, and "0" if the customer did not respond.

At this point, we begin model building using the responses from the starter campaign (which serve as the target values) and the corresponding customer demographics and other predictor attributes. This is done using an SQL *join* statement, which basically maps the RESPONSE column to the corresponding customer predictor attributes using the customer identifier in each table. For example, if the table containing the original information is CUSTOMERS and the sample table is STARTER_CUSTOMERS, the SQL statement used to create the training dataset looks like:

```
select c.*, sc.RESPONSE
   from STARTER_CUSTOMERS sc left outer join
        CUSTOMERS c on sc.CUSTOMER_ID = c.CUSTOMER_ID
   where sc.RESPONSE IS NOT null
```

For those not familiar with SQL, here is an explanation of the "left outer join" in this context. The statement will return all the customers contained in STARTER_CUSTOMERS (which is our sample list) for which the response has been provided (either 1 or 0) and join the information known about them contained in the CUSTOMERS table. Because the STARTER_CUSTOMERS list has been obtained from a sample of the CUSTOMERS table, as soon as the RESPONSE field is valid, this statement will return a table with one line for each customer in our sample and all the known information about these customers. This statement is created in the code of the method *buildSQLStatement*, shown between lines 2 and 6 in the next code listing.

Our specification mentioned that the campaign manager would have to select a number of attributes used to build models. To express this, we have two options: One is to use the JDM *LogicalData* feature that allows users to indicate if attributes are ACTIVE or INACTIVE via *AttributeUsageType*. The second is to design SQL select statements that retrieve only the columns (attributes) explicitly selected. We will show the use of logical data; however, the implementation of *LogicalData* is optional in JDM and should be checked through the capabilities of the particular data mining engine (DME).

The method *buildSQLStatement* is shown here:

```
1.   public String buildSQLStatement(){
2.     String lSQLStatement = "select c.*, sc.RESPONSE from "
3.         + mOutputTableName + " sc left outer join "
4.         + mInputTableName + " c on sc."
5.         + mIdentifierColumnName + " = c." + mIdentifierColumnName
6.         + " where (sc.RESPONSE IS NOT null)";
7.     return lSQLStatement;
8.   }
```

Now, we have to transform this SQL *select* statement into something that can be used by the JDM implementation as a *PhysicalDataSet* for use in the classification build task. In JDM, physical datasets are specified using a uniform resource identifier (URI) with a vendor-specific syntax. Hence, the code that translates the SQL statement into a dataset URI is vendor-specific. We have placed this code into the method *get-VendorJDMDataSetURI*.

A vendor implementation may allow the use of a select statement as part of the URI, perhaps creating a table using a CREATE TABLE AS statement, or, the vendor implementation may allow the use of a select statement directly, avoiding the creation of an intermediate table. The next code listing contains this vendor-specific code starting from an SQL statement at line 9. We set the case identifier attribute in lines 12 to 14.

Then, *LogicalData* is used to select the active attributes. The list of active attributes is provided by the campaign manager. We could use the *LogicalAttributeFactory* to create logical attributes and provide the *AttributeType* explicitly to the create method for *LogicalAttribute*. However, we will rely on the data mining engine (DME) to automatically create the logical attributes from the physical dataset. This is done at line 19. In this case, the DME assigns the *AttributeType* to each attribute, and declares all the logical attributes to be active by default. The *LogicalData* is saved at line 23. Note that all available attributes will be used to build the model if the user specifies an empty attribute list.

Next, a *ClassificationSettings* object is created and associated with the target attribute name RESPONSE, as shown at line 34. If the user has specified a list of active attributes, this *ClassificationSettings* object must reference the saved *LogicalData* and the active attributes must be specified. Recall that when logical attributes are created from the physical dataset, they are declared as active by default. We first set all logical attributes to inactive, and then the attributes provided as input arguments are set to active at lines 50 to 52. Once this operation is completed, the *ClassificationSettings* object is saved.

Finally, we create the *BuildTask* to associate the build settings, the build dataset, and the user-specified model name at line 61. This task is verified at line 67 and saved in the mining object repository (MOR) at line 72, and then executed at line 73. Upon successful execution of this build task, a model with the specified name can then be used for scoring.

Some advanced users could write equivalent methods to specifically build a decision tree or a neural network. All these models will be remembered by their names in the campaign optimization object. The next section shows that it is possible to compare models to select the best.

The following code assumes that the JDM implementation can build a model on "unprepared" data, as described in Chapter 7. If the JDM implementation requires data preparation, some specific code will have to be included to perform this preparation.

```
1.   public void buildModel(String iModelName, Collection iActiveAttributes)
2.       throws JDMException, InterruptedException {
3.     String lDataSetName = iModelName + "_DS";
4.     String lBuildDataSQLStatement = buildSQLStatement();
5.     mBuildDataSQL = lBuildDataSQLStatement;
6.     PhysicalDataSetFactory lPdsFactory =
7.       (PhysicalDataSetFactory) mJDMConnection.getFactory(
8.         "javax.datamining.data.PhysicalDataSet");
9.     String lDataSetURI = getVendorDatasetURI(lBuildDataSQLStatement);
10.    PhysicalDataSet lBuildData = lPdsFactory.create(lDataSetURI, false);
11.    lBuildData.importMetaData();
12.    PhysicalAttribute lAttr
13.      = lBuildData.getAttribute(mIdentifierColumnName.toUpperCase());
14.    lAttr.setRole(PhysicalAttributeRole.caseId);
15.    mJDMConnection.saveObject(lDataSetName, lBuildData, true);
16.    LogicalDataFactory lLDFactory =
17.      (LogicalDataFactory) mJDMConnection.getFactory(
18.        "javax.datamining.data.LogicalData");
19.    LogicalData lLogdata = lLDFactory.create(lBuildData);
20.    String lLogicalDataName = iModelName + "_LD";
21.    if (0 < iActiveAttributes.size())
22.    {
23.      mJDMConnection.saveObject(lLogicalDataName,
24.                    lLogdata,
25.                    true);
```

```
26.     }
27.     String lSettingsName = iModelName + "_S";
28.     ClassificationSettingsFactory lCsFactory =
29.         (ClassificationSettingsFactory) mJDMConnection.getFactory(
30.             "javax.datamining.supervised.classification"
31.             + ".ClassificationSettings");
32.     ClassificationSettings lClassificationSettings =
33.         lCsFactory.create();
34.     lClassificationSettings.setTargetAttributeName("RESPONSE");
35.     if (0 < iActiveAttributes.size()) {
36.         lClassificationSettings.setLogicalDataName(lLogicalDataName);
37.         Collection lLogAttributes = lLogdata.getAttributes();
38.         for (Iterator lAttrIter = lLogAttributes.iterator();
39.              lAttrIter.hasNext(); ){
40.             String lAttributeName =
41.                 ((LogicalAttribute)(lAttrIter.next())).getName();
42.             lClassificationSettings.setUsage
43.                 (lAttributeName,
44.                  LogicalAttributeUsage.inactive);
45.         }
46.         for (Iterator lActiveAttrIter = iActiveAttributes.iterator();
47.              lActiveAttrIter.hasNext(); ){
48.             String lAttributeName = ((String)(lActiveAttrIter.next())).
49.                 toUpperCase();
50.             lClassificationSettings.setUsage
51.                 (lAttributeName,
52.                  LogicalAttributeUsage.active);
53.         }
54.         lClassificationSettings.setUsage("RESPONSE",
55.                                          LogicalAttributeUsage.active);
56.     }
57.     mJDMConnection.saveObject(lSettingsName,
58.                               lClassificationSettings,
59.                               true);
60.     String lTaskName = iModelName + "_T";
61.     BuildTaskFactory lBuildTaskFactory =
62.         (BuildTaskFactory) mJDMConnection.getFactory(
63.             "javax.datamining.task.BuildTask");
64.     BuildTask lBuildTask = lBuildTaskFactory.create(lDataSetName,
65.                                                     lSettingsName,
66.                                                     iModelName);
67.     VerificationReport lVerifTask = lBuildTask.verify();
68.     if (lVerifTask != null) {
69.         reportError(lVerifTask.getReportText());
70.         return;
71.     }
72.     mJDMConnection.saveObject(lTaskName, lBuildTask, true);
73.     boolean lSuccess = executeTask(lTaskName);
74.     if (!lSuccess) {
75.         report("Did not manage to build classification model!");
76.         return;
77.     }
```

```
78.    mModelNames.put(iModelName, iActiveAttributes);
79.    mCurrentState = CampaignOptimizerState.ANALYZING;
80. }
```

The user can run the *buildModel* method several times, for example, keeping only the demographic attributes, then keeping only the behavioral data. This can be done by invoking the method described earlier with different values for the *iActiveAttributes* argument. All models successfully built are saved into a member variable of the *CampaignOptimizer* object called *mModelNames*, which is a map associating the name of the built model with the list of active attributes used by this model. This list of model names will be used to select the best model later. More complex scenarios could use specific algorithm settings to create several decision trees with different settings.

The next step will be to select the best model based on the cost structure, and associate this model with a specific threshold to decide whether or not mail should be sent to a given customer. As in any response model, the model predicts not only if the customer will respond, but also a probability that a customer will respond. The campaign manager must select a threshold probability such that customers scoring above that threshold will receive the offer. To tune this probability, we use the receiver operating characteristics (ROC) curve returned by the *TestMetrics* task.

The ROC curve was discussed in Chapter 7. Table 12-1 provides an example of data that is returned in the ROC object.

Table 12-1 *ROC Object—example data contents*

False Alarm	Hit Rate	True Neg.	False Neg.	True Pos.	False Pos.	Probability Threshold
0.0	0.0	37155	11687	0	0	1.000
0.05	0.526724	35297	5531	6155	1857	0.451
0.1	0.674433	33439	3804	7882	3715	0.365
0.15	0.768535	31581	2705	8981	5573	0.280
0.2	0.83775	29724	1896	9790	7431	0.212
0.25	0.887242	27866	1317	10369	9288	0.161
0.3	0.922603	26008	904	10782	11146	0.110

Table 12-1   *ROC Object—example data contents (continued)*

False Alarm	Hit Rate	True Neg.	False Neg.	True Pos.	False Pos.	Probability Threshold
0.35	0.945291	24150	639	11047	13004	0.075
0.4	0.960988	22293	455	11231	14862	0.071
0.45	0.973021	20435	315	11371	16719	0.039
0.5	0.982192	18577	208	11478	18577	0.034
0.55	0.988682	16719	132	11554	20435	0.012
0.6	0.992834	14862	83	11603	22293	0.007
0.65	0.995267	13004	55	11631	24150	0.006
0.7	0.997004	11146	35	11651	26008	0.004
0.75	0.998207	9288	20	11666	27866	0.003
0.8	0.998736	7431	14	11672	29724	0.003
0.85	0.999135	5573	10	11676	31581	0.002
0.9	0.999436	3715	6	11680	33439	0.002
0.95	0.9997	1857	3	11683	35297	0.001
1.0	1.0	0	0	11687	37155	0

The data points contained in this table are often depicted as the ROC curve gains chart, which shows the true positive rate, or *hit rate*, against the false positive rate, or *false alarm rate*, as shown in Figure 12-2. For each point on this curve, JDM also provides all elements of the confusion matrix associated with the probability threshold. In other words, the third row of Table 12-1 tells you that, if you select all the customers with a probability higher than 0.36 (value of the last column), it will return 7,882 + 3,715 "positive" customers (the sum of the true positive and false positive cases). Here, remember that positive/negative means selected/not selected by the model, and true/false means correctly/incorrectly classified. Table 12-1's first row entry means that the probability threshold is so high that no customers are selected. In the last row entry, the threshold is so low that all customers are selected. Now, to come back to the third row, 7,882 customers were correctly classified, which means that, in our scenario, they are buying the product proposed by HEW, and 3,715 were contacted but did not buy the product. The nice thing about all

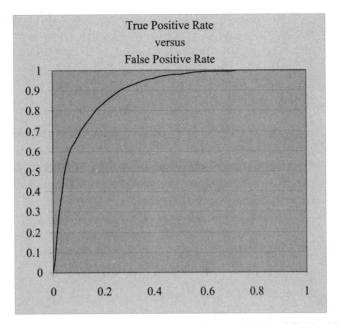

Figure 12-2   *The ROC Curve of data points of Table 12-1.*

these numbers is that they can be used to pick the probability threshold to optimize the revenue if we know the cost associated with each of the 3,715 negative responses and the profit associated with the 7,882 positive responses.

Given these numbers, we can select — for each model, based on the ROC curve obtained on the test dataset — the probability threshold that will maximize revenue. The following code shows how to perform that computation by creating a *TestMetrics* task for each model and asking for the ROC curve, which is specified at line 20. We scan through the different threshold candidates of the ROC curve. Each threshold candidate provides access to the elements shown in Table 12-1. In particular, we can get back the number of true positives and false positives, and compute the expected profit if we set the threshold at this level. The expected return will be the difference between the number of true positives (the customers that are contacted and responded positively) times the individual profit, and the number of false positives (the customers that are contacted but did not respond positively) times the individual cost.

Expected Return = (number of true positives × individual profit)
− (number of false positives × individual cost)

The loop started at line 35 selects the threshold candidate with the highest expected return at line 40. This expected return is associated with the model (it is the best functioning point of a given model), and the model with the highest expected return is then selected at line 45. For this, we need to provide the method with an individual cost (the cost of a mailing to a customer), an individual profit (how much does HEW get when a customer buys the product), and a fixed cost (usually the cost associated with the design/graphics of the mailing). The fixed cost, being the same for all models and all threshold candidates, is not taken into account in the selection of the best model but will be used to compute the expected profit.

```
1.    public void selectBestModel(double iGlobalCost,
2.                                 double iIndividualCost,
3.                                 double iIndividualProfit)
4.       throws JDMException, InterruptedException {
5.       mGlobalCost = iGlobalCost;
6.       mIndividualCost = iIndividualCost;
7.       mIndividualProfit = iIndividualProfit;
8.       ClassificationTestTaskFactory lTestTaskFactory =
9.          (ClassificationTestTaskFactory) mJDMConnection.getFactory(
10.        "javax.datamining.supervised.classification.ClassificationTestTask");
11.       String lBestModelName = null;
12.       double lModelsBestProba = 0.0;
13.       double lModelsBestValue = 0.0;
14.       for (Iterator lModelNameIter = mModelNames.keySet().iterator();
15.             lModelNameIter.hasNext();) {
16.          String lModelName = (String) lModelNameIter.next();
17.          ClassificationTestTask lTestTask = lTestTaskFactory.create(
18.             lModelName + "_DS", lModelName, lModelName + "_Metrics");
19.          lTestTask.computeMetric(
20.           ClassificationTestMetricOption.receiverOperatingCharacteristics,
21.           true);
22.          mJDMConnection.saveObject(lModelName + "_TT", lTestTask, true);
23.          boolean lSuccess = executeTask(lModelName + "_TT");
24.          if (!lSuccess) {
25.             return;
26.          }
27.          ClassificationTestMetrics lMetrics
28.             = (ClassificationTestMetrics) mJDMConnection
29.               .retrieveObject(lModelName + "_Metrics",
30.                               NamedObject.testMetrics);
31.          ReceiverOperatingCharacterics lROC = lMetrics.getROC();
32.          int lCount = lROC.getNumberOfThresholdCandidates();
33.          double lBestValue = 0;
34.          double lBestProba = 0;
```

```
35.        for (int lIdx = 0; lIdx < lCount; lIdx++) {
36.            long lTP = lROC.getPositives(lIdx, true);
37.            long lFP = lROC.getPositives(lIdx, false);
38.            double lValue = (lTP * iIndividualProfit) -
39.                              (lFP * iIndividualCost);
40.            if (lBestValue < lBestValue) {
41.                lBestValue = lValue;
42.                lBestProba = lROC.getProbabilityThreshold(lIdx);
43.            }
44.        }
45.        if (lModelsBestValue < lBestValue) {
46.            lModelsBestValue = lBestValue;
47.            lModelsBestProba = lBestProba;
48.            lBestModelName = lModelName;
49.        }
50.    }
51.    mBestModelName = lBestModelName;
52.    mBestModelProbaThreshold = lModelsBestProba;
53. }
```

Then, the selected model will be used to generate the probabilities associated with each individual customer. To do this, we create the appropriate *ApplySettings*, asking to generate the probability of being in the desired category (the *Responded* category). We show how to apply the model to customers for the large-scale campaign, and exclude those from the starter campaign. For this, we create an SQL statement with logic opposite from the one we used for the build dataset. The following SQL selects the customers for which we do not have any response during the starter mailing campaign.

```
select c.*
    from CUSTOMERS c left outer join
         STARTER_CUSTOMERS sc on c.CUSTOMER_ID = sc.CUSTOMER_ID
    where (sc.RESPONSE IS null)
```

When creating the *ApplyTask*, we specify the name of the dataset where the scored results, that is, probabilities, are placed. In our design, these results will be stored in an intermediate table as specified in the variable *iApplyOutputDataName* with an "_ALL" suffix, as shown at line 39. This table contains only intermediate results because we need to filter those customers meeting the probability threshold requirement. Those customers selected are placed in the final result dataset named in *iApplyOutputDataName*.

To perform this selection, a view is created in the OMDB to select only the customers with a probability higher than the threshold, which is executed at line 57. The contents of this view will be forwarded to TCA together with the names and addresses of the prospective customers to contact.

We can also report the expected number of responses prior to sending the mailing. This is obtained by summing the probabilities for all customers in this dataset. The expected number of responders can be used to compute the expected profit prior to sending the actual mailings. Again this is done in SQL and executed at line 63. Multiplying the individual profit by the expected positive responses and subtracting from this the individual cost times the expected negative responses leads to an estimation of the global profit of this campaign, as shown between lines 68 and 70.

```
1.    public void applymodel(String iTargetKey,
2.                         String iApplyOutputDataName)
3.        throws JDMException, InterruptedException, SQLException {
4.      String lApplyDSSettName = getBestModelName() + "_ApplyS";
5.      ClassificationApplySettingsFactory lApplySettFactory =
6.          (ClassificationApplySettingsFactory) mJDMConnection.getFactory(
7.      "javax.datamining.supervised.classification.ClassificationApplySettings");
8.      ClassificationApplySettings lApplySett = lApplySettFactory.create();
9.      lApplySett.mapByCategory(ClassificationApplyContent.probability,
10.                         iTargetKey,
11.                         "Proba");
12.     mJDMConnection.saveObject(lApplyDSSettName, lApplySett, true);
13.
14.     String lApplyDataSetName = getBestModelName() + "_ApplyDS";
15.     String lApplyDataSQLStatement = "select a.* from "
16.         + mInputTableName + " a left outer join "
17.         + mOutputTableName + " b on a."
18.         + mIdentifierColumnName + " = b." + mIdentifierColumnName
19.         + " where (b.RESPONSE IS null)";
20.     mApplyDataSQL = lApplyDataSQLStatement;
21.     PhysicalDataSetFactory lPdsFactory =
22.         (PhysicalDataSetFactory) mJDMConnection.getFactory(
23.           "javax.datamining.data.PhysicalDataSet");
24.     String lDataSetURI = getVendorDatasetURI(lApplyDataSQLStatement);
25.     PhysicalDataSet lApplyData = lPdsFactory.create(lDataSetURI, false);
26.     lApplyData.importMetaData();
27.     PhysicalAttribute lAttr
28.         = lApplyData.getAttribute(mIdentifierColumnName.toUpperCase());
29.     lAttr.setRole(PhysicalAttributeRole.caseId);
30.     mJDMConnection.saveObject(lApplyDataSetName, lApplyData, true);
31.     mApplyOutputDataName = iApplyOutputDataName;
32.     DataSetApplyTaskFactory lApplyTaskFactory =
33.         (DataSetApplyTaskFactory) mJDMConnection.getFactory(
```

```
34.                "javax.datamining.task.apply.DataSetApplyTask");
35.   DataSetApplyTask lApplyTask = lApplyTaskFactory.create(
36.       lApplyDataSetName,
37.       getBestModelName(),
38.       lApplyDSSettName,
39.       getVendorJDMDatasetURI(iApplyOutputDataName + "_ALL"));
40.
41.   VerificationReport lVerifTask = lApplyTask.verify();
42.   if (lVerifTask != null) {
43.       reportError(lVerifTask.getReportText());
44.       return;
45.   }
46.
47.   mJDMConnection.saveObject(getBestModelName() + "_ApplyT",
48.                             lApplyTask,
49.                             true);
50.   boolean lSuccess = executeTask(getBestModelName() + "_ApplyT");
51.   if (!lSuccess) {
52.       return;
53.   }
54.   String lSQLQuery = "create view " + iApplyOutputDataName
55.       + " as (select * from " + iApplyOutputDataName + "_ALL"
56.       + " where Proba > " + mBestModelProbaThreshold + ")";
57.   Statement lStatement = mJDBCConnection.createStatement();
58.   lStatement.executeQuery(lSQLQuery);
59.   String lSQLCountQuery = " select count(*), sum(Proba) from "
60.       + iApplyOutputDataName;
61.   Statement lStatementCount = mJDBCConnection.createStatement();
62.   ResultSet lResultSetCount
63.       = lStatementCount.executeQuery(lSQLCountQuery);
64.   lResultSetCount.next();
65.   mApplyCount = lResultSetCount.getInt(1);
66.   mExpectedResponses = lResultSetCount.getInt(2);
67.
68.   mExpectedProfit = ((mExpectedResponses * mIndividualProfit)
69.       - ((mApplyCount - mExpectedResponses) * mIndividualCost))
70.          - mGlobalCost;
71.   report("Expected Profit using model [" + getBestModelName() + "]: "
72.          + mExpectedProfit);
73. }
```

Once the full campaign is complete, the last operation is to check that the actual revenue is in line with the expected revenue. This can be done using the following method, which assumes that the responses have been collected in the table used to hold results of the apply of the model. The name of that table can be obtained through the member variable called *mApplyOutputDataName*. For example, assuming that the table name *iApplyOutputDataName* was set to SCORE in calling the method *applyModel*, the table SCORE_ALL was created with a column RESPONSE with only empty values. If we assume that this RESPONSE column is filled later with the actual responses of 1 (positive response), 0 (negative response), or it remains NULL if the customer has not been contacted, then we can use SCORE_ALL to check the expected revenue with the actual revenue generated by the campaign. Computing revenue, taking into account the cost structure, is exactly the same as the formula used to predict the expected profit, as shown in lines 13 to 15.

```
1.   public void checkRevenue()
2.           throws SQLException {
3.       String lSQLCountQuery = " select count(*), sum(RESPONSE) from "
4.           + mApplyOutputDataName + "_ALL "
5.           + "where RESPONSE IS NOT NULL and Proba > " + mBestModelProbaThreshold;
6.       Statement lStatementCount = mJDBCConnection.createStatement();
7.       ResultSet lResultSetCount
8.           = lStatementCount.executeQuery(lSQLCountQuery);
9.       lResultSetCount.next();
10.      int lResponseCount = lResultSetCount.getInt(1);
11.      int lActualResponses = lResultSetCount.getInt(2);
12.      doublelActualProfit = 0.0;
13.      lActualProfit = ((lActualResponses * mIndividualProfit)
14.          - ((lResponseCount - lActualResponses) * mIndividualCost))
15.              - mGlobalCost;
16.      report("Actual Profit using model [" + getBestModelName() + "]: "
17.          + lActualProfit + " to be compared with expected "
18.          + mExpectedProfit);
19. }
```

That concludes the project, in which JDM and JDBC were used to improve target marketing campaigns.

12.1.4   Scenario 1 Conclusion

The code in this section has been tested. It shows how to write an operational application using JDBC for basic data manipulation and JDM for data mining operations. One important aspect of the preceding code is that it did not require extensive data mining knowledge. The most complex part of the code implies a clear understanding of the values returned by the ROC curve obtained through a *TestMetrics* task. The second important thing to notice is the compactness of the code. The number of lines is small compared to its business value for HEW.

To achieve code compactness, we made two assumptions about the JDM implementation:

- Its ability to build classification models on unprepared data: If the JDM implementation does not work directly on unprepared data, the code presented above must be augmented with data preparation code. Because data preparation is algorithm-specific, the Java programmer must understand how to prepare data for the specific algorithm.

- Its ability to build classification models when the ratio of positive cases is small (such as 2 percent): If a JDM implementation does not offer an algorithm giving good results when the number of positive cases is low, the code presented earlier must be modified before building models. Specifically, the build dataset must be produced with all possible positive cases and a subsample of the negative cases — a stratified sample allowing a more balanced (50% to 50%) proportion of positive versus negative cases in the build dataset. When such stratified sampling is used, the JDM feature for specifying prior probabilities can be used in the *ClassificationBuildSettings*.

12.2   Business Scenario 2: Understanding Key Factors

HEW has used the *CampaignOptimizer* code to compare several JDM implementations in one experimental campaign, and was particularly impressed with the results, both in terms of ease of use and performance, but the campaign manager wanted more information about *how* the models were making their predictions. As an example, he would have loved to see which attributes were most used by the DME to compute the probability that a prospective customer will respond to that mailing.

12.2.1   Code Example

With this new objective, the user has decided to complement the *CampaignOptimizer* object with a feature to indicate key factors. This is a small enhancement to the previous project, which does not require any new design considerations.

In JDM, the notion of key factors can be obtained through attribute importance. There are two ways to obtain a list of the important attributes: (1) as a side effect of model building or (2) by building a specific model of type *AttributeImportanceModel*.

The first technique can be used by a business user to deepen his confidence in the quality of the models, and the second technique can be used before building any classification models to have a reduced set of attributes on which to build models.

We augment the *CampaignOptimizer* with these two possibilities. When several models have been built, one can use the method called *findKeyFactorsFromModels* to retrieve the important attributes from each model, or one can use the method called *findKeyFactors* to specifically compute the attribute importance independently of any classification model. Both methods take the number of attributes that the campaign manager wants to inspect.

Following is the code for *findKeyFactorsFromModels:*

```
1.    public void findKeyFactorsFromModels(int iAttributeCount)
2.          throws JDMException, InterruptedException {
3.      for (Iterator lModelNameIter = mModelNames.keySet().iterator();
4.           lModelNameIter.hasNext();) {
5.          String lModelName = (String) lModelNameIter.next();
6.          // We need to present the key factors to the campaign manager
7.          ClassificationModel lModel = (ClassificationModel)
8.              mJDMConnection.retrieveObject(lModelName,
9.                                    NamedObject.model);
10.         Collection lAttributes = lModel.getSignature().
11.             getAttributesByRank(SortOrder.descending);
12.         if (0 < lAttributes.size()) {
13.             intlAttrIdx = 1;
14.             for (Iterator lAttrIter = lAttributes.iterator();
15.                  (lAttrIter.hasNext()) && (lAttrIdx < iAttributeCount); ) {
16.                 AttributelAttribute = (Attribute) lAttrIter.next();
17.                 report("Attribute " + lAttrIdx
18.                        + " is " + lAttribute.getName());
19.                 lAttrIdx ++;
20.             }
21.         } else {
22.             report("This JDM DME does not support attribute ranking!");
23.         }
24.     }
25. }
```

In this method, we scan the different models that were built in the *CampaignOptimizer* instance. We retrieve them from the DME at line 8, and obtain their respective model signatures. As noted in Chapter 7, the attribute ranking information is stored in this signature and accessed using the method *getAttributesByRank*, as shown at line 11. The attributes, sorted in descending order, are reported to the user. If the JDM implementation does not support this feature, the size of the collection returned will be 0 and, thus, we report it to the campaign manager as shown by the test at line 12 and the message at line 22.

If the campaign manager wants to know, before building any model, which key factors affect predictions, he can execute the following method, called *findKeyFactors:*

```
1.    public Vector findKeyFactors(int iAttributeCount)
2.          throws JDMException, InterruptedException {
3.        Vector lFactors = new Vector();
4.        String lModelName = "KeyFactors";
5.        String lSettingsName = lModelName + "_S";
6.        AttributeImportanceSettingsFactory lCsFactory =
7.            (AttributeImportanceSettingsFactory) mJDMConnection.getFactory(
8.              "javax.datamining.attributeimportance"
9.              + ".AttributeImportanceSettings");
10.       AttributeImportanceSettings lAttributeImportanceSettings =
11.           lCsFactory.create();
12.       lAttributeImportanceSettings.setTargetAttributeName("RESPONSE");
13.       mJDMConnection.saveObject(lSettingsName,
14.                                 lAttributeImportanceSettings,
15.                                 true);
16.
17.       String lDataSetName = lModelName + "_DS";
18.       String lBuildDataSQLStatement = buildSQLStatement();
19.       PhysicalDataSetFactory lPdsFactory =
20.           (PhysicalDataSetFactory) mJDMConnection.getFactory(
21.             "javax.datamining.data.PhysicalDataSet");
22.       String lDataSetURI = getVendorDatasetURI(lBuildDataSQLStatement);
23.       PhysicalDataSet lBuildData = lPdsFactory.create(lDataSetURI, false);
24.       lBuildData.importMetaData();
25.       PhysicalAttribute lAttr
26.           = lBuildData.getAttribute(mIdentifierColumnName.toUpperCase());
27.       lAttr.setRole(PhysicalAttributeRole.caseId);
28.       mJDMConnection.saveObject(lDataSetName, lBuildData, true);
29.
30.       String lTaskName = lModelName + "_T";
31.       BuildTaskFactory lBuildTaskFactory =
32.           (BuildTaskFactory) mJDMConnection.getFactory(
33.             "javax.datamining.task.BuildTask");
34.       BuildTask lBuildTask = lBuildTaskFactory.create(lDataSetName,
35.                                                       lSettingsName,
36.                                                       lModelName);
37.       VerificationReport lVerifTask = lBuildTask.verify();
38.       if (lVerifTask != null) {
39.           reportError(lVerifTask.getReportText());
40.           return lFactors;
41.       }
```

```
42.      mJDMConnection.saveObject(lTaskName, lBuildTask, true);
43.      boolean lSuccess = executeTask(lTaskName);
44.
45.      // Check success/error
46.      if (lSuccess) {
47.          // We need to present the key influencers to the campaign manager
48.          AttributeImportanceModel lModel
49.              = (AttributeImportanceModel) mJDMConnection
50.                  .retrieveObject(lModelName,
51.                                  NamedObject.model);
52.          Collection lAttributes  = lModel.
53.              getAttributesByRank(SortOrder.descending);
54.          intlAttrIdx = 1;
55.          for (Iterator lAttrIter = lAttributes.iterator();
56.              (lAttrIter.hasNext()) && (lAttrIdx <= iAttributeCount); ) {
57.              StringlAttrName = (String) lAttrIter.next();
58.              report("Attribute " + lAttrIdx + " is " + lAttrName);
59.              lAttrIdx ++;
60.              lFactors.add(lAttrName);
61.          }
62.      }
63.      return lFactors;
64. }
```

In lines 1 to 42, all the objects needed to create an attribute importance model are created and saved. Then, the *BuildTask* is executed and, if successful, the model is retrieved from the MOR at line 50. The attribute names are extracted from the *AttributeImportanceModel* in descending order at line 53 and the most important attributes are collected into a vector, which is returned by this method at line 63. The vector of attribute names returned by this method can be directly fed into the argument *iActiveAttributes* of the *buildModel* method.

12.2.2   Scenario 2 Conclusion

The attribute importance-related code presented in this section will likely be used in conjunction with other modeling techniques. In the previous scenario, we designed our *CampaignOptimizer* methods in a way that makes it possible to directly take the output of the *findKeyFactors* method and to use it as the input for building a classification model.

Again, the assumption that we made here is that the JDM implementation can work on unprepared data for attribute importance.

12.3 Business Scenario 3: Using Customer Segmentation

HEW has been successfully using the previous applications to optimize direct marketing campaigns. The chief marketing officer (CMO) now wants to advertise in select mass media. For this, he needs to know more about the customer profiles to target the proper magazines and TV channels.

The marketing term for getting these profiles is *segmentation*. Customer segmentation can be done in many ways, and those familiar with the CRM space know that the subject of customer segmentation could fill a book of its own; in fact, many books have been written on the subject (see, for example, *Optimal Database Marketing: Strategy, Development and Data Mining* [Drozenko/Drake 2002]). Most customer segmentation efforts are designed to optimize promotional product offerings and are generally made in several stages. First, customer segments are made based on information available in the customer database, such as customers engaged in fraud, a "do-not-promote" segment of those who do not want to be contacted anymore, and high risk accounts to be discarded from the next mass mailings.

Then, the remaining population can be segmented using what is called *life-stage segmentation*, which is primarily based on demographic and psychographic data obtained internally or externally. These segments can be used to determine the future needs of HEW customers or to adapt promotions or messages to customer interests.

12.3.1 Customer Segmentation Specifications

To perform the customer segmentation operation, the CMO will buy psychographic data, such as customer hobby, music, movie, or book preferences, from an external service bureau or data enhancement facility. In this example, the service bureau is called "The Service Bureau" (TSB). This company can augment a file containing names and addresses with both demographic information, such as household size, household income, the age of the head of household in years, and psychographic information, such as interests and hobbies.

This data will be used to create a small number of clusters (between 5 and 10) for the entire HEW customer database. Then, these clusters will be characterized in terms of important demographic and psychographic attributes and each cluster will manually be assigned a descriptive name. Recognizing a good clustering from a bad one is difficult. There is no mathematical formula that can be used. A good clustering is one that "talks" to the marketers.

To get this profile information, we will use counts obtained from the OMDB to compare profiles from psychographic attributes for each obtained cluster, or we can use the profiles from buying patterns with respect to each product line. These profiles will be presented to and validated by the CMO. The marketing manager then uses this information to select, for each product line, appropriate magazines or TV channels.

Again, because the CMO expects this process to be done on a regular basis, especially because he would like to be able to compare profiles easily for each cluster, HEW has decided to build a "tool" to perform these operations. This tool will be referred as the *Customer Segmenter* in this section.

The following are the step-by-step operations that should be supported by this tool:

- HEW CMO commences the process of psychographic enhancement.

- The marketing manager uses the tool to start this process. The tool selects the customers without psychographic enhancement and extracts a file to be provided to the service bureau with the customer identifier, name, and address.

- HEW IT sends this extract to TSB for enhancement.

- TSB uses proprietary algorithms to match the name and addresses with their internal database and complement each customer with demographic and psychographic information. In this particular scenario, about 100 attribute values are assigned to each customer. TSB sends back a file with proper enhancement data to HEW.

- HEW IT department loads the enhanced data as a specific table in the OMDB.

- HEW marketing manager then builds the clustering models. In this scenario, HEW CMO estimates that this strategic segmentation should generate between 5 and 10 clusters. So the system will create different clustering models with different maximum numbers of clusters. A table associating each individual customer to cluster identifiers in the OMDB will be generated. These clusters are kept in a specific table

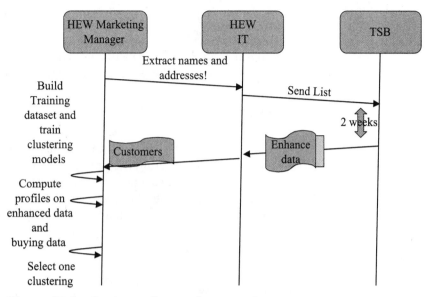

Figure 12-3   *Customer Segmenter scenario.*

of the OMDB. This table could in turn be used by an online analytical processing (OLAP) tool.

- HEW IT provides a table in the OMDB containing, for each customer, the number of products bought per product line in the past 12 months. In HEW, there are 10 product lines.

- HEW marketing manager then asks for profiles based on the enhanced data as well, and on the buying behavior per product line. For this, SQL count statements will be provided as reports to the marketing manager, who will prepare a thorough report to the CMO.

- The CMO selects one clustering model and associates cluster identifiers with names used for marketing purposes.

This process is presented in Figure 12-3.

12.3.2   Design of the *CustomerSegmenter* Object

Now that you've had success with the first two applications of JDM, you are asked to design and implement the business layer for this project. Some other team members will be in charge of the user interface layer and the infrastructure layer. Of course, you will use the same techniques: JDBC for some data manipulations and JDM to create clustering models.

Again, for the sake of simplicity, we will implement all services of the business layer in a single class called *CustomerSegmenter*.

12.3.3   Code Examples

This section details the code of the *CustomerSegmenter* class that follows the steps described in the previous section. As presented earlier, the constructor creates a new campaign optimization object with a name and a creation date. Because our object must deal with some basic data manipulations as well as data mining operations, we provide it with two valid connections (JDBC and JDM). This is reflected in the following constructor:

```
1.   public CustomerSegmenter(String iName,
2.                            java.sql.Connection iJDBCConnection,
3.                            Connection iJDMConnection) {
4.      mName = iName;
5.      mCreationDate = Calendar.getInstance().getTime();
6.      mJDBCConnection = iJDBCConnection;
7.      mJDMConnection = iJDMConnection;
8.   }
```

The following sections detail the code of the *CustomerSegmenter* class that follows the steps described earlier. The first step consists of extracting some file to be provided to TSB for enhancement. This code is very similar to the one described in the *CampaignOptimizer* project except that no sampling is involved. This code starts with the name of the table containing at least the customer identifier, name, and address as *iCustomerTableName*. These attributes are mandatory to allow the recognition of the individuals by the enhancement service and they are provided as a list of names in *iColumnNames*. The identifier attribute must also be provided because it will be the one used to reconcile the data provided by TSB with the customer database. Finally, the table name to be generated is provided in *iOutputTableName*.

```
1.   public void export(String iCustomerTableName,
2.              Collection iColumnNames,
3.              String iIdentifierColumnName,
4.              String iOutputTableName)
```

```
5.        throws SQLException {
6.        mCustomerTableName = iCustomerTableName;
7.        mColumnNames = iColumnNames;
8.        mIdentifierColumnName = iIdentifierColumnName;
9.        mOutputTableName = iOutputTableName;
10.       String lSQLQuery = "create table " + mOutputTableName + " as select ";
11.       lSQLQuery += mIdentifierColumnName;
12.       for (Iterator lColNamesIter = mColumnNames.iterator();
13.            lColNamesIter.hasNext();) {
14.         String lColName = (String) lColNamesIter.next();
15.         lSQLQuery += ", " + lColName;
16.       }
17.       lSQLQuery += " from " + mCustomerTableName;
18.       Statement lStatement = mJDBCConnection.createStatement();
19.       lStatement.executeQuery(lSQLQuery);
20.       String lSQLCountQuery = " select count(*) from " + mOutputTableName;
21.       Statement lStatementCount = mJDBCConnection.createStatement();
22.       ResultSet lResultSetCount = lStatementCount.
23.            executeQuery(lSQLCountQuery);
24.       lResultSetCount.next();
25.       int lSamplingCount = lResultSetCount.getInt(1);
26.       mCurrentState = CustomerSegmenterState.EXPORTED_FOR_ENHANCEMENT;
27.       report("Count for enhancement: " + lSamplingCount);
28. }
```

This code generates the SQL statement that creates the desired table from the *select* statement as shown in lines 10 to 17. The number of records produced is reported to the user, because it may be linked with payment to TSB.

Then some time is needed by TSB to enhance the data and return the enhanced file, which is loaded by the IT team into the OMDB. This enhanced table is used as the basis for building the clustering models. As described for this scenario, several clustering models with different numbers of clusters are built. This is done by the method called *buildModelAndApply*. Once the clustering models are built, they are used to assign each customer of the enhanced table with their cluster identifiers.

In the *buildModelAndApply* method, the parameter *iModelPrefix* is used together with the number of clusters found in that model to generate the model names. For example, if the prefix is "MyModel" and *iMinClusterCount* is set to 5, and *iMaxClusterCount* is set to 7, then the models "MyModel5," "MyModel6," and "MyModel7" will be built by this routine. The argument *iEnhancedTableName* is the table name containing demographic and psychographic data filled by the IT department from the file returned by TSB.

The parameter *iApplyOutputPrefix* is the prefix of the table used to contain cluster assignments. For example, if *iApplyOutPrefix* is set to "Clusters," and *iModelPrefix* is set to "MyCluster," the system will apply the clustering models to generate a table called "Clusters5" in which there will be an attribute for the customer identifier and an attribute called "MyCluster5" containing the clusters associated with the customers.

In fact, we have left the possibility for the user, through the Boolean member variable *mUseApplyOutPrefix*, to either create a new table for each clustering model (this is the default option that is described here) or to create a single table (in this case the prefix will not be concatenated with the number of clusters) with one column for each clustering model. In general, the second solution requires less database maintenance because fewer tables are created, but the applications of the different clustering models will require either inserting or updating in this table. The first clustering model will insert the lines for the first assignment between customer identifiers and clusters, but all the other models will have to update the values for the new clustering assignments and this update operation can be long if the number of customers is large.

Figure 12-4 shows the different situations when models with 5 to 7 clusters are built.

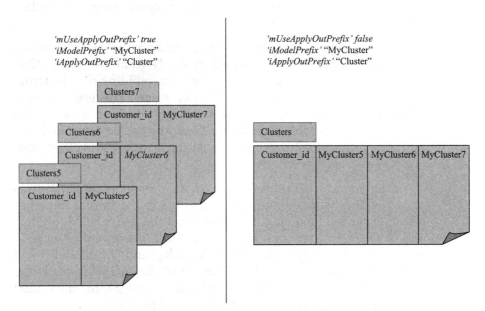

Figure 12-4   *Tables containing cluster association using different settings.*

```
1.   public void buildModelAndApply(String iModelPrefix,
2.                               int iMinClusterCount,
3.                               int iMaxClusterCOunt,
4.                               String iEnhancedTableName,
5.                               String iApplyOutputPrefix)
6.      throws JDMException, InterruptedException {
7.      mModelPrefix = iModelPrefix;
8.      mApplyOutputPrefix = iApplyOutputPrefix;
9.      String lDataSetName = iModelPrefix + "_DS";
10.     mEnhancedTableName = iEnhancedTableName;
11.     String lBuildDataSQLStatement = "select * from " + iEnhancedTableName;
12.     PhysicalDataSetFactory lPdsFactory =
13.        (PhysicalDataSetFactory) mJDMConnection.getFactory(
14.           "javax.datamining.data.PhysicalDataSet");
15.     String lDataSetURI = getVendorDatasetURI(lBuildDataSQLStatement);
16.     PhysicalDataSet lBuildData = lPdsFactory.create(lDataSetURI, false);
17.     lBuildData.importMetaData();
18.     PhysicalAttribute lAttr
19.        = lBuildData.getAttribute(mIdentifierColumnName.toUpperCase());
20.     lAttr.setRole(PhysicalAttributeRole.caseId);
21.     mJDMConnection.saveObject(lDataSetName, lBuildData, true);
```

In these first 21 lines, we created the *PhysicalDataSet* that is used for both building the model and then applying it to assign customers a cluster identifier. The following code creates models with increasing numbers of clusters from the minimum to the maximum specified by the user.

```
22.     for (int lClusterCount = iMinClusterCount;
23.          lClusterCount <= iMaxClusterCOunt;
24.          lClusterCount++) {
25.        String lModelName = iModelPrefix + "_" + lClusterCount;
26.        String lSettingsName = lModelName + "_S" + lClusterCount;
27.        ClusteringSettingsFactory lCsFactory =
28.           (ClusteringSettingsFactory) mJDMConnection.getFactory(
29.              "javax.datamining.clustering"
30.              + ".ClusteringSettings");
31.        ClusteringSettings lClusteringSettings =
32.           lCsFactory.create();
33.        lClusteringSettings.setMaxNumberOfClusters(lClusterCount);
34.        mJDMConnection.saveObject(lSettingsName,
35.                                  lClusteringSettings,
36.                                  true);
37.        String lBuildTaskName = lModelName + "_T";
38.        BuildTaskFactory lBuildTaskFactory =
39.           (BuildTaskFactory) mJDMConnection.getFactory(
40.              "javax.datamining.task.BuildTask");
41.        BuildTask lBuildTask = lBuildTaskFactory.create(lDataSetName,
42.                                  lSettingsName,
```

```
43.                                              lModelName);
44.        VerificationReport lVerifTask = lBuildTask.verify();
45.        if (lVerifTask != null) {
46.            reportError(lVerifTask.getReportText());
47.            return;
48.        }
49.        mJDMConnection.saveObject(lBuildTaskName, lBuildTask, true);
50.        boolean lSuccess = executeTask(lBuildTaskName);
51.        if (!lSuccess) {
52.            report("Did not manage to build clustering model!");
53.            return;
54.        }
```

The previous lines create as many build tasks as needed. These tasks only differ with the maximum number of clusters in the *ClusteringSettings* object, which is set at line 33. The purpose of this operation is to compare cluster models started with different maximum numbers of clusters. The JDM clustering mining function does not require that the effective number of clusters will be the same as the maximum number of clusters specified in the build settings. This is often dependent on the algorithm used. As such, it could be that some models built through this process have the same number of effective clusters. However, even if two models have the same effective number of clusters, their resulting clusters could be different, and comparing these cluster models could prove useful. The overall process will stop if any problem is found.

The following code applies the clustering model to the build dataset to assign customer cluster identifiers.

```
55.        ClusteringApplySettingsFactory lApplySettFactory =
56.            (ClusteringApplySettingsFactory) mJDMConnection.getFactory(
57.                "javax.datamining.clustering.ClusteringApplySettings");
58.        ClusteringApplySettings lApplySett = lApplySettFactory.create();
59.        String lApplyDSSettName = lModelName + "_AS" + lClusterCount;
60.        String lClusterAttributeName = iModelPrefix + "_" + lClusterCount;
61.        lApplySett.mapTopCluster(ClusteringApplyContent.clusterIdentifier,
62.                            lClusterAttributeName);
63.        mJDMConnection.saveObject(lApplyDSSettName, lApplySett, true);
64.        DataSetApplyTaskFactory lApplyTaskFactory =
65.            (DataSetApplyTaskFactory) mJDMConnection.getFactory(
66.                "javax.datamining.task.apply.DataSetApplyTask");
67.        String lApplyOutTableName = iApplyOutputPrefix;
68.        if (mUseApplyOutPrefix)
69.            lApplyOutTableName += "_" + lClusterCount;
70.        DataSetApplyTask lApplyTask = lApplyTaskFactory.create(
```

```
71.             lDataSetName,
72.             lModelName,
73.             lApplyDSSettName,
74.             getVendorDatasetURI(lApplyOutTableName));
75.         lVerifTask = lApplyTask.verify();
76.         if (lVerifTask != null) {
77.             reportError(lVerifTask.getReportText());
78.             return;
79.         }
80.         String lApplyTaskName = lModelName + "_ApplyT";
81.         mJDMConnection.saveObject(lApplyTaskName,
82.                                   lApplyTask,
83.                                   true);
84.         lSuccess = executeTask(lApplyTaskName);
85.         if (!lSuccess) {
86.             return;
87.         }
88.     }
89. }
```

As can be seen at line 60, we specify that we want to generate the cluster identifiers into an attribute with a name obtained with the model name prefix concatenated with the maximum number of clusters for this model. After this method is executed, we have clusters associated with the customers inserted into specific table columns.

Once each customer in the database is associated with clusters from the different clustering models, the next step is to decide which clustering model should be kept. The technique generally used to compare clustering models is called *profiling*. This consists of comparing the distributions of some attributes for customers belonging to each cluster with the distribution of the same attributes for the customers not belonging to this cluster, that is, the distribution between attributes values for cases assigned to a given cluster and the reaming cases is far apart). With this analysis, the marketer decides to name a given cluster with the attribute names and values that best describe the cluster.

For example, an attribute describing "work class" could be profiled for a specific cluster to see if this attribute has a distribution very different from the profile obtained on the population not belonging to this cluster. Profiling can be done on the attributes used to build the clustering model as well as other attributes. In our example, the clusters are made out of the psychographics data provided by the service bureau, but the marketer could very well profile the different clusters on attributes representing behavioral information, such as how customers buy the product.

OLAP tools can be used to get the basic counts and frequencies on the different populations of customers, but these tools do not really help when the user is looking for the most distinctive attributes. We will show code that computes the profiles on the population "belonging" and "not belonging" to a cluster, and that returns the distance between these two distributions. This distance can be used to sort the attributes. Attributes with the largest distance can be considered as distinctive for the specified cluster.

In the next section, we will show how to compare distributions of discrete variables for one cluster with respect to all the others. This will be done through expressions using the SQL "group by" statement. We have chosen this design for the method *computeProfile*. In this method, the user specifies a table name and an attribute name to be profiled. Again, this table does not have to be the one used for model building as long as there is an identifier attribute that can be used to merge the information from this table and the generated cluster assignments.

In the following code for method *computeProfile, iInputTableName* is the table containing the attribute to be profiled and *iAttributeName* is the attribute to be profiled. The argument *iClusterCount* is a way to point to interest, because each model was created with a different number of clusters, and *iClusterIdx* is the cluster identifier to be profiled against all the others. In this code, we assume that cluster identifiers are integers, which is normally the case.

```
1.    public double computeProfile(String iInputDataSet,
2.                          String iAttributeName,
3.                          int iClusterCount,
4.                          int iClusterIdx)
5.        throws JDMException, InterruptedException, SQLException {
6.        double lDistance = 0.0;
7.        String lClusterTableName    = mApplyOutputPrefix;
8.        String lClusterAttributeName = mModelPrefix + "_" + iClusterCount;
9.        if (mUseApplyOutPrefix)
10.           lClusterTableName +=   "_" + iClusterCount;
11.       String lSQLCountQuery = "select count(*), " + iAttributeName + " from "
12.           + iInputDataSet + " a left outer join "
13.           + lClusterTableName + " b on a."
14.           + mIdentifierColumnName + " = b." + mIdentifierColumnName
15.           + " where (b." + lClusterAttributeName + " = " + iClusterIdx + ")"
16.           + " group by a." + iAttributeName;
17.       Statement lStatement = mJDBCConnection.createStatement();
18.       ResultSet lResultSetCount =
19.           lStatement.executeQuery(lSQLCountQuery);
```

In these first lines, we have created the statement used to obtain the number of customers in the specified cluster for each possible value of the specified attribute. For example, if the selected attribute is "PurchaseA," which indicates how many times the customer bought product A in the last month, contained in the table "Purchases," and the selected cluster is 1 from a clustering done with 5 clusters, we will get the following statement:

```
select count(*), PurchaseA
From Purchases a left outer join CLUSTER_TABLE_5 b
on a.CUSTID = b.CUSTID
where (b.MyCluster_5 = 1)
group by a.PurchaseA;
```

In this statement, we have used "MyCluster" as the model name prefix and "CLUSTER_TABLE" as the apply table name prefix. Assume that we have customers that have bought product A 0, 1, 2, or 3 times. We will have, as a result of the execution of the previous statement, the number of customers that have bought this product 0, 1, 2, or 3 times belonging to cluster 1. The following lines show how to retrieve the results from this statement.

```
20.     int lTotalSize = 0;
21.     Map lCategories = new HashMap();
22.     while (lResultSetCount.next()) {
23.         int lCategorySize = lResultSetCount.getInt(1);
24.         String lCategory = lResultSetCount.getString(2);
25.         lTotalSize += lCategorySize;
26.         lCategories.put(lCategory, new Integer(lCategorySize));
27.         report("Category: " + lCategory + ": " + lCategorySize);
28.     }
```

If we want to compare the profiles of the distribution of the selected attribute, we must perform the same operation for the customers that are not in this cluster, and get back the number of customers for each possible value of this attribute, as shown below:

```
29.     lSQLCountQuery = "select count(*), " + iAttributeName + " from "
30.         + iInputDataSet + " a left outer join "
31.         + lClusterTableName + " b on a."
32.         + mIdentifierColumnName + " = b." + mIdentifierColumnName
33.         + " where (b." + lClusterAttributeName + " <> "+iClusterIdx + ")"
34.         + " group by a." + iAttributeName;
```

```
35.    lResultSetCount =
36.        lStatement.executeQuery(lSQLCountQuery);
37.    int lOtherTotalSize = 0;
38.    Map lOtherCategories = new HashMap();
39.    while (lResultSetCount.next()) {
40.        int lCategorySize = lResultSetCount.getInt(1);
41.        String lCategory = lResultSetCount.getString(2);
42.        lOtherCategories.put(lCategory, new Integer(lCategorySize));
43.        lOtherTotalSize += lCategorySize;
44.    }
```

To compute and compare frequencies in the two cases, we have used hash maps to store the results and we have collected the global number of customers in each case. For this, we scan through the two maps and compare both categories and report this to the user. If we go back to the situation in which we apply this to "PurchaseA," we could have received the following results for cluster 1:

```
Count   PurchaseA
2345    1
45603   2
21342   3
```

And the following results for the population not in cluster 1:

```
Count   PurchaseA
17546   1
31846   2
4275    3
```

These two result sets have been saved into two Java maps in order to compute the profile in terms of relative frequencies and compute the distance between these two distributions. The distance is based on the average between the frequencies of the categories for each population, as shown at line 58.

```
45.    Set lCategoryNames = lCategories.keySet();
46.    Iterator lIter;
47.    for (lIter = lCategoryNames.iterator();
48.        lIter.hasNext(); ) {
49.        String lCategory = (String) lIter.next();
50.        double lOtherCategoryFreq = 0.0;
```

```
51.        double lCategoryFreq =
              (double)(((Integer)(lCategories.get(lCategory))).
52.             intValue())/(double)(lTotalSize);
53.        if (lOtherCategories.containsKey(lCategory)) {
54.           lOtherCategoryFreq =
                 (double)(((Integer)(lOtherCategories.get(lCategory))).
55.                intValue())/(double)lOtherTotalSize;
56.        }
57.        report("Category: " + lCategory + ": " + lCategoryFreq +
58.             " to be compared to: " + lOtherCategoryFreq);
59.        lDistance += java.lang.Math.abs(lCategoryFreq -
                 lOtherCategoryFreq);
60.     }
```

We also scan through the second map to ensure that we do not neglect the categories present in this second map that do not appear in the first one.

```
61.     Set lOtherCategoryNames = lOtherCategories.keySet();
62.     for (lIter = lOtherCategoryNames.iterator();
63.          lIter.hasNext(); ) {
64.        String lOtherCategory = (String)lIter.next();
65.        double lCategoryFreq = 0.0;
66.        if (!lCategories.containsKey(lOtherCategory)) {
67.           double lOtherCategoryFreq = (double)(((Integer)
68.                     (lOtherCategories.get(lOtherCategory))).
69.                          intValue())/(double)(lOtherTotalSize);
70.           report("Category: " + lOtherCategory + ": " + lCategoryFreq +
71.                " to be compared to: " + lOtherCategoryFreq);
72.           lDistance += java.lang.Math.abs(lCategoryFreq -
                    lOtherCategoryFreq);
73.        }
74.     }
75.     return lDistance;
76. }
```

The returned distance can be used to sort the attributes, showing, for example, the ones that are the most different for the two populations. Another implementation could define an object that contains the compared profile for later graphic display of histograms, as shown in Figure 12-5, for example, which takes the values shown in the example of "PurchaseA" statistics.

This code can be extended through profiling of continuous attributes using binned ranges of possible values, or just report the difference between the minimums, maximums, averages and standard

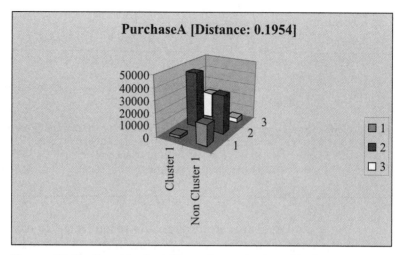

Figure 12-5 *Graphical profiling of one cluster with distance information.*

deviations of a continuous attribute in both cases (in or out of the specified cluster).

12.3.4 Scenario 3 Conclusion

We have shown in this section that, in conjunction with JDBC, the Java developer can easily complement clustering information with profiling. Profiling is a key element allowing business users to recognize a good clustering from a bad one.

12.4 Summary

This chapter demonstrated how to design and implement software to solve practical business problems using data mining. We used JDM and also JDBC since data manipulations such as filtering datasets or computing some aggregate values are needed in such projects and readily performed in SQL. We have shown how to mix data mining operations with cost structures to improve business performance and how the JDM *TestMetrics* can be used for this. And we have shown, through the use of *AttributeImportance* and *Clustering* models, how to help business users make greater use of business data.

We have taken examples from customer relationship management (CRM) since the foundations of CRM processes, such as marketing campaign optimization or customer segmentation, can be presented in a way that most readers will understand, making it possible for them to focus on the design and implementation of the use case scenario. CRM is also a domain in which data mining is becoming more frequently used.

With the advent of JDM, once the business problem is defined in terms of data mining (for example, using classification, regression, or any mining function associated with JDM), writing software becomes quite easy.

References

[Drozenko/Drake 2002] R. G. Drozenko, P. Drake, eds., *Optimal Database Marketing: Strategy, Development and Data Mining,* Sage Publications, 2002.

Building Data Mining Tools Using JDM

A tool is but the extension of a man's hand, and a machine is but a complex tool. And he that invents a machine augments the power of a man and the well-being of mankind.

—Henry Ward Beecher, *Proverbs from Plymouth Pulpit*

This chapter presents the design and implementation of three user interfaces developed in Java Swing. This exercise exposes design principles for writing tools that work with different vendor implementations. The proposed interfaces can connect to known data mining engine (DME) implementations, thereby realizing the benefits of standards-based interfaces. These interfaces have been tested on the vendor implementations that will be introduced in Chapter 16.

So far this book has looked at the main functional domains covered by the major data mining tools vendors; we now examine how these functions can be implemented on top of Java Data Mining (JDM) through three graphical user interfaces (GUI).

The first user interface provides access to named objects saved in a mining object repository (MOR). The second provides access to the main functions of the DME itself, such as building and saving models. The third interface can be used to compute test metrics on a previously saved model.

Whereas Chapter 12 was directed to developers supporting business users, this chapter is directed to users and developers of data mining tools.

13.1   Data Mining Tools

The previous chapter focused on practical application implementation. This chapter focuses more on showing the JDM features for the entire modeling life cycle, and on a vendor-independent implementation, by heavily using the JDM notion of *capability* introduced in Chapter 8.

One purpose of this chapter is to show how some traditional data mining functionalities, or modules, can be implemented using JDM. Tools are often aligned with data mining methodologies such as CRISP-DM (discussed in Chapter 3). This chapter shows how to easily build tools to cover aspects of:

- Data exploration
- Model building
- Model validation
- Model and task management

To illustrate these, we build graphical user interfaces (GUI). The purpose of these demonstration interfaces is not to show off fancy graphics but to be functionally usable. Hence, the user interfaces are straightforward and simple. We have based these GUIs on Java Swing classes because Swing is a portable graphical layer; it is relatively simple and powerful. None of the Java Swing classes are detailed in this implementation; only the code referring to JDM is commented on in the following sections.

The first user interface is designed to allow basic maintenance operations on an MOR, such as viewing saved objects like models, build settings, and tasks on a per class basis. This interface also allows deleting objects from the MOR and renaming them. DME capabilities are used to detect what classes can be persisted since implementations are not required to persist all MOR objects. The second user interface is designed to show the mining functions supported by the DME, to allow creating models for each of these functions, and using the general settings associated with each function. The third user interface allows reusing a previously built model to compute quantitative quality metrics on a dataset specified by the user.

Whenever possible, we highlight good JDM programming practices, such as use of the *verify* method to minimize the chance of exceptions after the tasks have been scheduled.

13.1.1 Architecture of the Demonstration Interfaces

The three graphical user interfaces, referred to as *consoles* hereafter, need five graphical windows, as shown in Figure 13-1.

The demonstration interface source code can be found under *http://www.kxen.com/products/analytic_framework/kjdm.php*. This source code is organized into the following files:

- JDMConsole.java contains the common methods defined for all three user interfaces. The class JDMConsole can serve as the basis for any Java user interface looking like a console (see following text).
- JDMAdminConsole.java contains the class defining the user interface to browse the objects persisted in the MOR.
- JDMBuildConsole.java contains the class defining the user interface to build models of all data mining functions supported by the DME.
- JDMTestConsole.java contains the class defining the user interface to apply a model previously built on new datasets.

These files are complemented by the following utility files:

- DescriptiveStatisticDisplayer.java contains the class defining the user interface to visualize descriptive statistics.
- TestMetricsDisplayer.java contains the class defining the user interface to display quantitative metrics about classification and regression models.

Finally, this file deals with exception handling:

- UnexpectedJDMException.java is another Java RuntimeException used to encapsulate JDM exceptions. In Java, a *RuntimeException* does not have to be explicitly declared and this feature can be beneficial, as discussed in the next section.

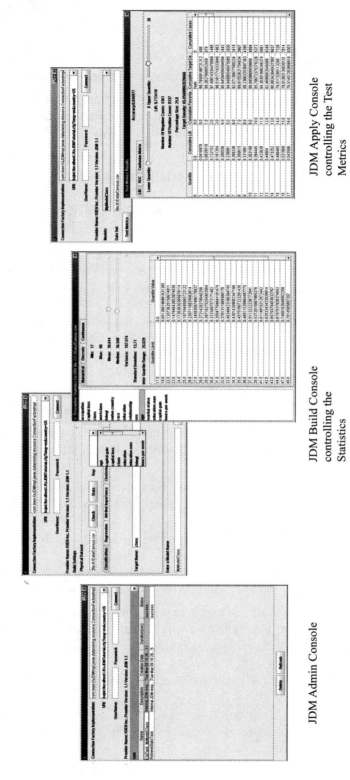

JDM Admin Console

JDM Build Console
controlling the
Statistics

JDM Apply Console
controlling the Test
Metrics

Figure 13-1 *A view of the three "consoles" with dependent windows.*

For brevity, the proposed user interfaces have no facility to view model details such as the rules of an association model, or the nodes of a decision tree model.

This chapter follows the same naming conventions as Chapter 12 about variable names used in the source code:

- Input arguments are prefixed with *i*.
- Output arguments are prefixed with *o*.
- Member variables of objects are prefixed with *m*.
- Local variables are prefixed with *l*.

13.1.2 Managing JDM Exceptions

One purpose of the tools developed here is to show how to deal with different JDM implementations. Since applications will have to deal with exceptions, it is worth spending some time on JDM exception management before writing portable JDM code.

How to deal with exceptions is a subject of debate among Java users; there is no clear consensus. For example, some Java projects make maximum reuse of the existing Java exception classes; others define a single root Java exception class for the functional domain of interest. For JDM, the expert group decided to create a single root for all JDM java exceptions, plus two specializations of runtime exceptions (see Chapter 8). Almost all methods of the application programming interface (API) have been declared to throw the generic JDM exception.

Regular exceptions defined by JDM are: *ConnectionFailureException, IncompatibleSpecificationException, InvalidObjectException* (decomposed into *DuplicateEntryException, EntryNotFoundException, ObjectExistsException, ObjectNotFoundException*), *InvalidURIException*, and *TaskException*. Except for the *ConnectionFailureException*, all exceptions can be avoided by proper design of the calling program. Through the use of capabilities and *verify* methods, JDM provides mechanisms to prepare arguments to invoked methods, and to check that these invocations are compatible with the connected DME. For example, when designing a graphical interface to ask a user to enter a dataset uniform resource identifier (URI), a programmer could either use the DME vendor documentation to write verification code to check that the provided URI has the proper syntax, or the programmer could provide the URI directly to the DME and handle the *InvalidURIException* with a message provided by the DME vendor. When the second design is chosen, the JDM exception classes allow easier fallbacks from the user interface: In the previous example, if the system receives an *InvalidURIException,* it can easily ask the user to enter a new one.

The two runtime exceptions defined by JDM are *JDMIllegalArgumentException* and *JDMUnsupportedFeatureException.* Runtime exceptions result from unanticipated application execution failure and may require stopping the application or, at least, restarting a session.

The JDM *ConnectionFailureException* has not been declared as a *RuntimeException* and thus could occur in many situations. This means that all methods using JDM calls should either process all JDM exceptions or declare them in their signature for transfer to the caller method. For the consoles we highlight in this chapter, we avoided exception management to improve code readability. We have created a specific *RuntimeException* that takes a *JDMException* as argument. In effect, this translates the *JDMException* into a Java *RuntimeException* and avoids chaining *JDMException* declarations in all methods. The code of *UnexpectedJDMException* is provided in the file *UnexpectedJDMException.java* and is shown below:

```
1.  public class UnexpectedJDMException extends RuntimeException {
2.      private JDMException mJDMException;
3.      public UnexpectedJDMException(JDMException iJDMException) {
4.          mJDMException = iJDMException;
5.      }
6.      protected final JDMException getJDMException() {
7.          return mJDMException;
8.      }
9.  }
```

13.2 Administrative Console

The first GUI demonstrates the use of JDM API services to list, rename, or delete the persistent representations of JDM named objects from the MOR. Of course, this assumes the vendor implementation exposes persistent named objects (such as model, tasks, or build settings).

Figure 13-2 depicts the GUI where the user has connected to a DME and asked to view the list of tasks in the MOR. Elements of this window will be explained later. Tasks are presented with their name, description, creation date, duration, and final status.

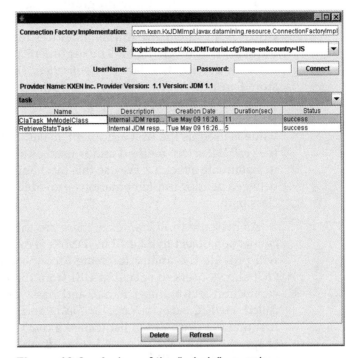

Figure 13-2 *A view of the "admin" console.*

The main graphical object of this user interface is a table displaying persisted objects. We have extended the graphical *TableModel* (this is a Java Swing notion) to show the description and creation date of each object. The table used when displaying *Tasks* has two additional columns showing the task execution duration and status, as shown in Figure 13-2.

Furthermore, the user can change the name of an existing object by typing a new name in place of the old one. Names displayed in the first column are editable. Name changes can be validated when the user hits the RETURN key after having edited the name of the object displayed in the first column or discarded when the user hits the ESC key.

13.2.1 Creating the Connection

The code to create the connection is the same for all three consoles presented. It is provided in a file called *JDMConsole.java*. All user interfaces presented in this chapter inherit from this basic console.

The entry point of any program using JDM is the creation of the *ConnectionFactory*. In this example, we show the ability to switch easily from one JDM implementation to another using the Java introspection mechanism. The argument provided in the text field associated with the label *"Connection Factory Implementation"* is stored in a *JDMConsole* member variable called *mConnectionText-Field*. This argument, including the full package path, is used as the Java class name to the vendor-specific *ConnectionFactory* class. This value is used as the first argument, called *iConnectionFactoryImpl*, of the *getJDMFactory* method and is used as a *Class.forName()* argument to instantiate a factory. We use this mechanism to dynamically switch between vendor implementations provided the correct jars are in the class path.

As presented in Chapter 9, there are three ways to create a valid connection object to a DME in JDM. It is expected that most vendors will provide the ability to create a connection through a URI. The GUI allows users to specify a URI from three text fields: the vendor connection factory, user name, and password. These text fields are called *mURICombo, mNameTextField,* and *mPasswordTextField*. The first one is a drop-down list (called a *combo box* or *combo* later in this chapter) because we provided some default values for the URI used to connect to a DME.

Once the user provides the required information, he can click on the *Connect* button. The following code is then called:

```
1.  private final void handlerConnectButton() {
2.      String lMsg = "";
3.      try {
4.          mDmeConn = getJDMConnection(mConnectionTextField.getText(),
5.                              (String)mURICombo.getSelectedItem(),
6.                              mNameTextField.getText(),
7.                              mPasswordTextField.getText());
8.          ConnectionMetaData lMeta = mDmeConn.getMetaData();
9.          if (lMeta != null) {
10.             lMsg = "Provider Name: " + lMeta.getProviderName() + " "
11.                 + "Provider Version:  " + lMeta.getProviderVersion() + " "
12.                 + "Version: " + lMeta.getVersion();
13.         } else {
14.             lMsg = "No Vendor Information";
15.         }
16.         mMaxNameLength = mDmeConn.getMaxNameLength();
17.         mMaxDescriptionLength = mDmeConn.getMaxDescriptionLength();
18.         start(mDmeConn);
19.     } catch (JDMException lException) {
20.         JOptionPane.showMessageDialog(this,
```

```
21.                                    "JDMException Occured: "
22.                                    + lException.getMessage());
23.        lException.printStackTrace();
24.    } catch (ClassNotFoundException lException) {
25.        JOptionPane.showMessageDialog(this,
26.              "The specified Connection factory was not found. "
27.              + "Verify the class name and the classpath.");
28.    } catch  (Exception lExce) {
29.        lMsg = "Error occured while collecting vendor information.";
30.    } finally {
31.        mMetaInfo.setText(lMsg);
32.    }
33. }
```

This code shows how to get a connection object. This connection instance will be used throughout each of the GUI examples. The code of *getJDMConnection* is explained later, but assuming that the connection is established, the code shows how to retrieve vendor information between lines 9 and 12.

If a JDM exception occurs at that point, it will be mainly a badly formed URI. The only thing the designer can do in this case is to display the vendor message obtained from lException.getMessage(). A more carefully designed application should use the vendor documentation to ensure that the URI is properly formatted. The *ClassNotFoundException* will be raised if the user provides a class name that does not correspond to any valid JDM connection factory class.

The code also shows how to retrieve the maximum length of the names and descriptions that can be associated with named objects. From an application perspective, it is important to retrieve this information since the GUI must ensure name length limitations to avoid DME-generated exceptions.

Once a connection is established, there is a call to *start*, which is defined by each console to initialize the graphical display, as shown at line 18.

The *getJDMConnection* method creates the factory from its Java class name, and uses this factory to create the connection. Its code is presented here:

```
1.  protected final static Connection getJDMConnection(
2.      String iConnectionFactoryImpl,
3.      String iURI, String iUserName, String iPassword)
```

```
4.      throws JDMException, ClassNotFoundException  {
5.          Class lClass = Class.forName(iConnectionFactoryImpl);
6.          ConnectionFactory lConnectionFactory;
7.          try {
8.              lConnectionFactory = (ConnectionFactory) lClass.newInstance();
9.              ConnectionSpec lCSpec = lConnectionFactory.getConnectionSpec();
10.             lCSpec.setURI(iURI);
11.             lCSpec.setName(iUserName);
12.             lCSpec.setPassword(iPassword);
13.             return lConnectionFactory.getConnection(lCSpec);
14.         } catch (InstantiationException lException) {
15.             lException.printStackTrace();
16.         } catch (IllegalAccessException lException) {
17.             lException.printStackTrace();
18.         }
19.     return null;
20. }
```

When using the introspection mechanism, we can receive an
InstantiationException or an *IllegalAccessException*. The *Instantiation-
Exception* would be raised if the specified class object cannot be
instantiated because it is an interface or an abstract class. The
IllegalAccessException would be raised if the application was trying to
reflectively create an instance but the currently executing method
does not have access to the definition of the specified class, field,
method, or constructor (if, for example, the constructor has been
declared as private). These two exceptions are low-level exceptions
that would be raised if the system can access the class specified by
the user but cannot use it for instantiation. Not much can be done to
offer any fallback in these scenarios. The *ClassNotFoundException*,
which is thrown when the user-specified factory Java class name is
invalid, is re-raised to the caller. As a result, the graphical interface
will show an error message to ask for another connection factory
implementation.

13.2.2   Retrieving the List of Classes That Can Be Saved

As presented in Chapter 7, vendors may choose to implement the
persistence of certain named objects into a repository. If objects are
not persisted, they are discarded when the connection is closed. The
first operation performed by the administrative (Admin) console is
to determine which of the named objects are persisted and to provide them as a drop-down list for selection by the user. This list is
stored into a graphical combo box, *mPersistentObjectsCombo*, which

we fill with a *ComboBoxModel* instance. A *ComboBoxModel* is the object underlying the graphical combo box that holds the values that can be accessed by position.

> It may be confusing in the following discussion that objects in Java Swing holding values for underlying graphical representations are called "models." We will nevertheless use this terminology, because it is the one used by user interface programmers. We will, however, be precise, when necessary, and specify the type of graphical model we are talking about, such as *ComboBoxModel* mentioned above or *TableModel*. All graphical "models" provide access to the values (for example, the values of a drop-down list) based on the position (or the rank) of the values.

We have created a small extension of a *DefaultComboBoxModel* to retrieve the names of the selected persisted named object classes. The *NamedObjectComboModel* extends the *DefaultComboBox-Model* and allows the returning of the object name at a given position but also the casting of this object as a *NamedObject* for further program use.

```
1.  protected void start(Connection iConnection) {
2.     mDmeConn = iConnection;
3.     try {
4.        final NamedObject[] lPersistence
5.           = mDmeConn.getNamedObjects(PersistenceOption.persistentObject);
6.        NamedObjectComboModel lComboModel =
7.           new NamedObjectComboModel(lPersistence);
8.        mPersistentObjectsCombo.setModel(lComboModel);
9.        handlerUpdateTableContent();
10.    } catch (JDMException lExce) {
11.       throw new UnexpectedJDMException(lExce);
12.    }
13. }
```

In line 5, the call to *getNamedObjects* returns the types of named objects persisted by this DME implementation. The JDM enumeration *PersistenceOption* provides two values: *persistentObject* and *transientObject*. In this example, we are only interested in persistent objects.

The method *handlerUpdateTableContent* executed at line 9 in the previous code obtains the GUI user-selected named object class, and then retrieves the names of the corresponding persisted mining objects. The *handlerUpdateTableContent* code is shown here:

```
1.  private void handlerUpdateTableContent() {
2.      NamedObject lNamedObject = getSelectedNamedObjectType();
3.      String[] lMiningObjects = getMiningObjects(lNamedObject);
4.      if (lNamedObject == NamedObject.task) {
5.          mDisplayObjectsTable.setModel(
6.                  new TaskTableModel(
7.                      mDmeConn,
8.                      lMiningObjects,
9.                      getSelectedNamedObjectType()));
10.     } else {
11.         mDisplayObjectsTable.setModel(
12.                 new MiningObjectsTableModel(
13.                     mDmeConn,
14.                     lMiningObjects,
15.                     getSelectedNamedObjectType()));
16.     }
17. }
```

This code fills the *TableModel* associated with the Java Swing graphical table used to display these objects. The graphical table used to display named objects has three columns to display their name, description, and creation date. The table used to display tasks has two more columns to display task duration and status, and thus, these columns have a specific *TableModel*. A *TableModel* is the object underlying the graphical component that holds the values accessed by row and column indices. The *TableModel* also provides the graphical component for the number of rows and columns to be displayed. The code of *getMiningObjects* is detailed in 13.2.3.

13.2.3 Retrieving the List of Saved Objects

Retrieving the list of object names for a given named object class is shown below.

```
1.  private String[] getMiningObjects(NamedObject iNameObject) {
2.      Collection lMiningObjects = null;
3.      try {
4.          lMiningObjects = mDmeConn.getObjectNames(iNameObject);
5.      } catch (JDMException lException) {
6.          throw new UnexpectedJDMException(lException);
```

```
 7.      }
 8.      return (String[])
 9.          lMiningObjects.toArray(new String[lMiningObjects.size()]);
10. }
```

This object name array is provided to the *MiningObjectsTableModel* or the *TaskTableModel*. As presented earlier these *TableModels* must provide to the graphical layer the values to display in the cell at a given row and column through the call to *getValueAt*. The constructors of these *TableModels* store the connection as well as the named object class to ask for information when required. Below is the code of the *MiningObjectsTableModel* constructor method. The *TableModel* has three member variables: the connection in *mModelConnection,* the list of the object names of the named object class in *mMiningObjects,* and the value of this named object class in *mModelNamedObject.*

```
1.      MiningObjectsTableModel(
2.          Connection iConnection,
3.          String[] iMiningObjects,
4.          NamedObject iModelNamedObject) {
5.      mMiningObjects = iMiningObjects;
6.      mModelConnection = iConnection;
7.      mModelNamedObject = iModelNamedObject;
8.      }
```

We provide here the code for the method *getValueAt* associated with the *MiningObjectsTableModel* because this code calls JDM functions. Mining objects other than tasks are represented in a table with three columns showing their name, description, and creation date. Column index 0 returns the name; column index 1 returns the associated description; and column index 2 returns the creation date.

```
 1.      public Object getValueAt(int iRowIndex, int iColumnIndex) {
 2.          String lMiningObject = mMiningObjects[iRowIndex];
 3.          try {
 4.              switch (iColumnIndex) {
 5.                  case 0: return lMiningObject;
 6.                  case 1:
 7.                      String lDescription = "No Description";
 8.                      try {
 9.                          lDescription = mModelConnection.getDescription(
10.                              lMiningObject, mModelNamedObject);
11.                      } catch (JDMUnsupportedFeatureException lException) {
```

```
12.                        // do nothing
13.                    }
14.                 return lDescription;
15.              case 2:
16.                 return mModelConnection.
17.                    getCreationDate(lMiningObject, mModelNamedObject);
18.              default:
19.                 throw new IllegalArgumentException("Bad Column Index");
20.           }
21.        } catch (JDMException lExce) {
22.           JOptionPane.showMessageDialog(null,
23.                                  "JDMException Occured: "
24.                                        + lExce.getMessage());
25.           return null;
26.        }
27.     }
```

To retrieve task duration and status, we provide a specific *TaskTableModel* class that inherits from the *MiningObjectsTableModel* and retrieves the duration and status by extending the *getValueAt* method shown here:

```
1.     public Object getValueAt(int iRowIndex, int iColumnIndex) {
2.        if (iColumnIndex < super.getColumnCount()) {
3.           return super.getValueAt(iRowIndex, iColumnIndex);
4.        }
5.        int lColumn = iColumnIndex - super.getColumnCount();
6.        try {
7.           Task lTask = mTaskArray[iRowIndex];
8.           ExecutionHandle lExecutionHandle = lTask.getExecutionHandle();
9.           switch (lColumn) {
10.            case 0:
11.              return lExecutionHandle.getDurationInSeconds();
12.            case 1:
13.              return lExecutionHandle.getLatestStatus().getState().name();
14.            default:
15.              throw new IllegalArgumentException(
16.                      "BadColumn Number: " + iColumnIndex);
17.          }
18.        } catch (JDMException lException) {
19.           JOptionPane.showMessageDialog(null,
20.             "JDMException Occured: " + lExce.getMessage());
21.           return "JDMException Occured";
22.        }
```

This code will work even if we later add new columns to the parent class.

13.2.4   Rename a Saved Object

In this Admin console, when the user enters a new object name in the "Name" column on the GUI screen and validates this new name by hitting the RETURN key, the Java graphical framework throws an event which is translated as a *setValueAt* method call on the underlying *TableModel*. The code of *setValueAt* is shown here:

```
1.     public void setValueAt (Object iValue,
2.                        int iRowIndex,
3.                        int iColumnIndex) {
4.         if (iColumnIndex == 0) {
5.             String lOldName = (String) getValueAt(iRowIndex, iColumnIndex);
6.             String lNewName = (String) iValue;
7.             try {
8.                 handlerRename(lOldName, lNewName);
9.             } catch (JDMException lException) {
10.                lNewName = lOldName;
11.                displayJDMException(lException);
12.            } finally {
13.                mMiningObjects[iRowIndex] = lNewName;
14.            }
15.        }
16.    }
```

This code shows that our system accepts only the first column to be edited as shown by the test at line 4. It resets the old value in case of error and displays the cause to the user. Of course, besides changing the value in the GUI, the action must rename the object in the MOR; this is the role of the method called *handlerRename* shown here:

```
1. private void handlerRename(String iOldName,
2.                        String iNewName) throws JDMException {
3.     NamedObject lNamedObject = getSelectedNamedObjectType();
4.     mDmeConn.renameObject(iOldName, iNewName, lNamedObject);
5. }
```

The call to *renameObject* at line 4 asks the DME to perform the operation in the MOR.

13.2.5 Delete a Saved Object from the MOR

When the user clicks on the *Delete* button, the intention is to remove the persisted object from the repository, and execute the *handlerDestroyButton* method from the *JDMAdminConsole* class. To show the result of this deletion, we must refresh the table showing the list of objects, which is contained in the *TableModel* object. This object can be obtained through the member variable *mDisplayObjectsTable* that is initialized when the graphical display is initialized. We have defined a method called *fireTableDataChanged* to refresh the values contained in the *TableModel*. The handler of the button is presented here:

```
1.  private void handlerDeleteButton() {
2.      NamedObject lNamedObject = getSelectedNamedObjectType();
3.      String lObjectToRemove = getSelectedObjectName();
4.      if (lNamedObject != null && lObjectToRemove != null) {
5.          try {
6.              mDmeConn.removeObject (lObjectToRemove, lNamedObject);
7.              ((MiningObjectsTableModel) mDisplayObjectsTable.getModel()).
8.                      fireTableDataChanged();
9.          } catch (ObjectNotFoundException lExce) {
10.             JOptionPane.showMessageDialog(this,
11.                             "Object: " + lNamedObject +
12.                                 " does not exist");
13.         } catch (JDMException lExce) {
14.             displayJDMException(lExce);
15.         }
16.     }
17. }
```

The call to *removeObject* in line 6 asks the DME to perform the operation on the MOR. This concludes the description of the first user interface.

13.3 User Interface to Build and Save a Model

The second graphical user interface demonstrates using JDM in practice to build models. Mining models created through this interface could then be used through Web services for real-time apply as demonstrated in Chapter 14, or other Java applications for batch or real-time apply. In this example, we focus on the mining function level, without addressing algorithm level interfaces. We start the code example from the exchange with the DME to determine the mining function it supports. We assume connections have already been addressed, as noted in Section 13.1.

13.3.1 General Introduction

The proposed graphical user interface is depicted in Figure 13-3. This GUI, designed to be simple, will not use *LogicalData*. It exposes the data mining functions supported by the vendor implementation, and allows building models for each supported function. A minimum number of parameters will be provided for each function. For classification and regression, parameters include the name of the target attribute. For attribute importance, parameters include the optional target, as well as the number of desired top attributes. For clustering, parameters include the maximum number of clusters. And for association, parameters include the minimum support, minimum confidence, and maximum rule length for association rules.

This user interface also exposes the URI to reference the build datasets. Recall that the URI syntax for such datasets is vendor-specific.

To allow experimentation with vendor implementations, we have added the ability to overwrite all objects saved in the connection. When the "overwrite" box is unchecked, an exception should be thrown if the user specifies an object with a name already in the MOR.

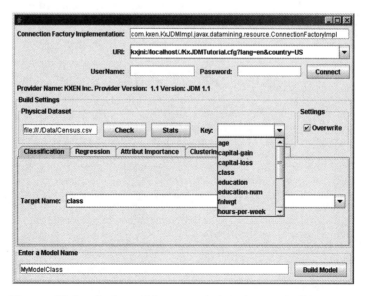

Figure 13-3 *A view of the generic interface to build and save models.*

The *Check* button imports the metadata on the dataset specified by the URI. JDM does not fully specify the results of import metadata, but the list of dataset attributes should be provided at that time. Some vendors may also compute some basic attribute statistics. This is why, when the user selects "Check," the drop-down lists containing the possible attribute names are updated. For example, on the screen shown in Figure 13-3, the drop-down list allowing the selection of the key attribute, and the one used to select a target attribute have been updated with the list of columns contained in the dataset referenced by the URI "file:///./Data/Census.csv."

The *Stats* button is only active when the vendor implementation supports the *ComputeStatisticsTask* interface. This allows quick data exploration, providing univariate statistics that are displayed in a pop-up window (described in Section 13.3.5).

Note that while the user specifies only the model name, this application uses this name as a base name from which to generate names of other persisted objects, such as tasks, build settings, and physical datasets. We will see that automated name creation must be validated against the maximum name length supported by the DME, assuming that uniqueness is guaranteed by the user-provided names.

The source code is contained in the file *JDMBuildConsole.java*.

As explained for the administration console, once a connection is obtained, the application invokes the *start* method. Following is the code for the *BuildConsole*:

```
1.  protected void start(Connection iConnection) {
2.      mDmeConn = iConnection;
3.      try {
4.          setDatasetSettingsEnabled(true);
5.          MiningFunction[] lFunctions = mDmeConn.getSupportedFunctions();
6.          List lFunctionList = Arrays.asList(lFunctions);
7.          mFunctionPane.setEnabledAt(ATTRINDEX,
8.              lFunctionList.contains(MiningFunction.attributeImportance));
9.          mFunctionPane.setEnabledAt(CLASSIFINDEX,
10.             lFunctionList.contains(MiningFunction.classification));
11.         mFunctionPane.setEnabledAt(CLUSTERINGINDEX,
12.             lFunctionList.contains(MiningFunction.clustering));
13.         mFunctionPane.setEnabledAt(REGINDEX,
14.             lFunctionList.contains(MiningFunction.regression));
15.         mFunctionPane.setEnabledAt(ASSOCINDEX,
16.             lFunctionList.contains(MiningFunction.association));
17.         handlerCheckDataSet();
18.     } catch (JDMException lException) {
```

```
19.        setDatasetSettingsEnabled(false);
20.        throw new UnexpectedJDMException(lException);
21.    }
22. }
```

The call to *setDatasetSettingsEnabled* at line 4 enables the buttons *Check, Stats,* and *Build Model* because the connection has just been established with the DME. In line 5, *getSupportedFunctions* returns the list of supported functions. Each mining function is then processed to enable its associated pane (sometimes called a *tab* in other environments) corresponding to the proper build settings. Once this is done, we also validate the default URI through the call of *handlerCheckDataSet.*

13.3.2   Getting the Metadata

When the user hits RETURN after changing the *Physical Dataset* URI text field, or when clicking on the *Check* button when creating the connection, the *handlerCheckDataSet* operation is performed as shown here:

```
1.  private void handlerCheckDataSet() {
2.      try {
3.          setCursor(Cursor.getPredefinedCursor(Cursor.WAIT_CURSOR));
4.          createDatasetAndImportMetaData(mPhysicalDataset.getText());
5.          String[] lAttributesNames = getAttributeNames();
6.          // Comment the following line if you want the natural order
7.          Arrays.sort(lAttributesNames);
8.          populateCombos(lAttributesNames);
9.      } catch (UnexpectedJDMException lException) {
10.         JOptionPane.showMessageDialog(this, "Exception Occured: "
11.                                 + lException.getMessage());
12.     } finally {
13.         setCursor(Cursor.getPredefinedCursor(Cursor.DEFAULT_CURSOR));
14.     }
15. }
```

At line 3, we set the cursor to a shape indicating that the user must wait because the metadata retrieval may take a while, for example, when the connection to a database must be initialized. The cursor is reset to its original shape at line 13.

Once the metadata has been populated, the list of attributes can be retrieved from the *PhysicalDataSet.* This list is used to update a number of combo boxes in the user interface to propose choices to the user. Depending on the vendor implementation, more information could be obtained, such as descriptive statistics, or simply the list of categories of the nominal attributes. These operations are performed by the method called *createDatasetAndImportMetaData*.

Integrators can comment (line 7) if they want to keep the list of attributes in the retrieved order as provided by the metadata, but it is sometimes easier to select attributes from a sorted list.

```
1. private void createDatasetAndImportMetaData(String iDatasetName) {
2.     try {
3.         PhysicalDataSetFactory lPdsFactory =
4.             (PhysicalDataSetFactory)mDmeConn.
5.             getFactory("javax.datamining.data.PhysicalDataSet");
6.         mBuildData = lPdsFactory.create(iDatasetName, false);
7.         mBuildData.importMetaData();
8.     } catch (JDMException lException) {
9.         throw new UnexpectedJDMException(lException);
10.    }
11. }
```

After this code is executed, the console member variable *mBuildData* references a valid *PhysicalDataSet* object populated with metadata information. The following code shows how to retrieve the list of attribute names from the *PhysicalDataSet* object.

```
1. private String[] getAttributeNames() {
2.     int lAttr = mBuildData.getAttributeCount();
3.     Vector lAttributesNames = new Vector();
4.     for (int i = 0; i < lAttr; i++) {
5.         lAttributesNames.add(mBuildData.getAttribute(i).getName());
6.     }
7.     return (String[]) lAttributesNames.toArray(new String[lAttr]);
8. }
```

The list of attributes is retrieved immediately once the metadata has been imported. More information could be extracted, such as the data itself. These attribute names are used in many combo boxes that are updated through the *populateCombos* method, as shown here:

```
1. private void populateCombos(String[] iAttributesNames) {
2.     mTargetNameAttr.setModel(
```

```
3.              new DefaultComboBoxModel(iAttributesNames));
4.      mTargetNameClassif.setModel(
5.              new DefaultComboBoxModel(iAttributesNames));
6.      mTargetNameRegression.setModel(
7.              new DefaultComboBoxModel(iAttributesNames));
8.      mKeyForAssociation.setModel(
9.              new DefaultComboBoxModel(iAttributesNames));
10. }
```

The reader should now be familiar with the notion of *ComboBox-Model,* which contains the data underlying the graphical components. The combo box updated at line 2 enables selecting the attribute that will be used as a target for the attribute importance mining functions. The one updated at line 4 is for the target of the classification function, and the one updated at line 6 is for the regression function. The one at line 8 allows the user to select a key (unique identifier) attribute. This is required for association rules, but the key attribute will also be forwarded to all build settings objects.

13.3.3 Computing Statistics

When the user clicks on the *Stats* button of the GUI, the following code is executed:

```
1. private void handlerRetrieveStatistics() {
2.     try {
3.         boolean lDoesSupport
4.         = mDmeConn.supportsCapability(null,
5.                                       null,
6.                                       MiningTask.computeStatisticsTask);
7.         if (!lDoesSupport) {
8.             displayLongMessage(this, "Unsupported feature",
9.                             "This implementation does not support "
10.                            + "the compute statistics task",
11.                            JOptionPane.INFORMATION_MESSAGE);
12.             return;
13.         }
14.         PhysicalDataSet lStatData = retrievePhysicalDataset();
15.         if (lStatData == null) {
16.             return;
17.         }
18.         JDialog lDialog = new JDialog(this,
19.                                     "Descriptive Statistics for URI:"
20.                                     + lStatData.getURI());
21.         lDialog.getContentPane().add(
22.             new DescriptiveStatisticDisplayer(lStatData));
```

```
23.        lDialog.pack();
24.        lDialog.setVisible(true);
25.    } catch (JDMException lException) {
26.        displayJDMException(lException);
27.    }
28. }
```

Statistical information is obtained through the *PhysicalDataSet* attribute information. It is expected that not all DME implementations will support statistics computations, so the capability *Mining-Task.computeStatisticsTask* must be tested. The actual work occurs in the *retrievePhysicalDataSet* method. To avoid redundant computation if the *Stats* button is clicked twice on the same URI reference, we will save the *PhysicalDataSet* into the MOR with its statistics (giving it the specific name *RetrieveStatsDS*); if we retrieve this dataset from the MOR with a URI equal to the one currently specified, we will not rerun the task to update the statistical information, as shown next:

```
1. private PhysicalDataSet retrievePhysicalDataset() throws JDMException {
2.     if (mDmeConn.doesObjectExist("RetrieveStatsDS",
3.                          NamedObject.physicalDataSet)) {
4.        PhysicalDataSet lPhysicalDS =
5.            (PhysicalDataSet) mDmeConn.retrieveObject(
6.                "RetrieveStatsDS", NamedObject.physicalDataSet);
7.        if (lPhysicalDS.getURI().equals(mBuildData.getURI())) {
8.            return lPhysicalDS;
9.        }
10.    }
11.    ComputeStatisticsTaskFactory lTaskFactory =
12.        (ComputeStatisticsTaskFactory) mDmeConn.getFactory(
13.            "javax.datamining.task.ComputeStatisticsTask");
14.    mDmeConn.saveObject("RetrieveStatsDS", mBuildData, true);
15.    ComputeStatisticsTask lTask =
16.        lTaskFactory.create("RetrieveStatsDS");
17.    VerificationReport lVerifTask = lTask.verify();
18.    if (lVerifTask != null) {
19.        displayLongMessage(this, "Wrong Task",
20.                      lVerifTask.getReportText(),
21.                      JOptionPane.INFORMATION_MESSAGE);
22.        return null;
23.    }
24.    mDmeConn.saveObject("RetrieveStatsTask", lTask, true);
25.    // Run the task.
26.    ExecutionHandle lBuildHandle =
27.        mDmeConn.execute("RetrieveStatsTask");
28.    if (monitorTaskExecution(lBuildHandle)) {
29.        return (PhysicalDataSet) mDmeConn.retrieveObject(
```

```
30.            "RetrieveStatsDS", NamedObject.physicalDataSet);
31.     }
32.     return null;
33. }
```

Line 2 checks if the *PhysicalDataSet* named *RetrieveStatsDS* exists in the MOR. If it does, we retrieve the *PhysicalDataSet* and check that its URI is the same as the one of the current console, which is stored in the member variable *mBuildData*. If so, we return the restored *PhysicalDataSet* that should contain statistical information from a previous execution of the *ComputeStatisticsTask* object.

When the *PhysicalDataSet* called *RetrieveStatsDS* does not match, we save a new version of the *PhysicalDataSet* named *RetrieveStatsDS* in the repository (note the last argument on line 14 overwrites any previous version). We then create the *ComputeStatisticsTask* associated with this dataset and save, verify, and execute. Note that the *PhysicalDataSet* was saved before task creation because the *ComputeStatisticsTaskFactory* needs a named *PhysicalDataSet,* as shown in line 16. When the task successfully completes, it saves a new version of this *PhysicalDataSet* with the statistical information.

In JDM, vendors are required to support synchronous execution; while asynchronous execution is optional. We have chosen to illustrate asynchronous execution for our tool examples. We monitor task execution using the method *monitorTaskExecution* for all tasks executed from the *JDMConsole*. The code for this method is provided here:

```
1.  protected boolean monitorTaskExecution(ExecutionHandle iExecHandle)
2.         throws JDMException {
3.      ExecutionState lState = iExecHandle.getLatestStatus().getState();
4.      boolean lIsTerminated = false;
5.      while (!lIsTerminated) {
6.         lState = iExecHandle.getLatestStatus().getState();
7.         lIsTerminated = (lState.equals(ExecutionState.success)
8.            || lState.equals(ExecutionState.error));
9.         try {
10.           Thread.sleep(100);
11.        } catch (InterruptedException lException) {
12.           JOptionPane.showMessageDialog(this,
13.                              "InterruptedException Occured: "
14.                              + lException.getMessage());
15.        }
16.     }
17.     return lState.equals(ExecutionState.success);
18. }
```

If task objects are persisted and executed asynchronously, any application that can login to the corresponding DME for the named user can check the execution status of that user's tasks. The *JDMAdminConsole* can be used to check task execution status as well. To perform synchronous execution, change lines 24 to 28 of the method *retrievePhysicalDataSet* with the following lines:

```
1.    ExecutionState lState = mDmeConn.execute(lTask, null).getState();
2.    if (lState.equals(ExecutionState.success)) {
```

In this case, the *ComputeStatisticsTask* need not have been persisted in the repository and synchronous execution ends when the statistical information is computed and stored in the *PhysicalDataSet*.

13.3.4   Retrieving the Statistics Information

After the statistics task completes, the statistics are displayed in a dialog that is filled with a *JPanel* called *DescriptiveStatisticDisplayer,* as shown in Figure 13-4. We do not describe the layout setup of this specific displayer. The basic layout is a list of attributes on the left side allowing the user to select one attribute. The right side of the

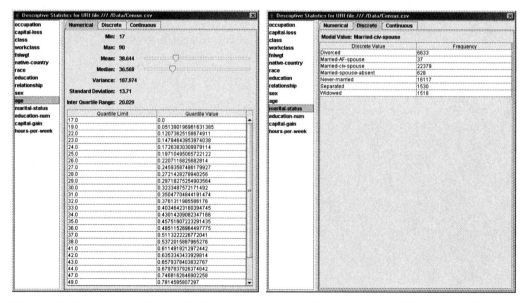

Figure 13-4   *A view of the statistics on an example of a numerical attribute, "age," and a discrete attribute, "marital-status."*

layout is filled with information on the selected attribute's statistics. We will focus on the methods of this class that retrieve information before displaying it. Three types of statistical information can be retrieved. Numerical attributes have statistics such as the minimum, maximum, and quantile information. Discrete attributes have statistics such as the frequency of attribute categories. Continuous attributes have statistics based on a segmentation of the values into bands described with their sum, frequency, and average.

The *DescriptiveStatisticsDisplayer* has several member variables to hold the graphical components and other member variables to hold the statistical information retrieved from the *PhysicalDataSet*. The main variables are:

- *AttributeStatisticsSet mAttributeStatisticsSet* is the set of statistics used to initialize the variable *mStatistics.*

- *Collection mStatistics* contains all retrieved statistics for all attributes.

- *ContinuousStatistics mSelectedContinuousStatistics* is the continuous statistics associated with the selected attribute.

- *NumericalStatistics mSelectedNumericalStatistics* is the numerical statistics associated with the selected attribute.

- *DiscreteStatistics mSelectedDiscreteStatistics* is the discrete statistics associated with the selected attribute.

When a *DescriptiveStatisticsDisplayer* object is created, the following code is executed:

```
1.  public DescriptiveStatisticDisplayer(PhysicalDataSet iPhysicalDataSet) {
2.      try {
3.          mAttributeStatisticsSet =
4.              iPhysicalDataSet.getAttributeStatistics();
5.      } catch (JDMException lException) {
6.          JOptionPane.showMessageDialog(
7.              this,
8.              lException.getMessage(),
9.              "JDMException",
10.             JOptionPane.WARNING_MESSAGE);
11.         lException.printStackTrace();
12.         return;
13.     }
14.     try {
```

```
15.        if (mAttributeStatisticsSet == null) {
16.            JOptionPane.showMessageDialog(
17.                this,
18.                "No Statistics Available",
19.                "Null Statistics",
20.                JOptionPane.WARNING_MESSAGE);
21.            return;
22.        }
23.        mStatistics = mAttributeStatisticsSet.getStatistics();
24.    } catch (JDMException lException) {
25.        JOptionPane.showMessageDialog(
26.                this,
27.                lException.getMessage(),
28.                "JDMException",
29.                JOptionPane.WARNING_MESSAGE);
30.        lException.printStackTrace();
31.        return;
32.    }
33.    if (mStatistics == null) {
34.        JOptionPane.showMessageDialog(
35.                this,
36.                "Descriptive Statistics not supported",
37.                "JDM",
38.                JOptionPane.WARNING_MESSAGE);
39.        return;
40.    }
41. ...
42. }
```

In this example, we removed the code dealing with graphical initialization. After the graphical component is created, the member variable *mStatistics* holds the collection of all attribute statistics. The code removed (noted by an ellipsis, ...) around line 41 contains graphical initialization as well as the following lines, which are also activated whenever the user selects a new attribute:

```
1.    String lVarName = (String) mVariableList.getSelectedValue();
2.    UnivariateStatistics lStats =
3.        mAttributeStatisticsSet.getStatistics(lVarName);
4.    mSelectedContinuousStatistics = lStats.getContinuousStatistics();
5.    ((AbstractTableModel) mContinuousStatisticsTable.getModel()).
6.        fireTableDataChanged();
7.    mSelectedDiscreteStatistics = lStats.getDiscreteStatistics();
8.    updateDiscreteStatistics();
9.    mSelectedNumericalStatistics = lStats.getNumericalStatistics();
10.   updateNumericalStatistics();
```

In line 3, the statistics of the selected attribute are retrieved and then the three kinds of statistics (continuous, discrete, and numerical) are retrieved and stored in the associated member variables. The DME will not produce statistics if the attribute type is not compatible, hence the result will be NULL. The code updating the Swing *TableModels* used to show the collected information is contained in *updateDiscreteStatistics* and *updateNumericalStatistics* that will be detailed later in the chapter.

The following code shows how the tool example obtains this information on distributions of numerical attributes.

```
1. private void updateNumericalStatistics() {
2.     ((AbstractTableModel) mNumericalQuantileTable.getModel()).
3.         fireTableDataChanged();
4.     if (mSelectedNumericalStatistics == null) {
5.         mNumericalMinLabel.setText("");
6.         mNumericalMaxLabel.setText("");
7.         mNumericalMeanLabel.setText("");
8.         mNumericalMedianLabel.setText("");
9.         mNumericalStandardDeviationLabel.setText("");
10.        mNumericalVarianceLabel.setText("");
11.        mNumericalInterQuartileRangeLabel.setText("");
12.        return;
13.    }
14.    NumberFormat lFormat = NumberFormat.getNumberInstance();
15.    lFormat.setGroupingUsed(false);
16.    double lMinValue = mSelectedNumericalStatistics.getMinimumValue();
17.    mNumericalMinLabel.setText(lFormat.format(lMinValue));
18.    double lMaxValue = mSelectedNumericalStatistics.getMaximumValue();
19.    mNumericalMaxLabel.setText(lFormat.format(lMaxValue));
20.    double lMeanValue = mSelectedNumericalStatistics.getMeanValue();
21.    mNumericalMeanLabel.setText(lFormat.format(lMeanValue));
22.    double lMedianValue = mSelectedNumericalStatistics.getMedianValue();
23.    mNumericalMedianLabel.setText(lFormat.format(lMedianValue));
24.    double lVariance = mSelectedNumericalStatistics.getVariance();
25.    mNumericalVarianceLabel.setText(lFormat.format(lVariance));
26.    double lInterQuartileRange =
27.        mSelectedNumericalStatistics.getInterQuartileRange();
28.    mNumericalInterQuartileRangeLabel.setText(
29.        lFormat.format(lInterQuartileRange));
30.    double lStandardDeviation =
31.        mSelectedNumericalStatistics.getStandardDeviation();
32.    mNumericalStandardDeviationLabel.setText(
33.        lFormat.format(lStandardDeviation));
34.    double lRange = lMaxValue - lMinValue;
35.    double lMeanPercent = (lMeanValue - lMinValue) / lRange;
36.    double lMedianPercent = (lMedianValue - lMinValue) / lRange;
37.    mNumericalMeanSlider.setModel(
38.        new DefaultBoundedRangeModel((int)(lMeanPercent * 100),
39.                                     1, 0, 100));
40.    if (lMedianValue > lMinValue && lMedianValue < lMaxValue)
```

```
41.        mNumericalMedianSlider.setModel(
42.            new DefaultBoundedRangeModel((int)(lMedianPercent * 100),
43.                                          1, 0, 100)));
44. }
```

Lines 2 and 3 update the *TableModel* used to display the quantile information and will be detailed later. The code shows that a lot of statistical information can be obtained for numerical attributes. We highlight the difference between the mean and median values by showing them on sliders scaled with the minimum and maximum values of the attribute. The standard deviation can also be compared to the interquantile range. The update of the quantile information is done with the following code extracted from the class *QuantileModel,* which extends the *AbstractTableModel* class.

```
1.    public Object getValueAt(int iRowIndex, int iColumnIndex) {
2.        if (mSelectedNumericalStatistics == null
3.            || mSelectedNumericalStatistics.getQuantileLimits() == null) {
4.            return null;
5.        }
6.        double lQuantileLimit =
7.            mSelectedNumericalStatistics.getQuantileLimits()[iRowIndex];
8.        switch (iColumnIndex) {
9.            case 0:
10.               return new Double(
11.                   lQuantileLimit);
12.           case 1:
13.               return new Double(
14.                   mSelectedNumericalStatistics.getQuantile(
15.                       lQuantileLimit));
16.       }
17.       return null;
18.   }
```

Note that the DME determines the number of quantiles and provides the associated quantile limits.

Since most numerical attributes are also continuous, we use the following code to extract continuous statistics from the class *ContinuousStatisticsModel,* which extends the *AbstractTableModel* class.

```
1.    public Object getValueAt(int iRowIndex, int iColumnIndex) {
2.        if (mSelectedContinuousStatistics == null) {
3.            return null;
4.        }
```

```
5.          Interval lInterval =
6.              mSelectedContinuousStatistics.getIntervals()[iRowIndex];
7.          switch (iColumnIndex) {
8.              case 0:
9.                  return intervalToString(lInterval);
10.             case 1:
11.                 return new Long(
12.                     mSelectedContinuousStatistics.getFrequency(
13.                         lInterval));
14.             case 2:
15.                 return new Double(
16.                     mSelectedContinuousStatistics.getSum(
17.                         lInterval));
18.             case 3:
19.                 return new Double(
20.                     mSelectedContinuousStatistics.getSumOfSquares(
21.                         lInterval));
22.         }
23.         return null;
24.     }
```

The code for *intervalToString* is shown below. It uses the closure type to produce a readable representation of the interval.

```
1. private static String intervalToString(Interval iInterval) {
2.     String lStart = "";
3.     String lEnd = "";
4.     String lString;
5.     if (iInterval.getIntervalClosure().
6.         equals(IntervalClosure.closedClosed)) {
7.         lStart = "[";
8.         lEnd = "]";
9.     } else if (iInterval.getIntervalClosure().
10.             equals(IntervalClosure.closedOpen)) {
11.         lStart = "[";
12.         lEnd = "[";
13.     } else if (iInterval.getIntervalClosure().
14.             equals(IntervalClosure.openClosed)) {
15.         lStart = "]";
16.         lEnd = "]";
17.     } else if (iInterval.getIntervalClosure().
18.             equals(IntervalClosure.openOpen)) {
19.         lStart = "]";
20.         lEnd = "[";
21.     }
22.     lString = lStart + String.valueOf(
23.         iInterval.getStartPoint()) + " ; "
24.         + String.valueOf(iInterval.getEndPoint()) + lEnd;
25.     return lString;
26. }
```

Finally, the information on the discrete attributes is obtained through the following code extracted from the class *DiscreteStatisticsModel,* which also extends the *AbstractTableModel* class.

```
1.    public Object getValueAt(int iRowIndex, int iColumnIndex) {
2.        if (mSelectedDiscreteStatistics == null) {
3.            return null;
4.        }
5.        Object[] lValues =
6.            mSelectedDiscreteStatistics.getDiscreteValues();
7.        Object lValue = lValues[iRowIndex];
8.        switch (iColumnIndex) {
9.            case 0:
10.               return lValue;
11.           case 1:
12.               try {
13.                   return new Long(
14.                       mSelectedDiscreteStatistics.
15.                       getFrequency(lValue));
16.               } catch (JDMException e) {
17.                   return "No Frequency";
18.               }
19.       }
20.       return null;
21.   }
```

This closes the section on retrieval of statistical information, which is rather complete in JDM for univariate statistics.

13.3.5   Saving the Physical Dataset, Build Settings, and Tasks

When the user clicks on the *Build Model* button, the *JDMBuildConsole* executes the method *handlerCreateModelButton.* The goal is to create an appropriate *BuildSettings* object and *BuildTask,* and then to execute the task. Because this method covers several pages of code, we will discuss it in sections.

```
1. private void handlerCreateModelButton() {
2.     try {
3.         setCursor(Cursor.getPredefinedCursor(Cursor.WAIT_CURSOR));
4.         createDatasetAndImportMetaData(mPhysicalDataset.getText());
5.         setDatasetKey((String) mKeyForAssociation.getSelectedItem());
6.         String lDSName = getDatasetName(mModelNameTextField.getText());
7.         if (lDSName != null) {
8.             saveDataset(lDSName, mOverwriteCheckBox.isSelected());
9.         } else {
```

```
10.            return;
11.         }
12.         int lSelectedFunction = mFunctionPane.getSelectedIndex();
13.         String lFunctionNameShort = "";
14.         BuildSettings lBuildSettings = null;
```

In line 3, we set the cursor to indicate to the user that the model build execution time can be long. We reuse the *createDatasetAndImportMetaData* method to ensure the *mBuildData* is aligned with the last dataset URI entered by the user and that the dataset metadata has been retrieved. The member *mKeyForAssociation* contains the name of the attribute selected by the user as a key, which will be used when creating the specific mining function *BuildSettings*. Line 8 shows that we use the check box value to ask the DME to overwrite objects already existing in the MOR. We get back the selected mining function through the associated selected pane (or tab). In line 13, we prepare a string to contain a short prefix depending on the user-selected mining function. This prefix will be used to generate names of objects, such as *BuildSettings* or *PhysicalDataSet,* to be saved.

```
15.         switch (lSelectedFunction) {
16.             //Classification
17.             case CLASSIFINDEX :
18.                 lFunctionNameShort = "Cla";
19.                 lBuildSettings = createClassificationSettings(
20.                     (String) mTargetNameClassif.getSelectedItem());
21.                 break;
```

We extract the user-selected target attribute name from the associated member variable pointing to a combo box. This is the only information needed for classification. The section for regression follows.

```
22.             case REGINDEX :
23.                 lFunctionNameShort = "Reg";
24.                 lBuildSettings = createRegressionSettings(
25.                     (String) mTargetNameRegression.getSelectedItem());
26.                 break;
```

We extract the user selected target attribute name from the associated member variable pointing to a combo box. This is the only needed information for regression.

```
27.          case ATTRINDEX :
28.              lFunctionNameShort = "AI";
29.              lBuildSettings = createAttributeImportanceSettings(
30.                  (String) mTargetNameAttr.getSelectedItem(),
31.                  ((Integer) mMaxAttributeCount.getValue()).intValue());
32.              break;
```

We extract the user selected target attribute name from the associated member variable pointing to a combo box and also the maximum number of attributes that should be returned by the attribute importance model.

```
33.          case CLUSTERINGINDEX :
34.              lFunctionNameShort = "Clu";
35.              Integer lNbCluster = (Integer) mClusterNumber.getValue();
36.              lBuildSettings = createClusteringSettings(
37.                  lNbCluster.intValue());
38.              break;
```

We extract the value selected by the user as the maximum number of clusters desired for the clustering model.

```
39.          case ASSOCINDEX :
40.              lFunctionNameShort = "Ass";
41.              int lMaxRule =
42.                  Integer.valueOf(mMaxRuleLengthTextField.getText())
43.                      .intValue();
44.              double lMinConfidence =
45.                  Double.valueOf(mMinConfidenceTextField.getText())
46.                      .doubleValue();
47.              double lMinSupport =
48.                  Double.valueOf(mMinSupportTextField.getText())
49.                      .doubleValue();
50.              lBuildSettings = createAssociationSettings(
51.                  lMaxRule, lMinConfidence, lMinSupport);
52.              break;
```

Association requires a minimum of three values to be set in their associated build settings.

```
53.          default :
54.              throw new IllegalStateException("Wrong Pane Index");
55.      }
```

This closes the section using the information entered by the user in the graphical interface to create the necessary build settings.

```
56.        VerificationReport lVerifBS = lBuildSettings.verify();
57.        if (lVerifBS != null) {
58.            displayLongMessage(this, "Wrong Settings",
59.                              lVerifBS.getReportText(), 0);
60.            return;
61.        }
```

The *BuildSettings* object is verified through the preceding code. If the user-provided values are not compatible with the selected mining function (for example, selecting a continuous attribute as the target for a classification model), we expect the DME implementation to provide a meaningful error report. We then save the build settings and execute the task.

```
62.        ExecutionHandle lBuildHandle =
63.            saveBuildSettingsAndExecuteTask(
64.                lFunctionNameShort,
65.                lDSName,
66.                lBuildSettings);
67.        if (lBuildHandle == null) {
68.            return;
69.        }
70.        boolean lTaskSucceed = monitorTaskExecution(lBuildHandle);
71.        // Check success/error
72.        if (lTaskSucceed) {
73.            JOptionPane.showMessageDialog(this, "Execution Successful");
74.        } else {
75.            JOptionPane.showMessageDialog(this,
76.                "Execution failed: "
77.              + lBuildHandle.getLatestStatus().getState().name() + " ["
78.              + lBuildHandle.getLatestStatus().getDescription() + "]");
79.        }
```

The code above reuses the same method to monitor the build task execution that we used to monitor the execution of the *Compute-StatisticsTask*.

Finally, the last section deals with the eventual exceptions that may be raised in the process.

```
80.        } catch (InvalidURIException lInvalidURIException) {
81.            JOptionPane.showMessageDialog(this,
```

```
82.                                   "Please verify the physical "
83.                                + "dataset URI, and try again.");
84.     } catch (JDMException lJdme) {
85.        JOptionPane.showMessageDialog(this, "JDMException Occured: "
86.                                + lJdme.getMessage());
87.     } finally {
88.        setCursor(Cursor.getPredefinedCursor(Cursor.DEFAULT_CURSOR));
89.     }
90. }
```

We have isolated the code that creates the minimum *BuildSettings* associated with each data mining function. The following is the code for classification and association; code for the other mining functions can be easily extrapolated from these. The code for classification is shown here.

```
1. private BuildSettings createClassificationSettings(
2.     String iTargetAttributeName) throws JDMException {
3.     ClassificationSettingsFactory lCsFactory =
4.         (ClassificationSettingsFactory) mDmeConn.getFactory(
5.             "javax.datamining.supervised.classification"
6.             + ".ClassificationSettings");
7.     ClassificationSettings lClassificationSettings =
8.         lCsFactory.create();
9.     if (iTargetAttributeName != null &&
10.        iTargetAttributeName.length() >= 0) {
11.        lClassificationSettings.setTargetAttributeName(
12.            iTargetAttributeName);
13.    }
14.    return lClassificationSettings;
15. }
```

The code for association is shown here.

```
1. private AssociationSettings createAssociationSettings(
2.         int iMaxRules,
3.         double iMinConfidence,
4.         double iMinSupport) throws JDMException {
5.     AssociationSettingsFactory lAssociationFactory =
6.         (AssociationSettingsFactory) mDmeConn.getFactory(
7.             "javax.datamining.association.AssociationSettings");
8.     AssociationSettings lAssociationSettings
9.         = lAssociationFactory.create();
10.    lAssociationSettings.setMaxRuleLength(iMaxRules);
11.    lAssociationSettings.setMinConfidence(iMinConfidence);
12.    lAssociationSettings.setMinSupport(iMinSupport);
13.    return lAssociationSettings;
14. }
```

To be complete, we expose the code of the *saveBuildSettingsAnd-ExecuteTask* method, which saves the task object before execution.

```
1.  private ExecutionHandle saveBuildSettingsAndExecuteTask(
2.        String iFunctionName,
3.        String iDatasetName,
4.        BuildSettings iBuildSettings) throws JDMException {
5.      String lBuildSettingsName =
6.        getBuildSettingsName(iFunctionName,
7.                    mModelNameTextField.getText());
8.      mDmeConn.saveObject(lBuildSettingsName,
9.                    iBuildSettings,
10.                   mOverwriteCheckBox.isSelected());
11.     BuildTaskFactory lBuildTaskFactory =
12.       (BuildTaskFactory) mDmeConn.getFactory(
13.         "javax.datamining.task.BuildTask");
14.     BuildTask lBuildTask =
15.       lBuildTaskFactory.create(
16.         iDatasetName,
17.         lBuildSettingsName,
18.         mModelNameTextField.getText());
19.     VerificationReport lVerifTask = lBuildTask.verify();
20.     if (lVerifTask != null) {
21.       displayLongMessage(this, "Wrong Task",
22.                     lVerifTask.getReportText(),
23.                     JOptionPane.INFORMATION_MESSAGE);
24.       return null;
25.     }
26.
27.     String lTaskName = iFunctionName + "Task_"
28.       + mModelNameTextField.getText();
29.     if (lTaskName.length() > getMaxNameLength()) {
30.       displayLongMessage(this, "String Too Long",
31.                     "The task name is too long, please change "
32.                     + "your model name.",
33.                     JOptionPane.ERROR_MESSAGE);
34.       return null;
35.     }
36.     mDmeConn.saveObject(lTaskName, lBuildTask,
37.                   mOverwriteCheckBox.isSelected());
38.     // Run the task.
39.     return mDmeConn.execute(lTaskName);
40. }
```

Both the *BuildSettings* and the *Task* are saved in this method. Note that the value of the check box indicating that the objects should be overwritten is used each time a named object is saved to the MOR. If this is not checked, the operation will fail if there is an object with the same name in the MOR. The *BuildSettings* name is based on the mining function name, a symbol indicating it is a *BuildSettings,* and the user-specified model name. It is returned by the *getBuildSettingsName* method. This method validates the length of the generated name per DME requirements. The *BuildTask* is initialized with the build dataset name, the generated build settings name, and the desired model name. As before, the *BuildTask* is verified before it is saved at line 19.

Then, the task name itself is generated using the prefix specific to the mining function, a symbol indicating it is a task object, and the model name. It is also checked for length compatibility with the DME implementation. The code of *getBuildSettingsName* is shown here:

```
1.  private String getBuildSettingsName(String iFunctionName,
2.                                  String iModelName) {
3.      String lBuildSettingsNameShort = "";
4.      lBuildSettingsNameShort = iFunctionName + "Sett" + iModelName;
5.      if (lBuildSettingsNameShort.length() > getMaxNameLength()) {
6.          displayLongMessage(this, "Too long string",
7.                      "The build settings name is too long, "
8.                      + " please change your model name.",
9.                      JOptionPane.ERROR_MESSAGE);
10.         return null;
11.     }
12.     return lBuildSettingsNameShort;
13. }
```

13.4 User Interface to Test Model Quality

In our example, we have also created a small user interface to compare model performance, either when the models are created through the same DME, or through tables of scores.

This graphical user interface allows users to select supervised models saved in the MOR and to create a test task using a selected model on the user-specified apply data. After connecting to a DME, the user selects a model and specifies a URI to a physical dataset, and executes the test task. Test metrics include a confusion matrix and lift and ROC curves for classification models, and for regression models, the mean absolute error, mean actual value versus the mean predicted value, root mean square error, and the R-squared error.

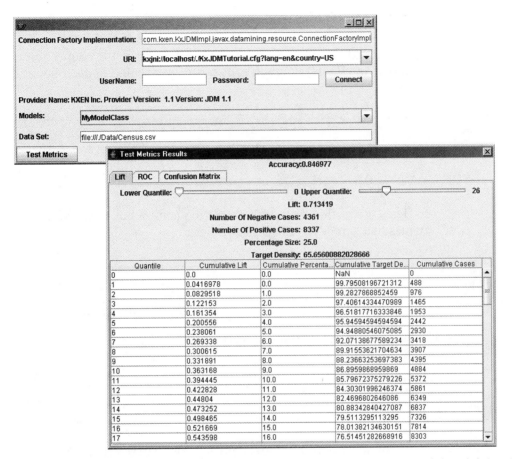

Figure 13-5 *Testing a model: the first window is used to select the model and datasets and the second to display resulting test metrics.*

For classification models, the user can interact with the lift object, as shown in Figure 13-5. The JDM lift object allows the user to select a segment of the population defined through a lower and upper quantile and to access the number of positive and negative cases within that segment, which effectively is the density of the positive cases.

The source code of the first window used to start the test metrics task is contained in the file *JDMTestConsole.java*. When the task completes, test metrics are displayed in a specific dialog called *TestMetricsDisplayer*. The structure of *TestMetricsDisplayer* is close to the one used to display statistical information. The source code of this dialog is provided in a file called *TestMetricsDisplayer.java*.

13.4.1   Getting the List of Saved Models

As explained for the administration console, once the connection is obtained, the *JDMTestConsole* calls *start*, as presented in the following code:

```
1.  protected void start(Connection iConnection) {
2.      mDmeConn = iConnection;
3.      mModelsCombo.setModel(new DefaultComboBoxModel(getModels()));
4.  }
```

The core of this method is to fill the combo box with the model names that can be tested, as shown here:

```
1.  private String[] getModels() {
2.      Collection lMiningObjectsNames = null;
3.      try {
4.          lMiningObjectsNames = mDmeConn.getObjectNames(NamedObject.model);
5.      } catch (JDMException lException) {
6.          throw new UnexpectedJDMException(lException);
7.      }
8.      return (String[])
9.          lMiningObjectsNames.toArray(
10.             new String[lMiningObjectsNames.size()]);
11. }
```

Obtaining the list of model names is easy. We select all the models from the MOR using the JDM enumeration *NamedObject.model*. We could have checked here whether the models are supervised (that is, can be tested), but we decided to illustrate the use of the verify method instead, which should send proper error messages otherwise.

13.4.2   Computing the Test Metrics

When the user clicks on the *Test Metrics* button, the following code is executed:

```
1.  private void handlerTestMetrics() {
2.      String lModelName = (String) mModelsCombo.getSelectedItem();
3.      Model lModel;
4.      try {
5.          lModel = (Model)
6.              mDmeConn.retrieveObject(lModelName, NamedObject.model);
```

```
7.        if (lModel == null)
8.            JOptionPane.showMessageDialog(this,
9.                                    "The Model Object for "
10.                                        + lModelName + "is null");
11.        MiningFunction lFunction = lModel.getMiningFunction();
12.        if (lFunction == null)
13.            JOptionPane.showMessageDialog(this,
14.                                    "The Mining Function for "
15.                                        + lModelName + "is null");
16.        if (lFunction == MiningFunction.association
17.                || lFunction == MiningFunction.attributeImportance
18.                || lFunction == MiningFunction.clustering) {
19.            JOptionPane.showMessageDialog(this,
20.                                    "Cannot use Test Metrics on "
21.                                        + lFunction.name());
22.        } else if (lFunction == MiningFunction.classification) {
23.            testClassificationModel(lModelName);
24.        } else if (lFunction == MiningFunction.regression) {
25.            testRegressionModel(lModelName);
26.        }
27.    } catch (UnexpectedJDMException lException) {
28.        JOptionPane.showMessageDialog(this, "Exception Occured: "
29.                                    + lException.getMessage());
30.    } catch (JDMException lException) {
31.        JOptionPane.showMessageDialog(this,
32.                                    lException.getMessage(),
33.                                    "JDMException",
34.                                    JOptionPane.WARNING_MESSAGE);
35.    }
36. }
```

First, we retrieve the selected name from the appropriate combo box and retrieve the model as shown in line 6. Since only supervised models can be used to compute test metrics, we obtain this information, as shown in line 11, and prepare the test metrics task only for classification or regression models. The code below shows the code for classification.

```
1. private void testClassificationModel(String iModelName) {
2.      try {
3.          PhysicalDataSetFactory lPdsFactory =
4.              (PhysicalDataSetFactory) mDmeConn.getFactory(
5.                  "javax.datamining.data.PhysicalDataSet");
6.          PhysicalDataSet lTestData =
7.              lPdsFactory.create(mDataSetTextField.getText(), false);
8.          mDmeConn.saveObject("myTestData", lTestData, true);
9.          ClassificationTestTaskFactory lClassificationTestTaskFactory =
10.             (ClassificationTestTaskFactory) mDmeConn.getFactory(
11.                 "javax.datamining.supervised.classification."
```

```
12.                          + "ClassificationTestTask");
13.          ClassificationTestTask lClassificationTestTask =
14.              lClassificationTestTaskFactory.create("myTestData",
15.                                                    iModelName,
16.                                                    "myMetrics");
17.          // Indicate the test option to compute.
18.          lClassificationTestTask.computeMetric(
19.              ClassificationTestMetricOption.lift,
20.              true);
21.          lClassificationTestTask.computeMetric(
22.              ClassificationTestMetricOption.
23.                 confusionMatrix,
24.              true);
25.          lClassificationTestTask.computeMetric(
26.              ClassificationTestMetricOption.
27.                 receiverOperatingCharacteristics,
28.              true);
29.          mDmeConn.saveObject("myTestTask",
30.                         lClassificationTestTask, true);
31.          ExecutionHandle lTestTaskHandle
32.              = mDmeConn.execute("myTestTask");
33.          boolean lTaskSucceed = monitorTaskExecution(lTestTaskHandle);
34.          if (lTaskSucceed) {
35.              ClassificationTestMetrics lTestMetrics =
36.                  (ClassificationTestMetrics) mDmeConn.retrieveObject(
37.                      "myMetrics",
38.                      NamedObject.testMetrics);
39.              JDialog lDialog = new JDialog(this, "Test Metrics Results");
40.              lDialog.getContentPane().setLayout(new BorderLayout());
41.              lDialog.getContentPane().add(
42.                  new TestMetricsDisplayer(lTestMetrics),
43.                                      BorderLayout.CENTER);
44.              lDialog.pack();
45.              lDialog.setVisible(true);
46.          } else {
47.              JOptionPane.showMessageDialog(this,
48.                  "Error during test: Last state: "
49.                  + lTestTaskHandle.getLatestStatus().getState().name()
50.                  + " -> "
51.                  + lTestTaskHandle.getLatestStatus().getDescription());
52.          }
53.      } catch (JDMException lException) {
54.          throw new UnexpectedJDMException(lException);
55.      }
56.  }
```

First, the URI selected by the user in the *mDataSetTextField* is retrieved. We use this URI to save a *PhysicalDataSet* object to the MOR under the name *myTestData*. This name will be used later in the test task. Then we use the *ClassificationTestTaskFactory* to create a test task setting the *PhysicalDataSet* name, model name, and resulting test metrics named in lines 14 to 16. We can further specify in the *Classification TestTask* which metrics to compute. Here we specify lift (line 18), confusion matrix (line 21), and ROC (line 25). Then the task is saved, executed, and monitored for success.

When the task completes, the results are obtained, as shown in lines 35 to 38.

The same class *TestMetricsDisplayer* is used for classification and regression but the graphical dialog layout is different for each. The creator of the *TestMetricsDisplayer* used at line 42 will look at the class of the argument *lTestMetrics* to select one of two proper layouts: (1) If the class is *ClassificationTestMetrics,* a layout based on three panes (or tabs), each of them leading to a table displayer, will be used; (2) if the class is *RegressionTestMetrics,* a very simple layout showing five scalar metrics values will be used.

A *TestMetricsDisplayer* has several member variables to store test metrics information:

- *JLabel mTestAccuracy* used to store the model accuracy to be displayed
- *JLabel mTestNumberQuantile* used to store the number of quantiles used to display the lift and ROC
- *Lift mLift* used to store the JDM lift structure obtained from the test metrics
- *ReceiverOperatingCharacterics mROC* used to store the JDM ROC structure obtained from the test metrics
- *ConfusionMatrix mConfusionMatrix* used to store the confusion matrix elements
- *Object[] mConfusionMatrixCategories* used to store the categories associated with the confusion matrix

Regression models produce five scalar values that can be displayed without needing to manage complex structures such as curves or a confusion matrix.

When a *TestMetricsDisplayer* is created with a *ClassificationTest-Metrics* object, the following code is executed:

```
1.  public TestMetricsDisplayer(ClassificationTestMetrics iTestMetrics) {
2.      mLift = iTestMetrics.getLift();
3.      mROC = iTestMetrics.getROC();
```

```
4.     mConfusionMatrix = iTestMetrics.getConfusionMatrix();
5.     setLayout(new BorderLayout());
6.     JPanel lMetricsGeneralInfos = new JPanel(new GridLayout());
7.     lMetricsGeneralInfos.add(new JLabel("Accuracy:", JLabel.RIGHT));
8.     lMetricsGeneralInfos.add(
9.        new JLabel(iTestMetrics.getAccuracy().toString()));
10.    add(lMetricsGeneralInfos, BorderLayout.NORTH);
11.    JTabbedPane lTabbedPane = new JTabbedPane();
12.    lTabbedPane.add("Lift", createLiftDisplayer());
13.    lTabbedPane.add("ROC", createROCDisplayer());
14.    lTabbedPane.add("Confusion Matrix",
15.                    createConfusionMatrixDisplayer());
16.    add(lTabbedPane, BorderLayout.CENTER);
17. }
```

We will not fully describe here the panes concerning the ROC or the confusion matrix since the reader has seen already how to fill graphical tables with information from JDM objects. However, we select the lift object, focusing on the *createLiftDisplayer*, to illustrate user interaction since that requires more explanation. We divide this code into several sections to explain this user interaction.

```
1. private JPanel createLiftDisplayer() {
2.     JPanel lLiftDisplayer = new JPanel(new BorderLayout());
3.     JPanel lSliderPanel = new JPanel(new FlowLayout());
4.     final JSlider lLowerIndexSlider =
5.        new JSlider(0, mLift.getNumberOfQuantiles() - 1, 0);
6.     final JLabel lLowerLabel = new JLabel("000");
7.     lSliderPanel.add(new JLabel("Lower Quantile:", JLabel.RIGHT));
8.     lSliderPanel.add(lLowerIndexSlider);
9.     lSliderPanel.add(lLowerLabel);
10.    final JLabel lUpperLabel = new JLabel("000");
11.    final JSlider lUpperIndexSlider =
12.        new JSlider(0, mLift.getNumberOfQuantiles() - 1, 0);
13.    lSliderPanel.add(new JLabel("Upper Quantile:", JLabel.RIGHT));
14.    lSliderPanel.add(lUpperIndexSlider);
15.    lSliderPanel.add(lUpperLabel);
```

The overall graphical component is the *lLiftDisplayer*, which is itself decomposed into two parts. The upper part displays two sliders to tune the lower and upper quantiles, defining a segment of the population managed by the *lSliderPanel*. The lower part displays the statistics about the selected segment, as shown here:

```
16.    JPanel lIndicatorsPanel = new JPanel(new GridLayout(5, 4, 5, 5));
17.    final JLabel lLiftLabel = new JLabel();
```

```
18.    lIndicatorsPanel.add(new JLabel("Lift:", JLabel.RIGHT));
19.    lIndicatorsPanel.add(lLiftLabel);
20.    final JLabel lNegativeCasesLabel = new JLabel();
21.    lIndicatorsPanel.add(new JLabel("Number Of Negative Cases:",
22.                                    JLabel.RIGHT));
23.    lIndicatorsPanel.add(lNegativeCasesLabel);
24.    final JLabel lPositiveCasesLabel = new JLabel();
25.    lIndicatorsPanel.add(new JLabel("Number Of Positive Cases:",
26.                                    JLabel.RIGHT));
27.    lIndicatorsPanel.add(lPositiveCasesLabel);
28.    final JLabel lPercentageSizeLabel = new JLabel();
29.    lIndicatorsPanel.add(new JLabel("Percentage Size:",
30.                                    JLabel.RIGHT));
31.    lIndicatorsPanel.add(lPercentageSizeLabel);
32.    final JLabel lTargetDensityLabel = new JLabel();
33.    lIndicatorsPanel.add(new JLabel("Target Density:",
34.                                    JLabel.RIGHT));
35.    lIndicatorsPanel.add(lTargetDensityLabel);
```

The preceding code defines the *lIndicatorsPanel* that contains the five elements that are updated each time the user selects a segment of the population. The following lines create the upper part as the *lNorthPanel* to contain both sections:

```
36.    JPanel lNorthPanel = new JPanel(new BorderLayout());
37.    lNorthPanel.add(lSliderPanel, BorderLayout.NORTH);
38.    lNorthPanel.add(lIndicatorsPanel, BorderLayout.SOUTH);
```

Then, a local listener class is defined to update the values of the selected segment's statistics.

```
39.    // Local listener
40.    ChangeListener lChangeListener = new ChangeListener() {
41.        public void stateChanged(ChangeEvent iE) {
42.            int lLowerValue = lLowerIndexSlider.getValue();
43.            lLowerLabel.setText("" + lLowerValue);
44.            int lUpperValue = lUpperIndexSlider.getValue();
45.            lUpperLabel.setText("" + lUpperValue);
46.            if (iE.getSource() == lLowerIndexSlider) {
47.                if (lLowerValue > lUpperValue) {
48.                    lUpperIndexSlider.setValue(lLowerValue);
49.                }
50.            } else {
51.                if (lLowerValue > lUpperValue) {
52.                    lLowerIndexSlider.setValue(lUpperValue);
53.                }
```

```
54.            }
55.         try {
56.            lLiftLabel.setText(
57.               mLift.getLift(lLowerValue, lUpperValue).toString());
58.            lNegativeCasesLabel.setText(""
59.               + mLift.getNumberOfNegativeCases(lLowerValue,
60.                                                      lUpperValue));
61.            lPositiveCasesLabel.setText(""
62.               + mLift.getNumberOfPositiveCases(lLowerValue,
63.                                                      lUpperValue));
64.            lPercentageSizeLabel.setText(
65.               mLift.getPercentageSize(lLowerValue,
66.                                           lUpperValue).toString());
67.            lTargetDensityLabel.setText(
68.               mLift.getTargetDensity(lLowerValue,
69.                                           lUpperValue).toString());
70.         } catch (JDMException e) {
71.            e.printStackTrace();
72.         }
73.      }
74.   };
```

Every time the graphical interface sends a change event on the values of a slider, this listener will be activated. It first looks for the values defined by the user through the two sliders, as shown in lines 42 and 44, and checks for the consistency of these two values (the upper quantile must be higher than the lower quantile). It then uses the convenient JDM calls on the lift object to retrieve the statistics between the two quantiles, as shown in lines 57, 59, 62, 65, and 68. These methods ease the integration work.

```
75.   lLowerIndexSlider.addChangeListener(lChangeListener);
76.   lUpperIndexSlider.addChangeListener(lChangeListener);
77.   lLiftDisplayer.add(lNorthPanel, BorderLayout.NORTH);
78.   lLiftDisplayer.add(new JScrollPane(new JTable(new LiftModel())),
79.              BorderLayout.CENTER);
80.   return lLiftDisplayer;
81. }
```

The last section of the *createLiftDisplayer* associates the defined listener to the two sliders, and finishes the graphical layout.

For regression models, we provide code for when the *TestMetrics-Displayer* is created with a *RegressionTestMetrics* object. In this case, the associated dialog can be filled directly with the five scalar values, as shown here:

```
1.  public TestMetricsDisplayer(RegressionTestMetrics iTestMetrics) {
2.      setLayout(new GridLayout(5, 2));
3.      add(new JLabel("MeanAbsoluteError: "));
4.      add(new JLabel(iTestMetrics.getMeanAbsoluteError().toString()));
5.      add(new JLabel("MeanActualValue: "));
6.      add(new JLabel(iTestMetrics.getMeanActualValue().toString()));
7.      add(new JLabel("MeanPredictedValue: "));
8.      add(new JLabel(iTestMetrics.getMeanPredictedValue().toString()));
9.      add(new JLabel("RMSError: "));
10.     add(new JLabel(iTestMetrics.getRMSError().toString()));
11.     add(new JLabel("RSquared: "));
12.     add(new JLabel(iTestMetrics.getRSquared().toString()));
13. }
```

This concludes the explanation of the source code of the *JDMTest-Console*.

13.5 Summary

This chapter presented the code for some graphical interfaces to illustrate how data mining tools can be developed using JDM. The source code can be freely downloaded and modified. The chapter developed three user interfaces: the first deals with model and task management, the second with data exploration and model building, and the third with quantitative model validation. They should be complemented later with tools to allow easy model apply and export/import of models to cover the deployment features currently offered by JDM. These are left as exercises for the reader.

Some extensions could be added to deal with data preparation that will be supported by JDM 2.0; this will allow a complete set of functions currently available in commercial and free data mining tools.

It is important to note that these data mining tools should work on any implementation compliant with JDM. Moreover, these tools could be used as seeds for more sophisticated data mining software, operating across different JDM implementations. These tools provide a user-friendly way to compare DME implementation behaviors such as:

- The behavior of DME implementations in the presence of errors (for example, user-friendly error messages, or type of exceptions raised)

- DME execution performance
- The visualization and exploration of regression and classification model quality against new datasets

Recognizing that these first examples of JDM tools are still somewhat crude, they should nevertheless facilitate the spread of JDM technology. We hope that they will open new avenues of development around JDM usage.

Chapter

14

Getting Started with JDM Web Services

The World Wide Web is more and more used for application to application communication. The programmatic interfaces made available are referred to as Web services.

—www.w3.org

Programming language independence of web services enables a legacy application to expose its functionality for other applications to use. This chapter extends the JDM web services discussion in Chapter 11 by presenting two examples. The first example illustrates how a non-Java application client can interact with JDM web services in the development of data mining applications. In this example, we use PHP [PHP 2005] — a popular web application scripting language — to develop a simple product recommendation application using JDM web services. The second example is a generic illustration of how to integrate calls to Web services (WS) from Java, which is useful for a Java programmer.

14.1 A Web Service Client in PHP

PHP [PHP 2005] is a widely used general-purpose scripting language that is especially well suited for Web development and can be embedded into HTML. PHP can be freely used, being related to the Apache foundation, and is one of the most commonly used languages for Web site development. We have chosen PHP to illustrate the examples in this chapter for its simplicity of integration with Web services. However, any programming language that integrates Web services layers, such as Visual Basic for Excel, can be used.

Recently, PHP has been extended with a package, specifically developed in PHP, called *NuSOAP*. This package enables the direct use of Web services from PHP scripts. HTML documents can easily include calls to external Web services in the pages accessed through Web browsers. The role of NuSOAP is to translate PHP structures into valid XML documents corresponding to SOAP messages. These SOAP messages allow developers to create and consume Web services based on SOAP 1.1, WSDL 1.1, and HTTP 1.0/1.1.

Web servers that answer HTTP requests can run PHP scripts. Figure 14-1 depicts a typical PHP application architecture and the process of connecting to Web service providers.

In this scenario, we use PHP to write a Web page accessible by a call center representative processing incoming calls. This page contains fields the representative will fill through a Web browser interface; each field corresponds to a question to be asked of the caller. When all questions have been answered (and fields populated), the system executes JDM Web services using *singleRecordApply* tasks on each model found in the mining object repository (MOR) with a name prefix *"Product."* We make two assumptions. First, all models whose name follows the pattern *"Product-<Name>"* will be classification models that predict the probability that the caller will buy a given product *<Name>*. And second, all models with names beginning with *Product* use the same apply input data. In our examples, we use three caller attributes: *education* to represent the education

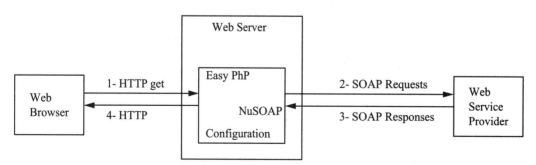

Figure 14-1 *PHP application architecture.*

level, *marital-status*, and *capital-gains*.[1] The system executes the *singleRecordApply* task using the selected models and collects the probability that the caller will buy each of the respective products.

The scenario works as follows:

- The Web page provides fields to be filled by the call center representative, who selects values from a drop-down list of discrete attributes, and types in values for continuous attributes. This portion of the HTML page is written in javascript code for the field value selection. The list of fields is defined at design time and will be the same for all models called from this page.

- When requested by the user of the Web browser (through the *Score* submit button shown in the screen shot), the system connects to a JDM Web services provider chosen at design time, obtains the names of models available in the MOR whose name begins with *Product*, and, expecting that these models are classification models, scores each input data record on each model and reports to the representative the probabilities returned by the models.

Figure 14-2 is a screen shot of the Web page.

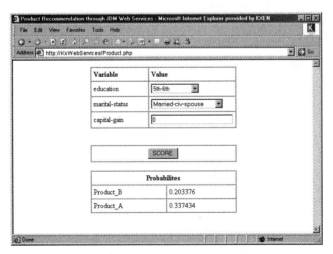

Figure 14-2   *Product recommendation PHP page.*

---

1   These three attribute names have been taken from a well-known dataset used in data mining packages called "census" and do not claim to be truly useful attributes for product recommendation.

The implementation is contained in a single PHP file, called *Product.php*. Portions of this file are discussed next.

14.1.1 Filling the Input Values Using Javascript

The first section of the source code of *Product.php* produces a form that presents the three attributes to be filled by the user. The first two attributes, *education* and *marital-status*, are discrete and a drop-down list supplies the possible values; the third attribute is a continuous attribute called *capital-gains*. The code below produces this form such that when the user clicks on the *Score* button, these values are forwarded and the PHP code is run.

```
1.  <html>
2.  <head>
3.  <title>Product Recommendation through JDM Web Services</title>
4.  </head>
5.  <script language="JavaScript" type="text/javascript">
6.  <body>
7.  <form method="POST" action="Product.php">
8.  <table cellpadding="5" cellspacing="0" border="1" width="50%">
9.  <tr>
10.     <td width="40%"><b>Variable</b></td>
11.     <td><b>Value</b></td>
12. </tr>
13. <tr>
14.     <td>education</td>
15.     <td align="Left"><select name="education" >
16.         <option value="5th-6th"> 5th-6th
17.         <option value="7th-8th"> 7th-8th
18.         <option value="9th"> 9th
19.         <option value="10th"> 10th
20.         <option value="11th"> 11th
21.         <option value="12th"> 12th
22.         <option value="Assoc-acdm"> Assoc-acdm
23.         <option value="Assoc-voc"> Assoc-voc
24.         <option value="Bachelors""> Bachelors
25.         <option value="Doctorate"> Doctorate
26.         <option value="HS-grad"> HS-grad
27.         <option value="Masters"> Masters
28.         <option value="Prof-school"> Prof-school
29.         <option value="Some-college"> Some-college
30.         </select><br/></td>
31. </tr>
32.
33. <tr>
34.     <td>marital-status</td>
35.     <td align="Left"><select name="marital-status" >
36.         <option value="Divorced"> Divorced
```

```
37.         <option value="Married-AF-spouse"> Married-AF-spouse
38.         <option value="Married-civ-spouse" selected > Married-civ-spouse
39.         <option value="Married-spouse-absent"> Married-spouse-absent
40.         <option value="Never-married"> Never-married
41.         <option value="Separated"> Separated
42.         <option value="Widowed"> Widowed
43.         </select><br/></td>
44. </tr>
45.
46. <tr>
47.     <td>capital-gain</td>
48.     <td align="Left"><input style="width:100%"
49.          type="text" name="capital-gain" value="0"/><br/></td>
50. </tr>
51. </table>
52. <br>
53. <table cellpadding="5" cellspacing="0" border="1" width="50%">
54. <tr align="center">
55.     <td><input type="submit" value="SCORE"></td>
56. </tr>
57. </table>
58. </form>
59. <br>
```

The following sections provide details of the PHP code, which calls JDM Web services. When calling SOAP invocations through NuSOAP, the programmer has two design choices: either he provides the "call" method with arguments directly in XML format, or he creates structures of recursive arrays that NuSOAP translates in the proper XML structure. These two options and their use will be discussed in later sections.

In this example, we assume that some models have been created in the MOR and are accessible through the data mining engine (DME) implementation.

14.1.2 Saving the ApplySettings Object

The file *Product.php* contains the HTML form as well as the call to the JDM Web services through PHP. Here, we describe how to use the NuSOAP library [NuSOAP 2004] to call the JDM Web services. The PHP section starts at line 60, as shown here:

```
60. <?php
61.   function beginsWith( $str, $sub ) {
62.        $str = strtoupper($str);
63.        $sub = strtoupper($sub);
```

```
64.       return ( substr( $str,0,strlen( $sub ) ) === $sub);
65. }
66. require_once('nusoap.php');
67. $namespace="http://www.jsr-73.org/2004/webservices";
68. $kjdmclient = new soapclient('http://myHost:1234/KxServices/services/
    IDataMiningPort');
69. $applySettingsName = "PHP-Product-ApplySettings";
70. $ParamAppSett = '<objectName>' . $applySettingsName . '</objectName>'
71.     .'<object xsi:type="ClassificationApplySettings"'
72.     .'xmlns="http://www.jsr-73.org/2004/JDMSchema">'
73.     .'<categoryMap category="1" content="probability"'
74.     .'destPhysAttrName="Probability"/>'
75.     .'</object>';
76. $SaveObjResponse = $kjdmclient->call("saveObject",
77.                     $ParamAppSett,
78.                     $namespace);
```

Lines 61 to 65 define the function used to filter the models. Line 66 includes the NuSOAP library, which is used at line 68 to connect to a specific Web services implementation using the call "new soapclient." This function takes the uniform resource identifier (URI) of the Web services implementation as an argument. In our example, it will look for the machine called *MyHost* on port 1234, which should be dedicated on this machine to listening to SOAP requests. In this example, KxServices is the name of the Web services context on MyHost.

Note that the JDM Web services definition does not forward the JDM class of *Connection* in any application programming interface (API) argument. Any JDM Web services implementation will use an internal default connection. From an application using JDM Web services, for example, there is no possibility to specify a user, password, or connection. On the other hand, SOAP can be used to specify credentials when connecting to the Web server. The connection details will be specified at the installation of the specific Web services implementation on MyHost.

Before executing a *RecordApplyTask* on each of the models, we first save a *ClassificationApplySettings* object that specifies that we want the probability the caller will purchase the particular product, that is, has a target value of "1". We show how to use JDMWS to save this object; however, a production implementation may assume that this *ClassificationApplySettings* is already saved in the MOR.

Here, we show how to create the XML document representing the argument of the call to *saveObject*. Looking at the jdm.wsdl file, we find that the argument must be of type *saveObject*, which contains a name and an object that is a subtype of *NamedObject*, and two optional Boolean flags, one indicating to overwrite the object and one indicating to verify the object.

The two required arguments are thus: objectName to be $apply-SettingsName, and "object" to follow the syntax of a *Classification-ApplySettings*

In the jdm.xsd file, the type *ClassificationApplySettings* is described by the following schema:

```
<xsd:complexType name="ClassificationApplySettings">
  <xsd:complexContent>
    <xsd:extension base="ApplySettings">
      <xsd:sequence>
       <xsd:choice>
          <xsd:element name="costMatrixName" type="xsd:string" minOccurs="0"/>
          <xsd:element name="costMatrix" type="CostMatrix" minOccurs="0"/>
       </xsd:choice>
        <xsd:element name="rankMap" type="ClassificationApplyMap"
                maxOccurs="unbounded"/>
        <xsd:element name="categoryMap" type="ClassificationCategoryMap"
                maxOccurs="unbounded"/>
        <xsd:element name="predictionMap" type="PredictionMap""
                maxOccurs="unbounded"/>
      </xsd:sequence>
    </xsd:extension>
   </xsd:complexContent>
  </xsd:complexType>
```

A valid XML may look like:

```
<object xsi:type="ClassificationApplySettings"
    xmlns="http://www.jsr-73.org/2004/JDMSchema">
...
</object>
```

We must fill "…" with a section representing a category map. The type *ClassificationCategoryMap* is described by the following schema:

```
<xsd:complexType name="ClassificationCategoryMap">
  <xsd:attribute name="content" type="ClassificationApplyContent"
          use="required"/>
```

```
  <xsd:attribute name="destPhysAttrName" type="xsd:string" use="required"/>
  <xsd:attribute name="category" type="xsd:string" use="optional"/>
</xsd:complexType>
```

This schema is used to generate the following XML string:

```
<categoryMap category="1" content="probability" destPhysAttrName="Probability"/>'
```

This explains how we have proceeded to create lines 70 to 75 preparing the argument to be provided to *saveObject* as an XML string.

14.1.3   Retrieving the List of Models

As noted earlier, for the sake of completeness, we use another mechanism to provide an argument to a Web service using NuSoap. To retrieve the models whose names begin with *Product*, we use PHP arrays to call the service *listContents* as shown at line 79 below:

```
79. $params = array('objectFilter' => array ('type' => 'model'));
80. $modelList = $kjdmclient->call("listContents", $params, $namespace);
81. $filter="Product";
```

NuSOAP uses the WSDL file representing Web services and the XML documents associated with the service arguments. PHP has a structure called array that can be used as a hash table, which is similar to the java.util.Map object in Java, where each field of the array can be retrieved with its name. NuSOAP creates a PHP array structure to represent web services request and response messages. The XML Schemas defined in the Web services are translated by NuSOAP into recursive arrays representing the XML documents presented in Chapters 10 and 11.

For example, the Web service *listContents* takes a single argument of type ObjectFilter. An *ObjectFilter* is defined in XML as a *complexType* with optional attributes *name, type, function, algorithm, creatorInfo, createdBefore, createdAfter, objectIdentifier,* or even *requestedContent*. This allows the user to specify different filtering criteria to retrieve objects contained in the MOR. This is seen by a PHP programmer as arrays of arrays. For example, "array('type' => 'model')" creates a PHP array with the value *model* associated with the key *type*, and this, in turn, is associated with a key called *objectFilter* into a generic array provided as argument. This structure representation allows NuSOAP to serialize this argument into an XML document such as: "<objectFilter> <type>model</type> </objectFilter>" or "<objectFilter type 5 "model"/>" when needing to generate the SOAP body.

If you use a debugging probe to track the SOAP requests on port 1234 of the machine MyHost, the call at line 71 will be translated into the following SOAP request:

```xml
<?xml version="1.0" encoding="ISO-8859-1"?>
<SOAP-ENV:Envelope
    SOAP-ENV:encodingStyle=http://schemas.xmlsoap.org/soap/encoding/
    xmlns:SOAP-ENV=http://schemas.xmlsoap.org/soap/envelope/
    xmlns:xsd=http://www.w3.org/2001/XMLSchema
    xmlns:xsi=http://www.w3.org/2001/XMLSchema-instance
    xmlns:SOAP-ENC="http://schemas.xmlsoap.org/soap/encoding/">
    <SOAP-ENV:Body>
        <listContents xmlns:="http://www.jsr-73.org/2004/webservices">
            <objectFilter> <type xsi:type="xsd:string">model</type> </objectFilter>
        </listContents>
    </SOAP-ENV:Body>
</SOAP-ENV:Envelope>
```

In the preceding code, we retrieve the SOAP body representing the call to *listContents* with the argument *objectFilter* set to "model." For arguments with simple structure, it is much more convenient to use the formulation used at line 79.

14.1.4 Executing RecordApplyTask on Models

NuSOAP applies the same principle for structures that are returned from Web service invocations. The call to *listContents* returns a sequence of *MiningObjectHeader*, which is stored in a variable called "$ModelsList." *MiningObjectHeader* is an extension of *MiningObject* with no specific attributes. So it contains a *description, name, type, creatorInfo, creationDate,* and *objectIdentifier.* NuSOAP will translate the returned XML document into an array. In this case, this array represents a list of models, which can be accessed by position. Each position contains a *MiningObjectHeader* representation providing access to the description, name, type, and so on. Line 81 defines the prefix used to select the models of interest from the MOR.

As seen in the screenshot in Figure 14-2, all probabilities of models will be shown in an HTML table that is prepared by lines 82 and 83 in the following code. The model headers are scanned at line 84. The model name is compared with the filter prefix at line 85. Note that attributes defined in the XML Schema must be fetched with a "!" before the attribute name, in line-85 "!name" is specified to fetch the name attribute of the MiningObjectHeader element.

```
82.  echo '<table cellpadding="5" cellspacing="0" border="1" width="50%">';
83.  echo '<th colspan="5">Probabilites</th>';
84.  foreach($modelList as $idx){
85.      if (beginsWith($idx['!name'],$filter)){
```

The goal is to prepare a *RecordApplyTask* using the HTML form-entered values. We create again an XML document representing the task, with its name, the model name, and its type in lines 87 to 90. We also loop over all attributes contained in the javascript form, as shown at line 91, to fill the values entered by the user. We then close the task XML document after setting the name of the *ClassificationApplySettings*.

```
86.  $TaskName = "Product_ApplyTask";
87.  $executeTaskParams  = '<task modelName="'.$idx['!name'].'" '
88.        . 'name="'.$TaskName.'" '
89.        . 'xsi:type="RecordApplyTask" '
90.        . 'xmlns="http://www.jsr-73.org/2004/JDMSchema">';
91.  foreach($_POST as $attrName => $attrValue) {
92.      $executeTaskParams = $executeTaskParams
93.          . '<recordValue name="'.$attrName.'">'
94.              . '<value xsi:type="StringValue">'
95.                  . '<string>'. $attrValue. '</string>'
96.                      . '</value>'
97.          . '</recordValue>';
98.  }
99.  $executeTaskParams = $executeTaskParams
100.      . '<applySettingsName>'.$applySettingsName
101.      . '</applySettingsName> </task>';
102. $executeTaskResponse = $kjdmclient->call("executeTask",
103.                    $executeTaskParams,
104.                    $namespace);
```

Because the task was provided as XML and not through its task name, the execution is synchronous and the response of the invocation can be checked directly. A *RecordApplyTask* returns a structure with an element called *recordValue*. This record value contains the returned probability. The probability is coded as a string for display in the HTML table at line 118 and is associated with its model name at line 117.

```
105.            $status = $executeTaskResponse['status'];
106.            if ($status['!state'] == "error") {
107.                    echo '<h3>The execution of the task has failed with the message: '
108.                        . $executeTaskResponse['description'] . '</h3>';
109.                die;
110.            } else if ($status['!state'] == "success") {
111.                    # echo '<h3>The execution of the task was a SUCCESS!</h3>';
112.            } else {
113.                    echo '<h3>Returned object is not valid.</h3>';
114.            }
115.            $RecordValues = $executeTaskResponse['recordValue'];
116.            $Value = $RecordValues['value'];
117.            echo '<tr><td>'.$idx['!name'].'</td>';
118.            echo '<td>'.$Value['string'].'</td></tr>';
119.        }
120.    }
121.    echo '</table>';
122.    unset($_POST);
123.    }
124.  ?>
125. </body>
126. </html>
```

This closes the product recommendation PHP file.

14.2   A Web Service Client in Java

Since this book focuses on Java technology, we have decided to add a section on how to write a Java client using JDM Web services. An easy way to build a Web service client in Java is to use a Web service framework. Chapter 11 presented JAX-RPC as one solution that generates the wrapper Java objects for the types defined in JDM WSDL and XML Schema. JAX-RPC can be used to generate server implementations or client implementations. Another solution is Axis from the Apache foundation. As the writer of a client application, you are shielded from the implementation details of writing XML code and SOAP-specific calls.

What is the usage of a Java client using Web services? Why not directly use a Java client on top of JDM? One reason is the security layers between the client and the server. The communication between a Java JDM client and the DME uses middleware that is vendor dependent. Some vendors could use Java RPC mechanisms; others could embed the DME into a database using JDBC internally; still others could use CORBA for remote procedure calls. A Java client written on top of Web services will use SOAP. System administrators can easily tune the security layer associated with the SOAP ports on the Web server: Some can use the credentials of the SOAP connection; some can use HTTPS for a secure transport layer. Using JDMWS allows leveraging security systems already in place.

On the other hand, Chapter 12 showed that a complete JDM application needs some data manipulation facilities, and dealing with a remote connection such as JDMWS will not facilitate the creation of datasets used to build or apply models. JDM 2.0 will introduce the data transformations to the standard to cope with this situation. Meanwhile, there is a lot that can be achieved through JDMWS in cases where the processes are well defined and the datasets are already prepared in a repository. For example, in customer relationship management (CRM), it is common for datasets representing a 360-degree view of customers to be prepared in a data warehouse. These datasets can then be reused to build multiple models and apply them on preconstructed filtered customer populations. We can then use JDMWS to automate business scenarios where the user has only to select datasets from an existing list to build or apply models.

This chapter uses the Apache Axis framework for two reasons: (1) it demonstrates that the WSDL provided with JDM is compatible with the current version of this framework, and (2) this framework is widely used and provided under open source. The following sections do not correspond to the implementation of an application but rather constitute a "how-to" guide to start a client implementation on top of JDMWS. For this, we show how to use Axis to generate Java classes and then provide source code to:

- Open a connection to the JDMWS live server
- Create and populate a build settings object with logical attributes
- Create and save a physical dataset
- Create, populate, and save a build task
- Execute the Build Task that places the model in the repository

This code could be used, for example, to create models that will be used for single record apply tasks presenting the PHP product recommendation, as shown in the previous section.

14.2.1   How to Generate Java Classes with Axis

The first step when using the Apache Axis framework [AXIS 2001], when provided with an existing WSDL file, is to use the

WSDL2JAVA tool. With just a few parameters, this program generates Java beans, services classes, and stubs containing the information to connect to the services server. In fact, this tool can be used to create the skeletons needed to write a Web service provider as well as a Web service client. We focus on the Web service client here.

The command lines that follow show an example that allowed us to generate the Java skeleton classes that we use to write our client. The first command line sets the path location where Axis has been installed on the software production machine. Then, the list of needed jar files is provided. Finally, the utility generating Java classes is executed, provided with the jdm.wsdl file. The option – *NStoPkg* allows control of the generated package names without using automatically created names.

```
set AXIS=.\axis\lib\
set AXISJARS=%AXIS%axis.jar;%AXIS%jaxrpc.jar;%AXIS%commons-logging-1.0.4.jar;
%AXIS%commons-discovery-0.2.jar;%AXIS%saaj.jar;%AXIS%activation.jar;
%AXIS%j2ee.jar;%AXIS%wsdl4j-1.5.1.jar;%AXIS%mailapi.jar
    java.exe -classpath %AXISJARS% org.apache.axis.wsdl.WSDL2Java --NStoPkg
http://www.jsr-73.org/2004/webservices=com.MyName.webservices.services --NStoPkg
http://www.jsr-73.org/2004/JDMSchema=com.MyName.webservices.beans -o "Java_Source"
"jdm.wsdl"
```

To use this script, you set the Axis project path (for the Java class path) and customize the package's name to tune the generated classes (e.g., by substituting your company name for MyName). The execution of this command generates a folder named *Java_Source* (the folder name can be changed).

The same process can be followed using Apache "ant" with the following code:

```
<target name= "all" description= "Builds the Java classes from wsdl.">
    <java classname= "org.apache.axis.wsdl.WSDL2Java"
            classpathref= "axis.classpath" fork= "yes ">
        <arg value= "--NStoPkg" />
        <arg value="http://www.jsr-73.org/2004/webservices=com.MyName.webservices.
        services"/>
        <arg value= "--NStoPkg" />
        <arg value="http://www.jsr-73.org/2004/JDMSchema=com.MyName.webservices.
        beans"/>
        <arg value= "--output" />
        <arg value= "${generated.dir}" />
        <arg value= "${local.wsdl}" />
    </java>
</target>
```

Many classes are generated; these can be grouped as follows:

- 23 classes associated with the possible services to execute.
- 4 classes for locating the data mining server (*DataMiningSer-vice.java* and *DataMiningServiceLocator.java*) and sending the Web services messages (*IDataMining.java* and *IDataMining-BindingStub.java*).
- 157 beans classes corresponding to all complex types defined in the XML schema.

Before using the generated classes, you must edit the default specification of the address to connect to a live JMDWS implementation in the file *com.MyName.webservices.services.DataMiningServiceLocator.java*, using the member variable *IDataMiningPort_address*. Here is an example corresponding to the same address as the PHP client application (the argument of the "new SOAP client" in the previous example):

```
// Use to get a proxy class for IDataMiningPort
private java.lang.String IDataMiningPort_address = "http:// MyHost:1234/KxServices/
services/IDataMiningPort";
```

14.2.2   Opening the Connection to a JDMWS Live Server

Once you have generated the service and bean classes, you can start writing the Java client. Here is a step-by-step procedure to develop your first Java Web service client to build a model. All methods provided below belong to a single class representing your simple Java client application.

The first step is to get a DME connection stub. You will then have a reference to the data mining services. Thanks to the Axis tool, all elements needed to connect to the server are already set in the skeleton classes. The following code is equivalent to connecting to a Web service provider, which in turn provides you access to a DME.

```
1.   private IDataMining initiateConnection() throws ServiceException {
2.       DataMiningService lServiceProvider = new DataMiningServiceLocator();
3.       IDataMining lServices = lServiceProvider.getIDataMiningPort();
4.       return lServices;
5.   }
```

In this simple method, getting a service stub is simple; there is no need for advanced knowledge of the JDM XML structure, as was the case with PHP. Once the Web service connection object is created, it is important to remember that the JDM connection is managed by the Web service provider application and, thus, the application can readily start.

14.2.3   Creating BuildSettings

The first step is to create and save the *BuildSettings* object to create a classification model. Axis has generated Java classes that fully map the XML structure provided with the XML Schema of JDM Web services. For example, in the following code the class *ClassificationSettings* has all the "setter" and "getter" methods to specify all its elements. Writing source code under any Java integrated development environment (IDE) such as Eclipse will provide you with the list of possible methods that can be used on an instance of such a class, making this a very easy exercise. In the following example, we assume that the target attribute is called *class* and that there is a weight attribute called *fnlwgt*. The methods called *createBuildAttributes* and *askToSaveObject* will be explained later in the chapter.

```
1.  public BuildSettings createBuildSettings(IDataMining iServices)
2.          throws RemoteException {
3.      ClassificationSettings lSettingsToSave =
    new ClassificationSettings();
4.      lSettingsToSave.setCreatorInfo("myClassifCreatorInfo");
5.      lSettingsToSave.setDescription("my First Classification Model");
6.      lSettingsToSave.setDesiredExecutionTimeInMinutes(new Integer(10));
7.      lSettingsToSave.setTargetAttributeName("class");
8.      lSettingsToSave.setBuildAttribute(createBuildAttributes());
9.      askToSaveObject(lSettingsToSave, "myBuildSettings", iServices);
10.     return lSettingsToSave;
11. }
```

We develop the method called *createBuildAttributes* as the first example using logical attributes. Logical attributes can be used in *Settings* to specify how the physical attributes should be interpreted by the algorithm, or outlier treatment, for example. In this simple example, we propose to associate a fixed set of four logical attributes to the *ClassificationSettings*. In the XML Schema, the specification of logical attributes in a *Settings* instance is presented as a sequence, which has been translated by Axis as an array of *BuildAttribute* objects. We show the initialization of this array at line 2 in the following code. Out of the four active attributes, three will be used as inputs (*education, marital-status,* and *capital-gain* as used in the product recommendation example), and one will be used as a target (*class*). Setting the *usage* to *active* is shown at lines 9, 17, 25, and 34. The second option we use is outlier treatment, which is set at lines 6, 15, 23, and 32. We have chosen, in this example, to let the system decide the treatment for *education* and *marital-status* but to leave the *capital-gain* "as is." Of course, more general code can be written, especially in conjunction with a user interface, to ask for attribute names, together with outlier treatment, usage, and others that can be tuned at the logical attribute level.

```
1. protected static BuildAttribute[] createBuildAttributes() {
2.     BuildAttribute[] lBuildAttributes = new BuildAttribute[4];
3.     BuildAttribute lBuildAttribute = new BuildAttribute();
4.     lBuildAttribute.setAttributeName("education");
5.     OutlierTreatment lOutlierTreatment =
6.         new OutlierTreatment(OutlierTreatmentStd.systemDetermined);
7.     lBuildAttribute.setOutlierTreatment(lOutlierTreatment);
8.     LogicalAttributeUsage lUsage
9.         = new LogicalAttributeUsage(LogicalAttributeUsageStd.active);
10.    lBuildAttribute.setUsage(lUsage);
11.    lBuildAttributes[0] = lBuildAttribute;
12.
13.    lBuildAttribute = new BuildAttribute();
14.     lBuildAttribute.setAttributeName("marital-status");
15.     lOutlierTreatment =
    new OutlierTreatment(OutlierTreatmentStd.systemDetermined);
16.     lBuildAttribute.setOutlierTreatment(lOutlierTreatment);
17.     lUsage = new LogicalAttributeUsage(LogicalAttributeUsageStd.active);
18.     lBuildAttribute.setUsage(lUsage);
19.     lBuildAttributes[1] = lBuildAttribute;
20.
21.      lBuildAttribute = new BuildAttribute();
22.      lBuildAttribute.setAttributeName("capital-gain");
23.      lOutlierTreatment = new OutlierTreatment(OutlierTreatmentStd.asIs);
24.     lBuildAttribute.setOutlierTreatment(lOutlierTreatment);
25.     lUsage = new LogicalAttributeUsage(LogicalAttributeUsageStd.active);
26.     lBuildAttribute.setUsage(lUsage);
27.     lBuildAttributes[2] = lBuildAttribute;
28.
30.     lBuildAttribute = new BuildAttribute();
31.     lBuildAttribute.setAttributeName("class");
32.     lOutlierTreatment =
    new OutlierTreatment(OutlierTreatmentStd.systemDetermined);
33.     lBuildAttribute.setOutlierTreatment(lOutlierTreatment);
34.     lUsage = new LogicalAttributeUsage(LogicalAttributeUsageStd.active);
35.     lBuildAttribute.setUsage(lUsage);
36.    lBuildAttributes[3] = lBuildAttribute;
37.
38.     return lBuildAttributes;
39. }
```

Line 9 of *createBuildSettings* is using a generic method called *askToSaveObject*. The method *askToSaveObject* has been defined in our example to save any named object to the MOR, forcing to overwrite existing objects (line 7) and asking for verification (line 8). Because of this verification, we need to be able to get back the verification report returned by the *saveObject* service invocation at line 10 if the verification was not successful as shown at line 13. Again, we see that Axis has streamlined the XML Schema into Java classes for the Java programmer to easily set and get subsections of this schema; this reduces the time needed to write client applications.

```
1.    protected static void askToSaveObject(MiningObject iMiningObject,
2.                                  String iName, IDataMining iServices)
3.          throws RemoteException {
4.        SaveObject lSaveObject = new SaveObject();
5.        lSaveObject.setObject(iMiningObject);
6.        lSaveObject.setObjectName(iMiningObject.getName());
7.        lSaveObject.setOverwrite(new Boolean(true));
8.        lSaveObject.setVerify(new Boolean(true));
9.        SaveObjectResponse lSaveObjectResponse
10.          = iServices.saveObject(lSaveObject);
11.       if (lSaveObjectResponse!= null) {
12.           System.out.println("Verification Report: "
13.               + lSaveObjectResponse.getReport().getReportText());
14.       } else {
15.           System.out.println("No object returned");
16.       }
17. }
```

We will use the *askToSaveObject* again in other parts of this example.

14.2.4   Creating a PhysicalDataSet

Creating a *PhysicalDataSet* from its URI is straightforward, provided that you know the specific URI format used by the implementation of the JDMWS. This means that it is likely that you will have to change the code at line 5. Because the JDM WSDL uses the generic URI type, Axis has translated this into a generic URI Java object. The last operation of this method is to save the object into the MOR, as shown at line 8.

```
1.  protected PhysicalDataSet createPhysicalData(IDataMining iServices) throws
2.          RemoteException, MalformedURIException {
3.      PhysicalDataSet lBuildPhysicalDataSet = new PhysicalDataSet();
4.      lBuildPhysicalDataSet.setName("MyODBCCensus ");
5.      String lBuildUri = "odbc:///ODBC_Source/CensusTable";
6.      org.apache.axis.types.URI lBuildUriAxis =
7.              new org.apache.axis.types.URI(lBuildUri);
8.      lBuildPhysicalDataSet.setUri(lBuildUriAxis);
9.      askToSaveObject(lBuildPhysicalDataSet, "MyODBCCensus", iServices);
10.     return lBuildPhysicalDataSet;
11. }
```

14.2.5   Creating a BuildTask

The task to build a classification model will use the *PhysicalDataSet* and *BuildSettings* previously built. This is done within the method called *createBuildTask*. The following code shows how to create the *BuildTask* from a *BuildSettings* object. Even if it has been previously saved to the MOR, the *BuildSettings* bean is provided as is, and thus will be expanded in its own XML in the SOAP message. We could have used the *BuildSettings* name instead of the object because JDM Web services allows both cases.

```
1.  protected final Task createBuildTask(IDataMining iServices,
2.                      BuildSettings iBuildSettings,
3.                      String iModelName,
4.                      PhysicalDataSet iBuildPhysicalDataSet)
5.          throws RemoteException {
6.      BuildTask lBuildTask = new BuildTask();
7.      lBuildTask.setBuildSettings(iBuildSettings);
8.      lBuildTask.setDescription("My First BuildTask");
9.      lBuildTask.setModelName(iModelName);
10      askToSaveObject(lBuildTask, "MyBuildTask_" + iModelName, iServices);
11.     return lBuildTask;
12. }
```

14.2.6   Executing a BuildTask

Finally, we need to create a method to execute the task we have just created, defined, and saved to the MOR. We use a code structure already presented in other environments: getting the execution status through the execution handle—a common usage scenario. There is an invocation of the *executeTask* Web service method at line 5. Following the specifications presented in Chapter 11, if the argument provided to the Web service *executeTask* is the task name (instead of the task itself), the execution is run asynchronously. We could have obtained the *ExecuteTaskResponse* to get the first execution status, but we preferred to show the use of the *getExecutionStatus* Web service. Invocation of this service returns an *ExecutionState* that can be accessed through *GetExecutionStatusResponse*, as shown at lines 9 and 10. As usual, the state can be monitored through a while loop, as shown by lines 11 to 18. If the task ends with an error, the description of this error is reported at line 21.

```
1.  protected void askToExecuteTask(IDataMining iServices, Task iTask)
2.          throws RemoteException, InterruptedException {
3.      ExecuteTask lExecuteTask = new ExecuteTask();
4.      lExecuteTask.setTaskName(iTask.getName());
5.      iServices.executeTask(lExecuteTask);
6.      GetExecutionStatus lExecutionStatus = new GetExecutionStatus();
7.      lExecutionStatus.setTaskName(lExecuteTask.getTaskName());
8.      GetExecutionStatusResponse lExecutionStatusResponse
9.          = iServices.getExecutionStatus(lExecutionStatus);
10.     ExecutionState lState = lExecutionStatusResponse.getStatus().getState();
11.     while (lState.equals(ExecutionState.executing)
12.             || lState.equals(ExecutionState.terminating)
13.             || lState.equals(ExecutionState.submitted)) {
14.         Thread.sleep(1000);
15.         lExecutionStatusResponse =
16.             iServices.getExecutionStatus(lExecutionStatus);
17.         lState = lExecutionStatusResponse.getStatus().getState();
18.     }
19.     if (lState.equals(ExecutionState.error)) {
20.         System.out.println("Error executing task: [" +
21.             lExecutionStatusResponse.getStatus().getDescription() + "]");
22.         return;
23.     } else {
24.         System.out.println ("Last state of execution: ["
25.             + lState.getValue() + "]");
26.     }
27. }
```

At this point, if the five methods described above are executed in sequence, a valid classification model will be accessible through the connection. This model, if given a name beginning with *Product*, can be used by the product recommendation Web browser front end shown in the PHP client application.

14.3   Summary

This chapter used code examples to introduce the use of JDMWS. We first looked at a Web service client in PHP to perform product recommendation. We then looked at a Web service client in Java, using a framework such as Axis or JAX-RPC. The chapter shows that tools exist to translate the JDM WSDL into structures integrated in both client environments (PHP or Java), allowing very fast development of such clients. The availability of JDMWS should open the path for integration of data mining into business processes frameworks.

References

[NuSOAP 2004] http://sourceforge.net/projects/nusoap.

[PHP 2005]http://www.php.net.

[AXIS 2001] http://ws.apache.org/axis.

Chapter

15

The Impact of JDM
on IT Infrastructure

I think there is a world market for maybe five computers.

—IBM Chairman Thomas Watson, 1943

Data mining can have a great impact on the infrastructure of information technology (IT). *Mining in the small*, that is, using small local datasets and maintaining a few models for short-term use, is unlikely to tax the IT environment. However, *mining in the large*—with multi-gigabyte and sometimes multi-terabyte datasets, hundreds or thousands of frequently changing datasets, obtaining datasets across the enterprise or beyond, and managing hundreds or thousands of models for deployment throughout the enterprise—places new demands for backup and recovery, data access, data staging, and ensuring proper levels of service. Moreover, data mining is often part of a larger business process requiring plugging into existing scheduling or workflow systems. There are also differences in how IT approaches database and non-database data mining engines (DMEs).

This chapter explores the impact that data mining can have on the IT infrastructure and what data and process administrators need to consider when mining in the large.

15.1   What Does Data Mining Require from IT?

This section explores some of the information technology components involved with data mining:

- **Computing hardware:** Data mining often requires CPU-intensive activity to build and apply models from large volumes of data. The amount and type of computation is often governed by the type of algorithm. For example, neural networks require many floating point operations, whereas naïve bayes algorithms rely more on co-occurrence counts. This computing hardware can range from off-the-shelf PCs to state-of-the-art high performance multiprocessor servers. The servers on which DME implementations run are called *modeling servers*.

- **Data storage hardware:** Obviously data mining needs data. Data is generally already present in the organization, so we focus here on the additional storage required for data mining, and how data mining affects the amount of data.

- **Database software:** Database software can be viewed as supporting not only the data storage and access requirements of data, but also the data mining capabilities. *Independent-server mining*, where data mining occurs in a separate process, often relies on databases for data storage. Increasingly, data mining programmers are leveraging the analytical capabilities in databases to avoid data movement. Modern relational database management systems (RDBMSs) provide data mining integrated with the database kernel, which we refer to as *in-database mining*. Some vendors may provide Java Data Mining (JDM) implementations on top of these in-database mining capabilities. Independent-server mining systems can also expose or use these in-database mining capabilities through their established user interfaces.

- **Data access:** In the case of independent-server data mining, the modeling server must access data contained in databases. This can impact the network between the modeling server and databases. This impact does not exist in the case of in-database DMEs where the database software runs on the same computing hardware as the DME. This may be less true in the case of hardware clusters where the large data exchange needed to build models will require careful implementation and parallel algorithms together with the data spread. However, this depends on the quality of the cluster software implementation.

- **Application execution performance:** Applications may utilize data mining results in batch (e.g., predicting which customers will respond to a campaign at one time and storing the results) or in real-time (e.g., predicting a customer's response to an offer while speaking to a customer service representative based on new customer profile information).

- **IT administration tools:** Most large organizations use tools to monitor software and hardware usage. The problem of backup and recovery is also of concern. In-database mining tools often leverage the existing backup and recovery mechanisms in place for the database. Independent-server tools either provide support in this area, or IT must rely on OS and file system-oriented tools.

15.2   Impacts on Computing Hardware

How much computing power will be required to mine data is often hard to determine. The time it takes to build a single model depends on many factors: the amount of data including both the number of cases and number of attributes, the complexity of the data itself, the choice of algorithm and settings, and the internal scalability of the algorithms as implemented in the DME (e.g., how these implementations may use multiple CPUs in parallel).

By complexity of the data, we mean the number of distinct values present in each categorical attribute, as well as the richness of patterns found in the data. For example, for an algorithm like k-means clustering, which accepts numerical data for its computations, each categorical attribute is exploded into indicator attributes. A binary attribute, one with two values, will become two attributes, whereas an attribute containing values for each of the 50 United States would become 50 attributes. In the case of association rules, two datasets with the same number of transactions, number of products, and items per basket can take radically different execution times based on the co-occurrences found in the data.

There is another dimension to data mining computing power requirements: the volume of mining activities. This volume includes the number and type of models built within a given time window, the number and type of models used to score datasets, and the real-time scoring requirements. In some circumstances, there are also incremental model building requirements that need to be factored in.

Consider an application that supports cross-sell—the recommendation of products to individual customers. One possible technique is to build a predictive model for each product to be recommended. If a business has 100 products, this would require the building of 100 models. If customer preferences change frequently, these models may need to be rebuilt, or *refreshed*, weekly or even daily. Let's say each model is built based on a dataset with 200 attributes and 500,000 cases. If a single model build takes 15 minutes to complete on a particular machine, that means that for the 100 models, this process would take 25 hours to complete if executed serially. If the objective is to rebuild these each night based on the previous day's data for use the following day, multiple such machines can be employed to allow building in parallel. Let's say we have a window of 5 hours in which to build the models; that would require 5 such machines, each building 20 models.

Model building is often performed on a much smaller number of cases in comparison to the number of cases used when applying models to data for making predictions, or *scoring*. Some businesses require scoring their entire customer base, where the number of customers may reach beyond 100 million. Moreover, such businesses often have a tight time window in which they can score these customers. The number of models applied to each customer may also increase the performance demands. Consider that for the 100 models built in the previous example, each model will have to be applied to each of the 100 million customers. Moreover, this may need to be completed overnight in an 8-hour time window. If a DME can score a million customers in 6 seconds on a given model, then it will take 600 seconds (10 minutes) to score those customers on all 100 models. With 100 million customers, this will take 1,000 minutes (16.7 hours). To ensure that scoring can be accomplished within the 8-hour time window, the data could be divided among three machines, which will allow the scoring to be completed in less than 6 hours.

This scenario assumes that the data mining steps have already been defined and are coded for repeatability. Another hardware consideration is the impact on the model building process when data miners are trying to come up with the appropriate data mining steps. More computing hardware can certainly speed up the data transformation, analysis, and model building of a data miner, which means long delays in seeing results will be avoided. However, many times the creative process of data mining involves time that dwarfs the individual transformations, analyses, or model building. For mining large datasets, there is a tradeoff between the data miner seeing results quickly versus the cost of hardware. This is clearly a business and resource issue.

In cases where a data mining tool automates much of the data mining process through trying various algorithms or settings automatically, more computing hardware can certainly improve throughput of mining results. Without the use of automatic modeling, it is not uncommon for the analysis and building of new models to take several weeks; buying a machine twice as big will not reduce the time it takes to design, build, and test models, because this time mainly involves human intervention. Automatic modeling can make use of the additional hardware such that the time to produce these models is generally in the ranges of hours.

Another factor to consider regarding hardware to mine larger datasets is the scalability of the particular algorithm (usually defined in terms of the number of attributes and number of cases used in the build data, but may also include attribute cardinality). Commenting on the scalability of specific algorithms is beyond the scope of this book; however, users of data mining software can request scalability figures from DME vendors. For example, if an algorithm scales as order n^2, where n is the number of cases, simply doubling the number of CPUs or using a CPU with double the speed will not provide the same performance when the dataset contains twice as many cases. This is especially true when considering the number of attributes because the performance of most classical algorithms is adversely affected by a larger number of attributes.

15.3   Impacts on Data Storage Hardware

Data storage and its associated costs are a normal part of virtually all businesses, and data volumes are growing. It is common to see Fortune 500 companies with terabytes of data, some adding terabytes per month. When considering data mining, data storage costs also include the storage of data mining models, intermediate datasets, especially if they are materialized as physical tables (as opposed to views), settings, test results, and apply results.

When considering the storage of data mining models, each algorithm typically has different model storage requirements. For example, a decision tree typically has a very compact representation consisting of a set of rules and tree nodes, perhaps on the order of tens. Each rule often consists of fewer than 10 predicates. In contrast, consider an association rules model that may contain tens of thousands of rules, each consisting of typically 2 to 5 items and a support and confidence value.

The architecture of the DME can also impact the amount of raw data storage required. Three architectures are described here:

- **In-database DME:** The DME resides within the execution engine of the database. It may be in the same process for optimal performance and data access. This does not include DMEs that are invoked only through a common SQL interface while the DME resides in a separate process space; this requires data to be transferred from the database engine to that separate DME process.

- **Independent-server DME with direct data access:** The DME is not hosted in the database, but can access database data directly stored in the database, either through proprietary data access interfaces or standard interfaces such as JDBC or ODBC. Such environments do not require data staging.

- **Independent-server DME with staging data:** The DME is not hosted in the database and requires temporary storage of data, possibly in a proprietary format or separate data marts. Some businesses may require data to be staged separately from operational data stores or the corporate data warehouse to avoid performance impacts, uncertain data storage impacts, or security concerns.

These three architectures are depicted in Figure 15-1.

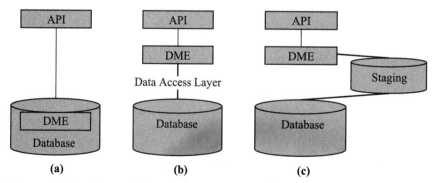

Figure 15-1   *Data mining engine data access architectures: (a) In-database DME, (b) Independent-server DME with direct data access, and (c) Independent-server DME with staging data.*

We distinguish among these DME architectures because the first and second cases do not require extra data storage. The third case, involving staging data, does of course require additional disk space as data is replicated for the purposes of mining.[1] So the question is, how much?

The correct answer is, "It depends…." Consider an example involving customer relationship management (CRM). Today, it is not uncommon to find build datasets with between 50 and 5,000 attributes, the median value being around 200; and the number of cases is often between 10,000 and 1,000,000, the median value being around 200,000. Whereas these are only the build datasets, the volumes for apply datasets are much larger. As cited earlier, a large organization as found in the telecommunications or banking industries could have a customer database dealing with 100 million customers. So we see here that corporate architectures requiring data staging require large disk capacity to store not only the data to be scored, but also the apply results.

Another impact could depend on specific DME requirements for dataset format. For example, a specific association rule algorithm could require the data in a multirecord case representation. In this situation, a single record representation for a million records with 100 attributes of 20 bytes each requires 2 gigabytes of space, but the corresponding multirecord case representation requires 7 gigabytes, assuming the case ID is 20 bytes and the attribute name is 30 bytes.

Modeling in the large also requires saving the models, the build settings, and all the objects declared as persistent by the DME implementation. In most cases, a model should be (much) smaller than its corresponding build dataset, because a model should extract knowledge from and find relationships in data. This is especially true when looking at the model details (i.e., the minimum information needed to apply a model), such as the tree nodes for a decision tree or the coefficients of a linear regression. Other models, such as support vector machine (SVM) for example, can take relatively more storage because they maintain the support vectors; similarly, an association rules model can contain hundreds of thousands of rules. In another aspect, some implementations keep not only the minimum model

---

[1] Note that when considering a tool's performance, the time required to export data from the database and import results back to the database must be included in the overall model build and apply time.

details, but also information such as the descriptive statistics of the input attributes for display purposes. This is the case for some clustering implementations, which are able to show the profiles for all input attributes for all clusters. Other models may maintain cross-statistics with the targets or all the input attributes.

In trying to optimize business performance, the number of predictive and descriptive models resulting from data mining techniques are increasing dramatically. For example, large telecommunications operators are now building more than 1,500 models a year, for their CRM activity alone! And they will expand this methodology later into risk management, which will dramatically increase the number of models built per year. This impacts the disk storage needed to persist not only the models, but also their build settings, apply settings, and various result objects. When building credit risk scoring models for example, it is not uncommon to have quality processes in place that require these settings be kept: it may be mandatory that a specific model's information can be retrieved, such as when the model was produced, what dataset was used to produce the model, and what were the test results. Often, a business wants or needs to keep track of the different model versions. This is considered an application level operation currently, because JDM does not include model versioning. As such, users will likely design naming conventions for their models, tasks, and datasets, and all the objects that are saved in the mining object repository (MOR) to externally manage the versioning of persisted objects. Consult your DME vendor for specifics concerning storage requirements for different models.

15.4   Data Access

Data access is needed in three major phases of a model's life cycle: (1) the build phase, where the model is created on a build dataset, (2) the test phase, where metrics are computed to understand model quality, and (3) the apply phase, where scores or forecasts are written back to storage for later use. In these phases, data must be accessed from the main repositories: data warehouses, operational systems, and so on. When the DME is an independent server, there must be data transfer between the data repository and the DME, which increases network traffic. If IT management does not allow mining the data in the actual data warehouses or operational data stores, in-database and independent-server (direct data access) DME may have to address the data staging issue, or introduce alternative hardware architectures (e.g., clusters or data segregation) to ensure reasonable non-interference with daily operations.

While the build task uses the data access layer embedded within the DME itself, there are other ways to perform the apply task and perhaps the test task; we will look at these tasks separately. Besides the architectural constraints, there is also the administration environment to consider.

15.4.1 Data Access for Model Building

As stated earlier, there are three types of DME architecture: in-database DME and two different layouts of independent-server DME. The in-database architecture does not require any data transfer since the algorithms exist where the data reside. The independent-server architectures requires data transfer, and there are two possibilities in this case: (1) either the DME implementation requires a copy of the data in a temporary or proprietary format, which implies a duplication of data together with additional disk space, or (2) the DME does not requires temporary or proprietary storage and accesses the data directly from the repository—this generates more data traffic but does not require additional disk space, and reduces data latency issues. However, the second case either requires large RAM to hold the data or efficient mining techniques to retrieve and process data in manageable chunks.

In most cases, the build dataset is of smaller size than the datasets used as input for apply. This can be attributed to one of two reasons. Either (1) the data is known only for a population concerned with an experience, which is generally reduced for cost reasons, or (2) robust models can be safely built on a sample of the entire population, resulting in smaller build times for similar model quality and robustness. In many practical situations, data access for the build phase is less demanding than for apply phase.

But the architecture of the DME and the volume of data are not the only points to take into account. As noted earlier, the policy of IT management against the use of data in the operational data environment may impact data access and force the staging of data to isolate the production environment from the modeling environment.

15.4.2   Data Access for Apply and Test

As noted earlier, a model can be applied to very large datasets, especially in terms of number of cases. This is why the possibility of exporting the model from the DME in a language that is supported by the scoring engine (e.g., a database) can be used. For example, IBM is proposing PMML interpreters for several databases; Teradata also proposes a PMML interpreter; and KXEN is able to export models either in SQL or in User Defined Functions for all major databases. In all these situations, the apply phases are done within the execution environment (e.g., the database) without external data transfer. This impacts the computing power of the database servers but it has no impact on network traffic.

In contrast, in-database DMEs, such as Oracle, perform apply and test at a layer below application-level SQL or User Defined Functions. This type of access eliminates overheads for security, process, and database data read overheads typically experienced by application level code. As a result, in-database scoring can achieve better performance than externally generated code.

15.5   Backup and Recovery

Backup and recovery plans are critical for any IT organization. IT staff are already quite familiar with performing database and file system backups on a regular basis. In-database DMEs or DMEs with database-hosted MORs make backup and recovery a part of normal database maintenance. Where models are maintained separately from the database (e.g., as flat files in either PMML or proprietary formats), users must rely on filesystem backups or ad hoc procedures.

15.6   Scheduling

In an IT environment where hardware is plentiful and software scales well with the addition of hardware, the consideration of when to execute data mining tasks can depend more on business requirements than on technical ones. However, most IT departments have budget constraints, both in terms of hardware purchases and personnel to manage and maintain their hardware and software. To this point, scheduling of data mining tasks becomes important to efficiently use existing hardware. This section assumes that the data mining process (e.g., specific data preparation and modeling steps) has been clearly defined and is largely amenable to automation. Where human resources are involved in the production of data mining models, standard human resource project scheduling techniques must be applied.

The business decisions for scheduling and workflows revolve around when the right data is available and when the information or knowledge, or mining results, are required. For example, if a business goal is to conduct a campaign leading up to the Labor Day holiday weekend, there is a hard deadline of when the mining results need to be available, perhaps several weeks prior so that appropriate printing activities can occur. If the data used for building the model or models will not change for the month prior to the needed results, preparing data and scoring customers for likelihood to respond can be performed more flexibly. If the data preparation and model build number-crunching will take 3 hours to execute, and the scoring of the potential respondees will take 6 hours, barring hardware, software, or other failures, such a model could be scheduled the day before the results are needed.

However, if hardware is scarce, or multiple activities are being performed on the same hardware, it may be appropriate to schedule model building and batch scoring activities during periods of low user or customer activity, for example, the middle of the night. It is fairly easy to use the Timer library in Java to implement Job Scheduling and there are several other libraries to perform job scheduling, such as Quartz [Quartz 2006]. JDM 2.0 introduces a basic scheduling interface that unifies scheduling within the JDM Connection *execute* method and can be implemented in terms of these specialized libraries.

15.7 Workflow

Some obvious but nonetheless important dependencies exist between data mining tasks that impact workflow design. As Figure 15-2 depicts, there may be separate workflow steps to support data preparation; these steps detail which data is brought together and the specific transformations that must be applied. If this process succeeds, a particular model or set of models is built according to prespecified build settings. To ensure that the resulting model(s) are valid, even if the build terminated successfully, the workflow should test the model to ensure a minimum level of accuracy or some other clearly defined

Figure 15-2   *Example of a data mining workflow.*

metric. If the model tests succeed, the model(s) may be deployed to their target environment, perhaps another application that is responsible for scoring, either in batch or real-time. The deployment may be as simple as providing the name of a data mining model stored in a database to the remote system, or may involve exporting the model as XML or a proprietary format and importing it at the target site. When at the target environment, the model may be applied to new data (e.g., to produce scores, segment customers, and so on).

Figure 15-2 depicts the success path; however, each workflow step also requires contingency tasks to handle failures. Depending on the sophistication of the workflow design, some automated measures may be taken to correct problems. For example, if test results do not meet specifications, the workflow could attempt to build different models with different algorithms and settings and reenter the test step.

There are considerations when redeploying a model in a production environment. In a real-time environment, perhaps where cross-sell recommendations are being made to online customers, models must be refreshed without interrupting scores for existing customers. In this case, if a model switch can be made atomically,[2] allowing pending requests to complete and new requests to be directed to the refreshed model, users should see no unusual effects such as missing recommendations. Once the old model is no longer servicing requests, it can be retired from service, having been fully replaced by the new model.

Note that both scheduling and workflow environments are slowly being addressed by business process environments, with frameworks such as BPEL [BPEL 2004] and BPML [BPML 2003]. Many of these environments allow inclusion of external services within business processes, and facilitate integrating services through Web services. JDM also defines a Web services interfaces so that DME providers that implement the Web services layer can easily be integrated in such business process environments.

---

2   That is, similar to the notion of an atomic database commit operation—either happening completely, or not at all.

15.8   Summary

This chapter explored the impact that data mining can have on IT infrastructure. In particular, several key IT areas were examined: computing hardware, data storage, data access, backup and recovery, scheduling, and workflows. In this effort, three main DME implementation architectures — one in-database and two independent-server — were contrasted; each has its own implications for IT.

References

[BPEL 2004] http://en.wikipedia.org/wiki/BPEL.

[BPML 2003] http://xml.coverpages.org/bpml.html.

[Quartz 2006] http://www.opensymphony.com/quartz/.

Chapter 16

Vendor Implementations

In general, an implementation must be conservative in its sending behavior, and liberal in its receiving behavior.

—Jonathan Bruce Postel

Vendor implementations are key to the success of any standard. This chapter provides an overview of two vendor implementations conforming to Java Data Mining (JDM), characterizing their architecture, capabilities, and extensions; readers are also directed to sources of more information on trying out the implementations and learning more about their feature sets. In addition, considerations for those pursuing a JDM implementation are discussed.

16.1 Oracle Data Mining

Oracle Corporation began offering an integrated in-database data mining engine (DME) as an option to the *Oracle 9i Database* release in 2001. Oracle continued to extend and enhance its mining function and algorithm offerings, while more deeply embedding data mining algorithms in the database kernel code. As a result, *Oracle Data Mining* (ODM) is able to leverage *Oracle Database*–inherent characteristics such as performance, scalability, and security. ODM is a key component of Oracle's in-database advanced analytics platform, which includes online analytical processing (OLAP), and spatial and statistics functions, also embedded in the database.

Oracle acquired Thinking Machines Corporation and its flagship data mining tool, *Darwin*, in 1999, which began Oracle's investment in data mining technology. *Oracle Database 10g Release 2* (10.2) includes all of the data mining functions supported under JDM 1.1, and several of the JDM 1.1 algorithms.

This section explores some details of ODM features, the architecture of the Oracle Java Data Mining (OJDM) implementation, JDM features supported by Oracle, using the JDM application programming interface (API) in the Oracle platform, Oracle-specific JDM extensions, OJDM capabilities, and a brief discussion of ODM's SQL data mining API, which is interoperable with OJDM-produced mining objects, and the Oracle Data Miner graphical interface, which uses OJDM.

16.1.1   Oracle Position on JDM

Oracle is a strong supporter of open standards, in particular, the Java standards developed under Java Community Process (JCP). The JDM standard (JSR-73) was initiated and led by Oracle under the JCP. ODM 10.2.0.1 supports JDM 1.0, while ODM 10.2.0.2 supports JDM 1.1 [JDM11 2005]. Oracle continues its support and interest in JDM as specification lead for JDM 2.0 (JDM 217).

16.1.2   Oracle JDM Implementation Architecture

OJDM is a thin-Java wrapper that conforms to the JDM standard and enables Java applications to integrate in-database data mining features of *Oracle Database*. OJDM uses the database as the DME and communicates with the database using JDBC. OJDM supports the use of any type of Oracle JDBC driver supplied with the database [ORAJDBC 2006]. Figure 16-1 shows the architecture of OJDM. Any type of Java application that is compatible with J2SE 1.4.2 can use the OJDM API consisting of the JDM standard API and Oracle-specific JDM API extensions.   The Oracle extensions are discussed further in Section 16.1.5.

OJDM maps the JDM named objects, such as mining model, task, settings objects, and test metrics, to database objects as shown in Table 16-1. The JDM mining model is mapped to the ODM mining model database object. Mining tasks are mapped to database scheduler jobs that can be executed either synchronously or asynchronously. Settings, cost matrix, and test metrics objects are mapped to

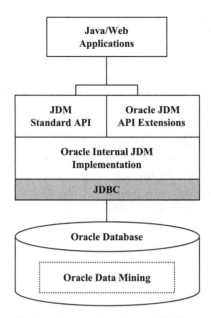

Figure 16-1 *Oracle Java Data Mining architecture.*

Table 16-1 *Oracle Java Data Mining named objects mapping to database object*

JDM Named Object	Oracle Database Object
Mining Model	Mining Model object in the database
Build Settings	Table that contains the settings details
Cost Matrix	Table that contains the cost details
Task	Database job created using the DBMS_SCHEDULER [ORADBADMIN]
Test Metrics	Table that contains the test metrics details
Apply Settings	Stored as transient object with the Connection
PhysicalDataSet	Stored as transient object with the Connection
LogicalData	OJDM API does not support this as database views provide JDM logical data capabilities.

database tables. By mapping JDM objects to database objects, OJDM requires no additional installation steps, such as additional schemas or server-side libraries. In addition, the database administrator (DBA) tasks for maintenance, such as backup and recovery, import/ export of models, and the migration of JDM objects during software upgrade, are greatly simplified.

16.1.3 Oracle JDM Capabilities

OJDM supports all the JDM 1.1 mining functions: *classification, regression, attribute importance, association,* and *clustering.* As an Oracle extension, OJDM also supports *feature extraction* and *one-class classifier,* also known as the mining function *anomaly detection.* In OJDM, applications can optionally select algorithms and their settings. Table 16-2 shows the OJDM supported functions, algorithms, and tasks. OJDM also supports export and import tasks for exporting and importing mining models in the *Oracle Database* format. OJDM allows data mining users to specify function level settings and have the database use a default algorithm.

Table 16-2 *Oracle Java Data Mining supported functions, algorithms, and function-level tasks*

Supported function	Supported algorithms	Supported function level tasks
Classification	*Naïve Bayes (NB)*	*BuildTask*
	Support Vector Machine (SVM)	*ClassificationTestTask*
	Decision Tree	*ClassificationTestMetricsTask*
	Adaptive Bayes Network (ABN)[*]	*DataSetApplyTask* *RecordApplyTask*
Regression	*Support Vector Machine (SVM)*	*BuildTask* *RegressionTestTask* *RegressionTestMetricsTask* *DataSetApplyTask* *RecordApplyTask*
Attribute importance	*Minimum Description Length[*]*	*BuildTask*
Association	*Apriori[*]*	*BuildTask*
Clustering	*k-Means*	*BuildTask*
	Orthogonal Partitioning (a.k.a. O-Cluster)[*]	*DataSetApplyTask* *RecordApplyTask*
Feature extraction	*Non-Negative Matrix Factorization (NMF)[*]*	*BuildTask* *DataSetApplyTask* *RecordApplyTask*
One-class classifier (a.k.a. Anomaly detection)	*Support Vector Machine*	*BuildTask* *DataSetApplyTask* *RecordApplyTask*

[*] Oracle-specific functions and algorithms

To simplify API usage, OJDM infers logical data settings from the data, and as such does not support the optional logical data specification. Recall that logical data provides the renaming of the physical attributes, attribute type specification, and attribute properties. In OJDM, attribute type is determined by the data type of the table column: VARCHAR2 and CHAR data type columns are inferred to be categorical attributes and NUMBER, FLOAT, and INTEGER data type columns are inferred to be numerical attributes. To change attribute type or rename attributes, a database view definition can be used. For a more detailed list of supported capabilities refer to *Oracle Data Mining Application Developer's Guide* [ORADMAPPDOC 2006].

16.1.4   Oracle JDM Extensions

Oracle Data Mining has introduced several extensions to the JDM standard API, as illustrated in Table 16-3. Package *oracle.dmt.jdm* is the base package for the Oracle extensions to JDM. OJDM follows the JDM standard framework for extensions. For example, OJDM introduces the *feature extraction* mining function, where a *feature* represents a combination of attributes that captures important characteristics of the data. (See Chapter 18 for a brief description of *feature extraction* in general, and *Oracle Data Mining Concepts* [ORADMCONCEPTS 2006] for further details.)

Using *MiningFunction.addExtension* and *MiningAlgorithm.addExtension* methods OJDM adds Oracle-specific mining functions and algorithms, so that applications can view the Oracle-specific functions from the standard interface. Feature extraction and other OJDM extension classes/interfaces extend the relevant JDM base classes/ interfaces to be consistent with the standard. For more details, refer to *Oracle Data Mining Java API Reference* [ORAJDMDOC 2006].

OJDM also provides interfaces for several of the data mining transformations (e.g., binning, normalization, clipping, and text). OJDM defines the API under the *oracle.dmt.jdm.transform* package. OJDM also introduces new tasks to more fully automate the data mining process. The high-level *predict* and *explain* tasks automate the data mining process by hiding the complexities of attribute filtering, data preparation, and the model build, test, and apply.

Table 16-3 *Oracle Java Data Mining extensions*

OJDM extension class/package	Description
oracle.dmt.jdm.resource OraConnectionFactory	This class provides an easy way to create Oracle-specific DME ConnectionFactory objects. It is particularly useful when applications do not have JNDI access.

oracle.dmt.jdm.featureextraction
    OraFeatureExtractionSettings
    OraFeatureExtractionModel
    OraFeature
    OraFeatureExtractionApplySettings
oracle.dmt.jdm.algorithm.nmf
    OraNMFAlgorithmSettings
	These classes and packages are used to define the feature extraction function and the Non-Negative Matrix Factorization (NMF) algorithm. OraFeatureExtraction-Settings is the build settings used to specify the maximum number of features that should be derived by the model. OraNMFAlgorithmSettings specifies NMF algorithm specific settings. OraFeatureExtractionModel and OraFeature classes represent the model that defines the extracted features. OraFeatureExtractionApply Settings is used to define the apply settings for feature extraction.

oracle.dmt.jdm.algorithm.abn
    OraABNSettings
oracle.dmt.jdm.modeldetails.abn
    OraABNModelDetail
	These classes and packages are used to define Oracle proprietary Adaptive Bayes Network (ABN) algorithm settings and associated model details.

oracle.dmt.jdm.algorithm.ocluster OraOClusterSettings	This package and class are used to define Orthogonal Partitioning Cluster (O-Cluster) algorithm settings. The JDM standard defined generic clustering model is sufficient to represent O-Cluster model.

oracle.dmt.jdm.task
    OraPredictTask
    OraExplainTask
	OJDM offers these non-JDM tasks that automate data mining processes in the database and produce final output. OraPredictTask is used to predict the target attribute of the input table/view. This task automates the model build, test, and apply operations and produces the final predictions as an output table. OraExplainTask is used to explain the specified target attribute of the input table/view. This task produces an output table that contains the attribute importance and rank. These two tasks produce reasonable quality results with minimum effort.

oracle.dmt.jdm.transform oracle.dmt.jdm.transform.binning oracle.dmt.jdm.transform.clipping oracle.dmt.jdm.transform.normalize oracle.dmt.jdm.transform.text	These packages are used to define the transformation-related classes. OJDM defines some of the common data mining data transformations, such as binning/discretization, clipping/outlier handling, normalization. Text data transformations convert text data in the datatypes such as CLOB to a nested table structure that can be mined using OJDM.

16.1.5 DME URI and Data URI

The JDM standard allows users to specify a uniform resource identifier (URI) string to represent the DME location and input/output dataset location. Since JDM implementations may differ in the URI syntax, we describe OJDM-specific URI syntax.

To connect to an Oracle DME, OJDM allows any JDBC-compatible URI specification to connect to the database. For example, to connect to the Oracle DME using the JDBC thin driver, the URI can be *jdbc:oracle:thin:@host:port:sid*, where *host* is the machine name, *port* is the port at which the database listener is running, and *sid* is the Oracle system identifier that is by default ORCL. Different types of DME URIs allowed in Oracle are listed in Table 16-4. For more details about these URIs, refer to *Oracle Database JDBC Developer's Guide and Reference* [ORAJDBC 2006].

Table 16-4 *Oracle JDBC drivers and associated DME URI syntax*

OJDBC *driver type*	*DME URI*
JDBC thin driver	*jdbc:oracle:thin:@host:port:sid or service_name*
JDBC OCI driver	*jdbc:oracle:oci:@host:port:sid or service_name, or*
	jdbc:orcle:oci:@(DESCRIPTION=(ADDRESS=(PROTOCOL=TCP)(HOST=hostname)(PORT=portnumber))(CONNECT_DATA=(SERVICE_NAME=service_name)))
Oracle JDBC Internal driver	*jdbc:oracle:kprb:*

Listing 16-1 *Connect to OJDM DME*

```
//Create OraConnectionFactory
javax.datamining.resource.ConnectionFactory connFactory =
         oracle.dmt.jdm.resource.OraConnectionFactory();

//Create ConnectionSpec
ConnectionSpec connSpec = connFactory.getConnectionSpec();
connSpec.setURI("jdbc:oracle:thin:@host:port:sid");
connSpec.setName("user");
connSpec.setPassword("password");

//Create DME Connection
javax.datamining.resource.Connection dmeConn =
         connFactory.getConnection(connSpec);
```

Listing 16-2 *Accessing data in OJDM*

```
//Create physical dataset that represents 'customer' table in the users schema
PhysicalDataSet pds = pdsFactory.create("customer", false );

//Create physical dataset that represents 'products' table in the user 'bob'
schema PhysicalDataSet pds = pdsFactory.create("bob.products", false);
```

Listing 16-1 illustrates how to connect to the OJDM DME using the JDBC thin driver. The OJDM connection logs in as a database schema user who can access the tables and views in their user schema and other user tables/views to which they have access.

Data URIs in OJDM are represented as *[schemaname.]tablename.* Datasets that are in the user's schema can be referred to simply by their *tablename* and other users' datasets can be referred to by *schemaname.tablename.* Listing 16-2 illustrates the code that uses data URI to create physical dataset objects.

16.1.6   Getting Started with OJDM

OJDM is installed with the data mining option of *Oracle Database Enterprise Edition 10g Release 2.* The software can be downloaded from the Oracle Technology Network (OTN) and installed by following the instructions in the *Oracle Data Mining Administrator's Guide* [ORADM-ADMIN 2006]. In addition, Oracle provides the OJDM plug-in (extension) for Oracle JDeveloper, which adds the "Oracle Java Data Mining" library and copies the demo programs to the   Oracle JDeveloper environment. For more details about this extension refer to [JDE-VOJDM 2006]. The OJDM sample programs use the sample schema tables that can be installed with the database. For more details about the installation of sample schema for data mining, refer to the *Oracle Data Mining Administrator's Guide* [ORADMADMIN 2006].

16.1.7   Other Oracle Data Mining APIs

In addition to the OJDM API, Oracle Data Mining provides an SQL-based API that can be used to develop database applications. This section provides a high-level overview of these APIs and references for further reading. Table 16-5 lists the PL/SQL packages and SQL functions supported in the Oracle Database. OJDM-created models are interoperable with the PL/SQL and SQL APIs. For example, a model created by OJDM can be used to make predictions using the SQL *prediction* operator. This allows application developers to use data mining capabilities through OJDM or the SQL-based interfaces. SQL operators in particular can enable complex data mining deployment scenarios, such as scoring multiple models in a single query or immediately combining the results of mining with other database SQL features involving spatial data and text analysis. For more details about these APIs, refer to [ORADMAPPDOC 2006].

Table 16-5 *Oracle Data Mining PL/SQL packages and SQL functions*

PL/SQL package	Description
DBMS_DATA_MINING	Provides the PL/SQL procedures and functions that can be used to build, apply, and test mining models.
DBMS_DATA_MINING_TRANSFORM	Provides the PL/SQL transformation procedures for binning, clipping, normalization, and missing value handling.
DBMS_PREDICTIVE_ANALYTICS	Provides the predict and explain procedures that automate complex data mining processes and produces final results.
SQL functions	**Description**
prediction prediction_probability prediction_cost prediction_set prediction_details	These prediction operators are used to compute prediction-related values using classification and regression models built using either OJDM or DBMS_DATA_MINING. The prediction operator returns the top prediction value of a case. The prediction_probablity operator returns the probability value for the top prediction. The prediction_cost operator returns the cost value of the top prediction if the cost matrix is specified at the model build. The prediction_set operator is used with classification models to return the collection of prediction, probability and cost values for all the class values of the target attribute in the model build data. The prediction_details operator returns the XML representation of the model details that describes how the prediction has been made for each case.
cluster_id cluster_probability cluster_set	These cluster operators are used to assign clusters for each case using the clustering models build using OJDM or DBMS_DATA_MINING. The cluster_id operator returns the case's top cluster id and cluster_probability operator returns the probability associated with the top cluster. The cluster_set operator returns the collection of cluster ids and their associated probabilities for all clusters in the model.
feature_id feature_value feature_set	These feature operators are used to find the feature associated with the case using the feature extraction model built using OJDM or DBMS_DATA_MINING. The feature_id operator returns the case's feature id that has highest coefficient value. The feature_value operator returns the coefficient value associated with the top feature for the case. The feature_set operator returns the collection of feature id and associated coefficient value for all features in the model.

16.1.8   Data Mining Graphical Interface Using OJDM

Oracle 10.2 Data Miner [ODMr102 2006] is a data mining workbench developed using OJDM and other in-database functionalities. Data Miner provides wizard- and activity-based guided data mining to allow a business analyst who may not be an expert data miner to produce good results quickly. For data mining experts, Data Miner also exposes interfaces for data preparation, fine-tuning algorithm settings, and viewing model details.

Figure 16-2 illustrates a few of the graphical interfaces available in Data Miner. The top left shows the main window with the menu to launch the guided analytics wizard. The top right shows the receiver operating characteristics (ROC) chart in the classification model test

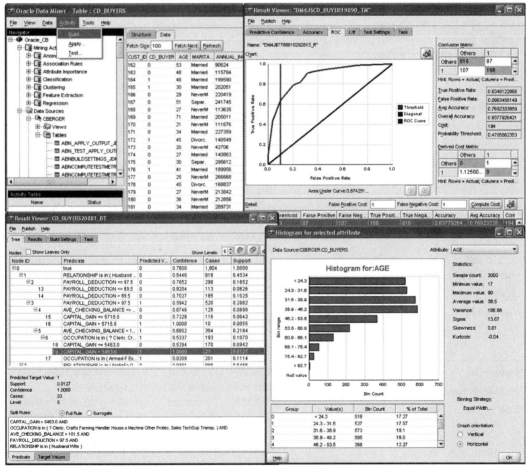

Figure 16-2   *Oracle Data Miner (ODMr) screen capture.*

metrics viewer. The bottom left shows the decision tree viewer enabling a structured view of the tree. The bottom right shows the data summary window depicting the distribution of AGE attribute values. Oracle Data Miner is an example where the JDM API has been used to build data mining tools.

16.2 KXEN (Knowledge Extraction Engines)

16.2.1 KXEN Data Mining Activity

KXEN's mission is to provide the technology to embed advanced analytics into existing enterprise applications. The KXEN Analytic Framework™ is a suite of predictive and descriptive modeling components that create robust analytic models faster and easier than in classical data mining environments.

KXEN believes that data mining should be a key element of corporate performance management. Initiatives such as campaign optimization, cross-sell, fraud detection, or risk assessment require extracting information from corporate data and turning it into actionable knowledge that can be used to predict and optimize business performance. Over time, the techniques used for this purpose have been assigned different names: statistics, data mining, machine learning, and lately, predictive analytics. New scientific discoveries, such as those of Vladimir Vapnik [Vapnik 1999], contributed to the evolution and refinement of these techniques, opening new doors toward efficient automation. Data mining was once the domain of specialists deploying their artful skills, but today the business of predictive modeling is gaining ubiquity with the emergence of modeling factories and time and productivity are now key issues.

Since 1998, KXEN has been a provider of data mining functions in all formats that are suited for easy integration, such as C++ library, CORBA server, COM/DCOM libraries and servers, and Java wrappers. KXEN provides its customers with the capability to set up their own factories for predictive and descriptive modeling. Their business units use the output of these factories to drive business performance throughout the company.

16.2.2 KXEN Position on JDM

KXEN joined the JDM standards group because the concepts that were beginning to emerge in this vendor group in 2002 were close to the architecture decisions KXEN made in 1998, when designing the KXEN Analytic Framework™. Besides the participation in developing the standard definition, one of the main contributions of KXEN has been the Reference Implementation (RI). The RI was used within the JSR to test the Technology Compatibility Kit (TCK) and can be used by integrators as a mock-up to test their developments.

KXEN was particularly attracted by the fact that JDM was one of the first attempts to rationalize a level of abstraction for data mining functions instead of providing a laundry list of known algorithms. That level of abstraction allows programmers to build applications and solutions based on best practices, without the constraints of specific algorithms' limitations. For KXEN, JDM is another way to provide its technology in a standardized form, which makes it easier to compare performance of data mining implementations at the same functional level or cost.

Another goal of KXEN was to apply the same standard to Web services because it truly opens the door to integrating data mining techniques within business workflow environments. Creating a set of Web services is not technically very difficult. The real problem is to federate a services community, made of both consumers and providers. KXEN believes that JDM Web services, an open standard, will open new opportunities for the proliferation of data mining within business environments across the enterprise. Since late 2005, KXEN provides KJDM as KXEN's JDM 1.1 implementation.

16.2.3 KXEN JDM Implementation Architecture

KJDM (KXEN Java Data Mining Implementation) is a commercial implementation of JDM built on top of KXEN technology. Technically, it can be seen as a Java "wrapper" on top of KXEN Analytic Framework. All data access and computations are done in C++ for efficiency and memory allocation purposes, but the Java wrappers give all the power of Enterprise wide application development.

KJDM can be switched at runtime between two architectures:

- In-process computing through a Java/JNI/C++ interface, allowing lightweight data mining embedding, or
- Out-process integration through CORBA.

The switch between the two architectures is done through the URI specified for the connection.

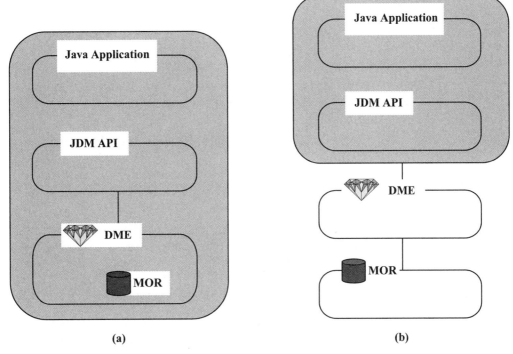

Figure 16-3 *KJDM choices of architectures.*

Figure 16-3(a) represents both the Java application and the JDM implementation in the same process. Figure 16-3(b) represents the Java application and the DME implementation in two different processes, which can be on the same machine or on different machines. For each case, the software architect has the choice of using an MOR accessible only on the machine, or an MOR residing on another environment: In this latter case, the data contained in the MOR will be accessed through open database connectivity (ODBC) by the DME itself. Figure 16-3(b) highlights a three-tier architecture.

16.2.4 KXEN JDM Capabilities

KXEN JDM (KJDM) supports all the JDM 1.1 mining functions: *classification, regression, attribute importance, association,* and *clustering*. There are some key features of KXEN JDM implementations:

- KJDM does not implement any specific algorithm: Java programmers can stay at the mining function level without any required knowledge about any algorithm implementation details.

- KJDM functions work directly on unprepared data, which is one of the key elements explaining the productivity improvement obtained by using KXEN. No need exists for specific processing of missing values, outliers, numeric, ordinal, or even categorical variables with high cardinality, such as ZIP code.

- KJDM classification, regression, and clustering functions work in very high-dimensional space without any need of a priori attribute selection: it is not uncommon to build classification models on 2,000 attributes for CRM applications with very good performance.

- KJDM can export classification, regression, and clustering models into a wide range of languages for optimized use of external scoring engines.

More information can be found at [KJDM 2006].

Table 16-6 shows the KJDM-supported functions and tasks. KJDM also supports export and import tasks for exporting and importing mining models in the KXEN proprietary format.

In KJDM, all named objects can be persisted in the MOR except taxonomy. Since persistence can be heavy on the management of the persisted objects, it can be useful to keep some classes of objects transient. KJDM enables this, and the process can be fine-tuned through a configuration file.

The application designer can use specific parameters in the URI specification to indicate the location of the MOR, as shown in the next section.

Logical description can be used to shield the physical descriptions from the models in KJDM: all data mining functions can use logical data and logical attributes, and can be used on discrete, bounded, ordinal, unprepared, numerical, and categorical attributes. Even if attributes are declared to be prepared, KXEN will process them.

In KJDM, there is no option for "outlier treatment" because KXEN proprietary algorithms are designed to resist perturbations due to outliers in the build datasets. In KJDM, there also is no option for "missing value treatment". Missing values are always

Table 16-6 *KXEN Java Data Mining supported functions, and function level tasks*

Supported function	*Supported function level tasks*
Classification	BuildTask ClassificationTestTask ClassificationTestMetricsTask DataSetApplyTask RecordApplyTask ComputeStatisticsTask ExportTask
Regression	BuildTask RegressionTestTask RegressionTestMetricsTask DataSetApplyTask RecordApplyTask ComputeStatisticsTask ExportTask
Attribute Importance	BuildTask ComputeStatisticsTask
Association	BuildTask ComputeStatisticsTask
Clustering	BuildTask DataSetApplyTask RecordApplyTask ComputeStatisticsTask ExportTask

processed in KXEN as if "missing" was a specific category and then encoded properly.

16.2.5 DME URI and Data URI Specifications

The only mechanism provided by KJDM to create a connection toward a DME is through a specification provided as a URI. Java 1.4 includes an implementation of URI representation and parsing in the package java.net that KXEN uses internally in KJDM. KXEN uses a hierarchical URI structure of the form:

[scheme:][//authority][path][?query][#fragment].

The KXEN URI for DME connections accepts only two schemes: *kxjni* to deal with in-process integration and *kxcorba* to deal with out-of-process integration. The KXEN URI uses the query section of the URI to transfer initial parameter settings to KXEN DME. The possible query keys are:

- Lang: the language used to forward error messages to the user (default is *en*).

- Country: the country used to localize error messages and reports to the user (default is *US*).

- MORClass: < Kxen.FileStore | Kxen.ODBCStore >. This is the KXEN class name of the repository; it can be either stored into files within directories or tables within an ODBC source (default is *Kxen.FileStore*).

- MORName: <Directory path containing MOR files | ODBC source name containing the MOR tables>: The default is "*/temp*".

- MORLogin: login to be used to open the MOR (default is) "".

- MORPwd: password to be used to open the MOR (default is "").

Table 16-7 provides some examples of URI to provide at connection creation time for in-process and out-of-process engines.

The first example in the table means to connect on the local machine to KXEN Analytic Framework through Java Native Interface, with the license file contained on the current directory "." called *KxJDM.cfg* (license files contain keys that activate KXEN components). The language and country are then specified: these settings are used to localize the error messages. Because the MOR is not specified, the default MOR will be used: temporary files on */tmp*.

The second example in Table 16-7 shows how to connect to the CORBA service referenced as *MarketingServer* on the name service accessed through port 12345 on the machine named *apollon*. This DME will be using a MOR accessed through the ODBC source called *MyBase* using the default login for this ODBC source.

Listing 16-3 shows a typical connection creation sequence of KJDM.

Table 16-7   *KXEN DME URI syntax*

Architecture	DME URI
In-process integration	*kxjni://localhost/./KxJDM.cfg?lang=en&country=US*
Out-process integration	*kxcorba://apollon:12345/MarketingServer?MORClass=Kxen.ODBCStore&MORName=MyBase*

Listing 16-3 *Connect to KJDM DME*

```
//Create OraConnectionFactory
javax.datamining.resource.ConnectionFactory connFactory =
        com.kxen.KxJDMImpl.javax.datamining.resource.ConnectionFactoryImpl();
//Create ConnectionSpec
ConnectionSpec connSpec = connFactory.getConnectionSpec();
connSpec.setURI("kxjni://localhost/./KxJDM.cfg?lang=en&country=US");
connSpec.setName("user");
connSpec.setPassword("password");
//Create DME Connection
javax.datamining.resource.Connection dmeConn =
        connFactory.getConnection(connSpec);
```

In KJDM, the URI syntax to access datasets allows access to either files or objects contained in databases. KXEN URI for dataset locations accepts only two schemes: file and odbc. Note that we have specified ODBC and not JDBC. This is because KXEN engines are written in C++ and access data sources through ODBC.

When "file" is selected the following structure is used:

- Host: <field ignored>
- Port: <field ignored>
- Path: <complete path to file>

This is an example:

```
file:///r:temp/mydata.csv
```

When "odbc" is selected, the following structure is used:

- Host: <field ignored>
- Port: <field ignored>
- Path: <odbc data source/table name or select statement>

These are some examples of valid KJDM URI:

```
odbc://kxen_Oracle/select * from TableName?user=foo&password=foo
odbc://kxen_SqlServer/table1?user=foo&password=foo
```

In the first KJDM URI example, a "select" statement can be directly used as a dataset to build or apply models, or compute statistics. This feature is particularly interesting when, for example, there is a need to filter lines or join information from different tables. The second example shows direct access to a table or a view prepared in advance. The user and password can be passed directly in the URI, but could also be assigned as default values in the odbc.ini parameter file to cope with some security issues. The access to all major databases from Windows and UNIX platforms is supported.

A specific extension can be associated with KJDM to read also proprietary formats of most commercial data mining vendors.

16.2.6   KXEN Extensions

The only extension that KXEN has implemented concerns the available languages in which classification, regression, and clustering models can be exported. The model resulting from an *ExportTask* execution will work on the data provided in the same format as for the *BuildTask* (which means unprepared data).

The possible exported formats are listed here:

- XML
- JAVA
- C
- VB
- PMML2_1
- PMML3_0
- SQL for MySQL
- SQL optimized for SQL Server
- SQL optimized for Teradata
- SQL for IBM DB2 and Oracle
- AWK
- SAS
- UDF for Oracle
- UDF for IBM DB2
- UDF for SQL Server
- UDF for Teradata

It should be noted that all models created through KJDM can be exported to UDF (user defined functions), which allows use of a database as a scoring engine without data transfer. Models exported in such a way are seen as native database functions and can be used as such in any SQL statements.

16.2.7 KXEN Web Services Implementation

KJDM provides a Web services implementation that has been developed with Apache-Axis. It can be safely installed on any J2EE server framework such as Apache Tomcat. KJDM Web services implements all Web services interface defined by JDM 1.1. The KJDM Web services architecture is shown in Figure 16-4.

KJDM Web services implementation is provided as a war file, *KxServices.war*, to be deployed under a J2EE server. It implements all JDM Web services: *saveObject, removeObject, renameObject, execute-Task, terminateTask, getExecutionStatus, getObject, listContents, getSub-Objects, getCapabilities,* and *verifyObject.*

KJDM Web services can be configured through a configuration file in which are specified the ConnectionClass, the ConnectionURI, the DME user name, and password; this implementation could be connected to any valid JDM implementation.

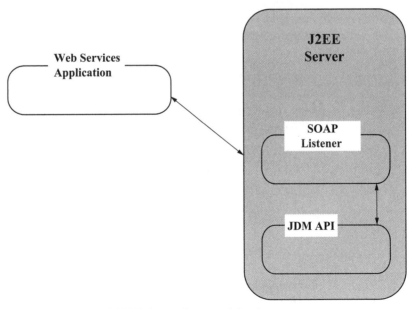

Figure 16-4 *KJDM Web services architecture.*

16.3   Guidelines for New Implementers

Guidelines for implementers[1] in developing a JDM implementation are described in Section 6 of the JDM specification. This section focuses on standards conformance, both in terms of a minimum JDM implementation and vendor extensions, and using the TCK.

16.3.1   Standards Conformance

Conformance to the JDM standard is easier than for many other standards due to JDM's á là carte capabilities mechanism. This mechanism allows implementing mainly the features a given product already supports. The expert group designed JDM with this in mind to lower the barrier to entry for new implementations. For example, a data mining vendor with a single decision tree algorithm may decide to offer only this algorithm as part of the classification mining function.

Of course, a JDM API implementation is written in Java. However, the DME itself need not be written in Java. As noted earlier, OJDM is a Java wrapper on top of data mining functions accessed through SQL, and KJDM is a Java wrapper on top of a C++ or CORBA library. The effort required to implement a Java wrapper on top of existing engines can be minimal: Implementers are encouraged to start from their existing product lines and expose them through JDM to minimize development effort.

The notion of capabilities allows implementers to adopt a phased approach to JDM implementation, perhaps offering a first version for a reduced feature set and then expanding the feature set. Implementers can shape their JDM implementation using the capabilities and the extension mechanism.

All JDM implementations share some core JDM functionality. The next section describes a "minimal" JDM implementation.

---

1   The term "implementers" includes both vendors of data mining tools and technology, and non-vendors. Non-vendors may include university students, researchers, or companies with internal data mining capabilities.

The Minimum Implementation

Because JDM is structured into packages, the implementer decides which packages to include. The packages required for all implementations are listed in the specification document:

- *Javax.datamining* must implement *Collection, Verification-Report, Exception,* and *ExecutionHandle* classes.

- *Javax.datamining.base* must implement *NamedObject, Mining-Object, BuildSettings, Models, Tasks,* and *TestMetrics* classes. *AlgorithmSettings* and *AttributeStatisticSet* can be left optional depending on the capabilities. Persistence can be supported for a given list of mining objects, so no extra effort is required from the vendor on required persistence.

- *Javax.datamining.resource* must implement the *Connection-Factory, ConnectionSpec,* and *Connection* interfaces. This connection contains the needed information about the physical connection to the DME, as well as the information related to the working session.

- *Javax.datamining.data* must implement the *PhysicalDataSet, PhysicalDataRecord,* and *PhysicalAttribute* with their associated factories, and *ModelSignature, SignatureAttribute,* and *Taxonomy* interfaces. *LogicalData* and *LogicalAttribute* can be left optional depending on the capabilities.

- *Javax.datamining.task* must implement the tasks that will be supported. The minimum implementation is to support only synchronous execution of the supported tasks, which would require minimum implementation effort in most situations.

- *Javax.datamining.statistics* must be implemented if the implementation supports the build statistics tasks.

JDM also defines a *scoring engine* conformance option that allows implementing only those JDM features required for scoring data (i.e., invoking model apply behavior). Details are provided in the JDM specification [JDM II 2006].

Vendor Extensions

Data mining implementers may have variations of the JDM standard functions/algorithms as well as new functions/algorithms that are not defined in the current standard. JDM is designed to enable extending the existing JDM functionality and adding new functionality. For example, a data mining vendor who provides non-JDM functionality, such as variations of the *decision tree* algorithm with additional settings, *time series* function, or a new *genetic algorithm* for *regression*, can extend the existing JDM interfaces by adding new interfaces/classes to support that functionality.

As discussed in Chapter 8, JDM packages are organized by mining function and mining algorithm. Settings interfaces are defined within each function and algorithm package. JDM implementations can add new functions and algorithms by defining new packages and including interfaces that inherit from the appropriate base interfaces. For example, a new *time series* mining function can be defined in a new package *com.xyzMiner.jdm.timeseries* with the *time series* build settings inheriting from the *javax.datamining.base.BuildSettings* interface.

When defining a new mining function or other feature, the appropriate enumeration must be updated. For example the *MiningFunction* enumeration, which lists the functions supported in the JDM standard, must be updated to include and entry for *time series*. To add vendor-specific extension enumerations to the standard extensions, JDM provides a static method called *addExtension(String enum)* in all enumerations.

16.3.2   Using the TCK

To validate that a given JDM implementation conforms to the standard, the implementer executes the Technology Compatibility Kit (TCK) on the new implementation. The TCK is available at the JDM Web site (http://www.jcp.org/en/jsr/detail?id=73). (From the latest Maintenance Release, follow the download instructions for "JSR073 for Implementation." The download will contain the latest specification document and the latest versions of the TCK and RI.)

This TCK includes a configuration file that the implementer modifies to conform to implementation-specific URI formats for datasets. It also includes Java package names where the TCK will find the proper connection factory implementations. The TCK runs a series of tests depending on the capabilities declared by the DME implementation and generates an HTML file containing a compatibility report.

Users of the TCK should realize that it is not a full unitary test suite. For example, the TCK does not validate that individual computations are correct, such as the standard deviation of a specific attribute returned by a *ComputeStatistics* task. It does not test the results of algorithm implementations, such as the correct number of rules for a given support and confidence level on a given dataset. Further, it does not test negative cases, that is, those involving error conditions. For example, if a vendor claims not to support a given capability, the DME implementation should return an *UnsupportedFeatureException* if a feature associated with this capability is invoked by the caller.

To run the TCK tests, you will need the following jar files:

- jdm.jar: the jar containing interfaces defined in JDM.
- junit.jar: the TCK is based on the JUnit unitary test framework [JUNIT 2006].
- jdmTCK1_1_0.jar: the jar containing the test scenarios to be run on the implementation.
- jdmTCKFramework1_1_0.jar: a jar containing utilities to start the test process.

The four jar files must be in the CLASSPATH of your runtime environment to be able to run the TCK. Then, assuming that the jar file containing your implementation is called MyJDMImpl.jar, you will have to perform the following operations:

- Create a test directory.
- Under the test directory, create (1) a *libs* directory in which the five jar files will be stored, (2) a *config* directory in which all eight configuration files provided with the download will be copied, and (3) a *reports* directory in which the TCK will produce the reports.
- Edit the configuration files. Most of them contain specifications for datasets that are expressed using URIs; thus, they must be edited because the URI syntax is vendor dependent and must point to valid datasets in the test environment. The master configuration file, called *tckconfig.pro*, points to six others, and a *connection.pro* that contains the class path used by the test framework to point to the JDM implementation connection factory.

Then, go to the test directory and launch the following command:

```
java.exe -classpath libs\jdmTCKFramework1_1_0.jar;libs\jdmTCK1_1_0.jar;
libs\jdm.jar;libs\junit.jar;libs\MyJDMImpl.jarjavax.datamining.testSuites.
JDMTCK/config/tckconfig.pro
```

This will generate reports in the *reports* directory. The HTML file called *TCKReport.html* is the main report. *CapabilitySummary.html* is a summary of the capabilities of your implementation, and specific error messages, if any, will be in the XML files associated with the ten remaining test suites.

Figure 16-5 shows a screen shot of the beginning of the report generated when running the TCK on KJDM.

As shown in Figure 16-5, there is one section for each data mining function and each supported algorithm. When there is a problem, an error report is generated. This report contains descriptions of each problem collated in an XML file. Figure 16-6 includes an example of a problem found by the TCK related to clustering.

In the error report shown in Figure 16-6, the problem is a wrong assertion. The TCK is based on JUnit and uses one of two problem

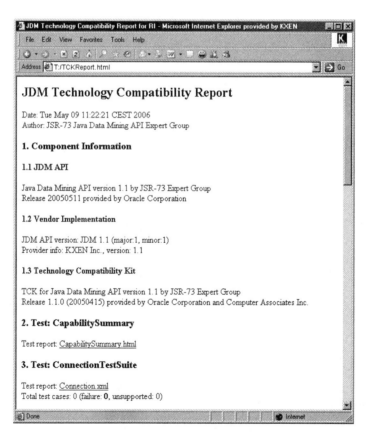

Figure 16-5 *Screen shot of the beginning of the report generated by TCK.*

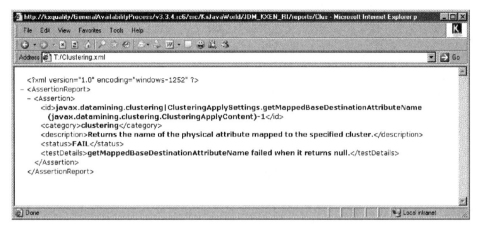

Figure 16-6 *Screenshot of an error report generated by TCK.*

report mechanisms: (1) some problems are due to the fact that the system does not behave according to its declared capabilities and these errors are reported as wrong assertions, and (2) some errors are due to processes finishing as exceptions and are reported as errors.

When there is a problem for a specific test suite, the test suite can be launched with a graphical interface using the following command (this example involves the regression test suite):

```
java.exe -classpath libs\jdmTCKFramework1_1_0.jar;libs\jdmTCK1_1_0.jar;
libs\jdm.jar;libs\junit.jar;libs\MyJDMImpl.jar javax.datamining.testSuites.
RegressionTestSuite -ga ./config/connection.pro
```

Problems that occur during these tests fall into one of two categories:

1. You identify the problem in your configuration or implementation. You may correct the problem and rerun the TCK for further validation.

2. You think that the problem comes from the TCK itself. For example, the TCK omits a check for a given capability prior to making a specific test related to this capability. In this case, you may want to communicate this to the TCK designers and implementers. To do this, go to *https://datamining.dev.java.net* and join the discussion forums (under the "Project Tools" section). One forum is dedicated to "TCK questions and issues."

Once you are satisfied with the global assessment of the TCK, you may share this report with the JDM expert group, together with the capabilities summary.

16.4   Process for New JDM Users

To use JDM, integrators will need a JDM implementation. Although the RI is provided as part of the JDM final specification, the RI is not a real JDM implementation because it does not implement any computations based on the data. The RI serves as a mock-up implementation to test the TCK and highlight API design issues. For example, when asked for a standard deviation of a numerical variable, the RI will always answer 3.4; when asked for a decision tree, it will always return the same tree structure with three nodes. The RI was purposely designed to test a large number of capabilities declared for tests that needed to be implemented within the TCK. Users new to JDM will want to contact JDM vendors to get real evaluation versions.

16.5   Summary

This chapter presented two commercial implementations of JDM and their specific features. These implementations correspond to good examples of implementation of in-database DMEs (Oracle) and out-of-database DMEs (KXEN). The chapter also provided some guidance for implementers new to JDM and described the JDM TCK framework.

References

[JDM11 2006] http://www.jcp.org/en/jsr/detail?id=73.

[JDEVOJDM 2006] http://www.oracle.com/technology/products/bi/odm/odm_jdev_extension.html.

[JUNIT 2006] http://www.junit.org/index.htm.

[KJDM 2006] http://www.kxen.com/products/analytic_framework/ apis.php.

[ORADMAPPDOC 2006] *Oracle® Data Mining Application Developers Guide*, 10g Release 2, http://www.oracle.com/pls/db102/portal.portal_db?selected=6.

[ORADBADMIN 2006] *Oracle® Database Administrator's Guide*, 10g Release 2, http://www.oracle.com/pls/db102/portal.portal_db?selected=4.

[ORADMADMIN 2006] *Oracle® Data Mining Administrator's Guide*, 10g Release 2, http://www.oracle.com/pls/db102/portal.portal_db?selected=6.

[ORADMCONCEPTS 2006] *Oracle® Data Mining Concepts*, 10g Release 2, http://www.oracle.com/pls/db102/portal.portal_db?selected=6.

[ORAJDBC 2006] *Oracle® Database JDBC Developer's Guide and Reference*, 10g Release 2, http://www.oracle.com/pls/db102/portal.portal_db?selected=5.

[ORAJDMDOC 2006] *Oracle Data Mining Java API Reference*, 10g Release 2, http://www.oracle.com/pls/db102/portal.portal_db?selected=6.

[ODMr102 2006] *Oracle® Data Miner*, 10g Release 2, http://www.oracle.com/technology/products/bi/odm/odminer.html.

[Vapnik 1999] Vladimir N. Vapnik, *The Nature of Statistical Learning Theory*, 2nd edition, New York: Springer, 1999.

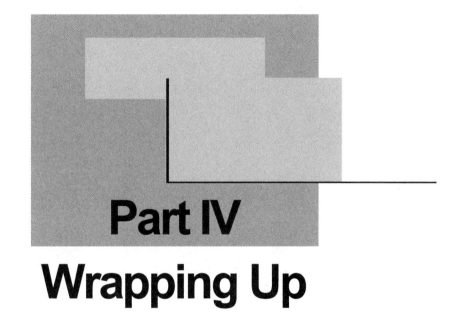

Part IV

Wrapping Up

Evolution of Data Mining Standards

*The reason why the universe is eternal is that it does not live for itself;
it gives life to others as it transforms.*

—Lao Tzu (600–531 B.C.)

Standards are not an end in themselves, but a means to an end. They often simplify the lives of individuals and, at the same time, both simplify and complicate the lives of vendors. A successful standard needs to grow and be adopted; it is through this process that the community reaps its benefits.

This chapter briefly explores several data mining standards[1]: what they are, who is defining them, their basic process, and any future directions. We then discuss the Java Community Process, by which Java Data Mining is derived, and briefly comment on why there are so many standards. Finally, we discuss future areas for data mining standardization.

---

1   We exclude the discussion of CRISP-DM in this chapter since it was covered in detail in Chapter 3 and it focuses on process, not implementaion.

17.1   Data Mining Standards

Java Data Mining (JDM) is not the first standard in the data mining space. The first standard in the data mining space was the Predictive Model Markup Language (PMML) developed by the Data Mining Group (DMG), which released version 1.0 in August 1999; the version is currently at 3.1. This was followed by the CWM data mining extension, developed through the Object Management Group (OMG), which started in 1999 and released version 1.0 in 2001 [CWM 2005]. The SQL/MM Part 6 Data Mining [SQL/MM DM 2006], part of the SQL standard from the Joint Technical Committee (JTC 1) of the International Standards Organization (ISO) [ISO 2006] and the International ElectroTechnical Commission (IEC) [IEC 2006], began in 1999 and made its first release in 2002. JDM began as JSR-73, starting in 2000, with its first release in 2004, and a second release is underway through JSR-247. These standards are discussed to provide a broader context for understanding JDM and the ways some of these standards may be used in combination with JDM.

17.1.1   Predictive Model Markup Language

PMML is an XML markup language for describing both statistical and data mining models. Its primary goal is to enable interchange of data mining models between systems as well as between vendor implementations. PMML supports the description of data mining model input (e.g., required data fields), the transformations necessary to prepare the data for scoring, as well as the parameters that define the data mining model [DMG 2005].

PMML emerged in 1997 because the need to exchange data mining models in a vendor-neutral format was viewed as important to moving the industry forward. PMML has evolved over the ensuing years, with successive releases becoming more precise in the definitions of data mining terminology and their use in specific types of models. Initially, PMML defined a set of the most common representations on which participating vendors could agree.

PMML is developed by the DMG—an independent, vendor-led group that develops data mining standards. The DMG is a voting-based organization; voting determines both direction and content. Membership consists of voting members and associate members. Generally, extensions and modification to the PMML standard come from one or more members taking the lead to modify a component of the standard. Multiple data mining vendors have implemented PMML in their released products, both those that are active in defining the standard through the DMG and those interested only in using PMML.

PMML, from its beginning, supported vendor-specific extensions. These were crucial to the initial success of the standard, since the core standard was not designed to cater to the full requirements of any given vendor but to represent a common set of required capabilities. However, by allowing vendor-specific extensions in XML, interoperability among vendors suffered, that is, it was not possible for vendors to exchange most models. One objective for model exchange is to be able to produce PMML in one vendor system (export) and consume it in another vendor's system (import and use). Yet, the seed was planted, the standard grew, gained acceptance, and continues to address the problems that limit interoperability. A key factor in ensuring interoperability will be the development of a conformance test suite. Then, vendors that claim compliance to the standard can validate their implementation more fully.

Some vendors produce PMML but do not consume their own or other vendor's PMML documents. Producer-only vendors allow third-party vendors to import that PMML for either scoring or visualization. Most vendors that support PMML, however, do produce and consume their own PMML models.

One of the limitations of an XML representation for data mining models is the impact that loading the model can have on real-time performance. Some models, such as association rules or clustering models can be quite large, involving megabytes or gigabytes of data. It can take a significant amount of time to load these models into memory for inspection or scoring. Such overheads may be acceptable in some situations; in other situations, where real-time response is required, the load-time requirement is unacceptable, even for relatively small models. Preloading such models and pinning them in memory help to overcome this concern. Other standards that provide support for applying models, such as SQL/MM DM and JDM, provide operations to load and pin a model in memory to facilitate real-time scoring, where multiple invocations will be made.

Over multiple releases, PMML has increased its breadth of model types supported, to the point where, today, quite a range of data mining models is supported. PMML continues to expand into new model representations while attempting to address the issue of transformations uniformly across models. PMML also strives to include functionality that will reduce the need for vendor extensions by working with the major vendors to standardize their extensions. While this helps to achieve the goal of having a standard that enables interoperability, it also adds to the complexity of the specification and the ability of vendors to fully implement it.

17.1.2   Common Warehouse Metadata for Data Mining

Common Warehouse Metadata (CWM) for data mining provides a metamodel for representing data mining metadata in XML. It is based on the more general CWM specification [CWM 2005].

> *The Common Warehouse Metamodel (CWM™) is a specification that describes metadata interchange among data warehousing, business intelligence, knowledge management and portal technologies. The OMG Meta-Object Facility (MOF™) bridges the gap between dissimilar meta-models by providing a common basis for meta-models. If two different meta-models are both MOF-conformant, then models based on them can reside in the same repository. [CWM 2005]*

In particular, CWM uses XML Metadata Interchange (XMI) to interchange data warehouse metadata, which is based on the more general CWM metamodel. The CWM metamodel is specified using the MOF model, allowing XMI to be used to (1) transform the CWM metamodel into a CWM document type definition (DTD), (2) transfer instances of warehouse metadata that conform to the CWM metamodel as XML documents, based on the CWM DTD, and (3) transform the CWM metamodel itself into an XML document, based on the MOF DTD for interchange between MOF-compliant repositories.

These specifications work together to allow warehouse metadata and the CWM metamodel to be interchanged using W3C's Extensible Markup Language (XML). CWM allows Interface Definition Language (IDL) to be used for specifying programmatic access to data warehouse metadata—based on the CWM metamodel. Other programming language APIs may be generated based on the CWM IDL and specific IDL programming language mappings (e.g., IDL-Java and CORBA-COM). The CWM DTD, CWM XML, and CWM IDL specifications are automatically generated from the CWM metamodel, as defined by the MOF and XMI specifications. (See Chapter 15 of [OMG 2001] for a detailed description of the data mining portion of the standard.)

OMG's charter is to produce and maintain specifications for interoperable enterprise applications in the computer industry. OMG membership includes nearly all large computer industry companies and some smaller ones. OMG maintains a board of directors. Participation is open to all companies; each member company receives one vote to ensure all participants have an effective voice in the standards-setting process. To initiate an OMG standard-setting activity, members must submit a Request for Proposal. Standards are approved by member voting.

The OMG's CWM for data mining formed an expert group comprised of representatives from IBM, Oracle, and Hyperion. Here, the goal was to define a complete specification of the syntax and semantics needed to export and import shared warehouse metadata and the common warehouse metamodel [CWMI 2000]. CWM/DM defined a set of objects and states to capture data mining metadata (e.g., objects for models, settings, and attribute usage, among others). CWM/DM was not intended to capture the details of individual models, but to serve as a framework that individual vendors could extend. Unfortunately, the scope and implementation requirements of CWM itself limited its adoption among some data mining vendors. Since the CWM 1.1 release, no further extensions to CWM/DM have been made.

17.1.3 SQL/MM Part 6 Data Mining

SQL/MM Part 6 Data Mining (SQL/MM DM) is geared toward SQL access to data mining in databases. SQL/MM DM took the standards effort a step further by recognizing the need for a standard SQL-based interface for building, testing, and applying models, while leveraging the model representation format available from PMML. SQL/MM DM does not specify how to represent models but suggests that standards such as PMML are likely candidates for model representations stored in database tables. SQL/MM DM began with the most commonly used data mining techniques: *classification, regression, clustering,* and *association*. It also prescribed the use of separate *settings* to control the behavior of the underlying algorithms.

SQL/MM DM used SQL *user-defined types* for the interface definition. Although this approach may be convenient from an implementation or user perspective, being object-based as opposed to defining syntactic extensions to the SQL language itself, the implementation of user-defined types by database vendors limits the flexibility of including data mining statements in complex SQL queries, also called *analytical pipelines*. Like PMML, SQL/MM DM continued to evolve, becoming more precise in its definitions, and expanding functionality to map to progress with PMML, CWM, and JDM.

SQL/MM is produced under JTC 1. The Joint Technical Committee (JTC-1) of ISO and IEC establishes international Information Technology (IT) standards. The scope of JTC 1 includes "… the specification, design and development of systems and tools dealing with the capture, representation, processing, security, transfer, interchange, presentation, management, organization, storage and retrieval of information" [JTC-1 2006]. The participants are national bodies, where each participating member country has one vote to affect the evolving and final standard.

The American National Standards Institute (ANSI), founded in 1918, "coordinates the development and use of voluntary consensus standards in the United States and represents the needs and views of U.S. stakeholders in standardization forums around the globe. ANSI is the official U.S. representative to the International Organization for Standardization (ISO) and, via the U.S. National Committee, the International Electrotechnical Commission (IEC). ANSI is also a member of the International Accreditation Forum (IAF)" [ANSI]. ANSI accredits Standards Development Organizations (SDOs) to develop standards in specific technology areas.

The International Committee for Information Technology Standards (INCITS) [INCITS 2006] is accredited by ANSI in the area of IT standards and represents US interests by serving as the Technical Advisory Group (TAG) to JTC-1. The INCITS/H2 Technical Committee on Database is responsible for database language standards including representing the US as TAG to the SQL/MM Data Mining effort within ISO/IEC JTC 1.

As this book goes to press, the second edition of SQL/MM DM is facing a final vote in a national body ballot. This version includes limited editorial changes. Currently, no further editions of this standard are expected.

17.2   Java Community Process

The Java Community Process (JCP) [SUN 2005] defines how the international Java community develops and evolves Java technology. Changes to Java technology begin with a Java Specification Request (JSR), which can be initiated by any JCP member. The JCP specifies several phases of standard development to enable timely and practical delivery of the Java standard application programming interface (API). These phases include *initiation, early draft, public draft,* and *maintenance.* In the initiation phase, any community member can initiate a JSR. Once the executive committee (EC) approves a JSR, the JSR specification lead forms an expert group—a team of industry experts from member corporations and individuals who will contribute to the requirements, design, and specification of the standard. The expert group produces an early draft for review by the Java community and the public. After further revisions, taking into account any early draft feedback, the expert group produces the public draft. Once approved, the reference implementation (RI) and technology compatibility kit (TCK) can be completed and submitted for final approval by the EC. The TCK is a suite of tests, tools, and documentation that tests a vendor's implementation for compliance with the specification. The RI is an implementation of the specification that can pass the TCK and in some instances serve as a basis for others to see how the specification is intended to be implemented. The maintenance phase is reserved for completed specifications that require further clarification, enhancement, or revisions.

Specification leads have significant latitude in how to organize and run the evolution of the specification and the completeness and complexity of the RI and TCK. However, there are some basic principles, such as taking a consensus-driven approach and iteratively reviewing the specification work products.

The JCP itself evolves using the JCP process, with change proposals initiated via a JSR, typically led by Sun and the JCP EC members serving as expert group members. The EC is responsible for approving specifications at the major phases or checkpoints noted above. EC members are drawn from a cross section of the Java community, including major stakeholders in Java technology.

17.3 Why So Many Standards?

Standards usually evolve to serve a particular need, supporting a particular technology, domain, or user group. Over the past century, many standards bodies have evolved (e.g., ANSI, JTC 1, IEC, ISO, OMG, JCP). Each applies different processes, requirements, and rigorousness to developing standards. In the domain of data mining, standards originated to support different communities and needs: the database community (SQL/MM), the data mining community in general (vendors and users) for model representation and interchange (PMML) and data warehouse metadata exchange (CWM, JDM XML Schema), the Service-Oriented Architecture community (JDM Web Services), and the data mining Java community (JDM).

When a user community recognizes the need for a standard, it will often look first to existing standards bodies before deciding to form its own standards body. Often, it is more convenient to fit into an existing framework with processes and recognition than to build one from scratch. However, issues of control, effort, and timing can lead a community away from existing standards bodies.

Some standards have strict guidelines concerning what can be specified, how it must be specified, and how changes are allowed in subsequent revisions. Others may have a rigorous process for submitting new material and revising existing material. This may require travel to remote or exotic destinations for days or even weeks as specifications are reviewed and edited. Time and resources are required to provide material in the proper format, and to ensure established procedures are followed.

In addition, the timing of when a standard becomes final can affect the choice of a standards body. If the release cycle is several years, a new user community may not be willing or able to wait for a standard to be published, with the chance that it may not be approved, requiring more editing and delay.

One of the challenges in having multiple standards in the same domain is unifying terminology and semantics. A brief survey of data mining literature will uncover numerous terms for the same concepts, or slight variations on the same concept. For example, an *attribute* in JDM can also be referred to as a *predictor, variable, column, feature,* or *field*. In different contexts, each of these terms can also have different semantics. For example, *field* could refer to a physical database table column, or a logical input to model build or apply. Table 17-1 maps some data mining terminology for JDM, PMML, CWM, and SQL/MM.

Some standards fit into an existing, highly evolved framework. CWM is one such standard that has a fairly complex and comprehensive data model. CWM/DM was required to fit within the overall CWM framework.

Sometimes standards overlap in both concepts and terminology, but have a different emphasis. For example, JDM focuses on execution of the data mining process including model build, test, and apply, and mining object import and export. PMML, on the other hand, focuses on the model representation and exchange using an XML representation.

Table 17-1 *Data mining standards terminology comparison*

JDM	PMML	CWM	SQL/MM
Attribute	MiningField	MiningAttribute	Column
{Y}Model {X}ModelDetail	{X}Model	MiningModel	DM_{Y}Model
ModelSignature	MiningSchema	ApplicationInputSpecification	DM_getFields ( )
BuildSettings {Y}Settings	N/A	MiningSettings {Y}Settings	DM_{Y}Settings
PhysicalDataSet	DataDictionary	MiningDataSpecification	DM_MiningData
TestMetrics	N/A	MiningModelResult	DM_{Y}Result
Target	Predicted	Target	Target
ApplySettings	N/A	N/S	N/S
LogicalData	N/A	AttributeUsageSpecification MiningDataSpecification	DM_LogicalDataSpec

X – {Tree, NeuralNetwork, etc.}   Y – {Classification, Regression, Clustering, etc.}   N/A Not applicable   N/S Not specified

PMML takes an algorithm-centered approach since each algorithm typically uses different data structures to maintain model state. Here the algorithm implementation drives the model representation, transformations, and algorithm-specific settings. Adding a new algorithm often requires creating a new set of XML Schema representations that fit into the PMML framework.

JDM takes a functionality-centered approach, focusing on higher-level mining functions such as classification, regression, and so on, but also provides for algorithm-specific representations for settings and model details.

Although terminology does not always coincide, the supported data mining technologies of the various data mining standards have a significant degree of commonality. Table 17-2 compares some of the more prominent features of JDM, PMML, CWM, and SQL/MM in terms of their support of various data mining and related technologies.

The other data mining standards—PMML, SQL/MM DM, and CWM/DM—served as the starting point for the JDM effort. With JDM, we saw the need to attempt to unify the various standards in concept, terminology, and structure. Due to the evolutionary nature

Table 17-2 *Data mining standards technology and capability comparison*

Technology	JDM Java interfaces for…	PMML XML representations for…	CWM Metadata for…	SQL/MM SQL Object interfaces for…
Transfor-mations	DME automated or external	Provided as Derived Fields	Transformation metadata	N/S Can leverage SQL
Mining Functions	Classification	Classification: *algorithm-specific*	Classification	Classification
	Regression	Regression and General Regression	Approximation	Regression
	Attribute Importance		Attribute Importance	
	Association	Association Rules	Association	Association
	Clustering	Clustering Sequence Analysis	Clustering	Clustering
Mining Algo-rithms	Decision Tree Naïve Bayes	Decision Tree Naïve Bayes	Decision Tree Naïve Bayes	N/S *Implementation defined*
	Neural Network SVM k-Means	Neural Network SVM Rule Set	Neural Network k-Means Self-Organizing Map Competitive Learn-ing *Names definition only*	
Tasks	Model Build Model Test Model Apply Export Import Compute Statis-tics	N/A	Model Build Model Test Model Lift Model Apply	Model Build Model Test Model Apply
Ensembles	N/S	Model Composition	N/S	N/S
Statistics	Univariate	Univariate	N/S	N/S
Test Metrics	Confusion Matrix Lift ROC	N/A	Confusion Matrix Lift	Confusion Matrix Lift

N/A Not applicable   N/S Not specified

of these standards and the need for backward compatibility, such unification proved difficult, if not impossible. However, through open communication and cross-pollination between standards when individuals participated in multiple standards efforts, progress was made. JDM leveraged concepts and terminology from PMML, SQL/MM DM, and CWM/DM while recommending concepts, terminology, and realizations back into these standards.

For the second release of JDM, the JSR-247 expert group plans to address data mining transformations, more advanced statistics, and the breadth of mining functions. The expert group also plans to provide a *generic interface* enabling the specification of settings as name-value pairs. Chapter 18 discusses these in more detail.

17.4 Directions for Data Mining Standards

With all this standardization, what remains to be done? What is needed in the data mining community? Generally speaking, there are a few key areas that are not adequately addressed:

- Model management
- Benchmarks for both model building and apply, with the emphasis on apply for batch and real-time.
- Test suites for conformance and interoperability certification
- SQL language extensions
- Conceptual and terminological convergence

Model management can take on many guises. One perspective includes the management and analysis of a large collection of data mining models [Liu/Tuzhilin 2006]. Model management is quickly becoming an issue of enormous concern for large-scale users of data mining. The ability to find models meeting certain characteristics or criteria is key where many users are building and testing many models, often hundreds or thousands. These criteria include models with a certain signature (required attributes), accuracy or model quality characteristics such as error rates, and performance factors such as model size. Model management also includes the ability to build many models efficiently as well as to score datasets using many models efficiently. This is the area in which APIs are often critical to success because graphical interfaces are often geared toward the building and use of a single or a few models, not hundreds or thousands. Model management also includes the ability to analyze deployed models, such as those that are underperforming or are being dominated by other models. Standards need to address these model management tasks.

The data mining community lacks standard benchmarks, either for model building or scoring. These benchmarks are needed across two dimensions: *performance* (or *speed*) and *accuracy* (or *quality*). One issue in this space is that it can be difficult to compare one vendor's implementation of a given algorithm against another's since they likely have dramatic differences in feature sets. For example, a given vendor's decision tree algorithm may differ on its support for missing value handling (surrogates), statistics, number of splits at a given node, and so on. However, progress can be made in defining benchmarks. Model build performance can be measured for several classes of mining functions, or even algorithms, based on the accuracy in the case of supervised models that the model is able to achieve in a given execution time. More readily comparable are scoring performance numbers. Using a given hardware platform, for example, how fast can a DME score a large dataset (e.g., 100 million customers), using 1 model or using 100 models? The accuracy of those scores can be validated relative to known values, essentially producing a JDM test metrics object.

One of the concerns for standards supporting interoperability is a lack of test suites for conformance or interoperability. Test suites for conformance determine whether the implementation meets the essence of the standard specification. For example, in JDM, conformance involves providing the required packages, classes, and methods defined by the standard and ensuring that certain minimal behaviors are met. Test suites for interoperability determine whether two vendors will be able to exchange models. For example, if a vendor has proprietary extensions, this will inhibit interoperability. However, if users and vendors can operate without using those proprietary extensions, interoperability is achievable. Currently, it is often up to individual vendors (or their customers) to determine what can be exchanged and what cannot.

Although SQL/MM DM has been defined, data mining vendors such as Oracle and Microsoft have chosen to extend the SQL language syntax to accommodate their database mining capabilities. As offerings of database mining mature and continue to extend SQL, having standard SQL language extensions will simplify the mining process for users. This includes both *data definition language* and *data manipulation language* for building models and scoring data.

Stepping back from specific features details or capabilities, let's consider data mining standards in general. The JDM effort started with several goals relative to data mining standards. The JDM expert group sought to provide a unified concept space for data mining that covered the core data mining objects as well as aspects of the data mining process, which included tasks such as build, apply, test, import, and export. This built upon many of the concepts introduced by SQL/MM DM and CWM/DM. As data mining standards continue to evolve, each needs to look at the other data mining standards to ensure as much as possible a congruence of terminology and capability. Moreover, each should ensure that one can fit seamlessly with the others where features dovetail. This means that concepts among standards should map cleanly and consistently, and where possible, terminology should be consistent and equivalent. Features introduced in one standard should be available in other standards as appropriate.

An ideal situation would be for definitions of concepts and terminology to converge to a single glossary. This is a difficult task, if for no other reason than backward compatibility. This is also difficult due to the many different schools of thought and areas of specialization that do not coordinate terminology. However, the community will be well-served if across different standards within the data mining community a unified glossary can evolve, with mappings between similar (or exact) concepts and terms.

An even more ambitious goal is the cross-pollination of data analytic standards in general (e.g., advanced data query, online analytical processing [OLAP], and statistics). It is clear that data mining is but one component of an overall analytics solution. Business analysts need the ability to use data mining results for designing OLAP data cubes, and use OLAP analysis to drive data mining analysis further. Having convenient points of integration through common objects can facilitate this for developers and users. The standards community is still far from attaining this goal.

17.5   Summary

Data mining standards have come a long way in a relatively short period of time. This chapter explored the various data mining standards, their history and future, and their relationship to JDM.

We introduced the JCP since this is the vehicle by which JDM became a standard. Some of the areas where data mining standards need to evolve were explored and areas of focus for future releases were discussed.

References

[ANSI] http://www.ansi.org.

[CWM 2005] http://www.omg.org/technology/cwm/.

[CWMI 2000] CWMI RFP, Final Submission Presentations, ADTF Denver meeting, March 2000.

[DMG 2005] Data Mining Group, http://www.dmg.org.

[JTC-1 2006] http://www.jtc1.org.

[IEC 2006] http://www.iec.ch.

[INCITS 2006] http://www.incits.org.

[ISO 2006] http://www.iso.org.

[Liu/Tuzhilin 2006] Bing Liu, Alexander Tuzhilin, *Managing and Analyzing Large Collections of Data Mining Models*, CACM, 2006.

[OMG 2001] Common Warehouse Metadata (CWM) Specification, Object Management Group, http://www.omg.org/cgi-bin/apps/doc?ad/01-02-01.pdf, Version 1.0, 2 February 2001.

[SQL/MM DM 2006] ISO/IEC JTC 1/SC 32 WG4, "Information technology—Database languages—SQL Multimedia and application packages—Part 6: Data Mining," ISO/IEC 13249-6:2006(E), April 26, 2006.

[SUN 2005] http://www.jcp.org.

Chapter

18

Preview of Java Data Mining 2.0

Without expectations, there's no future, only an endless present.

—François Jacob, winner of the Nobel Prize in medicine

As the first version of the Java Data Mining (JDM) standard (JSR-73) was being released, a new JSR, JSR-247, was submitted to continue the work started in JSR-73. Although the features for JDM 2.0 are still in flux, we have many expectations for its capabilities and use. At the time of this writing, JDM 2.0 is actively being specified, and the early draft review [JDM 2.0 2006], as specified through the Java Community Process (JCP), has been completed.

As with most software projects and specifications, some features do not make the cut for the first release. JSR-73 was no different. The JDM expert group identified many features for inclusion in the first release, but time and resource limitations required paring down the feature set to a manageable size that still reflected a range of commonly used data mining techniques. For readers interested in more detail of the JDM 2.0 specification, the latest available version can be downloaded at www.jcp.org.

With JDM 2.0, the goals are, in part, to expand the set of mining functions and algorithms to enable solving a broader range of data mining problems. These include time series analysis using ARIMA modeling, feature extraction using non-negative matrix factorization and anomaly detection. Further, the expert group strives to round out the existing functionality by including capabilities to apply association rules to generate cross-sell or up-sell recommendations using the apply task, to support multi-target models, and to include unstructured text as predictor attributes. Because the data mining process also involves data preparation and the ability to associate transformations with data mining models, the expert group addresses the ability to specify and perform transformations in a framework that fits with the overall JDM approach.

This chapter looks at some of the features proposed for JDM 2.0, including transformations, time series, apply for association, feature extraction, statistics, multi-target models, and text mining.

18.1   Transformations

A major part of the data preparation phase involves data *transformations*. Although not limited to the realm of data mining, transformations are often an essential part of the data mining process [Pyle 1999]. JDM 2.0 introduces a framework and representative set of transformations that provide a more seamless relationship between transformations and data mining models.

Traditionally, transformations would be modeled via a graphical user interface (GUI), or would be explicitly programmed (e.g., via SQL where the data is stored in a relational database). It was the application or user's responsibility to ensure that, if the model was exported to another environment, the transformations came along, since without these transformations the model is effectively useless. Recall from the discussion in Chapter 3 that the apply data needs to be prepared in the same way, using the same statistics, as it was for the build data.

JDM 2.0 integrates transformations at two levels: first at the task level, and second at the model level. At the task level, transformations are specified as a sequence of settings, where each settings object corresponds to a type of transformation. For example, there are numerical binning transformations, normalization transformations, and a sample transformation. A transformation task allows users to execute a transformation sequence to (1) compute transformation statistics, (2) produce a reusable transformation sequence object, and/or (3) apply a transformation sequence to data. An example of transformation statistics involves the shift and scale from a normalization transformation, which can be based on the maximum and minimum value range of the attribute. The transformation settings may be quite simple, for example, the percentage of cases to include in a random sample. Other transformation settings may be more involved, for example, providing a default normalization strategy for all input attributes while overriding several of these attributes with different normalization parameters.

At the model level, a model build task can be augmented with a transformation sequence object so that the transformations specified are applied to the data and the resulting transformation sequence is associated with the model. This allows the model to reference the transformations and when a model is exported, the transformations are also exported with the model. Similarly, when the model is applied to new data, the transformations associated with the model can be automatically applied to the apply data.

Transformations can be divided into several categories:

- **case filtering:** transformations that affect the number of cases (or rows) in the dataset, either by eliminating cases, or by dividing data into separate datasets as in sampling, or splitting data for building and testing.

- **attribute filtering:** transformations that affect the set of attributes remaining in a dataset. This can include indicating which attributes to exclude or include in the set according to some criteria.

- **attribute altering:** transformations that replace the values of attributes with new values, perhaps of a different data type (e.g., binning a numerical attribute into string-identified bins). These transformations may require obtaining statistics on attributes to perform the transformation.

- **attribute creating:** transformations that create new attributes, leaving existing attributes intact. These new attributes may be derived from multiple or single attributes.

- **pure function-oriented:** transformations that apply a function to each value in an attribute (e.g., square root, log, and so on).

JDM 2.0 provides interfaces for addressing each of these categories as part of *TransformationSettings* subclasses: *CaseFilteringTransformationSettings, AttributeFilteringTransformationSettings,* and *AttributeTransformationSettings*. The AttributeTransformationSettings include missing value and outlier treatment, normalization, binning, explosion, recoding, and general expressions. A key goal for JDM 2.0 transformations is to allow the transformation of very wide (in terms of number of attributes) datasets with minimal specification. For example, if a genomics dataset containing microarray data on 5,000 genes needs to have attribute values normalized between 0 and 1, the program should not have to specify the same normalization on each of the 5,000 attributes. Instead, JDM 2.0 allows users to specify a default normalization of all applicable attributes in the input dataset.

Consider the example illustrated in Figure 18-1, which shows a *TransformationSettingsSequence* instance consisting of three transformations: first take a 20 percent sample of the data, then remove columns that are determined to be "constants," (i.e., having the same value for 95 percent of the entries), and lastly, bin the *income* attribute into two bins.

We can now define a task, which consists of a *PhysicalDataSet* and *TransformationSettingsSequence* instance, to perform the transformations and produce a *TransformationSequence* object, which is depicted in Figure 18-2.

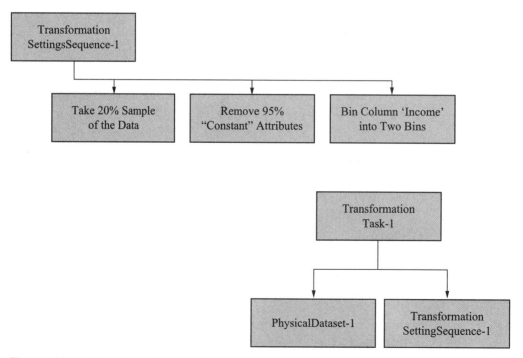

Figure 18-1 *Transformations settings sequence example.*

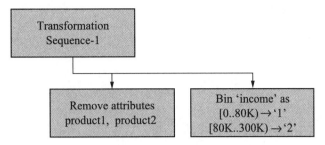

Figure 18-2 *Transformations sequence example.*

Generally, case filtering transformations are excluded from the reusable *TransformationSequence*. The first *Transformation* object defines which attributes to exclude from the dataset. Based on the specification to remove attributes found to be constants, the data mining engine (DME) removed product1 and product2. Here, perhaps all cases show that the product was purchased and hence the attributes provide no useful information for mining. The second *Transformation* instance contains the specific binning of the income attribute. Here, the DME selected $80K as the split point for the binning, assigning income values of $0 through $80,000 to bin 1, and $80,000 through $300,000 to bin 2.

18.2 Time Series

A *time series* is a sequence of numerical values, ordered in time. Examples of time series data include the Dow Jones Industrial Average (DJIA) daily values over the course of a year, a retailer's sales each day for the quarter, or the hourly rate of production on an assembly line dating back to the first production run. Figure 18-3 depicts the DJIA over the period April 2005–April 2006. This time series data is called the *signal* or, in data mining terminology, the *target attribute*. In some time series data, additional information can be provided, called *interventions*, such as a stock market crash, retail sale promotion, or failure of a key piece of equipment on the assembly line. Interventions consist of unusual or irregularly occurring events. They can be specified as one-time events, or events that occur over several periods in the time series, with a certain characteristic (e.g., a slow decay rate) or a constant impact over the period.

Time series analysis [Chatfield 2004] is the data mining technique that extracts the underlying patterns present in the time series data.

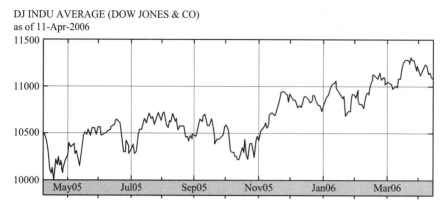

DJ INDU AVERAGE (DOW JONES & CO)
as of 11-Apr-2006

Figure 18-3   *Dow Jones Industrial Average time series data (graph courtesy Yahoo! Finance).*

These patterns are often characterized as *trend, cycle,* and *irregular* components — referred to as the *decomposition* of the time series. The trend reflects the long-term change in the average value of the time series signal. Here, long term depends on the sampling rate of the time series signal. The cycle reflects any repeating pattern of the signal, which can be characterized into *seasonality* or *periodicity.* If the cycle is seasonal, effects occur at specific times (e.g., "every Thanksgiving," "every quarter," or "every Friday"). If the cycle is periodic, the cycle repeats itself every *n* time periods. Cycles, in general, are described in terms of both a *period* and a *resolution.*

As with all data mining, the model produced from the data is imperfect. Not all the variation in the data can be expressed in regular trends or cycles. This residual difference, what is left over after removing everything that can be explained from the series, is referred to as the irregular component. Figure 18-4 illustrates the decomposition of a time series into its seasonality and trend with residual or irregular component.

As discussed earlier, time series analysis can help to show the structure or patterns found in the time series data, but it can also be used to forecast signal values in the future (e.g., forecasting the stock market and other economic indicators, retail product demand, and even weather predictions). Forecasts can be short range, such as the next period or few periods (which often maps to hours or days), but can also be long range, projecting results months or years ahead. Figure 18-5 illustrates a forecast for the time series data example. Since forecasts, or predictions, are in one sense statistical estimates,

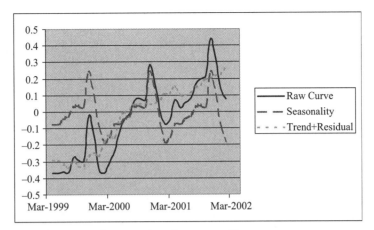

Figure 18-4   *Time series decomposition.*

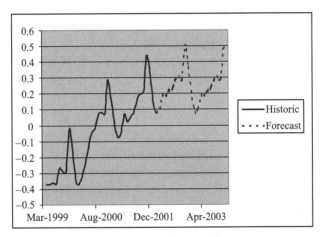

Figure 18-5   *Time series forecasting.*

the predicted signal value is often accompanied with a confidence band—a range of values that provides, for example, a 95 percent confidence of containing the correct outcome. Such confidence bands are also common in regression mining functions.

18.3   Apply for Association

Recall that the association mining function allows market basket analysis, producing rules of the form A → B, where A is one or more antecedent items, and B is a consequent item (e.g., "Portable DVD Player,

DVD → Noise Canceling Headset") with support and confidence. Since JDM 1.0, users can filter the rules according to various criteria, as discussed in Chapter 7. However, an interface to enable applying the model was lacking.

JDM 2.0 apply for association uses a rule filter to constrain the set of rules considered, if desired. The apply dataset consists of cases, each of which contains items for matching with the antecedent of filtered rules. Antecedent matching can be based on *exact match*, where the case items must match the rule antecedent exactly; *subset,* where the case items can be a subset of the items in the rule antecedent; or *superset,* where the case items can be a superset of the items in the rule antecedent.

The result from association apply is one or more consequent items, depending on the selection criteria specified. This criteria can include the top item with the highest support, confidence, or lift, or the top *n* items.

18.4   Feature Extraction

JDM 2.0 introduces the mining function *feature extraction* as an attribute reduction technique. In contrast to attribute importance, which ranks each individual attribute so that some top *n* can be selected, or some bottom *n* can be eliminated, feature extraction actually creates new *features*, or attributes, as linear combinations of existing attributes. This smaller set of attributes can result in deeper understanding of the original attributes, but can also improve model quality by presenting algorithms with fewer attributes that have richer content. In a sense, feature extraction can project a dataset with high dimensionality (many attributes) onto a smaller number of dimensions (e.g., two or three dimensions can enable effective visualization of complex data).

Feature extraction is particularly useful in domains in which there are many attributes, perhaps hundreds or thousands, and each attribute on its own has weak, even ambiguous, predictability. But when taken in combination, these weak predictor attributes produce meaningful patterns, topics, or themes. This occurs in text mining as well as life science data such as genomics. Other areas of application include data compression, data decomposition, and projection and pattern recognition.

Consider an example from text mining. To classify documents into categories, we first parse the text to extract important terms or words

	Features		
	A	**B**	**C**
Age	0.8	0.4	0.2
Income	0.8	0.5	0.7
HHSize	0.5	0.2	0.3
OwnHome	0.9	0.1	0.8
Employed	0.9	0.5	0.9

Figure 18-6 *Heat map example.*

using a separate text analysis tool. Once the terms, or words, are extracted, each word considered individually is often ambiguous or indeterminate in explaining what the document is about. For example, if we look at the word "hike," this word can be applied to the outdoors or interest rates. If we see "hike" in combination with "mountain," we may categorize the document with "outdoor sports." However, if we see "hike" in combination with "interest," we may categorize the document with "interest rates." These phrases could be provided directly to a classification mining algorithm. The feature extraction mining function produces a new attribute, or *feature*, as a linear combination of the original attributes, such as

$$feature\text{-}A = 0.8* \text{'}hike\text{'} + 0.7* \text{'}interest\text{'} + 0.01* \text{'}mountain\text{'}$$
$$+ 0.2* \text{'}word\text{-}x\text{'} + \ldots$$

An interesting visualization of feature extraction results involves displaying the coefficients in what is called a *heat map*. A feature heat map is a matrix, typically with the attributes represented along rows and the features as columns. An entry in the matrix is colored relative to the magnitude of the coefficient (e.g., values closer to 1 are colored red, values closer to 0 are colored blue, with color gradations in between). Figure 18-6 illustrates a heat map with three features for five attributes, where values below 0.3 are shaded black, values between 0.3 and 0.6 are shaded medium gray, and values above 0.6 are shaded light gray. This provides a quick visual assessment of feature-attribute relationships. Columns may be sorted by value to group a feature's related attributes more effectively.

18.5 Statistics

Even before data mining techniques were available, a first step toward data analysis was gathering statistics from the data. Data analysis could compute the *average, standard deviation,* or *variance,* and even more obscure "moments" of the attribute, such as the *skew* and *kurtosis* on continuous numerical data like *age* or *income*. Other statistics, such as the most frequently occurring value, or *mode*, apply to discrete or string data, such as marital status or satisfaction level. Since these are computed on individual attributes, they are termed *univariate statistics,* that is, they operate on a single attribute. The first release of JDM put in place a framework for addressing this type of statistics, as discussed in Chapter 7.

In JDM 2.0, the expert group is expanding the framework to include statistical calculations involving pairs of attributes, termed *bivariate* or more generally *multivariate statistics*. As with transformations, users should be able to specify many combinations of tests succinctly, across many attributes. For example, users can specify a set of predictor (independent) attributes and one or more target (dependent) attributes, and the system computes the requested statistical functions on the cross-product of independent and dependent attributes.

As with other types of objects in JDM, the statistics framework is intended to be extensible to include statistical functions not specified in the standard. Some of the multivariate statistical functions under consideration include F and T statistics, Kolmogorov-Smirnov, Mann-Whitney, and one-way ANOVA. These types of statistical functions can help users understand relationships in data prior to model building or when evaluating model quality.

In JDM, univariate and multivariate statistics can also be produced as a by-product of the model building process. By expanding the JDM *AttributeStatisticsSet* interface, vendors can immediately associate multivariate statistics with models as is currently possible for univariate statistics.

18.6   Multi-target Models

If a data miner wants to predict the probability with which customers will purchase each of 1,200 products, there are a few approaches. The data miner could define a classification problem with a target attribute containing the product purchased. However, building such models may require a very large number of customers. If insufficient data exists, model quality could be poor. Moreover, this type of model likely will not reflect when a given customer purchases multiple products.

Alternatively, the business analyst could build 1,200 individual classification models and use these models to score records and choose the top predictions. Challenges here include building the models separately (using separate tasks and largely redundant *Build-Settings* objects), managing the lifecycle of these 1,200 models, invoking the individual models for scoring (either in real-time or batch), and, finally, selecting the top predictions among 1,200 results. From the performance point of view, if all the models are using the same algorithm and same predictors, it is possible that much of the computation between the 1,200 model builds is redundant, but cannot be leveraged across the distinct model builds.

A better alternative is the use of multi-target models; with these, a single model build task can be executed by specifying multiple targets in that build. During the build process, the algorithm can optimize the computations and avoid recomputing the same intermediate results. Similar optimizations may be possible during model apply. One outcome is overall improved performance. Another benefit of multi-target models is the convenience of each target including the other $n - 1$ potential targets as predictors without having to specify those various combinations explicitly. Multi-target models also have the opportunity to include subtle interactions among the target attributes that impact predictions. If models are built separately on the different targets, they cannot take this interaction into account.

JDM 2.0 provides multi-target specification as a generalized supervised mining function that allows the specification of targets for classification, regression, or both in the same model. All the functionality present for classification and regression (e.g., involving test metrics or apply settings) is available for multi-target models.

18.7 Text Mining

"Text mining" is defined as follows:

> *Text mining, also known as* intelligent text analysis, text data mining, unstructured data management, *or* knowledge-discovery in text (KDT), *refers generally to the process of extracting interesting and non-trivial information and knowledge (usually converted to metadata elements) from unstructured text (i.e. free text). Text mining is a young interdisciplinary field that draws on information retrieval, data mining, machine learning, statistics and computational linguistics. As most information (over 80%) is stored as text, text mining is believed to have a high commercial potential value. [Wikipedia 2006]*

As noted, text data is far more prevalent than structured data (e.g., data stored in relational tables or XML). Typical use cases for text mining involve large repositories of text documents such as reports, technical papers, magazine articles, or e-mails that need to be automatically classified or grouped into appropriate hierarchical clusters. However, the ability to combine unstructured text data with structured data as found in relational tables can supplement the knowledge that data mining can extract. For example, customer service representatives in call centers type in notes from their interactions with customers. Physicians and nurses often provide textual notes on their patients and their progress. This valuable information is often excluded from the mining process due to a lack of convenient means to use it.

Although text mining is a field unto itself, with techniques ranging from statistical analysis of terms in documents to natural language processing, there are aspects that can be included in an application programming interface (API) to provide benefit to JDM users. A first-level objective for text mining in JDM is to provide a simple, minimal interface for mining text data. Specifically, JDM allows users to define an attribute as *text* or a *text reference*. A text attribute contains the text value in place, whereas a text reference attribute contains a uniform resource identifier (URI) indicating where the actual text resides.

At this stage, JDM leaves the details of preprocessing text attributes to the vendor. The vendor can make some assumptions about the nature of the text and, for example, perform term extraction and feed the results into a suitable algorithm. Alternatively, the vendor can extend the interfaces to enable the specification of supplementary settings such as stop word lists, thesauri, concept hierarchies, index specifications, and so on. Vendors may also choose to expose text mining–specific transformations.

18.8 Summary

This chapter introduced a few of the new features being considered for Java Data Mining 2.0. Because the expert group is still evolving this standard before its final release, concepts and details of the specific features, and even the features themselves, may change.

References

[Chatfield 2004] Chris Chatfield, *The Analysis of Time Series: An Introduction,* Boca Raton, FL: CRC Press, 2004.

[JDM 2.0 2006] "JavaTM Specification Request 247: Java™ Data Mining (JDM) 2.0," Early Review Draft, http://www.jcp.org/en/jsr/detail?id=247, November 30, 2006.

[Pyle 1999] Dorian Pyle, *Data Preparation,* San Francisco: Morgan Kaufmann, 1999.

[Wikipedia 2006] http://en.wikipedia.org/wiki/Text_mining.

Chapter

19

Summary

Every end is a new beginning.

—Proverb

Data mining is a journey, one where the arrival at insights and discoveries is the launching point for further inquiry—a new beginning. Having read this, and possibly other, books on data mining, you too are ready for a new beginning in applying data mining to your business or domain.

This book began by exploring data mining in the context of an overall strategy. Data mining was framed as a key strategic component for solving important business problems and the role of standards that support such a strategy was explored. As a technology, data mining is fascinating for what it can accomplish, the knowledge it can extract, and the speed at which it can extract it. However, technology for technology's sake is not sufficient—it must be put to use to solve practical and real business and scientific problems.

Part I highlighted general business (or cross-industry) problems, as well as problems specific to several industries to which data mining can be applied. The data mining process was examined in the context of another standard, CRISP-DM. Such a process helps to define data mining–related business problems with clear goals; as a result, higher quality results can be achieved. The various mining functions and algorithms supported by JDM were then introduced to give the reader a high-level sense of the domain. These mining functions are capable of addressing a wide range of problems. Since Part I focused on strategy, the specific strategic and tactical elements behind JDM were elaborated. Lastly, an example was given that leveraged both the CRISP-DM process and the JDM standard interfaces. This provided greater insight into the data mining process and use of JDM within that process.

Part II focused on the JDM standard itself, describing concepts from data mining generally, as well as JDM specifically. This was introduced through a series of examples organized by mining function. Becoming comfortable with data mining concepts is the first step toward being able to work with the technology. JDM concepts help the reader understand how JDM supports automation of, as well as detailed control over, the mining process. To assist JDM implementers and users to understand some of the JDM design principles, we discussed topics ranging from package design and object factories to exceptions and discovering data mining engine (DME) capabilities. Although JDM is focused on Java—targeting the Java API—we also explored the XML Schema for representing JDM objects and data mining Web services.

Part III brought data mining into practical focus, explaining how JDM benefits the application developer and how to use JDM to build applications. Through a series of full code examples, the use of the JDM API involving several data mining functions was illustrated in the context of specific business problems. An example of a data mining tool graphical interface was highlighted, illustrating the use of JDM's capability discovery mechanism to achieve code portability. To encourage the use of web services, two examples using JDM web services were introduced—one using PHP, and another based on JAX-RPC. Because data mining has an impact on the information technology (IT) departments of both large and small businesses, areas such as computing hardware, data storage and access, backup and recovery, scheduling, and workflow were examined. As with any standard, availability of implementations is key. Part III finished with an overview of architectures and JDM implementations from Oracle and KXEN. Some guidelines and insights into JDM implementation issues were discussed.

Part IV opened with the evolution of data mining standards, looking at PMML, CWM DM, and SQL/MM DM, and their relationship to JDM. The Java Community Process (JCP)—the means by which JDM came into being—was discussed, highlighting the phases of the process and the various participant roles. Some of the features of these standards were compared and directions for data mining standards were explored. A preview of some features proposed for JDM 2.0 was then provided, with a focus on capabilities that will further strengthen the standard and broaden its use.

We trust you found this book informative and useful, and that you will be able to enhance your applications and business with data mining technology to bring about greater insight and knowledge from your treasure trove of data.

Further Reading

M. Berry and G. Linoff, *Data Mining Techniques for Marketing, Sales, and Customer Relationship Management*, John Wiley & Sons, Inc., New York, 2004.

J. Han and M. Kamber, *Data Mining: Concepts and Techniques*, Morgan Kaufmann, San Francisco, 2001.

Tom Mitchell, *Machine Learning*, McGraw-Hill, Boston, 1997.

Dorian Pyle, *Data Preparation*, Morgan Kaufmann, San Francisco, 1999.

Ian H. Witten and Eibe Frank, *Data Mining: Practical Machine Learning Tools and Techniques*, 2nd ed., Morgan Kaufmann, San Francisco, 2005.

Glossary

The following glossary terms are provided from the Java Data Mining specification [JSR-73 2005, JSR-247 2006].

accuracy   In the context of a supervised model, accuracy refers to how well the model can make predictions.

algorithm   A specific technique or procedure for producing a data mining model. An algorithm uses a specific model representation and may support one or more functional areas. Examples include decision trees, backpropagation neural networks, naïve bayes algorithms for supervised mining functions, and apriori for the association mining function.

algorithm settings   A collection of settings, or parameters, to affect algorithm-specific behavior during model building.

anomaly detection   A mining function that produces models for detecting deviations from the norm in a dataset. The data provided for model building consists of normal cases from which an anomaly detection algorithm learns patterns that are captured in the resulting model. Applying the model flags cases that deviate or are unusual from the normal cases in some way.

antecedent   In an association rule, the left-hand side is called the antecedent. For example, in the rule "If A, then B," "A" is the antecedent. See also *consequent*.

API   Application Program Interface.

apply   The data mining operation that scores data using a data mining model (i.e., it applies a model to *apply data* to produce results according to *apply settings*). In JDM, apply is performed using an *apply task*.

apply data   The data used as input when applying a model.

apply settings   A user specification detailing the output desired from applying a model to data. This output may include predicted values, associated probabilities, key values, and other supplementary data.

apply task   A task that when executed applies the specified model to the apply data. The results are produced according to the *apply settings*.

association   A data mining technique that identifies relationships among items, producing *association rules*. One of the JDM mining functions.

association rules   Association rules capture co-occurrence of items among transactions. A typical rule is an implication of the form A$\rightarrow$B, which means that the presence of itemset A implies the presence of itemset B with certain support and confidence. The support of the rule is the ratio of the number of transactions where the itemsets A and B are present to the total number of transactions. The confidence of the rule is the ratio of the number of transactions where the itemsets A and B are present to the number of transactions where itemset A is present. See also *antecedent* and *consequent*.

attribute   A generic column of data, minimally with a name and datatype. There are several specializations of attribute; see *logical attribute*, *physical attribute*, and *signature attribute*.

Attributes are used in statistics, data mining, and other disciplines to describe observations, objects, data records, and other entities. Attributes are also referred to as variables, fields, columns, dimensions, features, and properties. Attributes are often categorized with regard to their mathematical properties, that is, in terms of the intrinsic organization or structure of the associated values (or value range or scale).

attribute assignment   The mapping of one attribute to another used to associate input data with a model's attributes, or a model's output with an output table.

attribute importance   A data mining technique that ranks the attributes in order of influence to predicting a target, or importance to model quality. One of the JDM mining functions. Also, a measure of the importance of an attribute within a model as recorded in the model signature.

attribute type   Specifies how a logical attribute is to be interpreted during model building. Commonly, four types of attributes are distinguished: nominal or categorical attributes, ordinal or rank attributes, interval attributes, and real or real-valued attributes (also called true measures). JDM restricts itself to three types: *categorical, numerical,* and *ordinal.*

attribute usage   Specifies how a logical attribute is to be used when building a model: *active, supplementary,* or *inactive.*

binning   A data mining transformation which maps a set of input values to a smaller set of bins. The input values may be discrete or continuous.

build   The data mining operation that produces a model.

build data   The data used as input to building a model. Sometimes referred to as the *training data.*

build settings   A collection of settings, or parameters, specifying the type of data mining model to build, including mining function and algorithm settings. Build settings exist for each of the mining functions, including: classification, regression, association, sequences, attribute importance, and clustering.

build task   A task that when executed builds a model as specified by the build settings.

case   A collection of related attribute values used as input to model building, testing, or scoring. In a simple table, a case corresponds to an individual record. In *transactional* format data, a case may be represented by multiple records, where columns play the roles of identifier, attribute name, and attribute value. See also *single record case* and *multi-record case.*

case identifier   The unique identifier associated with a case. Also referred to as "case id."

categorical attribute   An attribute where the values correspond to discrete categories. For example, *state* is a categorical attribute with discrete values (CA, NY, MA, etc.). Categorical attributes are either nonordered (nominal) like state, gender, and so on, or ordered (ordinal) such as high, medium, or low temperatures.

Categorical attributes tell us which of several categories a thing belongs to. For example, we can say that a beverage is BEER, LIQUOR, SOFTDRINK, or WINE. Categorical attributes exhibit the lowest degree of organization, since the set of categories such an attribute may assume posses no systematic intrinsic organization or order. The only relation between the categories of such attributes is the identity relation, that is, if two categories are equal. The lack of an order relation makes it impossible to tell if one attribute category is greater than another, or that one category is closer to another.

category A distinct value of a categorical attribute. Also referred to as a *class*.

category set A named collection of related categories.

centroid A cluster centroid is a vector that encodes, for each logical attribute, either the mean (numerical attributes) or the mode (categorical attributes) of the cases in the build data assigned to a cluster.

classification A supervised data mining technique that produces a model capable of classifying cases into categories or assigning cases to categories. A classification model requires a categorical target attribute in the build dataset. One of the JDM mining functions.

cluster A collection of cases that are similar to one another as determined by a clustering mining function. A cluster can be defined by its centroid, or by an area determined by an attribute vector space—a set of attribute value ranges (numerical) and attribute values (categorical). Predicate rules involving the cluster attributes are often used to define clusters in a human-understandable way.

clustering An unsupervised data mining technique that given a set of cases, each having a set of attributes, and a similarity measure among them, groups the cases into different clusters such that cases in the same cluster are more similar to one another while cases in different clusters are less similar to one another. One of the JM mining functions.

confusion matrix A table that counts of the actual versus predicted class values. It indicates where the model correctly predicted outcomes, and where it became *confused* or made mistakes.

consequent In an association rule, the right-hand side is called the consequent. For example, in the rule "If A, then B," "B" is the consequent. See also *antecedent*.

cost matrix A two-dimensional, $N \times N$ table that defines the cost associated with incorrect predictions. A cost matrix is typically used in classification models, where N is the number of distinct categories in the target, and the columns (reflecting predicted categories) and rows (reflecting actual categories) are labeled with target categories.

cross validation A method of evaluating the accuracy of a classification or regression model, typically used when there are relatively few cases to divide between build and test datasets. In cross validation, the build data is divided into several parts, with each part in turn being used to evaluate a model built using the remaining parts.

cycle   In time series, cycle describes the cyclic behavior of the target attribute, or signal. A cycle can be periodic, or regular, that is, having the same number of values within the cycle period. Alternatively, a cycle can be seasonal, or irregular, that is, having an irregular number of values within the cycle period. For example, monthly cycles have an irregular number of days per month, whereas a day has a constant number of hours. Time series can generate useful information about the periodicity or seasonality of a time series sequence.

data mining   The process of discovering hidden, previously unknown and usable information from a large amount of data. This information is represented in a compact form, referred to as a *model*.

data mining engine (DME)   The component in the JDM architecture that implements the algorithms to support data mining. The data mining engine may also support the persistent MOR.

data mining server (DMS)   The component in the JDM architecture that implements the data mining engine and persistent MOR. This is distinguished from the *data mining engine* since a server implies a separate component as in a client-server architecture.

data preparation status   An indication of whether a logical attribute provided as input to a build operation has been prepared by the user, or if the user expects the DME to perform automatic data preparation on the input data. A user may specify a logical attribute as *prepared* or *unprepared*.

DBMS   Database Management System.

descriptive data mining   Data mining that results in a *transparent* model that can be inspected to understand the process or behavior of a model. Effectively provides a characterization of a dataset in a concise and summary manner determined by the mining function and algorithm used. See also *predictive data mining*.

DME   See *data mining engine*.

DMS   See *data mining server*.

EIS   See *enterprise information system*.

ensemble model   A collection of primitive supervised data mining models (e.g., as produced from the classification mining function) that can be used together to improve model accuracy.

enterprise information system (EIS)   Generically, the application or enterprise system that supports a set of business processes and information technology infrastructure. The business processes are provided as a set of services. In support of data mining, an instance of an enterprise information system can be a set of backend component(s) that provide data mining functionality to the enterprise.

explode   A transformation that translates a discrete (categorical or ordinal) attribute into n attributes using the indicator or thermometer approach, where n corresponds to the cardinality of the attribute (number of distinct values). The indicator approach assigns the value 1 to the attribute that maps to the discrete value of the original attribute. The thermometer approach assigns the value 1 to the attribute that maps to the discrete value of the original attribute and all attributes that precede that value in the ordered sequence.

export   The operation that supports taking mining objects from within the DME and representing them in a transportable format for storage in an external system such as a file or database table cell, or for exchange with other systems or applications. In JDM, export is performed using an *export task*. See also *import*.

extension   A feature that is not covered by any of the relevant JDM specifications, or a nonstandard implementation of a feature that is covered.

feature extraction   An unsupervised mining technique that produces new attributes as combinations of input attributes, producing a reduced set of attributes containing more highly summarized information about those attributes.

feature selection   The process of selecting the features (attributes) that are deemed important to producing a quality data mining model. Feature selection is done based on the importance computed using attribute importance algorithms. See also *attribute importance*.

irregular component   In time series, the random or chaotic noisy residuals of data after the time-dependent components have been removed, namely, the trend, periodic, and seasonal components. It results from short-term fluctuations in the series that are neither systematic nor predictable. In a highly irregular series, these fluctuations can dominate movements, which will mask the trend and seasonality.

generic interface   An approach used in JDM 2.0 to enable vendors to specify name-value pairs of settings for build settings, algorithm settings, apply settings, and statistics settings. This provides a way for vendors to extend the standard settings while using a standard interface definition.

import The operation that supports taking mining objects from an external system such as a file or database table cell and importing them to the DME and MOR. In JDM, import is performed using an *import task*. See also *export*.

incremental learning An aspect of model building that refines or enhances an existing model by taking into account new data, thereby avoiding the need to rebuild the model on the complete dataset.

item An element that can be compared against another to determine if they are different. Typically used in the context of association models. For market basket analysis, an item may correspond to a retail product.

itemset A set of items, typically used as an antecedent or consequent in a rule, as produced from an association model. No item in an itemset can appear more than once. Itemsets can be compared to determine if they are different.

Java Data Mining A Java Community Process based standard supporting data mining, Java Specification Request 73 for JDM 1.x and Java Specification Request 247 for JDM 2.0.

Java Specification Request (JSR) The actual description of a proposed and final specification for the Java platform following Sun's Java Community Process. See http://www.jcp.org.

JDM See *Java Data Mining*.

JDM implementation A JDM technology-enabled client API data mining engine, and mining object repository.

JMI Java Metadata Interface (JSR-40)

JMS Java Messaging Service (JSR-914)

JSR See *Java Specification Request*.

lift A measure of how well a classification model improves identifying or prediction cases with the positive target value over a random selection given actual results. Lift may also be used as a measure to compare different data mining models. Since lift is computed using a dataset with actual outcomes, lift compares how well a model performs with respect to this dataset on predicted outcomes. Lift allows a user to infer how a model will perform on new data.

logical attribute A description of a domain of data used as input to mining operations. Logical attributes specify attribute type, data preparation status, among others.

logical data A set of logical attributes used as input to building a data mining model.

mining function   A major subdomain of data mining that shares common high-level characteristics. For JDM 1.1, functions include: classification, regression, attribute importance, association, and clustering.

mining object repository (MOR)   The logical or physical architectural component that stores JDM mining objects, such as tasks, models, settings, and their components.

mining result   The end product(s) of a mining operation. For example, a *build task* produces a mining model, a *test task* produces a test metrics object.

missing value   A data value for an attribute of a case that is missing because it was not measured, not answered, was unknown or was lost. Data mining methods vary in the way they treat missing values. Typically, they may ignore the missing values, omit any records containing missing values, replace missing values with the mode or mean, or infer missing values from existing values.

missing values treatment   A transformation that specifies how to replace missing values, for example, with the attribute mean or mode, a specific value, and so on.

model   A compact representation of patterns found using historical data. A model is the result of executing a *build task*. Model representation is specific to the algorithm used. A model can be descriptive or predictive. A descriptive model helps in understanding underlying processes or behavior. A predictive model is an equation or set of rules that makes it possible to predict an unseen or unmeasured value (the dependent attribute or target) from other, known values (independent attributes or predictors).

model comparison   A phase in the data mining process that involves comparing multiple models to select the model of highest quality or that best matches the needs of the business problem. Comparison can be based on various criteria, for example, maximum accuracy, minimum Type I error, and so on.

model detail   The specific representation of a model that is algorithm dependent. For example, a decision tree has specific model detail of the tree nodes and their relationships.

model signature   A collection of signature attributes, derived from the logical data used to build a model. The input data to a model for scoring must be compatible with the model signature.

MOF   Meta Object Facility.

MOR   See *mining object repository.*

multi-record case   A representation of physical data that uses multiple records to store a single case. The data typically has three columns with roles of sequence id, attribute name, and value.

multi-target model   A type of supervised model that can predict multiple targets, both categorical (classification) and numerical (regression). A multi-target model may be more efficient at representing the knowledge extracted during model building, and more efficient to compute.

normalization   A transformation that maps numerical values to a particular numerical range, typically 0 ... 1. There are several types of normalization (e.g., z-score, min-max, and shift-scale).

numerical attribute   An attribute whose values are numbers. The numeric value can be either an integer or a real number. See also *categorical attribute* and *ordinal attribute*.

OLAP   Online Analytical Processing.

ordinal attribute   An ordinal attribute is similar to a categorical attribute except that there is an order defined on the discrete categorical values, for example, *temperature* where the discrete values are high, medium, and low. There is an order defined on the values: high > medium > low.

Ordinal attributes define a total order relation on the categories. For example, if x, y, and z are ranked, 5, 6, and 7, we can tell $x < y < z$, but not if $(z - y) < (y - x)$.

Consider the ordinal attribute *speed* that takes the following ranked categories: STATIONARY, SLOW, FAST, VERY FAST, where rank (STATIONARY) = 1, rank (SLOW) = 2, rank (FAST) = 3, and rank (VERY FAST) = 4. We can tell that SLOW represents a smaller speed value than FAST. However, it is not possible to tell if, for example, the difference between two adjacent values is the same or not: is the difference between SLOW and FAST equal to, smaller or greater than the difference between FAST and VERY FAST.

outlier   A data value that does not (or is not thought to have) come from the typical population of data. Outliers are values that fall outside the boundaries that enclose most other values in the data. This can apply to values of an attribute, or of entire cases.

outlier treatment   The approach to replacing outliers in numerical data attributes. There are several techniques including specifying explicit boundaries, percentages in the tails of the distribution, and number of standard deviations, such that values outside the valid range are replaced either by null values or edge values.

percentage   A value between 0 and 100 that represents a part of a whole. For example, 75 percent indicates three quarters of a whole.

physical attribute   An object that corresponds to a field in a formatted file, or column in a database table.

physical dataset   Identifies data as a set of cases to be used as input to data mining. Using tasks, physical attributes can be mapped to logical attributes of a model's signature or logical data of a build settings object. The data referenced by a *physical dataset* object can be used in model building, scoring (apply), lift computation, statistical analysis, etc.

physical data record   A collection of named attribute values used as input and output for single or multi-record scoring.

predictor   A logical attribute used as input to a supervised model or algorithm to build a model. Also referred to as an independent variable.

predictive data mining   Data mining that results in a model by performing inference on build data, and attempting to predict outcomes for cases in apply datasets. See also *descriptive data mining*.

prior probabilities   The set of prior probabilities, or *priors*, specifies the distribution of categories, or classes, in the original population. Through skewed sampling, such as stratified sampling, prior probabilities will differ from the distribution observed in the build dataset. Priors allow the algorithm to adjust predictions to reflect original population distributions.

probability   A value between zero and one (0 … 1) that indicates the likelihood of an event. Zero indicates there is no chance of the event occurring. One indicates it is probabilistically certain the event will occur.

quality of fit   In clustering, a value between zero and one that is a measure of how well a given case fits in the predicted cluster. Values closer to zero indicate a poor fit; values closer to one indicate a good fit.

receiver operating characteristics (ROC)   A measure of comparison between individual models to determine thresholds that yield a high proportion of positive hits. ROC curves aid users in adjusting the cost matrix to minimizing error rates. ROC was originally used in signal detection theory to gauge the true hit versus false alarm ratio when sending signals over a noisy channel.

recode   A transformation that defines an explicit set of mappings, where each mapping involves an original value and replacement (or recoded) value. Upon performing the transformation on a column, all matching original values are replaced with the recoded values.

reference implementation   A software implementation of a JSR specification that validates the interface for practical implementation and usage. It must meet the tests defined in the TCK. See also *technology compatibility kit (TCK)*.

regression   A supervised data mining technique that predicts continuous targets. One of the JDM mining functions.

residual(s)   In *regression*, the difference between the actual target value and the predicted value. In *time series*, residual is what remains after accounting for trend, cyclic variations, and interventions.

return on investment   A measure used to make capital investment decisions. One possible calculation involves (increased revenue − costs)/investment.

ROC   See *Receiver Operating Characteristics*.

ROI   See *Return On Investment*.

rule   An expression of the general form *if X, then Y*. An output of certain models (e.g., association rules models or decision tree models). The *X* may be a compound predicate.

sample   (*n*) A representative set of cases taken from a larger data population. (*v*) To extract a set of cases from a larger population, typically at random to minimize bias in the dataset.

seasonality   In time series, this is a periodic effect due to the recurrence of certain drivers of the time series, for example strong sales around holidays. See also *time series* and *cycle*.

session   The duration of an open connection to the DME.

settings   The parameters used to control mining operations. See *build settings, apply settings, algorithm settings*.

signature attribute   A type of attribute used to define one of the inputs to a model for test and apply. See *model signature*.

single-record case   A representation of physical data that uses a single record to store each case. Each column contains data to be mined that can correspond to a logical attribute.

SOA   Service Oriented Architecture.

statistics   The science and practice of collecting, organizing, and analyzing data. In JDM, statistics refers to the type of summary data made available on individual attributes (univariate) and analysis of multiple attributes (multivariate). Univariate statistics include values such as the mean, mode, median, standard deviation. Multivariate statistics include tests such as F Tests and T Tests.

stratified sampling   A sampling technique such that the cases selected are based on percentages or counts of class values from a specific attribute. For example, a target attribute with values high, medium, and low, where the original distribution of cases is 75 percent, 20 percent, and 5 percent, respectively, may be stratified to ensure that there are equal number of cases in the sampled dataset.

structured data   Data that contains primitive data types such as integers, floats, or category strings. Examples include age, marital status, temperature.

supervised learning   The process of building data mining models using a known dependent attribute, referred to as the *target*. All classification and regression techniques are supervised.

system default   For an enumeration class, an implementation-defined default value that corresponds to one of the allowed values for the enumeration class. This default value may be different according to the context. Vendors must document the system default for each context.

system determined   For an enumeration class, a user may request the implementation to determine what is the best value for this enumeration. The implementation-selected value may take into account, for example other settings or data, to determine an enumeration value. JDM implementers are expected to document the behavior users can expect.

target   In supervised learning, the identified logical attribute that is to be predicted. Also referred to as a dependent variable.

taxonomy   A hierarchical grouping of a set of categorical values. For example, a geography taxonomy groups cities into states, states into regions, and regions into countries.

task   A container within which to specify arguments to data mining operations to be performed by the DME. Data mining tasks include: *model build, test, apply, import,* and *export*.

TCK   See *Technology Compatibility Kit*.

Technology Compatibility Kit   The suite of tests, tools, and documentation, as defined through the Java Community Process, that allows implementers of a specification to determine if their implementation is compliant with that specification.

test   The data mining operation that determines the accuracy of a model. This is typically performed by using held-aside (test) data identical in form to the build data, scoring that test data, and comparing the actual target value with the predicted target value. Testing is only applicable for supervised models. In JDM, test is performed using a *test task*.

test data   The input data used for testing a model.

test task   A task that when executed produces test results for supervised models.

text mining   A data mining technique for extracting patterns and insights out of unstructured, text data. Text mining goes beyond the notion of *search* in that previously unknown information can be discovered through the use of data mining algorithms.

time series   A data mining technique that supports the analysis of time series data. A series of values $X(t)$ are recorded according to some function of time and are thus ordered by an index describing the time (t) at which the values were recorded.

training   The step in the model building process that produces a possibly nonoptimized form of the model. For example, a tree algorithm may produce a full tree during training, but may require an evaluation phase to effectively select the best subtree. See *build*.

training data   See *build data*.

transformation   A function applied to data resulting in a new form or representation of the data. Binning and normalization are examples of data transformations. See also *binning, explode,* and *normalization*.

trend   In time series, this is typically considered to be a long-term change in the mean level of a series. What constitutes "long-term" depends on the sampling rate of the time series. See also *time series*.

UML   Unified Modeling Language.

URI   Uniform Resource Identifier.

unstructured data   Data that represents complex content, often with an inherent structure. Examples of unstructured data include text, images, audio, and video. See also *structured data*.

unsupervised learning   The process of building data mining models without the guidance (*supervision*) of a known, correct result. In *supervised learning*, this correct result is provided in the *target attribute*. Unsupervised learning has no such target attribute. Clustering and association are examples of unsupervised learning.

Web service A software application identified by a URI, whose interfaces and bindings are capable of being defined, described, and discovered as XML artifacts. A Web service supports direct interactions with other software agents using XML-based messages exchanged via Internet-based protocols.

weight A numeric value associated with an attribute or case. Weights associated with attributes instruct the DME to consider the contribution of attributes with greater weights more important than those with lesser weights. Weights associated with cases—by identifying an attribute as containing weight values—instruct the DME to consider the contribution of cases with greater weights more important that those with lesser weights.

References

[JSR-73 2005] "Java Specification Request 73: Java Data Mining (JDM)," Maintenance Release v1.1, June 2005, http://jcp.org/en/jsr/detail?id=73.

[JSR-247 2006] "Java Specification Request 247: Java Data Mining (JDM)," Early Review Draft Release v1.9, January 2006, http://jcp.org/en/jsr/detail?id=247.

Index

About the Authors

Mark Hornick — Sr. Manager, Data Mining Technologies, Oracle Corporation

Mark Hornick has led the Java Data Mining (JSR-73) expert group since its inception in July of 2000, and now leads the JSR-247 expert group working toward JDM 2.0. Mr. Hornick brings nearly 20 years' experience in distributed systems, in-database data mining, distributed object management, and Java APIs. Mr. Hornick is a senior manager in Oracle's Data Mining Technologies group.

Mr. Hornick joined Oracle through Oracle's acquisition of Thinking Machines Corporation in 1999. Prior to Thinking Machines, where he served as architect for TMC's next generation data mining software, he was a principal investigator at GTE Laboratories, involved in advanced telecommunications network management software, distributed transaction management research, and distributed object management research.

Mr. Hornick has contributed to several other data mining standards, including the Data Mining Group's PMML, JTC1 SQL/MM for Data Mining, and the Object Management Group's CWM for Data Mining. He has given talks at the International Conference on Knowledge Discovery and Databases, JavaOne, JavaPro Live!, and The ServerSide Symposium on data mining standards and JDM. He has also published various papers and articles over his career.

Mr. Hornick holds a bachelor's degree in computer science from Rutgers University, and a master's degree, also in computer science from Brown University, where he specialized in distributed object databases.

Erik Marcadé — Founder and Chief Technical Officer, KXEN

With more than 20 years of experience in the neural network industry, Erik Marcadé, founder and chief technical officer for KXEN, is responsible for software development and information technologies. He was a member of the expert group for the Java Data Mining standard developed under JSR-73 where he lead the development of the Reference Implementation (RI) and now he continues to actively participate as a member of JSR-247 expert group. He also supervised KXEN representation in the Data Mining Group's PMML effort.

Prior to founding KXEN, Mr. Marcadé developed real-time software expertise at Cadence Design Systems, accountable for advancing real-time software systems as well as managing "system-on-a-chip" projects. Before joining Cadence, he spearheaded a project to restructure the marketing database of the largest French automobile manufacturer for Atos, a leading European information technology services company.

In 1990, Mr. Marcadé co-founded Mimetics, a French company that processes and sells development environment, optical character recognition (OCR) products, and services using neural network technology.

Prior to Mimetics, Mr. Marcadé joined Thomson-CSF Weapon System Division as a software engineer and project manager working on the application of artificial intelligence for projects in weapons allocation, target detection and tracking, geo-strategic assessment, and software quality control. He contributed to the creation of Thomson Research Laboratories in Palo Alto, CA (Pacific Rim Operation—PRO) as senior software engineer. There he collaborated with Stanford University on the automatic landing and flare system for Boeing, and Kestrel Institute, a nonprofit computer science research organization. He returned to France to head Esprit projects based on neural networks technology.

Mr. Marcadé holds an engineering degree from Ecole de l'Aeronautique et de l'Espace, specializing in process control, signal processing, computer science, and artificial intelligence.

Sunil Venkayala—Principal Member of Technical Staff, Oracle

Sunil Venkayala is J2EE and XML group leader and Principal Member of Technical Staff at Oracle Data Mining Technologies. He was a member of the expert group for the Java Data Mining (JDM) standard developed under JSR-73 and now he continues to actively participate as a member of JSR-247 expert group.

Mr. Venkayala has more than five years' experience in developing applications using predictive technologies available in the Oracle Database and more than eight years' experience in working with Java and Internet technologies. He authored an article about JDM in *Java Developer Journal*.

Mr. Venkayala holds a bachelor's degree in engineering and a master's degree in industrial management from the Indian Institute of Technology, Kanpur.